Social Causes of Psychological Distress

Second Edition

SOCIAL INSTITUTIONS AND SOCIAL CHANGE
An Aldine de Gruyter Series of Texts and Monographs,
SERIES EDITOR
James D. Wright, *Tulane University*

V. L. Bengtson and W. A. Achenbaum, **The Changing Contract Across Generations**

M. E. Colten and S. Gore (eds.), **Adolescent Stress: Causes and Consequences**

Rand D. Conger and Glen H. Elder, Jr., **Families in Troubled Times: Adapting to Change in Rural America**

Joel A. Devine and James D. Wright, **The Greatest of Evils: Urban Poverty and the American Underclass**

Ann E. P. Dill, **Managing to Care: Case Management and Service System Reform**

G. William Domhoff, **The Power Elite and the State: How Policy Is Made in America**

G. William Domhoff, **State Autonomy or Class Dominance: Case Studies on Policy Making in America**

Paula S. England, **Comparable Worth: Theories and Evidence**

Paula S. England, **Theory on Gender/Feminism on Theory**

R. G. Evans, M. L. Barer, and T. R. Marmor, **Why Are Some People Healthy and Others Not? The Determinants of Health of Population**

George Farkas, **Human Capital or Cultural Capitol? Ethnicity and Poverty Groups in an Urban School District**

Joseph Galaskiewicz and Wolfgang Bielefeld, **Nonprofit Organizations in an Age of Uncertainty: A Study in Organizational Change**

Davita Silfen Glasberg and Dan Skidmore, **Corporate Welfare Policy and the Welfare State: Bank Deregulation and the Savings and Loan Bailout**

Ronald F. Inglehart, Neil Nevitte, Miguel Basañez, **The North American Trajectory: Cultural, Economic, and Political Ties among the United States, Canada, and Mexico**

Gary Kleck, **Point Blank: Guns and Violence in America**

Gary Kleck, **Targeting Guns: Firearms and Their Control**

James R. Kluegel, David S. Mason, and Bernd Wegener (eds.), **Social Justice and Political Change: Public Opinion in Capitalist and Post-Communist States**

Theodore R. Marmor, **The Politics of Medicare** (Second Edition)

John Mirowsky and Catherine E. Ross, **Social Causes of Psychological Distress** (Second Edition)

Thomas S. Moore, **The Disposable Work Force: Worker Displacement and Employment Instability in America**

Clark McPhail, **The Myth of a Madding Crowd**

James T. Richardson, Joel Best, and David G. Bromley (eds.), **The Satanism Scare**

Alice S. Rossi and Peter H. Rossi, **Of Human Bonding: Parent-Child Relations Across the Life Course**

Peter H. Rossi and Richard A. Berk, **Just Punishments: Federal Guidelines and Public Views Compared**

Joseph F. Sheley and James D. Wright, **In the Line of Fire: Youths, Guns, and Violence in Urban America**

David G. Smith, **Entitlement Politics: Medicare and Medicaid, 1995–2001**

David G. Smith, **Paying for Medicare: The Politics of Reform**

Linda J. Waite, et al. (eds.) **The Ties That Bind: Perspectives on Marriage and Cohabitation**

Les G. Whitbeck and Dan R. Hoyt, **Nowhere to Grow: Homeless and Runaway Adolescents and Their Families**

James D. Wright, **Address Unknown: The Homeless in America**

James D. Wright and Peter H. Rossi, **Armed and Considered Dangerous: A Survey of Felons and Their Firearms** (Expanded Edition)

James D. Wright, Peter H. Rossi, and Kathleen Daly, **Under the Gun: Weapons, Crime, and Violence in America**

Mary Zey, **Banking on Fraud: Drexel, Junk Bonds, and Buyouts**

Social Causes of Psychological Distress

Second Edition

JOHN MIROWSKY

CATHERINE E. ROSS

ALDINE DE GRUYTER
Hawthorne, New York

About the Authors

John Mirowsky and Catherine E. Ross are Professors in the Department of Sociology and Population Research Center at the University of Texas.

ALDINE DE GRUYTER
A Division of Walter de Gruyter, Inc.
200 Saw Mill River Road
Hawthorne, NY 10532

This publication is printed on acid-free paper ⊗

Library of Congress Cataloging-in-Publication Data

Mirowsky, John, 1949–
    Social causes of psychological distress / John Mirowsky and Catherine E. Ross.—2nd ed.
        p. cm. — (Social institutions and social change)
    Includes bibliographical references and index.
        ISBN 0-202-30708-5 (casebound : alk. paper)—ISBN 0-202-30709-3 (pbk. : alk. paper)
    1. Stress (Psychology)—Social aspects. 2. Social psychology. I. Ross, Catherine E., 1953– II. Title. III. Series.
    RC455.4.S87 M57 2002
    155.9′042—dc21

                                                            2002011167

Manufactured in the United States of America

10 9 8 7 6 5 4 3 2 1

Contents

Acknowledgments

The Aging, Status, and the Sense of Control (ASOC) survey was funded by a grant from the National Institute on Aging (RO1-AG12393) to John Mirowsky (principal investigator) and Catherine E. Ross (coprincipal investigator). The Community, Crime, and Health (CCH) survey was funded by a grant from the National Institute of Mental Health (RO1 MH51558) to Catherine E. Ross (principal investigator) and Chester Britt (coprincipal investigator). The Work, Family, and Well-Being (WFW) survey was funded by a grant from the National Science Foundation (SES-8916154) to Catherine E. Ross. The Illinois Survey of Well-Being was funded by a grant from the Research Board of the University of Illinois at Urbana-Champaign to Catherine E. Ross and John Mirowsky. The data collection, including sampling, pretesting, and interviewing, for all of our the surveys was conducted by the Survey Research Laboratory of the University of Illinois.

The National Institute on Aging and the National Institute of Mental Health supported our analysis and writing with the grants listed above, and with a grant from the National Institute of Mental Health to John Mirowsky (principal investigator) and Catherine E. Ross (coprincipal investigator) to study parenthood and psychological well-being (RO1 MH56543).

We are indebted to the National Institute on Aging and the National Institute of Mental Health for support of our research and writing. We thank the Ohio State University for the sabbatical that gave us time for writing. We thank Richard Hough, Dianne Timbers, and Joan Huber for giving us access to their data. We worked on the research reported in this book with a number of former graduate students in the Ohio State University Sociology Department, including Beckett Broh, Patricia Drentea, Karlyn Geis, Shana Pribesh, John Reynolds, Marieke Van Willigen, and Marylyn Wright. We thank them all.

Our book is dedicated to the people who started us thinking.

I

Introduction

1

Introduction

UNDERSTANDING THE CONNECTIONS BETWEEN SOCIAL AND PERSONAL PROBLEMS

Why are some people more distressed than others?

Imagine a man who left his inner-city high school at the first opportunity, without a degree and without basic skills; who spent years unemployed or underemployed; who finally got a factory job that he managed to hold onto long enough to make a down payment on a house and to start a family; who was among the first laid off when the product his factory produced could not compete with those made where labor costs are lower; and whose unemployment compensation has run out.

Imagine a woman who married young because she was pregnant; who had two more children by unplanned pregnancies in quick succession; who took a boring and unpleasant job at minimum wage because her husband couldn't support the family; whose husband says she trapped him into marriage, is embarrassed that she has a job, and gives her little help with the children and housework; who can't always find someone to look after the children, can't afford day care, and can't afford to miss work; whose boss gave her a bad report for being absent or late too often; and who has just learned that she is pregnant again.

The despair these people feel is deeply personal. Their problems are deeply social (Mills 1959). More than that, it is the despair that identifies the social facts as social problems.

One of the core interests of sociology is the study of social stratification—the inequalities in income, power, and prestige. Few persons would care about such inequalities if the poor, powerless, and despised were as happy and fulfilled as the wealthy, powerful, and admired. Sociology springs from humanistic empathy and concern as much as from scholarly and scientific curiosity. A sociologist might observe that black Americans are disproportionately poor, and investigate the racial differences in education, employment, and occupation that account for the disproportionate poverty. A table comparing the additional income blacks and whites can expect for each additional year of education is as interesting in its own

3

right as any dinosaur bone or photo of Saturn. But something more than curiosity underscores our interest in the table. Racial differences in status and income are a problem in the human sense as well as in the academic. This is what brings attention to them. The inequality in misery makes the social and economic inequality meaningful.

The traditional division of academic turfs can mask the connection between personal and social problems (Pearlin and Lieberman 1979). Researchers who study personal problems often rely on speculation in drawing connections to the social milieu. Those who study the structure of society and its institutions often guess about consequences for the subjective quality of life. Speculation and guessing have their hazards. The researcher who thinks a particular social condition is distressing may simply project personal values, preferences, and emotional responses not shared by people in the situation. An error of that sort is unacceptable in social science.

The cautious researcher often concentrates on the social condition and leaves its emotional consequences unmentioned. This creates a reassuring appearance of objectivity. Speak of status mobility, but don't mention the bitterness of failure or the pride of success. Speak of marital status, but don't mention the comforts of marriage or the loneliness and hardship of divorce. Speak of employment status, but don't mention the reassurance of a regular paycheck or the worries and doubts of unemployment. This avoids the appearance of attributing one's own feelings to others.

Critics of value-free social science say that researchers project their own values, beliefs, and feelings whether or not they admit it and whether or not they know it. The demographer who studies divorce rates knows that becoming divorced is usually a disturbing transition and being divorced is often a lonely and impoverished state. Even if the researcher computes rates that represent the currents of marital dissolution without prejudice or bias, the very choice of divorce as an object of study is value laden. Critics argue that researchers should drop all pretense of value-free social science and be unabashed advocates of openly declared causes.

The trouble with advocacy is that it begins with the choice of a conclusion. The advocate then selects or creates arguments and facts that support the chosen conclusion. Advocates believe that debate and struggle result in a natural selection of the truest and most correct arguments and facts. The arguments and facts that evolve from the debate and struggle of advocates may simply appeal to the prejudices and self-interests of the greatest number. Or they may simply represent the prejudices and self-interests of the wealthy or powerful—those who can afford or control advocates. Whatever the role of advocacy in politics, its value in scholarship is limited: a temporary stance for the development of hypotheses. Advocacy provides possibilities, but not answers.

There are two ways that social scientists avoid advocacy. The first way is to resist projecting personal beliefs, values, and responses as much as possible, while recognizing that the attempt is never fully successful. Social science can be relatively value-free, if not absolutely. The value-free social scientist looks at society in ways that do not demand moral agreement. Two demographers can calculate the same divorce rate, even if one sees it as a measure of human tragedy and the other as a measure of human liberation.

The second way social scientists avoid advocacy is by making the values of the subjects the values expressed in the research. Typically, this takes the form of opinion or attitude surveys. Researchers ask respondents to rate the seriousness of crimes, the appropriateness of a punishment for a crime, the prestige of occupations, the fair pay for a job, or the largest amount of money a family can earn and not be poor, and so on. The aggregate judgments, and variations in judgments, represent the values of the subjects and not those of the researcher. They are objective facts with causes and consequences of interest in their own right. In addition, they provide "objective" definitions of value-laden terms such as "serious," "fair," and "poor." They are objective in the sense that they are not mere reflections of the researcher's own feelings.

The two approaches are useful, but they have their limits. The demographers can calculate divorce rates without deciding whether the rates indicate suffering or release from suffering. Ultimately, though, if the divorce rate is increasing, people want to know which it is. The survey researcher can ask the public's opinion, but does the public really know? Respondents might simply project cultural stereotypes. And what if judgments differ among the happily married, unhappily married, never married, currently divorced, and divorced but remarried? To whose opinion do we give the greatest weight?

There is a way to evaluate the subjective quality of social conditions without imposing the judgments of the researcher or public: Explicitly and objectively measure feelings such as fear, anxiety, frustration, anger, guilt, despair, depression, demoralization, joy, fulfillment, and hope. Then map the frequency and intensity of such feelings across social conditions and positions. Suppose that women with jobs outside the home are happier than housewives. It is not the researcher's opinion. It is not the public's opinion. It is a social fact. This is the alternative we have chosen. It is the focus of our book.

The inequality of misery is the essential inequality. The founders of the United States recognized this in the second sentence of the Declaration of Independence, which says that the pursuit of happiness is an unalienable and self-evident right. When sociologists and economists study the unequal acquisition and accumulation of valuables, they study the pursuit of happiness. The subjective quality of life is the ultimate valuable. Goods, service, wealth, and prestige are the means or markers of acquired value, but not the value itself. As means, they may or may not be effective. As markers, they may or may not coincide with happiness. The correspondence is a matter for study. Our study of unequal distress has three primary aspects:

Distress as a Sign

The misery, demoralization, or distress a person feels is not the problem. It is a consequence of the problem. Misery is not only real, it is realistic. Suffering contains a message about the causes of suffering. The message can be read, understood, and acted upon. We are not looking for a drug to suppress the misery. We realize that such drugs have humane uses, but they are palliative. A drug that suppresses anguish does not remove the cause of the anguish. We are not looking for a way to talk people into believing things are better than they seem. An illusion cannot dispel a distressing reality. It just makes the reality more perplexing. We *are* looking for information on how people feel under various circumstances. Individuals can use that information to make decisions about personal and communal lives. If someone would rather not be distressed, and would rather that others not be distressed, then the information may be useful.

Gradations in Distress

Distress has many forms, suffered more or less. Situations are not either good or bad, they are better or worse. We do not see our task as dividing people into two categories: happy and fulfilled, or miserable and distressed. We certainly do not see our task as dividing people into the categories "sane" and "insane," or "well" and "ill." We think that mental illness and psychiatric diagnoses are largely categorical names for the extremes of graded traits, like the words "tall," "fat," or "smart." We see no great divide, no natural boundary, between common and uncommon misery. We look at all the shades and tones of distress.

Ordinary People in the Community

The inequality of misery is a fact of everyday life produced by unequal resources, opportunities, limitations, and demands. There are many kinds of ordinary people. Social scientists often speak of them as a composite— the mythical "average person" who is 55 percent female, 70 percent married, has 1.7 children, completed 12.5 years of education, etc. The averages flatten a great range and variety of experiences and situations. By comparing the various types of ordinary people, the dimensions and textures of social reality become visible. The lives of ordinary people in the community constitute a huge natural experiment beyond anything we could or would produce in a laboratory. The contingencies and exigencies of life differentially frustrate, strain, challenge, and empower. We compare the rich, middle-class, and poor; those with good jobs, bad jobs, and no jobs; men and women; young, middle-aged, and old; the single, married, divorced, and widowed; blacks, whites, and Hispanics; parents and nonparents; the dropouts, graduates, and postgraduates. Practically and ethically, no laboratory can affect the personality, mind, and emotions with the force and power of everyday life. To the extent that human action creates society, it experiments in the causes of misery and happiness. We observe and report the outcomes of that experiment—the lives and fortunes of ordinary people out in the world.

PREVIEW

Part I: Introduction

Social Causes of Psychological Distress is, first and foremost, a statement of our view and our understanding. Much of what we see and understand comes from the work of other scholars, including sociologists, demographers, psychologists, epidemiologists, psychiatrists, and social workers. Throughout the book we strive to give credit where it is due and to describe accurately the ideas and findings attributed to the work of others. However, *Social Causes of Psychological Distress* is not a textbook summary of the field. We look to the findings of others to answer questions, and we look to the ideas of others to stimulate and discipline our own. Our colleagues gave us a lot of good material to work with. We cut and assembled that material into our own construction—our representation of the social causes of distress. This second edition of *Social Causes of Psychological Distress* summarizes, synthesizes, and elaborates our observations and thoughts from two decades of research. It also presents many new results discovered by us and others since the publication of the first edition in 1989. This volume has five major parts. Part I is this introduction, in which we sketch our view and outline subsequent chapters.

Part II: Researching the Causes of Distress

In Part II (Chapters 2 and 3) we describe how sociologists study psychological distress. The sociologist's approach to studying the causes of psychological distress differs from that of the psychiatrist or psychologist.

Part II highlights two distinctive elements of the sociological approach: looking for gradations in distress rather than diagnosing mental illness, and interviewing people in the community rather than experimenting in laboratories.

Chapter 2: Measuring Psychological Distress.

We begin by describing psychological distress and the ways of measuring its gradations. By psychological distress we mean the unpleasant subjective states of depression and anxiety, which have both emotional and physiological manifestations. We call the emotional component mood, and the physiological component malaise. We contrast the diagnostic approach of psychiatry with our own approach. The diagnostic approach assumes that psychological problems result from discrete disease entities that invade and disturb the human organism. We think the presumed entities are mythical—a linguistic throwback to eighteenth- and nineteenth-century science of infectious diseases.

In the last part of Chapter 2 we evaluate three distinct hypotheses about the relationships among forms of psychological symptoms. The galaxy hypothesis says that symptoms of the same type (e.g., depression) generally appear together and symptoms of different forms (e.g., depression versus schizophrenia) generally do not. The nebula hypothesis says that all forms of psychological symptoms tend to appear together, in an amorphous mix. The spectrum hypothesis says that symptoms of similar type go together more than symptoms of different types, but gradually shade from one to another (e.g., anxiety to depression to paranoia to schizophrenia). A map of the correlations among ninety-one symptoms in a community sample shows a spectrum of symptoms with an overall pattern analogous to a color wheel.

Chapter 3: Real-World Causes of Real-World Misery.

Next we contrast our population-based survey method with the experimental method of psychology. Chapter 3 begins with a summary of the way that human sciences infer causal relationships. There are three formal criteria for establishing cause: (1) association—two things go together more than expected by chance; (2) nonspuriousness—the association is not just accidental because the two happen to result from the same prior condition; and (3) causal order—one of the two things cannot cause the other, so it must be the consequence.

Survey researchers talk to large numbers of people in the community who are representative of the larger population. We discuss the way survey research meets the three criteria of cause, using as an example the idea that low income causes depression. We discuss causal order in particular detail, because it is the most difficult criterion to establish. Practically, population researchers like sociologists look to six kinds of information to judge causal order: the things that do not change, common sequences, "relative stickiness," common knowledge, longitudinal data, and patterns and their explanations. Because explaining patterns is the heart of modern causal analysis, we discuss it in the most detail, contrasting the "social selection" versus "social causation" views on the association between low income and depression.

Next we talk about experimental studies of distress. The essence of an experiment is that a researcher manipulates a hypothesized cause and randomly assigns subjects to different levels of exposure. We discuss the practical, inherent, and philosophical limitations of experiments. Practical limitations include stable traits that cannot be manipulated, weak manipulation, trivial manipulation, analog manipulation, and unrepresentative subjects. Although the practical limitations of experiments can be reduced, the inherent limitations cannot. The core inherent limitation is that the laboratory is not the world. As a consequence, experiments cannot show patterns of distress in the real world; they cannot show causal direction in the real world; and they cannot explain why observed patterns of distress exist. The philosophical limitation of experiments is that they treat subjects as objects.

Despite practical, inherent, and philosophical limitations, the prestige of randomized, controlled experiments is so great in the scientific community that many social psychologists are loath to give it up. We describe strategies that preserve the *appearance* of a randomized, controlled experiment while skirting the substance. A genuine experiment on the causes of distress would manipulate personalities, worldviews, or social characteristics in a way calculated to make some subjects more distressed than others. But a researcher cannot produce a personality, worldview, or social characteristic in a one- or two-hour laboratory session that is more salient than those the subject came in with. On close examination, most experiments seemingly on the causes of distress simply evoke the different responses of individuals with different personalities, worldviews, or levels of distress.

Part III: Social Patterns of Distress

Even the most elementary information about the social patterns of distress is remarkably recent. The earliest community surveys were done at the very end of the 1950s and beginning of the 1960s, and published in the sixties (Gurin, Veroff, and Feld 1960; Srole et al. 1962; Leighton et al. 1963). These and subsequent studies published by the early 1970s (Dohrenwend and Dohrenwend 1969; Myers, Lindenthal, and Pepper 1971; Warheit,

Holzer, and Schwab 1973) discovered and confirmed some basic social patterns. Forty years of subsequent research reaffirmed some patterns and added more. A few patterns that were new in 1989 when the first edition of this book was published are now well-established.

Chapter 4: Established Patterns.

In 1989 the associations of sex, marriage, undesirable life events, and socioeconomic status with distress were well-established. Research since then establishes two new patterns: the associations of age and the presence of children in the home with distress. Both were new patterns in 1989 but have since been replicated many times. Chapter 4 outlines and discusses the six established patterns: (1) higher socioeconomic status—indicated by education, occupational status and work conditions, and economic well-being—is associated with less distress; (2) married people are less distressed than the unmarried; (3) parents with children at home are somewhat more distressed than nonparents; (4) women are more distressed than men; (5) undesirable life events are associated with distress; and (6) young adults are the most anxious and depressed, middle-aged people are the least depressed, but older people are the least anxious.

Much research of the past decades attempted to confirm the six patterns, specify them precisely, rule out spuriousness, and discover whether the association represented social cause or social selection. The six established patterns emerged as likely social causes of distress. They also explained some other patterns. In particular, blacks are more distressed than whites largely because of lower income and education, worse jobs, poorer neighborhoods, greater unemployment, and the like.

The established patterns are common knowledge now, but they were far from it in 1960. Cultural myths and human variety often cloud the facts. Many persons believed that men, who must face competition, uncertainty, responsibility, and noxious environments on the job, are more distressed than housewives in the relatively protected environment of the home. Many believed that single people with few responsibilities or restrictions are less distressed than married people constrained by family ties and responsibilities. Many believed that the executive or employer scrambling to make deadlines, meet payrolls, and negotiate conflicting demands is more distressed than the employee who simply has to punch a clock and do as told. All of these beliefs proved untrue. Research establishing the social patterns of distress contradicts these myths. Almost forty years of research into the social causes of psychological distress may have changed cultural beliefs somewhat. (Although to this day many persons, including many researchers, remain reluctant to believe women face more burdens and constraints than men.) The two newer patterns have been established only for about fifteen years. Perhaps they will dispel the myth that raising children brings joy to those with little else in life and to those who make it their life, and the myth that youth is the best time of life.

Most parents love their children and see them as one of life's great joys and blessings. Because of this many individuals believe that children increase parents' sense of well-being. On the contrary, surveys show that people with children at home are more distressed than those without. Parents sometimes find it difficult to support and care for their children. Love may make the burden worth carrying. It does not make the burden light.

America's youth-oriented popular culture portrays early adulthood as the best time of life, as a time of hope with boundless prospect and vigor. It's all down hill from there. Or so we thought. Surveys show that depression and anxiety are highest among young adults. Anxiety decreases progressively in subsequent age groups. Depression decreases up to the forty-five-year-old group, stays low until age fifty-five, then increases progressively in groups sixty and beyond. This pattern has been stable for at least a decade, suggesting that it reflects the life cycle in our society, and not the different historical events experienced by people currently of different ages.

Chapter 5: New Patterns.

Next we describe results from recent avenues of research on the life course and on neighborhood conditions. Three of the new patterns in Chapter 5 examine life course aspects of distress, identifying transitions early in life with persistent consequences or patterns that unfold across the life course. Some transitions and conditions compound and cumulate through life, shaping subsequent conditions that have consequences for mental health years later. Parental divorce in one's childhood increases distress throughout life. So does an early transition to parenthood oneself, particularly for women. On a related front, the gender gap in depression grows from the beginning of adulthood well into late middle age, as men and women experience their different lots in life.

Two other new patterns refer to the context in which individuals live. Life in a neighborhood with high rates of poverty and mother-only households increases distress, apart from the economic and family situation in one's own household. Disadvantaged neighborhoods are awash in distressing signs of physical decay and social disorder. Residents in disadvantaged neighborhoods report that there are too many people hanging around on the streets, using drugs, and drinking; that there is a lot of crime, graffiti, and vandalism; and that their neighborhood is not safe. Disadvantaged individuals find life distressing in their neighborhoods

characterized by crime and harassment, where neighbors seem untrust-
worthy, and danger, trouble, and crime are common.

Part IV: Explaining the Patterns

With the basic patterns established, and new ones emerging, the purpose
of research shifts to explaining the patterns. If the observed patterns are not
a mirage, then why do they exist? Establishing the facts is a big step forward, but only the first step. We want to know why gender, age, marital status, parenthood, undesirable events, and socioeconomic status influence
distress. We especially want to know if there is a common thread connect-
ing these and other social causes of distress. We need to advance understanding beyond the raw observation and confirmation of patterns and
causes. If possible—if reality supports it—we want to reduce the growing
set of observed patterns to a smaller set of underlying explanations.

Two steps are needed to explain the social patterns of distress. The first
is generative: thinking of the possibilities and seeing if there is anything to
them. The second is selective: pitting one explanation against another and
seeing which explains more. Current research is somewhere in the middle
of this process. As it stands, the basic patterns sparked at least nine distinct
explanations. Ideally, we would like to reduce that to one. "Explaining the
Patterns" describes each possible factor, and the reason it might be the
explanation for the social patterns of distress.

Chapter 6: Life Change: An Abandoned Explanation.

One early candidate for an explanation of the social patterns that
researchers have found has largely been rejected. Not long after the results
of the first community surveys were published one explanation became
rapidly and widely accepted. The popularity of the explanation was phenomenal, despite weak supporting evidence. It took a decade or more of
accumulating counterevidence to put the explanation to rest in scientific
circles. No doubt there are many in the general public who still believe it.

Life events mark major change in a person's daily life. They include
transitions such as the death of a spouse, birth of a child, move to a new
home, loss of a job, getting married, finishing school, and so on. Each event
is relatively infrequent in any one person's life, but likely within the lifetime and common in the community as a whole. Despite impressive rationales based on endocrinology and biological equilibrium, there was never
much evidence that change itself is distressing. The early studies failed to
distinguish between desirable and undesirable changes. It turns out that
only the undesirable changes are associated with distress (Ross and
Mirowsky 1979; Vinokur and Selzer 1975).

It is not the change itself, or even undesirable change, that is most important. Two critical factors largely determine the psychological impact of life events: (1) the conditions that produce the events and follow from them (Gersten, Langner, Eisenberg, and Orzek 1974); and (2) an active and instrumental response to the events, rather than a passive and fatalistic one (Wheaton 1980, 1983; Pearlin, Lieberman, Menaghan, and Mullen 1981). These, more than the events themselves, account for the social patterns of distress.

Chapter 7: Alienation.

Five alternatives displaced life change as the most likely and important explanations of the social patterns of distress. Alienation is a rift between the individual and society. Subjective alienation is a sense of that disconnection. Theorists define five basic types of subjective alienation: powerlessness, self-estrangement, isolation, meaninglessness, and normlessness (Seeman 1959, 1983). Although they are subjective they are not "just in your mind." For the most part they are realistic perceptions of objective social conditions. Speculation about the emotional impact of alienation leads social scientists to predict five corresponding social-psychological requirements for well-being: control, commitment, support, meaning, and normality. They link social conditions to emotional well-being. According to theory, each type of subjective alienation arises from a specific corresponding objective condition.

Control. Objective powerlessness is a condition in which the individual is unable to achieve desired ends. It leads to subjective powerlessness, which is the sense that important outcomes are beyond one's control, determined instead by chance, fate, or powerful others. People need to feel they are effective forces in control of their own lives. The sense of control bolsters the will to think about problems and do something about them. A person who feels powerless sees little reason to think about the causes of problems and possible solutions, and little reason to try to solve the problems. The tragedy of a sense of powerlessness is that it is destructive even if largely justified. When many bad things happen to a person that are unavoidable and genuinely beyond control the person develops a general sense of powerlessness. As a consequence, the person does not see that many problems can be avoided or solved, and thus does not take effective action. A firm sense of personal control makes a person attentive, active, and (ultimately) more effective. Beyond that, it indicates a self-assurance that directly counteracts demoralization and distress.

Commitment. Alienated labor is a condition in which a worker does not decide what to produce, does not design the production process, and does not own the product. Self-estrangement is a corresponding sense of being separate from that part of one's thoughts, actions, and experiences given over to the control of others. Work is drudgery. It has no intrinsic value. There is no pride in it. Rewards lie outside the activity itself. At best one is compensated. At worst one is forced by circumstances to submit. Work is unalienated if the person participates in decisions, controls the work process, and feels the work is a part of him- or herself. Unalienated labor is typified by participation in churches, political parties, civic or charitable organizations, clubs, and hobbies. Because these activities are voluntary and unpaid, they are necessarily self-expressive rather than self-estranged. Commitment to one's activities implies an identification that gives purpose and meaning to life. One's actions express rather than subjugate one's self. Freedom of action is a principal value, inherent in the human organism. The frustration of one's freedom is distressing.

Support. Isolation is a condition of detachment from networks of mutual communication, obligation, and liking. Social integration is the opposite condition, indicated by the density of a person's social network, the number of relationships, and the frequency of contact. Social support is the corresponding sense of being someone important in the eyes of others, being cared for and loved, being esteemed and valued as a person, and having someone who will listen, understand, and help when needed. Social integration is necessary, but not sufficient, for a sense of social support. Social support reduces distress by increasing the sense of being cared for and loved, which produces a sense of security. Social support is clearly an important component of well-being. However, there are many indications that integration and mutual obligation can be excessive and overly restrictive, limiting personal freedom and thus counteracting the desirable aspects of social support.

Meaning. Disorganization is a condition in which there are no guidelines, or a welter of inconsistent guidelines, for action and evaluation. Meaninglessness is the corresponding sense that the world is unintelligible, that life is without purpose, and that action is inherently discordant. A sense of meaningful existence seems important to well-being for two reasons. A world that cannot be understood cannot be controlled. In a chaotic world, all outcomes are chance. Beyond the issue of control, people may require a sense of purpose, significance, and value in their lives. Like a grammatical sentence, a delightful song, a stirring speech, or a beautiful sight, a meaningful life may conform satisfyingly to unarticulated standards. If the standards are in disarray, or if the world seldom conforms, the consequence may be a vague and general dissatisfaction, with consequent distress.

Normality. Structural inconsistency, role stress, and a disordered life-cycle make it difficult or impossible to meet normal expectations. Structural inconsistency is a condition in which standard goals are reinforced but access to effective legitimate means is restricted. Role stress is a disjunction or inconsistency in the system of roles, so that normal obligations cannot be met. A disordered life cycle is one in which the usual sequence of major transitions is disrupted or contravened.

Structural inconsistency produces normlessness, which is the belief that socially unapproved behaviors are required to achieve one's goals. Lack of faith in community standards often leads normless individuals to displace the pursuit of prestige and respect with the pursuit of elementary pleasures. The normless individual falls back on intrinsic gratification and pragmatic efficiency as guides that do not require faith in others. Other people exist to be manipulated, cheated, robbed, or used. They provide gratification but not comfort. Because of the need to disguise actions and purposes, and protect against preemption and retaliation, normlessness results in mistrust, paranoia, and anxiety.

Role stress produces role strain, which is the frustrating sense of not being able to understand or meet the normal expectations of one's roles. There are three types of role stress. Role conflict exists when two legitimate expectations produce incompatible or mutually exclusive demands. Role ambiguity exists when it is not clear what is expected. Role overload exists when expectations imply demands that overwhelm the resources and capabilities of the individual. Most people, most often, want to meet their obligations as spouses, parents, children, friends, citizens, employees, coworkers, and members. The inability to do so produces frustration and guilt, with consequent distress. The plight of employed women with children is an outstanding example of role stress in contemporary American society. The current reality is that most adult women hold jobs outside the home. Many couples have not fully adjusted their marital and family lives to the new reality. Women still have primary responsibility for work around the house and for child care. Employment is emotionally beneficial for women on average. However, the average conceals a large minority of employed women who have children, who get little or no help with child care from their partners, and who find it very difficult to arrange day care. These women are extremely distressed.

A disordered life cycle is a condition quite similar to role stress in its nature and effects. Each society tends to have a normal sequence of roles, statuses, and transitions over the lifetime. Transitions that happen out of their usual sequence create moral and practical dilemmas. Getting married is normal after graduation, but a problem while in high school. Getting pregnant is normal after marriage, but a problem before. Losing one's parents is normal by age sixty, but a problem at age six. The more common a given sequence of events and transitions, the greater the cultural, social, and personal preparation for it, and the less distress it engenders.

Chapter 8: Authoritarianism and Inequity.

Although life change and alienation are the most commonly offered explanations of the social patterns of the distress, there are two other contenders. Both have long histories as ideas and issues in the humanities and social sciences. They are authoritarianism and inequity.

Authoritarianism. Authoritarianism has two components most relevant to distress: inflexibility and mistrust. Authoritarianism is a complex worldview that grows from situations that limit horizons and opportunities, and that demand conformity and obedience. Insular personal networks and a lack of exposure to the views of other cultures, historical periods, and sectors of society create a sense that the familiar, traditional order has a universal and unique validity that transcends time, place, and situation. Tradition and authority are seen as compelling guides to behavior. Compliance with the dictates of tradition and authority are considered ethical and effective.

Inflexibility. Inflexibility in dealing with practical and personal problems is one aspect of the authoritarian worldview. Authoritarians see each problem as having a single correct solution known intuitively by everyone. Inflexibility produces distress in two ways. It limits the person's ability to solve practical problems because it makes the search for a range of possible solutions and a means of evaluating solutions seem moot. To the authoritarian, if things are done the proper way, ineffectiveness and undesirable consequences are irrelevant, or are a sign of evil forces contradicting and undermining proper order. Inflexibility also limits the person's ability to solve interpersonal problems. If there really is only one right way, available through intuition, then any contradictory desire, belief, or action of another is necessarily invalid and malicious. Any difference evokes moral outrage and righteous indignation. Such responses make negotiation nearly impossible. In an authoritarian world, there is no incentive to understand and express individual desires and beliefs, much less to adapt oneself to the individual desires and beliefs of others.

Mistrust. Mistrust is probably the most distressing aspect of authoritarianism. Early scholarly interest in mistrust developed out of interest in the authoritarian worldview. In land-based peasant economies, one person can have more only if another person has less. Land is essentially fixed in quantity. If land is the basic measure of wealth, then one person's wealth increases only at the expense of another's. The "zero-sum" view has intrinsic appeal if technology and productivity stagnate. If community wealth does not visibly increase, it will appear that one person's wealth creates another's poverty. If there is an inherent scarcity of wealth, power, and prestige, then people must constantly be alert to the threat of exploitation and victimization. Under the circumstances, many consider it rational to exploit and victimize others, believing it is a matter of "eat or be eaten." The consequent fear and guilt are distressing in themselves. By blocking coalition, cooperation, and negotiation, the atmosphere of mistrust also increases distress by reducing effectiveness.

Theoretically mistrust arises from conditions of scarcity, threat, and powerlessness. In this edition we apply these ideas to new interests in neighborhoods and trust. We show how disorder, crime, harassment, and threat generate mistrust among neighborhood residents; how the sense of powerlessness also results from neighborhood disorder; and how powerlessness makes the effect of disorder on mistrust even worse. We call this general paradigm structural amplification of disadvantage. We reexamine mistrust's origins in authoritarianism and suggest that its importance to distress probably lies elsewhere—in alienation.

Inequity.   Ideas about inequity go back to Aristotle. Human beings have a sense of right and wrong. Injustice and unfairness arouse frustration and anger in the victim and sympathizers, and apprehension and guilt in the exploiter. While other theories predict that the victims of an unfair relationship are distressed by it, equity theory is distinct in predicting that the exploiters also are distressed by it. People have a conscience—a built-in mechanism for self-punishment. People can choose to be unscrupulous, but at an emotional price. Furthermore, even an exploiter devoid of guilt must fear retaliation and retribution from the victim and sympathizers. Exploitative relationships also may be less productive than cooperative ones. Victims often resist and frustrate the will of exploiters. The exploiter may have more control than the victim, but still less than could be had through cooperation. Equity theorists generally argue that exploiters are less distressed than victims, but more distressed than people who are neither victim nor exploiter.

Part V: Conclusion

Chapter 9: Why Some People Are More Distressed Than Others

Control of One's Own Life.   Of all the things that might explain the social patterns of distress, the sense of control over one's own life stands out. All the established and emerging social patterns of distress point to the sense of control as a critical link. The patterns of distress reflect the patterns of autonomy, opportunity, advantage, and achievement in America. The realities of socioeconomic status—education, unemployment, family income, and economic hardship—profoundly influence the sense of control. Minority status also lowers the sense of control, partly because of lower education, income, and employment, and partly because any given level of achievement requires greater effort and provides fewer opportunities for members of minority groups. Undesirable events also decrease the sense of control. Unwanted, their occurrence implies powerlessness to avoid them. Older age is associated with low control. As resources, networks, health, and social power decline, so does the sense of control and well-being. Living in a neighborhood where disadvantage, danger, and threat prevail undermines the sense of personal control. Early life course disruptions such as teenage parenthood produce consequences that limit real opportunities, producing a sense of powerlessness to achieve goals.

The barriers of class and status, the misfortunes of life, and the losses of old age are impersonal oppressors. The personal world of the family holds out the hope of an alternative source of power. That hope can be realized, but it also can be undermined. Marriage increases the sense of control for both men and women by increasing the average household income and by creating a partnership of mutual effort. However, marriage increases control more for men. For some women, marriage increases subordination and dependency, which can counteract the positive effects of marriage on the sense of control. Parenthood can provide meaning and bring purpose to life, but the realities of too many children, or children born too early in life before parents have well established jobs or economic security, undermine the sense of personal control by creating a constant struggle to pay the bills, find affordable child care, and pay for food, medicine and shelter.

As we said earlier, knowing the facts helps, and explaining the facts helps more. Explaining the facts succinctly helps the most. In the business of explanation, less is more. Powerlessness, self-estrangement, isolation, meaninglessness, normlessness, inflexibility, mistrust, and inequity all explain at least a part of what we know. Each concept has a body of theory and research. Each is a plausible factor in the social patterns of distress. Each captures some of the truth, but we see one explanation that contains the others. We see a single thread that connects all the explanations—control. The occurrence of undesirable events and conditions implies powerlessness to deter them. Self-estrangement is the enslavement felt when labor is alienated. Isolation leaves a person without allies and supporters. Meaninglessness implies a chaotic world beyond control. Normlessness and role stress arise when standard approaches and understandings are taxed beyond their limits. Inflexibility reduces the ability to solve problems and negotiate solutions. Mistrust undermines the ability to cooperate and achieve mutual goals. The victims of inequity suffer a situation not of their preference and choosing. The exploiters mistake power over others for the power to achieve ends. Every other explanation refers, directly or indirectly, to the individual's sense of control. Self-estrangement, isolation, meaninglessness, normlessness and role stress, inflexibility, mistrust, victimization, and perhaps even exploitation undermine the sense of being master of your own fate—of being the main force that shapes your own life.

Control improves well-being, but there are limits to the psychological benefit of control. Autonomy improves psychological well-being, but authority does not. Control over another in marriage implies inequity. Control over others at work often implies conflict and frustration. Supportive relationships are based on the ability to negotiate and compromise, not on the ability to get one's way in opposition to others. Inequity, conflict, and lack of support are distressing. Emotionally beneficial power is the ability to achieve goals, not the ability to win conflicts.

A decade of research since the first edition of this book was published confirms the sense of personal control as the primary link between social conditions and psychological well-being.

Social Causes: How Important Are They?   First, how much of all distress is attributable to social factors? Second, how serious is the distress that is socially patterned? To address the first question we look at the collective impact of seven social factors on depression. These include economic hardship, education, gender, age, the sense of personal control, social support, and mistrust. We divide symptoms of depression into two parts: base and excess. The base represents the symptoms we would find if all segments of the society had the same level of symptoms as the best decile, defined in terms of the seven social traits. Of all the symptoms reported, 37.1 percent are in the base, and 62.9 percent are excess. At least half of all the symptoms of depression are attributable to social factors. In the worst social decile, 85 percent of all symptoms are excess above the base—symptoms the people would not have if they were in the most advantaged decile of society.

Social factors account for a great deal of distress, but do they account for severe psychological distress? To address this second question, we defined extreme distress as a level of symptoms greater than 95 percent of the population. Most of these people would qualify for a psychiatric diagnosis (Boyd et al. 1982). If we split society into two halves, better and worse, the worse half of society has 78.5 percent of all severe distress. The advantaged half has only 21.5 percent of the severe distress. Stated another way, the odds of being severely distressed are 7.5 times greater in the worse half than in the better half.

Genetics and Biochemistry as Alternative Explanations.   The current popularity of genetic and biochemical explanations of distress comes from advances in genetic theory and psychopharmacology in recent decades. Despite the impressive bodies of research in these areas, neither genetic nor biochemical factors have been shown to account for any substantial part of the measurable differences in levels of distress found in our society. In particular, there is no evidence that the social patterns of distress reflect genetic or biochemical abnormalities.

What Can Be Done to Prevent Distress?   We summarize our views on preventing psychological distress under three main headings: (1) education: the headwaters of well-being, (2) a good job: one that provides an adequate income, provides a measure of autonomy and opportunity for creative productivity, and minimizes strain between the demands of work and family, and (3) a supportive relationship: fair and caring. These three conditions help people control their own lives and promote psychological well-being for themselves and others.

Humans are social. We think. We feel. These things come from the organism. The basic link between powerlessness and distress comes from the organism. But the man out of work, the employed woman wondering if her children are all right, the divorcee alone and uncertain, the old person losing everything, the young family struggling to make ends meet—these things come from the world we create for ourselves and each other. They come from society. They are the social causes of distress.

II

Researching the Causes of Distress

2

Measuring Psychological Well-Being and Distress

WHAT IS PSYCHOLOGICAL DISTRESS?

Depression and Anxiety; Mood and Malaise

Distress is an unpleasant subjective state. It takes two major forms. Depression is feeling sad, demoralized, lonely, hopeless, or worthless, wishing you were dead, having trouble sleeping, crying, feeling everything is an effort, and being unable to get going. Anxiety is being tense, restless, worried, irritable, and afraid. Depression and anxiety each take two forms: mood and malaise. Mood refers to feelings such as the sadness of depression or the worry of anxiety. Malaise refers to bodily states, such as the listlessness and distraction of depression or the restlessness and autonomic ailments such as headaches, stomachaches, or dizziness of anxiety. Depression and anxiety—both mood and malaise—are related in two ways: the maps of their social high and low zones are very similar, and a person who suffers more than usual from one also tends to suffer more than usual from the other (although not necessarily at the same time). Figure 2.1 shows some examples of symptoms of depression and anxiety, distinguishing mood and malaise.

Sociologists typically measure distress by asking questions about depressed and anxious mood and malaise. The researcher makes an index by counting the number of symptoms a person reports. The more symptoms, the more severe the problems. Many of the indexes were developed to screen for persons who might need further psychiatric evaluation. For example, Langner (1962) developed an index that was used widely in the 1960 and 1970s. Langner made a checklist of twenty-two questions that he chose from a much longer list because they best distinguished between persons in psychiatric treatment and persons not in treatment whom psychiatrists judged mentally well or normal. The more of the symptoms a person has, the more likely that the person would be considered mentally ill by a psychiatrist. The items selected on this basis turn out to be questions about

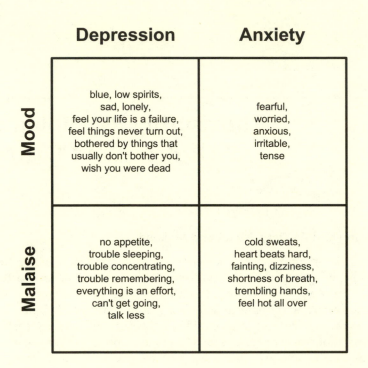

Figure 2.1. Examples of items measuring depression and anxiety, separated into mood and malaise components. Respondents are asked how often they feel this way (i.e., have trouble concentrating). The depression items are from the Center for Epidemiologic Studies' Depression Scale (CES-D) and the Diagnostic Interview Schedule (DIS); anxiety items are from the Langner index and the DIS. In the case of depression, mood may also be thought of as having two components: depressed mood and lack of positive mood. The latter includes the absence of feeling happy, enjoying life, and feeling hopeful about the future.

depression and anxiety, although Langner was not trying to measure any specific type of psychiatric problem. Almost all mental patients suffer from depression or anxiety, even if they are in treatment for other kinds of problems such as hallucinations or paranoid delusions. The index has questions about depressed mood (Do you sometimes wonder if anything is worthwhile anymore? In general, would you say that you are in very good spirits, good spirits, low spirits, or very low spirits?) and depressed malaise

(Have you had times when you couldn't take care of things because you couldn't get going?). It also has questions about anxious mood (Are you the worrying type?) and anxious malaise (Do you feel weak all over much of the time? Are you bothered by acid or sour stomach several times a week? How often are you troubled with headaches or pains in the head?). Langner's index was developed as a quick and easy way of screening individuals for further psychiatric evaluation and possible treatment. Its greatest success, though, was in measuring and comparing the level of psychological distress in different segments of the population.

The typical content of indexes measuring distress changed over the years. Many early community studies asked mostly about malaise such as cold sweats and heart palpitations and other physical symptoms (Gurin, Veroff, and Feld 1960; Srole et al. 1962). Current studies ask more questions about mood, such as feeling worried, lonely, or sad. The contrast between the Gurin index and the Center for Epidemiologic Studies' Depression Scale (CES-D) typifies the transition. In *Americans View Their Mental Health,* one of the earliest community mental health surveys, Gurin et al. (1960) measured distress with an index composed entirely of items referring to malaise such as dizziness, trembling hands, and difficulty getting up in the morning. This index was also used in Myers' New Haven follow-up study (Myers et al. 1975; Thoits 1983). In contrast, the more recent CES-D contains mostly questions about emotions such as feeling depressed, fearful, lonely, and sad or not feeling as good as other people, hopeful about the future, or happy, and not enjoying life (Radloff 1977; Ross and Mirowsky 1984). The CES-D is used in the National Center for Health Statistics' Health and Nutrition Examination Survey (HANES) (Eaton and Kessler 1981), in a large-scale public health survey in Los Angeles (Frerichs, Aneshensel, and Clark 1981), in a national survey of married couples (Ross, Mirowsky, and Huber 1983), and many others (e.g., Lennon 1982; Tausig 1982), and has largely replaced the Langner index as the standard.

Two sets of observations drive the shift from physiological to psychological indicators of distress. First, researchers discovered that people are far more willing to report their feelings in community surveys than anyone expected. Researchers ask questions about headaches, sweaty palms, heart palpitations, lethargy, and loss of appetite partly to mask their intent of measuring the respondent's emotional state. In the early days of community mental health studies the researchers thought people might be insulted or disturbed by direct questions about emotional states. Some early studies hired psychiatrists and psychologists to cautiously ask questions about emotions. The surveyors gradually discovered that direct questions about emotions create little or no unease. Some individuals seem less forthcoming than others, perhaps because they are less attuned to their own emotional states. Generally speaking, more people will report a physical symptom such as lethargy than a corresponding emotional one such as sadness. That could reflect a reluctance among some individuals to report emotions, or the physical symptoms might really occur more often. Luckily, both types of measures show the same social patterns of distress—the same profile of high and low zones across social statuses and conditions. Today, telephone surveys using lay interviewers with essentially the same training as interviewers for an opinion poll produce the same quality of results as earlier, more cautious surveys using mental health professionals.

A growing interest in the relationship between physical and mental health created a second reasons for the switch. Some studies suggest that malaise may indicate physical health problems as well as emotional ones, particularly in aging populations (Johnson and Meile 1981) or other groups that have high rates of health problems (Wheaton 1982). The impact of chronic and acute disease, hospitalization, injury, and disability on emotional well-being is an important issue. The use of physiologic symptoms of distress could bias results in favor of an association, making it seem stronger than it really is (Thoits 1981). Many researchers feel that it is safer to use purely psychological indicators. On the whole though, studies of "physiogenic bias" find that it exists but is not great and does not account for the major social patterns of distress (e.g., Mirowsky and Ross 1992). Measures of dread, anxiety, sadness, hopelessness, worthlessness, guilt, enervation, listlessness, and distraction are interrelated. For most purposes they provide interchangeable indications of distress (Dohrenwend et al. 1980). Sometimes different types of distress (such as depression and anxiety) have different patterns that provide insight into the nature of a particular social condition (e.g., Mirowsky and Ross 1984; Wheaton 1983), but more often the patterns match and tell the same story about who is distressed and why.

The Opposite of Well-Being

Well-being and distress are opposite poles on a single continuum: more well-being means less distress and more distress means less well-being. Well-being is a general sense of enjoying life and feeling happy, hopeful about the future, and as good as other people. Lack of these positive feelings is related to depression and anxiety. It is useful to think of a continuum from happy and fulfilled at the well-being end to depressed and anxious at the distress end. As well-being goes up, distress goes down. Figure 2.2 illustrates, using data from our 1995 U.S. Aging, Status, and the Sense of Control (ASOC) survey. It shows the average number of days of sadness reported by persons reporting no days of happiness, one day, two

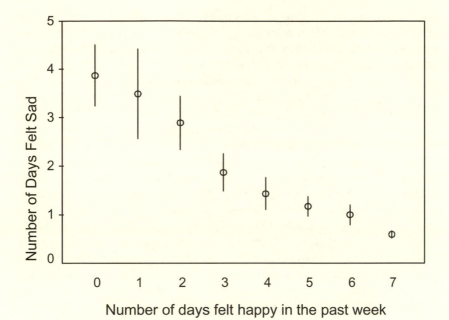

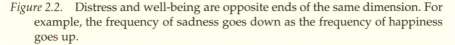

Figure 2.2. Distress and well-being are opposite ends of the same dimension. For example, the frequency of sadness goes down as the frequency of happiness goes up.

days, and so on. (The vertical lines represent the 95 percent confidence interval, sometimes called the sample's margin of error.) As the figure illustrates, the average number of days of sadness goes down as the number of days of happiness goes up.

The fact that well-being and distress are opposite poles of the same emotional dimension is so obvious that many readers may think it does not need to be said. Yet some researchers say that positive and negative emotions are distinct dimensions of mood, and not just opposite poles (e.g., Bradburn 1969). The reason given is that the negative correlation between measures of well-being and of distress is not perfect (not –1.0). Depending on how well-being and distress are measured, the estimated correlation ranges from –.50 (Ross and Mirowsky 1984) to near zero (Bradburn 1969). These correlations seem to suggest that well-being and distress are at least partially independent moods.

There are three reasons why the negative correlation between well-being and distress is less than perfect, even though they are opposite poles of a single dimension of mood. The most important is random measurement error. There is always a certain amount of randomness in the processes of communicating and recording. Like the background noise in a radio broadcast, this randomness can be minimized but never totally eliminated. Random error in measures of well-being and distress reduces the size of their apparent correlation, because the random part of one measure is necessarily uncorrelated with the random part of the other. However, it is possible to estimate the percentage of the recorded communication that is random, and then estimate the correlation that would be found if communication and recording were perfect. By our estimate, the corrected correlation is approximately −.70 (Ross and Mirowsky 1984).

The negative correlation between distress and well-being also is less than perfect because of differences in emotional expressiveness and volatility. Some people express their feelings less than others. Differences in expressiveness crosscut differences in mood. The worse a person's mood, the less well-being and more distress he or she reports, but the less expressive a person is the less of *both* he or she reports. In addition, questions about distress generally cover a period of time such as the past week or month. Most individuals are happier on some days than on others. Some individuals go up and down more than others.

Differences in expressiveness and volatility are easy to take into account, and investigations show they have little effect on the results of studies (Ross and Mirowsky 1984; Gove et al. 1976; Gove and Geerken 1977). In particular, women are more expressive than men but this does not account for the higher levels of anxiety and depression reported by women, as detailed in Chapter 4. Other sociodemographic differences in expressiveness are not as great as that between the sexes, and do not account for the social patterns of distress. Well-being increases and distress decreases with greater education and income, with fewer personal losses and economic hardships, and with marriage. Well-being and distress have opposite sociodemographic patterns because they are opposite ends of the same continuum.

Not Dissatisfaction or Alienation

In contrast to some other researchers (notably Campbell, Converse, and Rodgers 1976), we do not consider dissatisfaction a part of distress. Well-being and distress are the poles of one dimension; satisfaction and discontent are the poles of another. Satisfaction implies a convergence of aspiration and achievement that reflects resignation as much as it does accomplishment. Whereas distress often results from deprivation, dissatisfaction results from deprivation *relative to one's expectations*. Although the two may often go together, the instances in which they do not are important to sociological theory. For example, education increases expected income and thus increases both well-being and satisfaction with one's income; but among people in the *same* income bracket, higher education increases well-being but *de*creases satisfaction with that level of income (Mirowsky 1987). By the same token, a worker is more satisfied with low pay, but also more distressed, if he or she has a high school education rather than a college education. Rising expectations tend to reduce satisfaction with a given level of achievement, while simultaneously enhancing the sense of well-being.

Subjective alienation also is not distress. Alienation is a state of mind, distress is a state of feeling. An alienated person has a sense of not controlling outcomes in his or her own life, or of being an agent of someone else's intentions, or of life having no meaning or purpose, or of not being someone of importance and value to others, or of the social rules being in disarray, inapplicable, or hostile to his or her own interests. These perceptions may be profoundly distressing, but they are not distress itself. Distinguishing between subjective alienation and distress allows researchers to ask several empirical questions that are of theoretical interest: To what extent are alienation and distress correlated? Under what conditions is the correlation stronger or weaker? To what extent, and under what conditions, do those who suffer as a consequence of alienation recognize the cause of their distress?

Not Mental Illness

Only the most extreme, persistent, or inexplicable distress would get labeled as mental illness. Most people in the community do not have severe or abnormal emotional problems, although a substantial minority do. Much distress is the psychiatric equivalent of a cold or flu. Even when severe, much distress reflects threatening or discouraging circumstances that most individuals can resolve.

Distress differs conceptually from a number of other mental problems often considered mental illness. In particular, most researchers treat cognitive problems such as schizophrenia as conceptually distinct from affective problems such as depression. Anxiety, guilt, anger, and lack of positive feelings are basically emotional. Problems such as schizophrenia are basically cognitive—a disorder of the thought processes rather than the emotions. Although affective problems can have cognitive components, and vice versa, their defining characteristics are different. Cognitive symptoms include seeing things other people do not see, hearing things other people do not hear, believing other people can hear your thoughts, feeling possessed or controlled by forces or beings, thinking you have enemies who want to harm you, being sure everyone is against you, believing you are being plotted against, having nightmares, and having unusual thoughts. Many of these symptoms indicate the delusional thinking of paranoia. The term "distress" also does not refer to personality disorder such as being antisocial or hostile, to intellectual deterioration resulting from old age or drug abuse, to manic states or emotional volatility, or to alcoholism or other chemical dependencies. Distress often results from those other types of problems or the situations that created them, but it is seen as distinct from them.

A Human Universal

If distress is not mental illness, why bother to study it? There are several reasons. The most important is that misery is still misery, even if it is a normal response to a stressful situation rather than a symptom of disease. Most people, perhaps all, prefer to avoid depressed and anxious mood and malaise. That makes it a universal common yardstick. Measuring distress allows researchers to quantify the quality of life in terms that embody universal human values. The researchers who produce the information about distress and the individuals who learn that information and use it do not have to share the same ideology, religion, politics, or attitudes. Measuring distress allows researchers to provide information that individuals can use to make their own lives and communities better without the researchers having to superimpose their own views of what is good for those individuals and communities.

Distress also has social costs. Some are obvious. The person who can't sleep at night and feels tired and listless during the day may have trouble working or getting along with others. Some are less obvious. People with backaches, stomachaches, headaches, and other forms of malaise often seek medical care. At least 20 percent of all visits to primary care physicians turn out to be for malaise with no detectable physical cause (Locke and Gardner 1969; Hiday 1980). Because the same symptoms can result from serious medical illness, the physician takes a history, does a physical, follows up with diagnostic tests, and, because false positives are inevitable, sometimes treats people for illnesses they do not have. This is an expensive, dangerous, and ineffective way to care for people who are depressed or anxious. Psychological distress creates problems in our medical care system.

For sociologists there is a final reason to study distress. The maps of emotional high and low zones tell us a great deal about the nature and quality of life in different social positions.

DIAGNOSIS: SUPERIMPOSED DISTINCTIONS

Psychological Problems Are Real, But Not Entities

Psychological problems are not discrete. They are not something that is entirely present or entirely absent, without shades in between. Psychological problems are not entities. They are not alien things that get into a person and wreak havoc. Nevertheless, psychiatrists speak of depression and other psychological problems as if discrete entities enter the bodies or souls of hapless victims. The psychiatrist detects the presence of an entity, determines its species, and selects an appropriate weapon against it. The imagery of detection follows from the language of discrete entities. This categorical language is the legacy of nineteenth-century epidemiology and microbiology. A person is diseased or not. The disease is malaria or not, cholera or not, schistosomiasis or not, etc. A language of categories fits some realities better than others. It fits the reality of psychological problems poorly.

The Linguistic Legacy of Infectious-Disease Epidemiology.

In the eighteenth and nineteenth centuries, the fledgling science of epidemiology made its first major advances. Epidemiology studies the causes of disease by comparing the amount of disease in different groups of people. In the early days, epidemiologists gathered the birth, death, and census data collected by churches and local government. Much of this information had been kept for the purpose of tithing and taxation, or to warn wealthy urbanites of impending plagues (Susser 1973). The early epidemiologist counted the number of deaths in an area and divided by the number of persons living in the area. The ratio was compared with similar quantities for other areas or for the same area at other times, and correlated with environmental differences between areas or changes over time. Counts of persons and counts of deaths lent themselves naturally to a language of categories. When London parishes began recording counts of death due to cholera, John Snow discovered the connection between outbreaks of the disease and the contamination of drinking water with sewage. Snow demonstrated the power of the new science by closing a contaminated well and thus stopping an epidemic (ibid.). Based on his observations, Snow thought cholera might be caused by an invisible, self-reproducing organism living in contaminated water. His speculation was confirmed thirty years later, when Koch and Pasteur showed that the cholera *Vibrio* is the responsible agent.

As the science of epidemiology developed, it spawned a host of concepts based on the underlying method of sorting and counting people, and comparing ratios of various counts. These are the concepts familiar to anyone who studies epidemiology today: point prevalence, period prevalence, incidence, attack rate, risk, relative risk, attributable risk, standardized morbidity, proportionate mortality, and so on. Every one of these concepts presupposes the ability to sort people into two groups: those who have the disease and those who do not. This distinction is not always easy to make. Another set of concepts describes the ability to detect the true underlying presence or absence of the disease: sensitivity, specificity, true positive rate, false positive rate, true negative rate, false negative rate, likelihood ratio, and so on. In essence, these concepts measure how much one is more or less certain a person does or does not have the disease. Alternatively, we could say they measure how well a particular piece of information, or the information on a particular patient, fits our concept of the disease. These terms stretch the dichotomy at the heart of epidemiology to cover a dimensional and shaded reality. So do others, such as infectivity, pathogenicity, virulence, and resistance. In a time when health problems such as hypertension, alcoholism, diabetes, hypercholesterolemia, and obesity are forcing the language of epidemiology and medicine to describe gradations, and not just distinctions, psychiatry has developed a passion for diagnostic schemes.

Reification of Categories in Psychiatry.

Why does psychiatry use and promote a categorical language if psychological problems are not discrete entities? Today, psychiatry wants to look and sound like other medical specialties. The older Freudian psychiatry was not always well received in the world of medicine. Physicians familiar with talk about lesions, toxins, and organisms felt queasy when the talk turned to repression, transference, and wanting to sleep with your mother and kill your father. To the extent that Freudian analysis was considered the treatment for all psychological problems (or at least all neuroses), exact and uniform diagnostic categories and procedures were not essential. The insight of a specific analysis was the important thing. In other medical specialties, professional authority was (and is) based on the claim of having the proper treatment for each disease and the proper diagnosis for each patient. Diagnosis links the problem presented by a particular patient to the cataloged information and accumulated lore of medicine.

Psychiatry has come to equate categorical assessment with true science. The method of research and the form of ideas in nineteenth-century epidemiology and microbiology are built into the official language of medicine, and if psychiatry is medicine then it must use the official language. Instead of shaping the methods and language of psychiatry to suit its dimensional and graded subject, psychiatrists and psychiatric epidemiologists insist that there must be discrete entities hidden in the shades of psychological problems. The following quote is from a debate in the *Archives of General Psychiatry*:

> Without some diagnostic criteria for who is "in" or "out" of a diagnostic class, such as depression, it is not possible to decide whether a given person or group of persons are [sic] clinically depressed as distinct from unhappy

and discontented because of social deprivation or the frustration of their personal wishes. Nor is it possible to assess risk in a way that would generate more specific clues to possible etiologies. The concept of "risk" implies "risk for what?" The "what" we maintain, are discrete disorders. (Weissman and Klerman 1980:1424)

This statement is saying that clinical depression is and must be a discrete entity because otherwise the concept of risk, and the standard machinery of clinical and epidemiologic research, would not apply. There is a word that is not used much in everyday conversation, but it is used by philosophers, linguists, cultural anthropologists, and others who study the relationship between ideas and the things they represent. The word is "reify." Reifying is treating an abstraction as if it had material existence. This is known as "the fallacy of misplaced concreteness" (Srole and Fischer 1980). The person who feels bad is real. The person's feelings are real. The psychiatrist's act of classifying the patient's problem is real. The consequences of the psychiatrist's act of classification are real. "Major depressive disorder" is *not* real. It is a linguistic pigeonhole that some cases are put in and others are not. Speaking of the diagnosis of depression as if it *is* depression is reifying. The manmade shape of the pigeonhole is mistaken for the shape of reality.

The Alternative: The Type and Severity of Symptoms.

The fact is that researchers do not have to place people in diagnostic categories in order to know which subpopulations suffer more than others. Counting the number of persons in a diagnostic category is easily replaced by counting the number of symptoms of a particular type that various people have. The latter strategy avoids the proliferation of disease categories, each with its own name and mythical status as a unique, discrete entity. One needs to remember, though, that a category of symptoms is a mental pigeonhole too. People are the real entities. The symptoms are merely things that some people feel or think or do more than others, for reasons we would like to understand. Some of those things appear together more frequently than others, and seem alike in their nature, and those are the ones we treat as a single type of symptom.

It is useful to think in terms of the *type* and *severity* of psychological problems. Depression is a type of psychological problem. So is anxiety. Each type of problem ranges from not at all severe to very severe, on a continuum. People score at all points on the continuum, from very few symptoms to many symptoms. People can get a severity score for each type of psychological problem. Contrast this with the diagnostic approach. Imagine two people on either side of some arbitrary cutoff that defines depression. One has just enough symptoms to get a diagnosis, the other is just short of enough. Although the type and severity of their problems are very similar, one is diagnosed as depressed and the other is not. The categorization ignores their similarity. Imagine another two people. One is happy, fulfilled, and productive. The other is demoralized, hopeless, and miserable, but just short of meeting the criteria for a diagnosis of depression. The categorization ignores their differences. Diagnosis throws away information on the similarity of some cases and on the dissimilarity of others.

Reliability versus Certainty: The Fallacy of the Two-Category Scale.

Throwing away information hinders understanding rather than promoting it. Many people, including many scientists, erroneously believe that making crude distinctions improves the accuracy of an assessment. For example, a typical bathroom scale measures weight accurately within a range of plus or minus 2 pounds. This means that if a person's true weight is 140 pounds, there's a 95 percent probability that the bathroom scale will say the person's weight is in the range from 138 to 142 pounds. It is unlikely the scale will give the person's exact, true weight, and it would be sheer chance if the scale did. Nevertheless, the bathroom scale is almost certain to register within 2 pounds of the person's true weight. Although the bathroom scale will rarely tell us a person's true weight, it will usually tell us correctly which 5- or 10-pound range the person's weight is in. The broader the ranges, the more likely a bathroom scale tells us correctly which range the person's weight is in. The broadest range would divide everybody into two categories: heavies and not heavies. Almost everyone would be correctly classified. The current bathroom scale, which almost never shows a person's true weight, could be improved so that it only shows whether a person is heavy or not. Now suppose you are trying to lose weight. Which bathroom scale would you choose? The old one that is almost never correct, or the new and improved one that is almost always correct?

The fallacy of the two-category scale lies in confusing certainty and reliability. In psychometrics (the science of measuring psychological states and traits), reliability is the exactness of reproduction that can be achieved with a given measure. Reliability in psychometrics is analogous to fidelity in electronics. Fidelity is the degree to which a system, such as a radio or television, accurately reproduces the essential characteristics of its input. The symphony one hears on the radio is never exactly like the symphony one hears in the concert hall, but no one would ever suggest improving the broadcast by reducing all sounds to the presence or absence of a single tone. Imagine listening to a broadcast altered in that way and trying to figure out what music is being played. Reliability increases with the precision of assessment. A measure of length is more reliable if the ruler is marked in inches than if the ruler is marked only in feet. Reliability is lowest if measurement is dichotomous—a simple yes or no, in or out, heavy or not, diagnosed or not.

As an assessment becomes broader, it becomes less sensitive to meaningful changes or differences, *and the ratio of information to noise declines*. This may seem strange, given that broader categories increase the certainty of an assessment. Once again, though, it is reliability and not certainty that we need. After all, if we reduced everything to a single category, our certainty would be perfect, but meaningless. The bathroom scale that has a random error of plus or minus two pounds has exactly the same amount of random error when we paint out all the little marks and replace them with a red zone for heavy and a white zone for not heavy. The crude split eliminates almost all of the information without eliminating any of the random error.

When the full range of symptoms is split into two categories (enough for a diagnosis of depression, or not enough), most of the information is lost, but all the random error remains. A diagnosis of depression is a profoundly insensitive measure. As a consequence, it can be difficult to find meaningful changes or differences in diagnosed depression. For example, one community study finds education and family income do not predict whether a person gets a diagnosis of depression or not (Weissman 1987). One of the researchers concludes that "depression equally affects the educated and uneducated, the rich and poor, White and Black Americans, blue and white collar workers" (ibid.:448). Nothing could be further from the truth. No theory, whether social, psychological, genetic, or environmental, predicts that the poor, the uneducated, the blacks, and the blue-collar workers have the same exposure to the causes of depression as the rich, the educated, the whites, and the white-collar workers. With a sufficiently insensitive measure, psychiatric epidemiology cannot hear the suffering of millions and cannot see the causes.

A Person Does Not Have to Be Diagnosed to Be Helped.

Often the argument for categorizing people as ill versus well is that those categorized as ill can be treated. A diagnosis may or may not be handy, but it is not necessary. Anyone who feels very depressed and seeks treatment or is referred for treatment can be treated for depression. We do not need to label people as depressives, schizophrenics, or alcoholics in order to recognize that they feel bad, that their thoughts are disorganized and bizarre, or that they have problems with alcohol. Certainly, we need to assess the type and extent of a person's problems, but the assessment does not need to be categorical. A person does not have to be diagnosed to be helped.

Once a person is diagnosed, the diagnosis may be treated as the person's preeminent trait. Mark Vonnegut is a good example. He writes of his experiences with serious psychological problems in *Eden Express* (1975). Mark Vonnegut had severe levels of schizophrenia (thought disorder). His functioning was impaired, and his problem lasted for months or more. He was diagnosed as schizophrenic. Within the diagnostic paradigm, this was correct. However, Mark Vonnegut had many other psychological problems. His anxiety was so severe he often would panic. His depression led to long crying spells, black moods, and suicide attempts. Because Mark Vonnegut was "schizophrenic," his depression and anxiety were ignored or treated as merely secondary. His label blinded those who were trying to help him (and Mark himself after he accepted the diagnosis) to his other problems. Mark Vonnegut was a person who had high levels of schizophrenia, depression, and anxiety. He was not treated for depression and anxiety because he was a "schizophrenic." In reality, many people with problems of one type also have others too.

Even if types of symptoms are distinct, it does not mean that we can neatly assign individuals to a set of mutually exclusive diagnostic categories, saying some are depressed, others are anxious, and others are schizophrenic. Attempts to produce a set of exhaustive and mutually exclusive diagnostic categories led to a proliferation of diagnoses that describe people who happen to have symptoms from more than one cluster. Thus, we get diagnostic categories like "schizo-affective," which is given when the clinician can't decide whether to diagnose schizophrenia (disorganized and bizarre thoughts and perceptions) or affective disorder (severe depression and anxiety). Worse than the introduction of unnecessary complexity, such a practice may obscure the fact that the causes of some symptoms on which a diagnosis is based are different than the causes of other symptoms on which it is based. Even with a profusion of categories for people who are between categories (schizo-affective disorder) or just outside a category (schizophreniform disorder), many patients are difficult to classify (Srole and Fischer 1980).

How a Diagnosis Is Made

Although current diagnostic schemes vary somewhat, all are based on descriptions in the *Diagnostic and Statistical Manual of Mental Disorders* (DSM); now in its fourth edition) of the American Psychiatric Association. The general criteria for diagnosis are the presence and duration of symptoms. Each criterion has a cutoff point below which the person does not qualify for a diagnosis of a particular disorder. Some diagnostic categories are considered mutually exclusive, so alternative diagnoses must be ruled out. For example, the diagnosis of major depressive disorder rules out cases with signs of schizophrenia such as hallucinations or delusions, cases apparently resulting from bereavement or substance abuse, and cases with a history of manic episodes.

There are four steps in making a diagnosis. The first is *assessing* the level of symptoms, extent of impaired functioning, and duration of problems. Note that level, extent, and duration all refer to assessments of degree or amount. The second is *splitting* each assessed amount at some cutoff point, so that differences in degree are collapsed into two categories: amounts that meet the criterion and amounts that do not. The third is *totting up* so that all possible combinations of met/unmet on the three criteria are represented in a single overarching split. The fourth is *excluding* cases that also meet other criteria considered preeminent (such as recent bereavement).

Diagnosis combines assessment with judgment. Questioning, observing, and recording symptoms, functioning, and duration is assessment. Using the answers, observations, and records to assign a case to a category is judgment. The two kinds of tasks can be divided in time or between actors (e.g., nurse and physician). In research they are often divided into a questionnaire or protocol for assessment, and an "algorithm" or set of rules for making a judgment. In early community mental health studies, the judgments were made by psychiatrists who examined the records of assessed symptoms, functioning, and duration. Today, the judgments are often made by computers following preset rules.

Diagnosing Schizophrenia.

Many people might agree that depression is not a categorical problem; that this is a reified notion of disease that does not reflect reality. But the same people might disagree about schizophrenia, arguing that the diagnostic approach *is* appropriate here. We do not think so. Symptoms of schizophrenia also can be measured by a continuous scale. Wheaton (1985) uses a scale of schizophrenic (cognitive) symptoms, each scored according to how often the respondent reported it (never, rarely, sometimes, often, very often) and then added together. The symptoms are:

- felt that your mind was dominated by forces beyond your control
- felt sure everyone was against you
- heard voices without knowing where they came from
- had trouble thinking
- believed you were being plotted against
- thought people were saying things about you behind your back
- saw things that other people did not see
- heard your thoughts being spoken aloud
- heard your thoughts being broadcast or transmitted

- felt you did not exist at all
- felt possessed by the devil
- felt you had special powers
- had trouble thinking
- had visions
- makes up words
- gives answers that have little to do with the questions.

We are most aware of people who have severe symptoms of schizo-phrenia, who cannot function, and who have had the problem for a long time—those who would qualify for a diagnosis of schizophrenia. In fact, cognitive symptoms, like affective ones, can be scaled, and people can be placed along the continuum of intensity. People can score from no cognitive symptoms, to mild, moderate, and severe. There are actually many people in the community who have mild or moderate cognitive problems, who sometimes see things others do not, or feel their mind is controlled by outside forces, but whose problems are not severe and do not interfere with functioning. Even with schizophrenia, the diagnostic approach does not reflect reality. As with depression, information on possible social, psychological, and genetic causes should be collected and correlated with schizophrenia. So should information on the duration and consequences of schizophrenia. But nothing is gained, and much is lost, by reducing that information to a diagnosis. It is likely that susceptibility, onset, severity, duration, and dysfunction have different causes that obscure each other when everything is thrown into a single diagnostic pot.

A Sea of Troubles

Two things are classified in diagnosis: people and symptoms. People are hard to classify. They often have more than one type of psychological problem, and each type is graded and variable, not just present or absent. Perhaps the symptoms are readily classified, even if people are not. Each person could have a profile of scores representing their levels of anxiety, depression, schizophrenia, and so on. Each score counts the person's symptoms of the respective form. But how do we know which symptoms belong in which index? How unambiguously distinct are the forms of psychological problems?

The Patterns of Symptoms: Galaxies, Nebulae, or Spectra?

There are two predominant opposing views about the distinctiveness of the forms of psychological symptoms. Both are compatible with the fact that individual persons can have mixed and graded problems. One we

Galaxies   Nebula   Spectrum

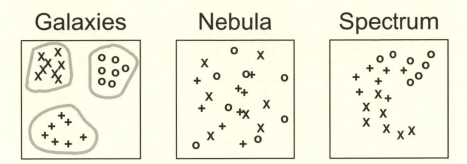

Figure 2.3.   The galaxies, nebulae, and spectra hypotheses. O, +, and x each represent a type of symptom such as paranoia, depression, and anxiety.

will call the galaxy hypothesis, and the other the nebula hypothesis. The
galaxy hypothesis says that symptoms cluster together by type. Symptoms of a similar type often go together and symptoms of different types
usually do not go together. Imagine a map showing pairs of symptoms
closer together the more often they occur together in the same persons. In
this view symptoms of the same type form clumps or "galaxies" separated
by large, empty regions from the symptoms of other types. Clusters may
be close to each other or far apart. For instance, depression and anxiety
clusters may be closer than depression and schizophrenia clusters. However, each is a distinctive cluster, separated from the others by empty
space. The types of problems are clearly separate. In contrast, the nebula
hypothesis says that symptoms are randomly distributed. Symptoms do
not cluster according to type. They are an undifferentiated pool. The only
meaningful quality of the nebula is its overall severity. Types are not distinct (see Figure 2.3).

Do the types of psychological problems form distinct galaxies, or
merely a random, undifferentiated nebula of symptoms? Debates over this
issue are often acrimonious (for example, Srole and Fischer (1980) versus
Weissman and Klerman [1980]). The weight of scientific opinion shifts one
way or the other from time to time, but the issue is not settled, largely
because the debate is over conceptual schemes with little reference to the
data on real people and real symptoms.

There are two alternatives to the opposing galaxy and nebula views.
Dohrenwend and his colleagues present one compromise view. They
argue that there is a large pool of symptoms indicating "nonspecific psychological distress" (Dohrenwend et al. 1980). Like fever or pain, the nonspecific symptoms tell us whether or not a person has a problem, but not
which problem the person has. Then there are specific symptoms that

distinguish one type of problem from another, such as false beliefs and perceptions, mania, guilt, or problem drinking. In our analogy, this would be a large random nebula with definite galaxies interspersed.

Another alternative is the spectrum hypothesis. According to this view symptoms of each type cluster together. Symptoms of depression cluster together, symptoms of anxiety cluster together, and so on. However, the clusters overlap. One type shades into the next. Symptoms of depression cluster together, as do symptoms of anxiety, but no clear boundary separates them. Their areas shade from mostly depression to mostly anxiety.

Mapping the 4,095 Correlations among Ninety-One Symptoms.

Using modern psychometric techniques, we mapped the location and clusters of ninety-one symptoms in correlational space. The map shows what symptoms are associated with each other. Importantly, we did this without having to guess in advance what the pattern looks like. The map does not superimpose any assumptions or preconceptions about the types of psychological problems. The map illustrates what people report. Using a technique called multidimensional scaling, we look at the pattern of correlations among symptoms (Kruskal and Wish 1978; Schiffman, Reynolds, and Young 1981). We also show the diagnostic category associated with each symptom in standard diagnostic schemes. That shows how well or poorly the diagnostic categories reflect actual patterns of correlation among symptoms.

Before showing the actual map that we derived, we need to summarize how the method works, what the results mean, the nature of the data we used, and why we chose that data. The map making begins by selecting a set of symptoms, a sample of people, and a way of noting each individual's symptoms. All pairs of symptoms are correlated across individuals. The correlation is a number that theoretically ranges from –1 to +1. The correlation is positive if the two symptoms tend to be present together and absent together. In other words, if a person in the sample has one of the symptoms, he or she is more likely than average to have the other one too. If a person in the sample does not have one of the symptoms, he or she is less likely than average to have the other. The more this is true, the larger the positive correlation. If two symptoms always appeared together, and never appeared without each other, the correlation would be +1. (In practice, correlations are usually much smaller.)

The technique of multidimensional scaling draws a map of the correlations among the symptoms. Each symptom has a location on the map, just as each city or town has a location on a road map. The proximity of two symptoms on the map represents the size of their correlation with each other and the similarity of their profiles of correlations with all the other symptoms. The map summarizes the correlations among all the symptoms. Without the map it is very difficult to see and think about all the relationships at once. In our analysis, we look at the correlations among ninety-one symptoms—a total of 4,095 correlations. That's more numbers than anyone can think about at once. Ninety-one points on a map are relatively easy to comprehend. The closer two symptoms are on the map, the higher the correlation between them and the more similar their patterns of correlation with the other symptoms.

To make the map, the program begins by giving each symptom a random location. Then it measures the distance between all the pairs of locations and compares the distances to the respective correlations. If two symptoms are farther apart than their correlation says they should be, the program moves them closer together. If the symptoms are too close, the program moves them farther apart. The program keeps shuffling the points around until the fit of the distances to the correlations stops improving.

The correlations we use come from a community survey of 463 people living in El Paso, Texas, and Juarez, Mexico, called the Life Stress and Illness Project. We use this survey because it has, to our knowledge, the most complete list of symptoms of all forms of psychological problems of any community study. The symptoms were chosen from standard research indexes and diagnostic questionnaires, and from the *DSM*. They represent the symptoms found in survey research measures such as the Langner, Gurin, and CES-D indexes, and in diagnostic instruments such as the Schedule for Affective Disorder and Schizophrenia and the Diagnostic Interview Schedule. A complete list of the ninety-one symptoms is given in the appendix to this chapter. *These are the symptoms on which psychiatric diagnosis is based*. They represent the problems of the overwhelming majority of all patients seen and diagnosed by psychiatrists.

The persons interviewed in the study were selected by careful random-sampling. They represent the typical range of people living in El Paso and Juarez. Most people in the community have symptoms that range in severity from mild to moderate. Very few are psychiatric patients or have ever been psychiatric patients, although some may be. All were interviewed in their homes, in English or Spanish, depending on the person's preference. One of the original purposes of the study was to find out if the pattern of correlations among symptoms depends on the subjects' language and culture. In these data, it does not. The patterns are essentially the same for the Mexicans as for the Anglos (Mirowsky and Ross 1983). The two groups are therefore combined. For most of the symptoms, the people were asked how often they had it or how often it happened in the previous twelve months. The response categories were never, almost never, sometimes, fairly often, and very often (coded 0 through 4, respectively). Seven of the items are based on the interviewer's observation of the person's behavior during the interview, with specific behaviors noted as observed or not (1 or 0). Most people do not have, or rarely have, most of the symptoms, but everyone has some symptoms, and every symptom is reported by some people.

In order to show the relationship between the pattern of correlations and diagnostic concepts, we've classified symptoms into five main categories: depression, anxiety, schizophrenia, paranoia, and alcoholism. These distinctions help us read the map, *but they do not determine the findings.* Our assignment of symptoms to categories follows standard research and diagnostic practice (American Psychiatric Association 1980; Wheaton 1985). We've subdivided the symptoms of depression and anxiety into two subgroups: mood and malaise. The feelings and body states typically go together, but survey researchers sometimes separate the two to avoid "physiogenic bias"—the possibility that an illness could create malaise that has nothing to do with underlying depression or anxiety (Johnson and Meile 1981).

A Circular Spectrum.

Our final map is shown in Figure 2.4. The pattern is like a spectrum with the ends connected. It is not separate galaxies. It is not an amorphous nebula. It is not separate galaxies against a backdrop of an amorphous nebula. It is a circle of association—a circumplex. It is like a color wheel, shading from blue to green to yellow to orange to red to purple to violet to blue. In order to fit all the words on the map, we stretched the horizontal axis (in a ratio of 3:2 compared to the vertical axis). Although it looks like an oval in Figure 2.4, the actual pattern is close to a perfect circle. There are regions of similarity on the circumference that correspond roughly with research and clinical distinctions. Beginning at 12 o'clock and moving counterclockwise, there is schizophrenia, paranoia, extreme depression and anxiety, a large amorphous area of depression and anxiety, sleep problems, physical symptoms of anxiety, signs of restlessness and tension during the interview, signs of alcoholism during the interview, drinking problems, and then schizophrenia again.

The symptoms of schizophrenia cluster together at the top of the map. Seeing things other people don't see, having visions, hearing things other people don't hear, thinking your thoughts are broadcast or spoken aloud, feeling dead, and feeling possessed and dominated by forces beyond your control cluster together. Notice, however, that heavy drinking is also associated with hearing voices, seeing things, and feeling dominated by forces beyond your control.

At the top left of the map, symptoms of paranoia cluster together between schizophrenia and depression/anxiety. They shade into both.

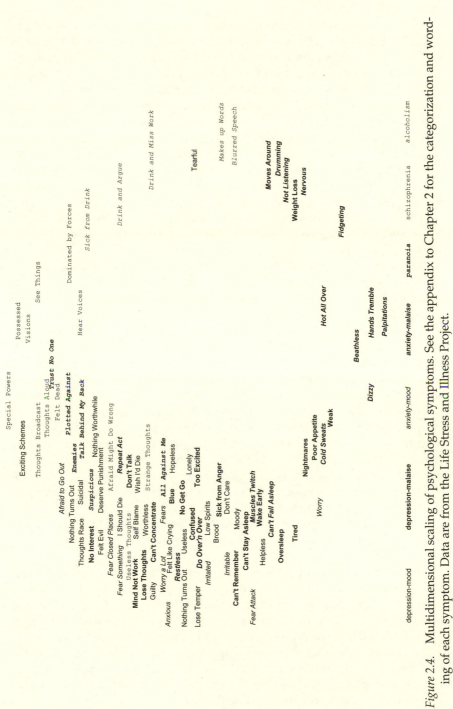

Figure 2.4. Multidimensional scaling of psychological symptoms. See the appendix to Chapter 2 for the categorization and wording of each symptom. Data are from the Life Stress and Illness Project.

Paranoia is a cognitive problem. In the lexicon of psychiatry, it is a delusion. The heart of the delusion is that others are out to harm you. Paranoid schizophrenia is the most common type of schizophrenia and some think all schizophrenia has a paranoid component (Meissner 1978). According to psychiatric diagnostic schemes, cognitive problems are clearly distinct from emotional (or affective) problems like depression and anxiety. Yet the results of the multidimensional scaling show paranoid beliefs are strongly associated with depression. The beliefs that you have enemies who wish to harm you, that others are talking about you behind your back, that you are being plotted against, and that everyone is against you are strongly associated with depression, especially with the feelings that nothing is worthwhile, that nothing ever turns out right, feeling suicidal, and that you deserve punishment. In the community, suspicion and paranoia are associated with other cognitive symptoms of schizophrenia *and* with feelings of depression.

Following the circle of symptoms counterclockwise, we see a large group of symptoms of depression and anxiety, including both mood and malaise. Even though depression and anxiety seem different because they feel different, in reality people who have a lot of one tend to have a lot of the other. Although the map does not indicate it directly, depression and anxiety are the most common forms of psychological problems. That is why there are so many variations on these forms. Like Eskimos having lots of words for the qualities and kinds of snow, we have lots of symptoms of the most common problems. The large cluster includes serious symptoms of depression like wishing you were dead and feeling that others would be better off if you were dead at the top, followed by blaming yourself and feeling worthless and guilty as we continue around the circle, and by feeling blue, lonely, hopeless, and that nothing ever turns out right. Interspersed among symptoms of depression are symptoms of anxiety, including feeling irritable, anxious, restless, and worried. Toward the bottom of this large cluster are the sleep problems characteristic of depression (and anxiety), including trouble falling asleep, waking early and not being able to get back to sleep, feeling tired, sleeping too much, and having nightmares.

At the bottom of the map are symptoms of malaise that indicate anxiety. These include cold sweats, feeling weak, dizzy, out of breath, hot all over, and that your heart is beating hard. These symptoms shade into behavioral symptoms of anxiety as recorded by the interviewer's observations: that the person is restless, fidgeting, not listening, and nervous.

On the right of the map are symptoms of alcoholism, including the interviewer's ratings of the person's behavior like blurred speech, and the person's reports of troubles due to drinking. Notice that the interviewer rating that the person cried during the interview, while conceptually a measure of depression, is actually associated with drinking. Drinking problems shade into seeing things, hearing things, and feeling dominated by forces beyond your control. We are back to schizophrenia.

This map of people's reports of their symptoms makes it clear that, while there are distinctive regions, they shade into each other. Depression and anxiety, including mood and malaise, go together. Paranoia, a cognitive symptom, associates closely with the affective symptoms of depression and anxiety. People who think enemies are out to get them, plotting against them, and talking behind their backs are likely to feel depressed. Schizophrenia forms a relatively distinct cluster, but in some cases the symptoms result from heavy drinking.

The conceptual overlay reflects the pattern of association, but the correspondence is far from perfect. The correlations among symptoms indicate that psychological problems are not clearly distinct, nor are they completely nebulous. There are loci of association, but the regions overlap and blend from one to the next. The symptom correlations form a spectrum of association in which the ends are linked, called a circumplex. The large, amorphous area of depression and anxiety on the left at first seems consistent with Dohrenwend's idea about "nonspecific psychological distress." However, it is not nonspecific. It is clearly depression and anxiety. It shades into paranoia toward the schizophrenia end. Furthermore, it is not simply a backdrop for more specific forms. It is as much a distinct place on the circular spectrum as is schizophrenia or alcoholism.

Several things are not apparent from the figure, but should be mentioned. First, the symptoms in one place in the circle correlate positively with the symptoms in any other place. To some extent this reflects the fact that all the forms of psychological problems are more common among persons with lower education, less desirable jobs, lower family income, and less comfortable living conditions. To some extent it reflects a cascade of problems, with one type resulting in another. The diagnostic insistence on mutually exclusive categories (that a person *cannot* be depressed if he or she is schizophrenic, for example) does not reflect reality. The positive correlations also belie the notion that one type of symptom displaces another. For instance, some might claim that the poor and the well-to-do face the same amount of stress in life but respond to it differently: the well-to-do become depressed, the poor become alcoholic or psychotic. This implies that one problem displaces the other and therefore correlates *negatively* with it. Such is not the case. Different types of problems go together.

Second, as mentioned earlier, depression and anxiety are the most common types of psychological problems, experienced by everyone to some degree at some time. Using symptoms of depression and/or anxiety as indicators of a person's emotional well-being captures the most common problems. In looking at social patterns of distress, we focus on depression and anxiety. In most cases, the patterns would be the same if we examined other forms of psychological problems, but not in all. When we speak of psychological distress, we are referring to symptoms of depression and anxiety. However, in Part IV, we look briefly at other psychological forms on the map, particularly paranoia and schizophrenia.

The Multiplication of Diagnoses

Psychiatry's efforts to speak and think about the correlated, overlapping, shaded, and graded troubles in categorical terms creates three kinds of pseudoknowledge: the proliferation of categories, the social construction of prevalence and "unmet need," and the elaboration of "comorbidity." Efforts to define each seemingly distinctive combination of emotional, cognitive, and behavioral problems proliferates the number of official diagnostic categories. Figure 2.5 shows the multiplication of psychiatric categories over the past century. The chart begins with Kraepelin's nineteenth-century definition of two main types of psychiatric disorder (Horwitz 2002:39): affective psychosis (extreme emotional disorders), and dementia praecox (Latin for premature cognitive disorder, later called schizophrenia). The first standard U.S. psychiatric nosology in 1918 had twenty-two categories, developed to classify persons in mental hospitals for an upcoming census. The first official DSM of the American Psychiatric Association appeared in 1952, with 112 categories, or a fivefold growth in the number of categories. The growth continued, with the number of official categories reaching 374 in the 1992 DSM IV. Throughout the twentieth-century the number of psychiatric categories grew at a compounding rate of 3.25 percent a year, doubling the number of categories every twenty-two years.

Each defined category provides an implicit definition of need for psychiatric treatment. Regardless of how arbitrary the criteria for a specific diagnosis might be, it gets justified on two grounds: two persons using the same rules tend to agree on who fits in the category, and some people in treatment fit the category. Researchers then estimate the number of people not in treatment who "need" psychiatric services because they fit a pattern similar to that of some people in treatment (Kessler and Zhao 1999). Anyone fitting a category but not in treatment gets counted as having an unmet need. This kind of research seeks not to discover the causes of problems but "to develop interventions aimed at increasing the proportion of people with mental disorders who receive treatment" (Kessler 2000:464). Such measurement of unmet need assumes and implies that psychiatric treatment should be provided to everyone who qualifies for a diagnosis but is not currently in psychiatric treatment. Many of the people with psychological problems but not receiving psychiatric treatment do not want

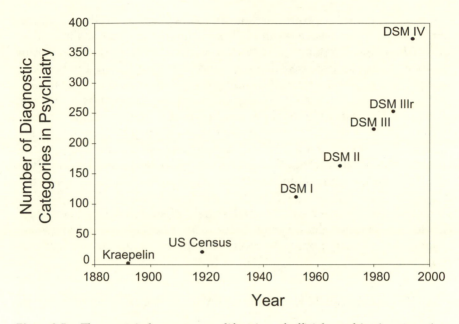

Figure 2.5. The twentieth-century proliferation of official psychiatric categories, doubling every twenty-two years.

to seek help, do not feel comfortable consulting a psychiatrist, and would rather deal with their problems on their own or in other ways (Lin and Parikh 1999). Studies look for ways to convince such refractory individuals to view themselves as having a problem that should be treated with drugs or other psychiatric therapies. Need gets defined and measured as a projection of psychiatric concepts and services, rather than as people wanting help they cannot find or afford. When combined with the proliferation of categories, the social construction of unmet need creates exponential growth in the target market for psychiatric interventions.

Over the years psychiatric epidemiologists eased constraints on diagnostic rules in various ways, such as dropping the requirement that a person seek help or have impaired role performance. Since the first edition of this book, researchers began dropping rules that treat diagnoses as mutually exclusive. This allows each individual to qualify for a variety of diagnoses (and implicitly for a variety of treatments). A surge of publications measures what the psychiatric epidemiologists call "comorbidity": the likelihood that someone who fits one category also fits another. Not surprisingly, researchers find that when they eliminate the exclusion rules individuals tend to qualify for multiple diagnoses. In particular, individuals who fit the definition of an anxiety disorder such as phobic, obsessive-compulsive, panic, or post-traumatic stress disorder generally also fit the definition of a depressive disorder. This "comorbidity" results from two things. First, the symptoms used to categorize individuals do not separate neatly in reality, as discussed above. Second, many symptoms can be taken as signs of different disorders depending on the other symptoms that coincide with them. For example, irritable mood can be seen as indicating generalized anxiety, antisocial personality, borderline personality, cyclothymia, dysthymia, manic or hypomanic episode, major depression, paranoid personality, or oppositional-defiant personality depending on the combination of other things that appear with it. The apparent distinctiveness of various combinations exists largely or entirely in the eyes of the beholders. The current 374 diagnostic categories create 69,751 possible comorbidities—an effectively boundless field of study for psychiatric epidemiology. The one thing such studies must find is the one thing their diagnostic preconceptions must fail to see: the problems are not discrete, not entities.

CONCLUSION: THE STORY OF A WOMAN DIAGNOSED

Superimposing a diagnosis on a person's symptoms and situation does not add information—it takes information away. Worse than that, it entices us to believe a hidden entity has been revealed. The mythical entity insinuates itself into the role of a named actor, and the symptoms and situation dissolve into mere signs of its presence. Current psychiatric theory favors the view that the detected entities are physiological dysfunctions that arise from occult abnormalities that developed because of a pathological genetic inheritance. This explanation is often firmly believed, despite the fact that diagnoses are made without reference to direct measures of genetic inheritance, anatomy and histology, or physiology. Diagnoses are almost always made entirely by reference to symptoms and history. Nevertheless, the *presumed* presence of the entity justifies biochemical treatment and obviates a continuing search for social and environmental causes. To illustrate, we end this chapter with the story of a woman diagnosed.

The story appeared as an "in-depth report" of an evening news program aired nationally on the Public Broadcasting System (PBS). The program is well-known for its balanced and revealing exploration of opposing views on political issues. Unfortunately, the same techniques often are not applied to coverage of health issues. The "medical miracles" format often supersedes the "opposing views" format. The story in question had a clear and simple message: Depression is an illness that can be diagnosed by doctors and treated with drugs; if you have the telltale signs, see your doctor.

The woman is in her late twenties or early thirties. She sounds intelligent and educated. She is married, a mother of preschool-aged children, and a full-time housewife. Her husband has a good job and provides for the family. They live in a pleasant home with a yard the children can play in. She has not suffered any major failure, loss, threat, or undesirable event: no death of a loved one, no life-threatening disease, no breakup of her marriage. As far as she can tell, she has no reason to feel bad. Nevertheless, she found herself drifting into a deepening state of apathy, lethargy, and melancholy. As her energy dwindled, she found herself becoming unresponsive to the children and letting things go around the house. She went to her family doctor, who found no evidence of the medical problems that might produce a profound lethargic state (e.g., anemia, fever, infection, vitamin deficiencies). Her physician diagnosed major depression, prescribed standard antidepressive medication, and referred her to a psychiatrist. Unfortunately, her symptoms did not respond to drug treatment, so her psychiatrist enrolled her in a clinical trial of a new drug. During the interview, she said she felt a little better than before, but far from well. She expressed her belief that the origin of her problem is organic, and (somewhat less certainly) that her psychiatrist would find the right drug to solve her problem.

Within the context of psychiatry, the woman's diagnosis of major depression is correct. She has the symptoms of mood and malaise that characterize depression: she feels sad, blue, hopeless, lethargic, and distracted. The symptoms have been around more than a few weeks. She sought help. Her family physician ruled out medical disease. She does not have symptoms of schizophrenia or other psychiatric disorder. She, her physician, and her psychiatrist can see nothing in her recent history or present circumstances that would normally be depressing. By default, they presume she is suffering the consequences of an insidious and unseen organic dysfunction that may be the result of an unfortunate genetic inheritance.

Apparently, the woman, her physician, and her psychiatrist are unaware that the role of housewife and mother of young children is not the idyllic state our culture says it is. As we detail in parts of Chapters 4, 5, and 7, women who are solely housewives are, on average, more depressed and anxious than women who also have jobs outside the home; women with young children (whether employed or not) are more depressed and anxious than women with older children or no children in the home. The combination of being a housewife with young children at home is particularly distressing. The differences in distress cannot be attributed to differences in other traits of the women, such as age, education, or family income. This is not to say that all housewives and mothers of young children are miserable. But many women find the economic dependency, restrictions, isolation, and menial labor distressing.

The combination of cultural values and preconceptions, along with genuine love of the children and husband, make it difficult for many women to recognize or admit that they find the role of housewife and mother ungratifying. These women may find the psychiatric interpretation of their symptoms appealing, to the extent it helps them avoid an interpretation they are inclined to avoid. In such a case, drug treatment does not solve the basic problem, but it may make the situation more tolerable to the woman, and improve her performance in it. (Also see Chapter 3, Figure 3.2.) If she is treated long enough for her children to get older, her emotional state may improve, and she can be taken off the drug and declared cured. The woman's diagnosis of major depression is functional in that it provides an interpretation and response that does not challenge or threaten her preconceptions, values, and family relationships. The diagnosis is dysfunctional in that it helps her hide from a problem she must recognize and understand in order to solve.

APPENDIX OF SYMPTOM INDEXES

Schizophrenia

dominated by forces: felt that your mind was dominated by forces beyond your control
hear voices: heard voices without knowing where they came from
see things: have seen things or animals or people around you that others did not see
visions: had visions or have seen things other people say they cannot see
possessed: felt that you were possessed by a spirit or devil
special powers: felt you had special powers
felt dead: felt that you did not exist at all, that you were dead, dissolved
thoughts aloud: seemed to hear your thoughts spoken aloud—almost as if someone standing nearby could hear them
thoughts broadcast: felt that your unspoken thoughts were being broadcast or transmitted, so that everyone knew what you were thinking
afraid might do wrong: felt afraid that you might do something seriously wrong against your own will
strange thoughts: had unusual thoughts that kept bothering you
useless thoughts: had useless thoughts that kept running through your mind

Paranoia

trust no one: felt it was safer to trust no one
plotted against: believed you were being plotted against
talk behind back: felt that people were saying all kinds of things about you behind your back

enemies: felt you had enemies who really wished to do you harm
suspicious: have been very suspicious, didn't trust anybody
all against me: have been sure that everyone was against you

Depressed Mood

nothing worthwhile: wondered if anything was worthwhile anymore
suicidal: thought about taking your own life
nothing turns out: felt that nothing turned out for you the way you wanted it to
deserve punishment: felt you deserved to be punished
should die: felt that others would be better off if you were dead
felt evil: felt that you have done something evil or wrong
wish I'd die: wished you were dead
worthless: felt very bad or worthless
self blame: blamed yourself for something that went wrong
hopeless: felt completely hopeless about everything
lonely: felt lonely
felt like crying: felt like crying
guilty: felt guilty about things you did or did not do
useless: felt useless
lose temper: lost your temper
low spirits: have been in low spirits
brood: brooded over unpleasant thoughts or feelings
don't care: just didn't care what happened to you
moody: have been moody and unhappy
helpless: felt completely helpless
tearful: the respondent cried or was tearful

Manic Mood

exciting schemes: had times when exciting new ideas and schemes occurred to you one after another
thoughts race: became so excited that your thoughts raced ahead faster than you could speak them

Depressed Malaise

don't talk: become very quiet and didn't talk to anyone
no interest: have shown no interest in anything or anybody
can't concentrate: had trouble concentrating or keeping your mind on what you were doing
lose thoughts: kept losing your train of thought

mind not work: felt that your mind did not work as well as it used to

blue: had periods of feeling blue or depressed that interfered with your daily activity

no get go: had periods of days or weeks when you couldn't take care of things because you couldn't "get going"

confused: felt confused; had trouble thinking

sick from anger: got angry and afterward felt uncomfortable, like getting headaches, stomach pains, and cold sweats

can't remember: began having trouble remembering things

can't stay asleep: had trouble staying asleep

wake early: had trouble with waking up too early and not being able to fall asleep again

oversleep: had trouble with oversleeping: that is, sleeping past the time you wanted to get up

tired: troubled by feeling tired all the time

nightmares: have been bothered by nightmares

poor appetite: had poor appetite

weak: felt weak all over

weight loss: experienced any weight loss of 10 lb (5 kg) or more over the past year, without going on special diets

Manic Malaise

too excited: felt so great (excited, talkative or active) that it was difficult to concentrate

Anxious Mood

worry a lot: worried a lot about little things

anxious: felt anxious about something or someone

irritated: got easily irritated

irritable: have been bothered by being irritable, fidgety, or tense

worry: are a person who is the worrying type

Panic

afraid to go out: felt afraid to leave the house because you were afraid something might happen to it

fear closed places: have been afraid to be in closed places

fear something: feared something terrible would happen to you

fears: had special fears that kept bothering you

fear attack: feared being robbed, attacked, or physically injured

Anxious Malaise

Autonomic muscles twitch: had trouble with your muscles twitching or jumping
can't fall asleep: had trouble falling asleep
cold sweats: had cold sweats
dizzy: had dizziness
breathless: had shortness of breath when you were not exercising or working hard
hands tremble: had your hands tremble
palpitations: had your heart beating hard when you were not exercising or working hard
hot all over: suddenly feel hot all over

Behavioral

restless: had periods of such great restlessness that you could not sit in a chair for very long
fidgeting: the respondent kept fidgeting and squirming
nervous: the respondent appeared nervous and fidgety
not listening: the content of the respondent's answers often have little or nothing to do with the questions asked
drumming: the respondent drums on surfaces with fingers or taps on floor
moves around: the respondent kept getting up and moving around restlessly

Obsessive

repeat act: had to repeat an act over and over again though it is hard to explain to others why you did it
do over 'n over: found yourself doing the same things over and over again to be sure they were right

Alcoholism

blurred speech: the respondent's speech was blurred
makes up words: the respondent makes up new words
drink and miss work: missed work or been late to work because of drinking
drink and argue: had arguments with your family because of your drinking
sick from drink: had trouble with your health because of drinking

3

Real-World Causes of Real-World Misery

ESTABLISHING CAUSE IN THE HUMAN SCIENCES

Why are some people more distressed than others? That is the question, the issue, the thing to be explained. The answer is found in the reality of people's lives: the hard facts and tough realities, the problems that must be faced, and the problems that cannot be faced. It is not found in fantasies or the subconscious, or in laboratories and clinics.

To learn why some people are more distressed than others, we must first find out *who* is more distressed: who feels happy, energetic, fulfilled, and hopeful; who feels miserable, run down, empty, and worried. The "who" is a list of attributes pointing to a reality shared by some that is different from the reality shared by others. It includes being wealthy, middle-class, working-class, or poor; having a college degree, a high school degree, or no degree; having a job or not; being white or black, male or female, single, married, divorced, or widowed; young, middle-aged, or old; being the boss or the bossed.

Once we know the social patterns of distress, we look for explanations. The patterns suggest and reveal the social causes of psychological well-being and distress. In this chapter we show how researchers in the human sciences—the sciences that study people—determine whether one state causes another. We discuss the criteria used in all the human sciences to establish cause, and compare the two major study designs: surveys and experiments. We argue, in contrast to what many other scientists believe, that surveys and not experiments are the best way to find out why some people are more distressed than others.

Finding Causes: The Three Criteria

How do we know one thing causes another? In common English, a cause is that which produces an effect, result, or consequence; the person, event, or condition responsible for an action or result. Logically, a cause must exist for an effect to occur. In modern human sciences, the effect is viewed as an alteration of probabilities, rather than a determination of outcomes. Probabilities can be altered by individual or communal choice and effort, aggregate behavior, historical trends, environmental constraints, biological events, and so on. The probability of an American earning more than the average income is increased by finishing college compared to only finishing high school, and by having been born white rather than black. Thus, education and race both cause variation in earnings, even though one is an achieved status and the other ascribed, even though some high school–educated blacks earn more than some college-educated whites, and even though the causal connections might not exist in another society or in the future.

Philosophers interested in cause have argued for centuries about necessity, sufficiency, responsibility, and inevitability. The debates get especially thick where humans are the objects of study, because of human free will. Many scientists are tired of the debate. Some try to avoid using the idea of cause. More commonly, scientists use terms that express the underlying idea without using the actual word: terms such as increased risk, increased probability, effect, determinant, or risk factor. Whatever the terms, the idea is much the same.

Human sciences say that one thing causes another if three criteria are met: association, nonspuriousness, and causal order (e.g., Hirschi and Selvin 1967; Cole 1972; Mausner and Bahn 1974). Things are associated if they appear together more than would be expected by chance. The association is not spurious if it exists for reasons other than historical coincidence and other than the two simply resulting from a common cause. The association is ordered if one thing leads and the other follows, rather than vice versa. Association, nonspuriousness, and causal order are individually necessary and collectively sufficient to show that one thing causes another.

The relationship between cigarette smoking and lung cancer is a good example of an established cause (Mausner and Bahn 1974). Smoking is associated with lung cancer: People who smoke are more likely to get lung cancer than people who do not. After four decades of research, there is no sign that the association is spurious: Smoking is connected with lung cancer by more than historical accident or a common antecedent. For example, men smoke more than women, and also have higher rates of lung cancer. It is possible that men have more lung cancer than women for some reason other than smoking. Thus, it is possible that cigarette smoking and lung cancer are associated because men smoke more than women, and coincidentally happen to have more lung cancer than women. If this were the whole reason for the association, then men who smoke would have the same rates of lung cancer as men who do not. In reality, just the opposite is true: men who smoke have higher rates of lung cancer than men who do not, and women who smoke have rates of lung cancer similar to those of men who smoke. Compare smokers and nonsmokers matched in age, education, type of job, race, ethnic origins, weight, drinking habits, and anything else that can be measured, and the smokers have higher rates of lung cancer than the nonsmokers. The real difference is between smokers and nonsmokers.

Researchers have not tried every imaginable comparison and never will, but they have tried a great many, and the connection between smoking and lung cancer remains. However, it is *possible* that a gene makes some people susceptible to both tobacco addiction and lung cancer, with no other connection between the two. If so, then the association between smoking and lung cancer is spurious, and both are simply due to a genetic factor that researchers did not take into account. In reality there is no evidence that such a gene exists. No one has shown that smokers and nonsmokers matched on genotype have the same rates of lung cancer. The "what if" argument is nothing more than speculation.

What is the order of the connection between smoking and lung cancer? Can we rule out the possibility that lung cancer causes smoking? It seems we can. Smokers usually pick up the habit in their teenage or young adult years. Lung cancer appears thirty or forty years later, in late adulthood. Among people who used to smoke but quit, the rate of lung cancer decreases as the number of years since they smoked increases. Lung cancer does not cause smoking. Smoking causes lung cancer.

As the example shows, evaluating an association requires judgment. The evidence is never totally unequivocal. There is no way to check off "yes" or "no" for each criterion without thought, no matter what the study design. The data provide evidence, but the researcher makes the judgment. It is possible, given everything we know, that smoking does not cause lung cancer. The evidence is not absolute proof. It is also hard to believe, given everything we know, that smoking does not cause lung cancer. The evidence of association, nonspuriousness, and causal order is substantial.

Population Studies of Distress.

Sociologists ask people about their lives in the community, at work, and at home—the world that they live in. Mostly, this is done by phoning or visiting large numbers of people. They are selected randomly, so as to represent the entire population. Everyone has an equal chance of being interviewed: those who sought help and those who did not, the middle class and the poor, men and women, those for whom visiting a psychiatrist is shameful and those for whom it is acceptable, those with access to care and those without it. Unlike clinical studies, this avoids the biases of basing conclusions on people in treatment: those who were unable to avoid or solve the problem on their own and had the time, access, and inclination to visit a psychologist or psychiatrist.

Statements about social causes are statements of probability. Suppose we say that poverty causes depression. This means that the poor have higher average levels of depression than the well-to-do. Not all poor people are depressed. In fact, many poor people are not. Not all depressed people are poor. Some poor persons are less depressed than some rich persons. Poverty increases a person's risk of depression. It puts one at a *relative* disadvantage. Also, social causes are not sole causes. When we say that poverty causes depression *we do not mean it is the only cause*. There are many causes of depression. Poverty is one.

Survey research establishes cause the same way all research on humans does: by meeting the three criteria. As an example, let's look at the idea that lower income causes higher depression.

Association.

First, is lower income associated with higher depression? To see if this is the case, we must compare persons at various levels of income. A sample of poor people alone would not do. Suppose poor people average twenty symptoms a week. What does that mean? If people who are not poor also average twenty symptoms a week, there is no association. This point may seem so obvious that it is not worth mentioning. Unfortunately, a lot of studies miss this essential point. It is amazing how often researchers interested in the effects of poverty only talk to poor people, or those interested in the effects of being female only talk to women, or those interested in the effects of being in a minority only talk to blacks or Hispanics, or those interested in the causes of depression only talk to the depressed. Comparison is essential for establishing an association. By taking random samples, the survey researcher assures a representative range of comparisons and contrasts. A random sample contains people at all levels of income, in much the same proportion as in the population. The very rich sometimes refuse to talk to interviewers. The extremely poor are often out of contact, especially those living on the street or staying wherever they can find shelter. Nonetheless, random community samples usually have the variation needed for comparison.

Nonspuriousness.

Second, are low income and high depression really connected, or is the association spurious? We know that blacks, Hispanics, women, and young adults are both poorer and more depressed than non-Hispanic whites, men, and middle-aged adults. Maybe there are hidden genetic, organic, or cultural factors that make these groups both poorer and more depressed. If so, then there may be no causal connection between low income and high depression, except that the two have common antecedents. However, when we look at people of comparable race, ethnicity, gender, and age, we still find that those with lower income have higher depression. This would not be the case if the association merely reflected differences in race, ethnicity, gender, and age. There is no evidence that the association is spurious.

Causal Order.

Third, does low income cause depression, or is it the other way around? This is the really tough question. We know that depression is associated with lethargy, listlessness, and malaise. These qualities do not make for success. On the other hand, we know that housewives are more depressed the less their husbands earn. A housewife's depression is less likely to cause her husband's lack of success than her own. Similarly, young people just entering the labor force are more depressed the less their parents earn. The son's or daughter's depression seems unlikely to cause the parents' lack of success. Taking these facts together, we think that low income causes depression.

Of the three criteria, the easiest one to judge is association. All we need to do is think of the appropriate questions, ask them of a representative sample of people, and correlate the responses. Ruling out a spurious association is a bit more difficult. We need to think of what might make the things we're interested in correlated without one causing the other. Then we need to measure those things as well, and take them into account. Usually this requires adjustment of the association, using statistical methods such as multiple regression (Tufte 1974; Pedhazur 1982). Technically, we never completely rule out spuriousness because we never adjust for every imaginable possibility. Practically, though, as we rule out more and more possibilities we become more convinced the association is not spurious. Of the three criteria, the most difficult one to judge is causal order. Which is the cause and which the consequence? There's a reason why the old conundrum about the chicken and the egg has been around so long. In the paragraphs that follow, we describe six ways that sociologists judge causal order.

Things That Don't Change.   Sometimes the causal order is obvious. This is usually the case if one of the variables is an ascribed status. For example, women are more depressed than men. The association is not spurious. It is implausible that depression causes people to become women. The fact is that gender is fixed at birth. The social status is attached to the individual's morphology before the first cry. So we say that something about being female is a cause of depression, rather than the other way around. Ascribed statuses, such as gender, race, year of birth, and national origin, are largely fixed by accidents of birth. For the most part, they are not optional, not a matter of choice, and not changeable. They are not produced by the individual's attitudes, feelings, beliefs, or experiences, so causal order is not a question.

Common sequences. Causal order is established by common and well-known sequences. For instance, people usually finish school, then get a job, which pays a certain wage. We might ask people what kind of job they have, how much money they make, and what the highest grade or year of school is that they have completed. If we find an association between level of education and prestige of job, we can assume with good reason that education preceded their job status. We can also assume that certain jobs pay certain wages, not that one's wages determine what kind of job one gets. Other well-established sequences might include: the status of one's first job precedes the status of one's second job, service in World War II precedes attitudes in 1980, grades in high school precede grades in college, marriage precedes divorce, etc.

Relative stickiness. Causal order can be established by the "relative stickiness" of the variables (Davis 1985). We know that some things do not change easily: where a person lives, their religion, the kind of job they have. Other things change more easily: preferences and attitudes, especially for certain political candidates, brands of products, etc. Therefore if a persons' religion is associated with their preference for a political candidate, we can assume that the person's religion affected preferences, rather than that the person's preference for a certain candidate led them to become Protestant, or Catholic, or Jewish. This is not to say it could never happen the other way around. Just that switching is unlikely to account for much of any association. Research shows that 90 percent of adult Americans are in the same religion they were brought up in. About 5 percent switched to having no religion. Most of the rest switched from one Protestant denomination to another, higher-status one. Information such as this often allows us to judge the causal order of an association.

Common knowledge. Causal order is judged based on understandings about the world. For example, we find that women who have jobs *and* children *and* husbands who do not share the child care responsibilities are very depressed compared to employed women without children, or employed women with children whose husbands share the child care. One could argue that a woman first becomes depressed (for organic reasons, say), then the depression leads her to get a job, have children, and do all the child care herself. This is possible, but implausible. We know that depression decreases motivation. It seems unlikely that depression drives women to take on the jobs of employee, mother, and sole caretaker of the children. It is more likely that role strain, overload, and conflict increase depression.

Longitudinal data.   Causal order is established with longitudinal data—information collected from the same people at two or more points in time. We can ask people about their income and symptoms in 1995, then ask the same people again in 1998. Then we can see if poverty in 1995 is associated with an *increase* in depression over the subsequent period. Low income at the beginning of the period cannot result from subsequent increases in depression, so we assume that low income caused the increase. A number of longitudinal studies find that low socioeconomic status increases psychological distress (Pearlin et al. 1981; Wheaton 1978). It is also the case that distress retards socioeconomic progress (Kohn and Schooler 1982), but this rebound effect is a relatively small part of the total association. Interestingly, to our knowledge the longitudinal studies in community mental health have never shown the causal order assumptions of previous cross-sectional analyses to be wrong. So far, the causal order judgments based on other considerations proved correct when tested.

Patterns and their explanations.   Causal order is established by explaining the association. If an association is causal, what are the mechanisms? If being female causes depression, how does it? If being black causes depression, how does it? If having low income causes depression, how does it? What are the consequences of being female, black, or poor that might be depressing? If we measure those consequences, and show that they account for the association with depression, then we have explained the association. *Patterns plus their explanations* are the essence of causal inference. Because explaining patterns is the heart of causal analysis, we give an extensive example of the process below.

We know that low income is associated with depression. In general, we think that the reality of day-to-day lives affects well-being. Perceptions and feelings do not just spring out of people's heads; they come from experience. What consequence of low income might result in depression? One real possibility is economic hardship—difficulty meeting the family's needs. A family is an economic unit bound by emotional ties. It is in the home that the larger social and economic order impinges on individuals, exposing them to varying degrees of hardship, frustration, and struggle. The chronic strain of struggling to pay the bills and feed and clothe the family on an inadequate income takes its toll in feelings of depression—in feeling run down, that everything is an effort, that the future is hopeless, that you can't shake the blues. Nagging worries make restless sleep. There isn't much to enjoy in life. When life is a constant struggle to get by, when it is never taken for granted that there will be enough money for food, clothes, and medical care, people feel worn down and hopeless. There is no relief from the struggle—it pulls at the person day after day in the form of another bill, an unexpected injury or sickness that needs treatment, or beginning the week before pay day with less than a week's worth of food money.

Does economic hardship explain the association between low income and depression? Economic hardship is assessed by asking, "During the past twelve months, how often did it happen that you did not have enough money to afford food for your family? Clothes for your family? Medical care for your family? How often did you have trouble paying the bills?" (Pearlin et al. 1981). A random sample of 680 married couples throughout the United States was interviewed by telephone and asked these questions, as well as questions about family income and symptoms suffered in the past week (Ross and Huber 1985). The answers are summarized in indexes of income, economic hardship, and depression.

Let's look at the pattern of association. The amount that a pair of variables go together is measured with a correlation coefficient, which is positive if more of one goes with more of the other and negative if more of one goes with less of the other. (In theory, correlation coefficients can range from –1.0 to +1.0, but in practice most are between –0.5 and +0.5). The correlation between income and hardship is about –.35; the correlation between hardship and depression is about +.30; the correlation between income and depression is about –.10 (Ross and Huber 1985). To see what this pattern tells us, let's look at two competing causal models.

The "social cause" model says that income reduces economic hardship, and economic hardship increases depression. As illustrated in Figure 3.1, the social status of having low income results in the psychological state of depression through economic hardship. The numbers over the arrows are the correlation coefficients reported above. According to the model, the total causal effect of income on depression is $(-.35) \times (+.30) = -.105$. This value, predicted by the social cause model, is very close to the actual correlation of –.10 between income and depression reported above.

The "social selection" model says that depression causes low income, and that income reduces economic hardship. As illustrated in Figure 3.1, the psychological state of depression increases the family's economic hardship through low income. According to the model, the total causal effect of depression on economic hardship is $(-.10) \times (-.35) = +.035$, which is *not* close to the observed correlation of +.30 reported above.

Social Cause Model

-.105 = (-.35)(.30)
-.105 = predicted correlation between family income and depression
-.100 = observed correlation between family income and depression
 .005 = observed - predicted

Social Selection Model

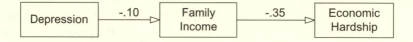

+.035 = (-.10)(-.35)
+.035 = predicted correlation between depression and hardship
+.300 = observed correlation between depression and hardship
 .265 = observed - predicted

Figure 3.1. Social cause and social selection models of the association between income and depression. Data are from the Women and Work Study. (See the Appendix to this book for the measurement of the variables and description of the sample.)

The observed pattern of correlations fits the social cause model much better than the social selection model. Looking at this information as a whole strongly suggests that low income causes depression. Other pieces of information also strengthen the judgment. For example, education should help people get more out of their money. The results show that higher education reduces the association between low income and economic hardship, which in turn reduces the association between low income and depression (Ross and Huber 1985). Other research shows that economic hardship results in a sense of powerlessness—of not being master of one's own life (Pearlin et al. 1981). The sense of powerlessness connects economic hardship and depression, as well as low income and depression. The way the pieces fit together says a lot about cause and effect. The patterns and their explanations tell us who is more distressed, and why.

Experimental Studies of Distress

The modern experiment holds out the hope of meeting the three criteria of cause without requiring judgment—without depending on common knowledge or outside information. Wherever there is room for judgment, there is room for misjudgment. Social scientists are acutely aware that common knowledge, assumptions, and presuppositions can represent false stereotypes, prejudices, and mistaken beliefs. The process of judgment is one of stating the assumptions, questioning them, looking for implications, and checking them against objective information. The modern experiment seems to offer a logical sword that will cut through this Gordian knot. Indeed, for many purposes the modern experiment works very well. For many other purposes, it does not work at all. In particular, experiments cannot tell us why some people are more distressed than others. To show you why, we will describe the theory behind experiments, and then the practical, inherent, and philosophical limitations of experiments.

The Theory behind Randomized Experiments.

Here's how a randomized experiment works. The researcher enlists a number of subjects, who are divided into two or more groups. Each subject is assigned to a group based on the outcome of a random process, such as flipping a coin. The researcher puts the individual members of the groups through experiences that are alike in every way except one. That one difference is the experimental treatment, which is the same for all members of the same group, and different for all members of different groups. The researcher assesses the outcome in all subjects, using the same means of assessment for all. Measures of the outcome are averaged for all members of the same group, and the averages are compared across groups.

The experimenter attempts to create an association by exposing the groups to different treatments. If the difference between groups in average outcome is greater than might typically be found by chance, then the results demonstrate an association between treatment and outcome.

The experimenter attempts to eliminate spuriousness by randomly assigning subjects to treatments. It is totally a matter of chance which persons wind up in which group. As a result, the groups are roughly comparable in terms of the proportion of females, average age, average IQ, proportion of democrats, average family income, average distress, and any other factor, known or unknown, imagined or unimagined, that might affect the outcome. The larger the number of subjects, the more this is true. If the groups are reasonably large, then any association between treatment and outcome is probably not due to pretreatment differences in the composition of the groups. In other words, the association is not spurious.

The experimenter attempts to establish causal order by actually manipulating the independent variable—the supposed cause. The groups are alike to begin with. The only consistent difference in their experiences is the one introduced by the experimenter. If there is an association between the manipulated experience and the assessed outcome, it cannot be that the outcome caused the experience. It must be that the experience caused the outcome.

The essence of an experiment is that an experimenter does something to the subjects. The observational researcher does not do anything to the subjects. He or she just observes the natural variation in the real world. Like any other form of research, the experiment is designed to meet the three criteria of cause. In an experiment, though, the researcher produces variation in the presumed cause and sees whether it affects the presumed consequence. In an observational study like a survey, the researcher examines whether the natural variation in the presumed cause produces the presumed consequence.

Experiments are the best way to evaluate the effectiveness of treatments. This is because treatments, such as drugs, surgery, or counseling, are interventions. They are actions taken by a therapist or researcher to produce a desired effect. Because intervention is the essence of an experiment, the randomized controlled trial is the preferred method of evaluating treatments. The power of experiments to evaluate treatments makes it the preferred method of psychology, even if the research question is not about treatments.

Practical Limitations of Experiments.

There are practical limitations of experiments on human subjects. To some extent they flow from the ethical limitations on doing things to human beings to see what happens, but to some extent control is simply beyond the experimenter's powers. There is a limit to how effectively one human being's life can be designed by another. No one can completely constrain another person. Some things require cooperation. At some level, freedom is not just a right, it is a fact.

The major practical limitations of experiments are stable traits, weak manipulation, trivial manipulation, analog manipulation, and unrepresentative volunteers.

Stable traits pose a special problem for experiments. Some are beyond manipulation, such as sex, race, or age. Others could be manipulated in theory, but the practical problems would be great. Personality traits fall in this category. Personality is, by definition, a set of stable traits shaped over the years. It is the sum of experiences and developmental changes. Personality is shaped by a substantial and enduring reality. Experiments tend to be brief experiences limited in scope. It is very difficult to change, in a few hours, the presuppositions, habits, preferences, and inclinations built up over years.

Weak or limited manipulation plagues many experiments. It is unethical to push some things too far. Strain, threat, and helplessness are in this category. In practice, it is unethical to push anything that, in theory, causes depression, anxiety, or malaise too far. It may be ethical to manipulate some things but impractical to manipulate them greatly. Experiments often manipulate money rewards over a range of five to ten dollars. This is tiny compared to the rewards ranging from thousands to millions of dollars manipulated in the corporate world. The experimental manipulation is two to six orders of magnitude weaker than the forces it supposedly represents.

Problems with stable traits and weak manipulation lead some experimenters to substitute trivial manipulations. For example, we know there is a correlation between overweight and blood pressure. Does overweight elevate blood pressure? To answer the question experimentally, we would have to randomly assign subjects to gain weight, stay the same weight, or lose weight. Then we would have to follow them long enough for substantial gains or losses to occur, and look at the differences in blood pressure across groups. The practical difficulties are obvious. A typical trivial end run would look like this. The experimenter divides the subjects into two groups: overweight and not overweight. Within each weight class the subjects are randomly assigned to experience or not experience a loud and unexpected bang. Blood pressure is measured. The difference in blood pressure between bang and no-bang conditions is greater for the overweight subjects than for the ones who are not overweight. So what? The experiment still doesn't tell us if overweight causes high blood pressure, because it does not manipulate body weight.

Many experiments on human subjects are simply analogies to reality that may or may not be apt. For example, much depression might result from being overwhelmed by difficult or impossible circumstances. To see if frustration and failure cause depression, the experimenter gives one group an anagram that can be solved and gives another group something that looks like an anagram but is not, and cannot be solved. The experimenter finds that the subjects doomed to failure report being more frustrated and annoyed with the task than do the subjects with a solvable problem. In what way is the unsolvable anagram like a life of poverty, like being laid off, or like having cancer? Can it really represent them? How much is the experimentally induced frustration and annoyance like the demoralization, powerlessness, depression, anxiety, and malaise felt by the poor, the unemployed, and the sick?

The final practical problem with experiments is that the samples are usually biased. The subjects are an odd group of uncertain similarity to the population as a whole. Typically, experiments use convenient samples of college students, or of people in an institution such as the army or prison. The subjects rarely represent the general population. The results can only be generalized to others like the subjects in the experiment, but it is not exactly clear who fits in that category. Experimental researchers often assume that people are people, and that the things we have learned in experiments on college students taking psychology courses apply to everyone. The assumption is false. Going to college is a social advantage. About 25 percent of Americans have a college degree or more. About half the people in the United States have not been to college—the half with less opportunity. Students also are younger and less experienced than the general population. Even among students in general, the ones in experiments are paid to participate, required to participate, or voluntarily donate their time. There is no reason to think the experimental subjects represent students in general, even at their own schools.

Inherent Limitations of Experiments on Causes.

The practical limitations of experiments on humans can be reduced by effort, ingenuity, and resources. The inherent limitations cannot. In the last analysis, the laboratory is not the world. The relevance of effects induced in the laboratory to phenomena observed in the world is inherently uncertain. Experiments cannot show patterns of distress in the real world; they cannot show causal direction in the real world; and they cannot explain why observed patterns of distress exist.

Experiments cannot show patterns: they cannot show who is more distressed than others. The core inherent limitation of experiments is that they do not account for observed differences in distress because they do not observe the differences that are out there. The cause manipulated in an experiment may not be the important one. One example comes from epidemiology. It is possible to produce high blood pressure in rats by inducing lesions in the blood vessels of the kidney (renovascular lesions). When the same lesions are found in human hypertensives, the hypertension can usually be cured with vascular surgery. It is quite clear from cross-sectional surveys such as the National Health and Nutrition Examination Survey that very little of the hypertension observed in the community is due to renovascular disease. The vast majority of high blood pressure is caused by obesity and a sedentary lifestyle—which are difficult to manipulate in experiments. Nevertheless, diet and exercise are things that individuals can and often do control, so the information is quite useful to people interested in reducing their blood pressure. This is just one example of an established experimental cause that is largely irrelevant as a cause (in this case, of high blood pressure) in the population.

The uncertain relevance of the cause found in an experiment to real-world variation means that experiments do not resolve the question of causal order in the real world. Doing something to the subjects and seeing what follows establishes the causal order within the experiment. Finding an effect of the manipulation does not rule out the possibility or primacy of the opposite effect. Suppose an experimenter randomly assigns subjects to two groups. One is given a drug that makes them feel depressed, the other is given a placebo. On average, the subjects given the drug feel and act more helpless than the ones given the placebo. Thus, depression causes helplessness in the experiment. This does not rule out the possibility that helplessness also causes depression. It does not tell us which effect accounts for the association between helplessness and depression in the community. In theory, doing both experiments might provide an answer, if an experimental effect is demonstrated in one direction but not the other. Practically, though, the failure to find an effect in one direction might be due to weak manipulation or an odd sample. At best, the experiment demonstrates a possibility.

Establishing causal order is supposedly one of the strengths of experiments. It is the reason that many researchers use experimental methods when they are inappropriate, impractical, or cannot answer the real question. Yet experiments cannot say which is the cause and which the effect in the real world. They can only make conclusions within the experiment. We are left with the unsettling question of how much (if anything) the experiment tells us about the real world. Perhaps it is better to relinquish the simplicity of unreality for the complexity of reality.

Experiments can show whether or not the manipulation has an effect, but they cannot explain why the effect does or does not exist. Experiments can measure different outcomes, but they cannot show the links among outcomes. They cannot tell us which outcome is the explanation and which is the ultimate consequence. To answer that question we must return to the logic of observational research and causal analysis.

Let's look at an example. Unemployment and poverty are common among mothers who are single, divorced, and separated, and may be a cause of the high levels of depression in these groups. Say we are considering a policy of providing unmarried mothers with jobs that pay a decent wage, and we want to evaluate the policy with an experiment. We randomly assign some unmarried mothers to an intervention in which they receive employment, while the control group receives no treatment. We might find that the experimental group—those mothers who got jobs—had lower depression than the control group after six months. Jobs decrease depression among unmarried mothers. The policy is a success, and even though we do not know why the jobs decreased depression, we know that they do. We can speculate that jobs decrease depression by decreasing poverty, or by increasing self-esteem, or by increasing the control these women feel over their lives, or by increasing interaction with and support from coworkers. We could even measure various outcomes, say, earnings, self-esteem, and depression. But we cannot know from the experiment whether higher earnings decrease depression, or whether higher self-esteem decreases depression, or whether lower depression increases self-esteem or earnings.

Now let's say the experiment had a different outcome. The experiment might have found no differences in depression between the control and experimental group. In this situation, we have no idea what is happening. Possibly, jobs just don't affect mental health. However, sometimes an experimental intervention has unintended side effects that counteract the desired effect. If this is the case the independent variable appears to have no effect on the outcome. This is because two intervening processes counteract each other. Possibly, employment among unmarried mothers has some positive effects and some negative effects, which, in essence, cancel each other out. The experiment cannot tell us why we found no effect, just that we did. Maybe this is what is happening. Jobs have the positive effects of decreasing poverty, and increasing self-esteem, personal control, and social support, as described above. But jobs have another effect on unmarried mothers. They greatly increase time pressures, compared to staying home. When a mother gets a job, she has to arrange child care, get her child to day care in the morning and pick him or her up after work, cope somehow when the child is sick, etc. This mother now has a double workload of paid work and child care. Possibly, jobs increase depression on the one hand by way of increasing time demands and work overload, but decrease depression on the other hand by way of decreasing poverty and increasing control, esteem, and support. The experiment cannot show why the independent variable had an effect or no effect on the outcome.

An experiment can tell us the consequences of the intervention but not the relationships among the consequences. The experiment itself could show that jobs increase time pressures on mothers, and that jobs increase depression among mothers. It cannot show the association between time pressure and depression within the experiment. This part is purely observational. We can correlate the two and conclude that jobs increase depression by increasing time pressure. This is nonexperimental evidence, though. It could be that jobs increase felt time pressures by increasing depression. We must assume a causal order between the two. Because the experiment itself does not tell us the sequence of its consequences it cannot explain its own consequences.

Patterns plus their explanations are the essence of cause. Experiments cannot show the patterns of distress in the real world, cannot show the causal direction in the real world, and cannot explain the patterns.

Inherent Limitations of Experiments on Treatments.

As we said earlier, experiments are the best way to evaluate the effectiveness of treatments because treatments, such as drugs or counseling, are interventions. However, many misinterpret the meaning of treatment experiments. They think that the effectiveness of a treatment says something about the cause of the problem. This is not correct, for two reasons.

First, we cannot know what makes patients depressed unless we compare them to people who are not depressed. An experiment evaluating the effectiveness of drugs versus counseling in reducing depression only has subjects who are depressed.

Second, we cannot discover the cause of depression by seeing what treatments are effective in reducing depression. For example, novocaine may relieve the pain of a toothache. Drilling and filling the tooth may eliminate the pain. But the cause of the toothache was not the absence of Novocain or filling. The cause was probably too much sugar in the diet and poor dental hygiene or the lack of fluoride. Likewise, psychiatric or psychological treatment studies do not tell us what causes depression. Just because a drug works to alleviate depression does not mean the original cause was chemical. Treatments do not eliminate the cause of depression. At best, they counteract it (see Figure 3.2).

Effectiveness of treatments does not tell us what causes depression. An effective treatment may not be as effective as removing the cause. And an effective treatment may be a net deficit if it deters the search for the problem causing the depression and a solution to the problem. This brings us to what we, as sociologists, see as the philosophical limits of experiments.

Philosophical Limitations of Experiments

Possibly the most important limitation of experiments is their view of the relationship between researcher and subject. The whole point of an experiment is to develop ways that objects and outcomes can be manipulated. The philosophical problem arises when the objects are humans, and the outcomes are human thoughts, feelings, and actions. The intent of an experiment is to give control to the manipulator, not to the manipulated. The validity of treating actors as objects is uncertain at best. There is a world of difference between manipulating and informing. Recall the blood pressure example. Informed individuals can and often do control their own

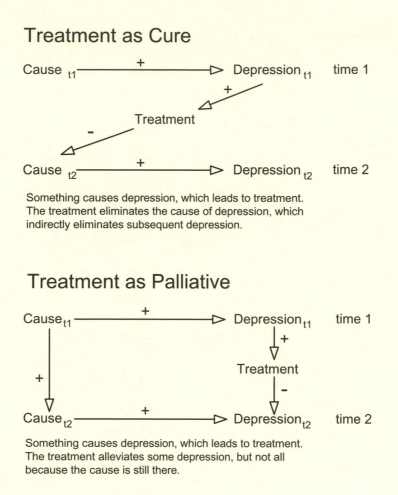

Treatment as Cure

Cause $_{t1}$ ——————— + ——————→ Depression $_{t1}$ time 1

Treatment

Cause $_{t2}$ ——————— + ——————→ Depression $_{t2}$ time 2

Something causes depression, which leads to treatment.
The treatment eliminates the cause of depression, which
indirectly eliminates subsequent depression.

Treatment as Palliative

Cause$_{t1}$ ——————— + ——————→ Depression$_{t1}$ time 1

Treatment

Cause$_{t2}$ ——————— + ——————→ Depression$_{t2}$ time 2

Something causes depression, which leads to treatment.
The treatment alleviates some depression, but not all
because the cause is still there.

Figure 3.2.   Treatment as cure versus treatment as palliative.

blood pressure by exercising and eating right. The big money, though, is in selling and prescribing antihypertensive medication. By their very nature, experiments look for a lever to put in the hands of a professional. The value of manipulating rather than informing is uncertain enough in a case such as hypertension. When we talk about psychological distress, the wisdom of giving control to the professional rather than the person becomes extremely uncertain. By all indications, distress is caused by helplessness, powerlessness, and the sense that others and chance control one's life. The search for experimental and professional means of manipulating these states is ironic, and probably futile.

EXPLAINING REAL PATTERNS

Laboratory experiments are never going to tell us why some people are more distressed than others. By their very nature, laboratory experiments shut out the world that people live in. When the experimenter hangs up his lab coat, shuts the light, and locks the door, the experimenter steps into the forces that make some people more distressed than others. He says good night to the student lab assistant, who did poorly on a statistics test the day before. He says good night to the secretary, who is on the phone trying to find out if her child got home from an early school closing all right. He passes the janitor, who is unlocking the broom closet and thinking that the university's budget cut means a new round of layoffs. He gets on the bus behind an old woman, who pauses at each step to rest and has difficulty counting the right change to give the driver. On the way home, the bus takes the experimenter past the hospital, where an ambulance has just arrived, around the edge of the slums, where there are kids playing in the street and teenagers hanging out and adults sitting on stoops or at windows staring, past the graveyard, where he sees a fresh mound of dirt next to a precise rectangle cut in the earth, into the pleasant suburb where he signals the driver to stop at his block. Unless the experimenter thinks about what he has seen on the ride home, unless he finds some way to talk to the people he passed, he will never learn why some people are more distressed than others.

III

Social Patterns of Distress

4

Basic Patterns

This chapter outlines and discusses the six basic patterns of distress discovered and confirmed in U.S. community surveys over the past forty years: (1) the higher one's socioeconomic status (education, job, and income) the lower one's level of distress; (2) married people are less distressed than the unmarried; (3) parents with children at home are more distressed than people who are not raising children; (4) women are more distressed than men; (5) the greater the number of undesirable changes in one's life the greater one's level of distress; (6) middle-aged people are the least depressed, but older people are least anxious.

The six basic social patterns of distress are well-established now. Many independent studies have confirmed each basic pattern. The observations may seem obvious today, but forty years ago many people would not have guessed them. Before community surveys, many theorists believed that responsibility, commitment to work, and upward mobility were stressful, whereas dependency, protection, and freedom from responsibility reduced stress. Many people still think that executives and others at the top of the hierarchy are tense and anxious from the responsibilities while workers at the bottom are carefree and content. Harried executives, rushing to the next meeting, might envy laborers with few responsibilities, but in fact the executive's power, income, and creative control reduce distress. Likewise some think that married people, especially married men, face burdensome restrictions, whereas singles lead a free and happy life. In fact, married people have lower levels of distress than singles, and this is especially true of men. On the other hand, many people believe that children increase parents' psychological well-being. Most parents love their children, and see them as one of the great joys and blessings of life. Even so, surveys show that adults with children at home are more distressed than those without. At one time most women were stay-at-home moms and men carried all the household's economic responsibility. Men had to go out and beat the world or be beaten by it, daily braving the rigors of commuter traffic and workplace tension. Women could stay home contentedly ministering to the needs of the family, safe within the circle guarded by protecting males, or so people thought. Many were surprised by the finding that women have higher levels of distress, and that employment generally lowers women's levels of distress, despite the added burden of conflicts between work and family responsibilities. On a related front, ours is a youth-oriented culture. Americans often think of early adulthood as the best time of life—a period of hope, vigor, and joy. In fact, surveys find the greatest distress among young adults struggling to establish sustaining relationships and careers, often while raising families that strain interpersonal and economic resources.

The six basic patterns first stood as fascinating new discoveries, then as core facts in the growing body of research. After it became clear that they are robust and replicable findings, the focus of research switched from *demonstrating* the facts to *explaining* them. Just as astronomy was once driven by the desire to explain the recorded motions of the sun, moon, and planets, research on psychological distress is currently driven by the desire to explain the recorded association with gender, marriage, events, status, and age. Here we describe the established social patterns of distress. In Part IV we will discuss some of the discoveries of the past forty years that may explain the six facts.

First we need to make clear the nature of these facts. To begin with, they are probabilistic. When we say that women are more distressed than men we do not mean that all women are more distressed than all men. We mean that, on average, women are more distressed than men, and that a randomly chosen woman is more likely to be distressed than a randomly chosen man. Second, social facts are hard facts, but they are not eternal. The facts about distress can change as society changes. In particular, the difference in distress between men and women could disappear if certain trends continue. The reasons why social differences in distress exist are also reasons why the differences might disappear.

COMMUNITY MENTAL HEALTH SURVEYS

Before the 1960s scientists knew little about the social patterns of emotional well-being and distress. Mental health studies looked at people in psychiatric treatment or in total institutions such as the military or mental hospitals. Most ideas about social stress were based on clinical interviews with small numbers of patients or on the records and reports of individuals exposed to extreme war-related stressors such as combat or prison camps. Studies limited to patients had no way of discovering the traits or personal histories that keep individuals from becoming mental patients. In the 1950s some early studies compared demographic and socioeconomic traits of patients in treatment with those of the general population in the same city. Researchers quickly realized that such studies could not distinguish the traits associated with poor mental health from the ones associated with getting treated of those experiencing mental health problems.

Beginning in the 1960s, American researchers began to do large-scale mental health surveys of persons in the general community. The researchers interviewed hundreds or thousands of individuals selected at random from the general population. Taking random samples avoided the biases of observations based solely on individuals who sought treatment or were pressured into it. Everyone had an equal chance of being selected: individuals facing many difficulties and those with few, persons managing their problems reasonably well and others overwhelmed by their problems, those who sought help and those who did not, the middle-class and the poor, men and women, those for whom visiting a psychiatrist is shameful and those for whom it is acceptable, those with access to care and those without it. The private and anonymous interviews, conducted in the home or later by telephone, let individuals report their situations and symptoms without repercussion. The data from those structured anonymous interviews of randomly selected members of the general population gave researchers an unprecedented view of the social patterns of distress.

All the findings we discuss come from community surveys of mental health and use advanced statistical methods to summarize and analyze the respondents' answers. In the 1970s community mental health researchers adopted digital computers to handle the large amounts of data generated by their surveys. Calculations that previously required several months of person-hours took only five or ten minutes on a computer—most of that time standing in line to submit the job. Soon after, basic sorting, counting, and cross-tabulating gave way to advanced but computationally intensive statistical techniques such as factor analysis and multiple regression analysis. Those methods made it much easier for researchers to do three important things. They could find out which symptoms had similar patterns of correlations with other symptoms and with characteristics such as age, sex, race, education, income, marital status, employment status, and parenthood, as discussed in Chapter 2. They also could adjust for many possible confounders, as discussed in Chapter 3. For example, a researcher wanting to know the effect of income on distress could readily estimate the differences in distress across levels of income for individuals otherwise similar in age, sex, race, and education. Finally, they could test hypothetical explanations, as discussed in Chapter 3 and in Part IV.

SOCIOECONOMIC STATUS

The daily grind—the problems that are always there—wear at the nerves and demoralize the spirit. Some people have many problems and fewer resources to solve them. They are the poor and uneducated, working at menial jobs or living on public assistance in run-down neighborhoods where crime is a constant threat. Some people have few problems and many resources to cope with them. They are the well-to-do and educated, working at challenging and fulfilling jobs and living in pleasant neighborhoods. The difference in distress between these two groups is remarkable. It dwarfs the difference between men and women or between the married and unmarried. The first basic pattern of distress is this: high socioeconomic status improves psychological well-being. Low socioeconomic status increases psychological distress (Glenn and Weaver 1981; Kessler 1982; Lennon and Rosenfield 1992; Link, Lennon, and Dohrenwend 1993; Mirowsky and Ross 1989, 1995; Pearlin et al. 1981; Ross and Huber 1985; Ross and Mirowsky 1989; Ross and Van Willigen 1997; Reynolds and Ross 1998).

Socioeconomic status is a person's relative position in the distribution of opportunity, prosperity, and standing. It indexes one's place in the unequal distribution of socially valued resources, goods, and quality of life. Researchers generally measure socioeconomic status by reference to education, occupational status and work conditions, and economic well-being as indicated by household income and freedom from economic hardships such as difficulty paying bills or not having money to buy necessities. People with college educations, employed at good jobs, with high incomes, and little economic hardship have high socioeconomic status. Although there is some value in looking at overall standing, there is more value in considering each component separately. The level of education, quality of work, and degree of economic well-being represent distinct aspects of socioeconomic status. Schooling indicates the accumulated knowledge, skills, values, and behaviors learned at school, as well the credential that structures employment opportunities. The quality of work measures the opportunity for rewarding and rewarded self-expression through physical or mental activity (paid or not) directed toward production or accomplishment. Income and freedom from economic hardship indicate material prosperity and security. In addition to representing distinct aspects of social status, education, work, and economic well-being represent sequential causal levels in America's distributive system.

Education Is Key

Education is the key to an individual's position in the stratification system. It forms the main link between the socioeconomic status of one generation and the next, and the main avenue of upward mobility in American society. Higher education decreases the likelihood of being unemployed and gives people access to good jobs with high incomes. Part of education's effect on psychological well-being is mediated by employment status,

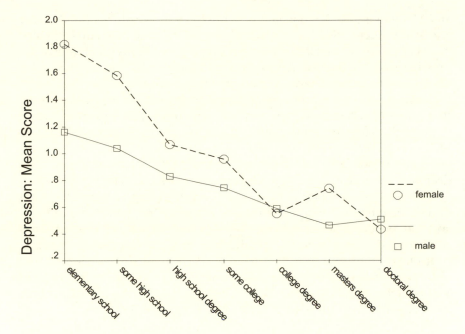

Figure 4.1. Average frequency of men's and women's depression by level of education. Data are from the ASOC survey.

work, and economic resources, but much is a direct benefit of being well-educated. Figure 4.1 shows the association between education and depression in the 1995 Aging, Status, and the Sense of Control (ASOC) survey. In general, the higher the levels of education the lower the depression. Education decreases depression for both sexes, but more strongly for women than for men. Men with less than a high school degree feel depressed about 80 percent more often than men with college degrees or higher. Women with less than high school degrees feel depressed about 170 percent more often than women with a college degree or higher. Higher education improves the emotional well-being of both sexes, while also narrowing the gap between women and men.

Employment Status and Work

Well-educated individuals are more likely to be employed, and more likely to be full-time rather than part-time, than persons with little education (U.S. Department of Education 1992). Employment, especially when full-time, is associated with higher levels of psychological well-being (Gore and Mangione 1983; Lennon and Rosenfield 1992; Pearlin et al. 1981; Ross and Van Willigen 1997; Reynolds and Ross 1998). The well educated also have better jobs. The well educated have more prestigious occupations, but prestige is not the important thing about jobs for psychological well-being. The better educated also do work that is more autonomous and creative, which are two of the most important aspects of work for well-being. Work that provides substantial autonomy, freedom from close supervision, and opportunities for workers to make their own decisions improves emotional well-being. Work that is creative, nonroutine, involves a variety of tasks, and gives people a chance for continued learning and development also decreases distress. Autonomous and creative work is nonalienated work. It gives workers the chance to use their skills in the design and implementation of the their own work; and it gives them the freedom to use thought and independent judgment in doing different things in different ways rather than doing the same thing in the same way in a process designed and controlled by others. These qualities of work decrease distress directly and also by boosting the sense of personal control over one's own life (Ross and Van Willigen 1997; Reynolds and Ross 1998; Mirowsky, Ross, and Reynolds 2000; Kohn 1976; Kohn and Schooler 1982; Kohn et al. 1990).

Economic Resources

One often hears that "money can't buy happiness." Certainly money cannot *guarantee* it. Nothing can. Even so, money makes happiness a lot more likely. Figure 4.2 shows the association between household income and depression in the 1995 ASOC survey. The higher the level of income, the lower the depression. (Household income decreases the depression levels of men and women about equally, so we show the pattern for both sexes combined.) Americans with incomes in the bottom 20 percent feel depressed and anxious an average of twice as often as those with incomes in the top 20 percent. Put another way, there is 100 percent more distress among those with low incomes than among those with high incomes.

Figure 4.2 shows another important aspect of the relationship between income and distress. The impact of an additional $10,000 a year is largest at the low end, getting smaller and smaller at higher levels of income. The benefit of additional income seems to level off around $65,000. About one-third of incomes are above that level and two-thirds are below it. Beyond that level more income makes little difference to the average frequency of depression. That pattern, called a diminishing marginal effect, has important implications. It suggests that raising incomes near the bottom will eliminate more distress than would raising incomes across the board.

Differences in economic hardship account for much of the differences in distress across levels of income. People find it very distressing to lack the

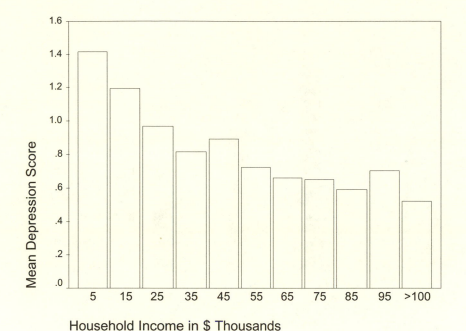

Figure 4.2. Mean depression scores by household income. Data are from the ASOC survey.

money needed to pay bills or buy things the household needs like food, clothes, or medical care. The struggle to pay bills and to feed and clothe the family takes a toll in anxiety and depression (Pearlin et al. 1981; Ross and Huber 1985; Reynolds and Ross 1998; Ross and Van Willigen 1997). Households at all levels of income can get into economic difficulties, but low income sharply elevates the risk.

The impact of additional income on the risk of economic hardship also follows a pattern of diminishing marginal effect. More money reduces economic hardship the most for households at the lowest levels of income. There are two reasons for that. First, the minimum cost of getting by is more or less similar for all families with the same numbers of adults and children. Households with middle-class incomes and up generally can avoid economic hardship by spending more carefully, and perhaps drawing on assets such as savings. Households with low incomes have less room to cut back and little or no assets to cash in on. Second, persons with low income also tend to have low education. Because education develops effective abilities it helps individuals avoid the economic hardship associated with low income. Given the same income and similar family composition, persons

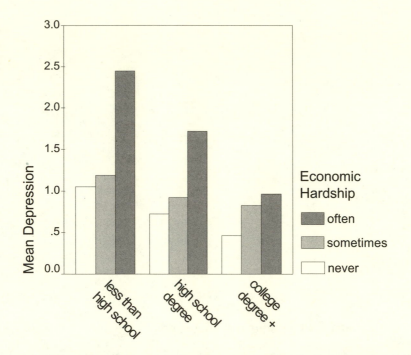

Figure 4.3. Mean depression scores by education and level of economic hardship (trouble paying bills or buying necessities). Data are from the ASOC survey.

with higher education avoid economic hardship better than those with lower education. Low education leaves individuals less able to manage on low income, while also making them more likely to have low income. The correlation between low education and low income, and their synergistic effect on economic hardship in combination, helps create a steep increase in hardship toward the bottom of the economic ladder.

Low levels of education further deprive people of the problem-solving resources needed to cope with the stresses of economic hardship. Ross and Huber (1985) find synergistic effects of low education, low income, and economic hardship on depression. Each makes the effects of the others worse. Figure 4.3 illustrates the interaction, using data from the 1995 ASOC survey. It shows that the relationship between depression and economic hardship gets weaker at higher levels of education. The interactions on this level also contribute to the pattern of diminishing marginal effect shown in Figure 4.2. People with low incomes tend to have low education too. That makes them less able to avoid economic hardship at their level of income, and less able to manage the emotional strains of economic hardship. On the other end, people with high incomes also tend to have high education. That education helps them depend less on income to avoid economic hardship and helps them manage better emotionally when faced with economic hardship. As a result, differences in income have less impact on depression at the high end than at the low end.

Sense of Control

In a way, the impact of socioeconomic status and achievement on distress seems obvious. Even so, there is a cultural myth of the successful person as driven by a sense of inadequacy, loneliness, or neurotic anxiety. This myth is not accurate. In fact, the typical successful person is active, inquisitive, open, and self-assured. If ever there was a formula for psychological well-being, this is it. How do some people get there, and others find themselves so far away?

The reasons for the vast difference in distress between the upper and lower ranks of society are intimately linked to the reasons those ranks exist. It is a self-amplifying process. Some people begin with fewer advantages, resources, and opportunities. This makes them less able to achieve and more likely to fail. Failure in the face of effort increases cognitive and motivational deficits. Those, in turn, produce more failure and distress. These forces have been examined in studies by Kohn and his colleagues (Kohn 1972; Kohn and Schooler 1982), Pearlin and his colleagues (Pearlin and Schooler 1978; Pearlin et al. 1981), Wheaton (1978, 1980, 1983), and by us (Mirowsky and Ross 1983, 1984). We paint the broad outlines of the results here, and give details in Chapters 7 and 8.

There are two things that combine to produce psychological distress. One is a problem. The other is inability to cope with the problem. A person who can solve his or her problems is, in the long run, happier than a person with no problems at all. There are two crucial characteristics of people who cope with problems successfully. The first is a sense of personal control, which is the belief that you control your own life, that outcomes depend on your own choices and actions, and that you are not at the mercy of powerful people, luck, fate, or chance. When a problem comes up, the instrumental person takes action. He or she does not ignore the problem or passively wait for it to go away. Furthermore, the instrumental person takes action before problems occur, shaping the environment to his or her advantage. A second crucial characteristic is cognitive flexibility. The flexible person can imagine complex requirements for solving a problem, multiple solutions to the problem, and many sides to an issue. He or she does not cling to habit and tradition. When necessary, the flexible person can negotiate and innovate. Instrumentalism and flexibility together eliminate the impact of undesirable events and chronic stressful situations on distress (Wheaton 1983).

A sense of personal control and cognitive flexibility are needed most where they are found least. Personal control is learned through a long history of successfully solving more and more difficult problems, and cognitive skills are learned by solving more and more complex problems. Instrumentalism and cognitive flexibility are mostly learned in school and on the job, but only jobs that are complex, unsupervised, and not routine have the desired effect (Kohn and Schooler 1982). Kohn and his colleagues interviewed a representative sample of 3,101 employed men in the United States at two points in time. They found that jobs that are simple, closely supervised, and routine reduce cognitive flexibility. The people at the bottom of society are the ones most burdened with chronic economic hardship, barriers to achievement, inequity, victimization, and exploitation. Their perceived control is reduced by demoralizing personal histories. Their cognitive flexibility is reduced by limited horizons and constraining jobs in which they are told what to do rather than making their own decisions. Wheaton made a distinction between coping ability and coping effort: Low cognitive flexibility reduces the ability to cope with problems and low personal control reduces the motivation to use whatever energy and resources are available (1980). Without the will or ability to cope with the overwhelming stressors present at the bottom of the social hierarchy, the unsolved problems of the poor and poorly educated accumulate. This combination of more problems and fewer resources to cope with them increases the psychological distress of the disadvantaged.

MARRIAGE

Married people are less distressed than unmarried ones, which is the second major social pattern of psychological distress. Compared to married adults of the same age, those who are single, divorced, cohabiting, or widowed have higher levels of depression, anxiety, and other forms of psychological distress (Gore and Mangione 1983; Gove, Hughes, and Style 1983; Kessler and Essex 1982; Ross, Mirowsky, and Goldsteen 1990; Ross 1995). The one exception is that very young adults who get married do not experience lower depression levels than those who remain single (Horwitz and White 1991). The positive association of marriage with well-being is strong and consistent, and selection of the psychologically healthy into marriage or the psychologically unhealthy out of marriage cannot explain the effect (Booth and Amato 1991; Horwitz and White 1991; Menaghan 1985). Figure 4.4 shows the relationship between marital status and depression (adjusting for age) in the 1995 ASOC survey. Married persons are less depressed than unmarried persons of all types. The widowed

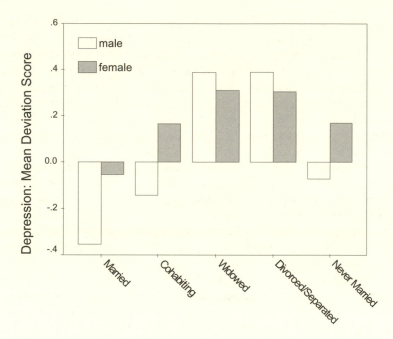

Figure 4.4. Average levels of men's and women's depression across marital statuses, adjusting for age. Data are from the ASOC survey.

and divorced or separated have the highest levels of depression, followed by persons who have never married and cohabitors.

Some researchers argue that marriage protects men's psychological well-being more than women's (Gove and Tudor 1973). Studies generally find bigger differences in distress between men who are married and those who are not than between women who are married and those who are not (Ross, Mirowsky, and Goldsteen 1990). We consistently find that marriage seems especially important to the mental health of men. For example, the average level of depression changes more across marital statuses for men than for women, as illustrated in Figure 4.4. The gap in depression between men and women is largest among the married. Divorce and widowhood, on the other side of the coin, are especially depressing to the men. In fact, men have somewhat higher levels of depression than women in those statuses. Single persons and cohabitors fall in between the married and the widowed, divorced, or separated in their depression levels, and men's advantage over women is almost as large in these statuses as in marriage.

Although marriage does seem generally better for the mental health of men than of women, the size of that difference can depend on the type of distress and the composition of the nonmarried category (Umberson and Williams 1999). For example, when we compare married persons to all nonmarried persons combined, we find a bigger sex difference in the overall effect of marriage on depression than on anxiety in the ASOC data. Even so, the differences across the five marital statuses in average levels of anxiety are larger for men than for women. The same is true for marital-status differences in other types of problems such as anger or heavy drinking. Details also can depend on the specific nonmarried category in question, or the mix combined into one "not-married" category. For example, cohabiting men are not more anxious than married men, although cohabiting women are much more anxious than married women. Also, among the widowed, divorced, or separated, the women are more anxious even though the men are more depressed.

Despite the interesting and important details, the basic fact remains. Married adults generally feel less distressed than do nonmarried adults of the same sex and age. Marriage generally improves emotional well-being despite the substantial "side effects" from strains of raising children and conflicts between work and family discussed later in this chapter. Those strains and conflicts burden women more than men, which largely accounts for women's smaller emotional gains from marriage. Even so, women as well as men generally benefit psychologically from marriage.

Social Integration

Why does marriage improve psychological well-being? One possibility is social integration. Studies of social relationships typically distinguish between social integration and social support. Social integration is the objective social condition indicative of more or less isolation, like the number of people in the household, whereas social support is the sense of having fulfilling personal relationships. At first researchers thought that the simple presence of another adult in the household might explain why marriage improves well-being. A person who lives alone may be isolated from an important network of social and economic ties. These ties may help create a stabilizing sense of security, belonging, and direction. Without them a person may feel lonely and unprotected. Since unmarried people often live alone but married people live with another adult, this could explain why unmarried people are more distressed. Contrary to expectation, however, Hughes and Gove (1981) found that unmarried people who live alone are no more distressed than those who live with other adults. The difference is between married people and others, not between people who live alone and others. The unmarried, living alone or with others, are significantly more distressed than the married. The presence or absence of other adults in the household does not appear to explain the effect of marriage on well-being (ibid.).

Supportive Relationships

Social support and the quality of relationships better explain why marriage is associated with psychological well-being. Compared to being unmarried, marriage provides emotional support—a sense of being cared about, loved, esteemed, and valued as a person (Cobb, 1976; Kessler and McLeod 1985; Turner 1981). Although some level of social integration makes emotional support possible, it does not guarantee that support (Pearlin et al. 1981). The quality of relationships, rather than simply the quantity, bolsters well-being. In general, married people have higher levels of emotional support than the nonmarried, and support, in turn, reduces depression and anxiety (Gerstel, Riessman, and Rosenfield 1985; House, Landis, and Umberson 1988; Kessler and McLeod 1985; LaRocco, House, and French 1980; Ross, Mirowsky, and Goldsteen 1990; Wheaton 1985).

Married people are also happiest with their partners. We asked everyone who reported any kind of close relationship, married or not, How happy would you say you are with your marriage (or relationship)? Would you like to change many parts of your relationship, change some things about it, or have it continue the way it is going now? In the past twelve months, how often would you say that the thought of leaving your husband/wife/partner has crossed your mind? (Ross 1995). Before our study, researchers had asked only married people about the quality of their relationships, which did not allow comparison of married to nonmarried. Until we asked people who were not married about the quality of their relationships, researchers could only speculate that married people had more fulfilling and happy close relationships than people who are not married. We find that they do. Married people are happier in their close relationships than others, which decreases depression, and partly explains why married people have low levels of depression (Ross 1995).

Although married people report more emotional support and better relationships than the nonmarried on average, the marriages vary considerably on supportiveness. A close, confiding relationship protects men and women against stressful events (Pearlin et al. 1981). On the other hand, when a spouse expects more than he or she is willing to give back, acts like the only important person in the family, and cannot be counted on for esteem and advice, men and women feel demoralized, tense, worried, neglected, unhappy, and frustrated (Pearlin 1975). The emotional benefits of marriage depend on the quality of the marriage. Gove, Hughes, and

Style (1983) found that it is better to live alone than in a marriage characterized by a lack of consideration, caring, esteem, and equity. The 62 percent of married people who report being very happy with the marriage are less distressed than unmarrieds. The 34 percent who only say they are pretty happy with the marriage are no less distressed than the unmarrieds. The 4 percent who say they are not too happy or not at all happy with the marriage are *more* distressed than unmarrieds of all types (ibid.). We found the same thing. People who report that their relationships are unhappy, that they often consider leaving their spouse or partner, and that they would like to change many aspects of their relationship have higher distress levels than people without partners (Ross 1995). It is not enough just to have someone around. It is better to live alone than in a marriage characterized by a lack of consideration, caring, and support. Luckily, though, most married people are happy with their relationships.

It is easy to imagine that the victim of an unfair marriage is distressed by the situation, but what about the exploiter? Does a person gain or lose psychologically by talking unfair advantage of a spouse? The cynical view is that each spouse is least depressed the more they get things their own way. Because one partner's dominance is the other's submission, it follows that one partner's well-being is the other's depression. The optimistic view is that exploiters, as well as victims, are more distressed than they would be in an equitable relationship. According to equity theory, exploiters face the disapproval of others, worry about retaliation and punishment, feel guilty, and must live with the obstruction and hostility of the victim. In their hearts the husband and wife both know what is fair; if they do what is right they will both lead happier and more productive lives.

Using data on 680 married couples in the Women and Work study, we found some truth in both the cynical and the optimistic view (Mirowsky 1985). The respondents were asked who decides what house or apartment to live in, where to go on vacation, whether the wife should have a job, and whether to move if the husband gets a job offer in another city. The scale of responses ranged from the wife deciding, to sharing the decisions equally, to the husband deciding. Mapping the average levels of depression across this scale revealed U-shaped patterns for wives and for husbands. Each spouse is least depressed if decisions are shared to some extent. However, the balance of influence associated with the lowest average depression is slightly different for husbands and wives: Each spouse is least depressed by somewhat more of their own influence. Similarly, while husbands and wives both feel best sharing major decisions, a spouse who dominates in decisions feels better than the one who submits. (See Chapter 8 for more details.) Analysis of the 1,217 persons with partners in the 1995 ASOC survey finds that shared decision-making increases the sense of social support (Van Willigen and Drentea 2001). The actual influence in these major decisions typically is closer to the balance that would minimize the husband's depression than it is to the balance that would minimize the wife's depression. This is one reasons why wives tend to be more depressed than their husbands.

Economic Resources

Married persons enjoy greater economic support, in addition to greater emotional support. Married people have higher household incomes than the nonmarried (Bianchi and Spain 1986). The economic benefits of marriage hold for both women and men, even adjusting for age, minority status, employment status, and education (Ross 1991). The economic advantages of marriage (or disadvantages of nonmarriage) are greater for women than for men (Cherlin 1981; Weiss 1984). Overall, marriage cuts the percentage reporting frequent economic hardship by a third among men and by a half among women in the ASOC data. Children in the household greatly increase the risk of economic hardship, as discussed below. Whether a household has children or not, marriage cuts the percentage reporting frequent economic hardship in half, as shown in Figure 4.5. Because marriage cuts that risk in half, marriage makes the biggest difference to the economic well-being of persons with children. Economic well-being, in turn, has a large positive effect on mental health, as shown earlier in Figure 4.3 (Pearlin et al. 1981; Ross and Huber 1985). The higher household incomes and lower levels of economic strain among married people partly explain their low levels of depression (Ross 1995).

Together economic well-being and supportive relationships largely explain why married people are less distressed than others (Ross 1995). Both men and women gain economic and emotional support from marriage, although marriage may be more of an economic benefit to women and an emotionally supportive benefit to men (Gerstel et al. 1985). People who have been widowed for less than five years have high levels of distress that are not completely explained by a lack of social and economic support (Ross 1995). Many among the recently widowed still bear the grief of their loss. For other nonmarried groups, though, the greater distress compared to married persons results from lower levels of social and economic support.

CHILDREN AT HOME

Marriage is good for psychological well-being, but raising children generally is not. This finding may surprise some. Many people have strong values about children. People often believe that children bring joy and happiness. Without children, women especially are said to feel empty,

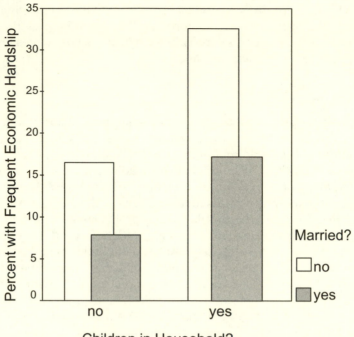

Figure 4.5. Frequent economic hardship by marital status for households with and without children, adjusting for age, sex, and education. Data are from the ASOC survey.

lonely, and unfulfilled. People who decide not to have children sometimes are viewed as selfish or immature. Although strict sanctions against stay-ing childless have abated somewhat, norms concerning the value of having children remain strong. The fact that almost all married persons, and many unmarried ones, have children suggests the strength of the norms favoring parenthood. Traditions treat the birth of a child as an occa-sion for congratulations and celebration. What does research suggest about the effect of children on parents' psychological well-being and dis-tress? Does it support the myths?

The evidence shows that having children in the home usually does not improve psychological well-being and often makes it worse (Gove and Geerken 1977; Pearlin 1975; Cleary and Mechanic 1983; Ross, Mirowsky, and Huber 1983; Ross and Mirowsky 1988; Radloff 1975; Lovell-Troy 1983; Gore and Mangione 1983; Kessler and McRae 1982; Brown and Harris 1978; McLanahan and Adams 1987). Children in the household create sit-uations that increase distress, including economic hardships, decreased

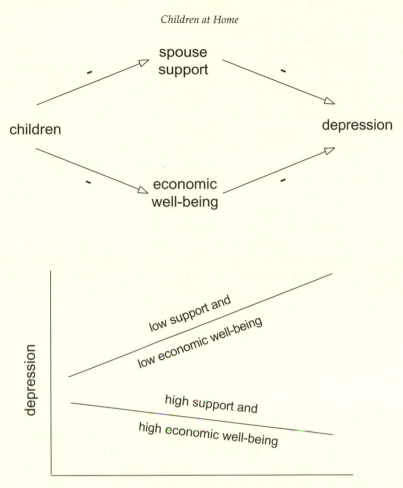

Figure 4.6. Effects of children in the home on depression, mediated (top panel) and moderated (bottom panel) by spouse support and economic well-being.

support from one's spouse, greater dissatisfaction with the marriage, inequity in child care responsibilities, and a tension between work and family, including difficulty arranging and paying for child care while parents are at work. However, in the rare circumstance when none of these stressors are present, having children at home can improve psychological well-being as illustrated in the bottom panel of Figure 4.6.

Mothers raising children are more distressed than other women (Gove and Geerken 1977; Pearlin 1975; Ross and Mirowsky 1988; Ross and Van Willigen 1996). The very group that cultural myths say most benefits from raising children actually shows the greatest associated distress. Having children in the household is most detrimental to the mental health of single and divorced mothers (Brown and Harris 1978; Pearlin 1975; Aneshensel, Frerichs, and Clark. 1981; Alwin, Converse, and Martin 1984; Kandel, Davies, and Raveis 1985). Children appear to have less of a negative effect on the mental health of fathers.

Why would children increase psychological distress? Children tend to be valued and loved (although the disturbing facts about the prevalence of child abuse betrays the myth somewhat). How could children be loved and valued and still increase distress? In large part, children in the home increase distress because they decrease economic well-being and create marital tensions the interfere with spouse support, as illustrated in the top panel of Figure 4.6. Parents who avoid economic hardship and maintain supportive relationships with each other actually benefit emotionally from raising children. Unfortunately, the presence of children sharply increases the risk of economic hardship and strains marital relationships, eroding the very resources needed to moderate the distress associated with raising them.

Economic Hardships

Children increase economic strains on the family, as illustrated earlier in Figure 4.5. At the same level of family income, a family with children feels greater economic pressures than one without children (Ross and Huber 1985). Each dollar must go further, must buy more food, clothes, and medical care. Having children often increases the pressures to buy a home. An apartment may seem too small or the couple may prefer a house with a yard as a better place to raise children. Those and other added expenses are considerable. Two parents raising a child require about 2.5 times the income of a childless couple to have an equally low risk of economic hardship (Mirowsky and Ross 1999). Adults raising children often take on stressful levels of debt from home mortgages, car loans, and credit cards (Drentea 2000). At the same time that raising children increases the need for money, it often undermines the wife's economic contribution to the household. She may quit her job while the children are young, or work part-time, further increasing the family's risk of economic hardship. If she continues employment, family funds often must pay for day care. If she returns to work, her period of absence puts her further back in the queue for well-paying positions. Whether she remains continuously employed or not, conflicts between work and family can undermine job performance and thus pay. Frequent economic hardship sharply increases distress, as illustrated earlier in Figure 4.3. The chronic strain of struggling to pay bills and feed and clothe the children drains the joy from life, creating nagging worries that make sleep restless and the future seem hopeless, leaving the body fatigued and the spirit exhausted.

Economic hardship especially burdens single and divorced mothers. A single parent raising a child requires about twice as much income as two parents in order to have an equal risk of economic hardship (Mirowsky and Ross 1999). Mothers head about 84 percent of the single-parent households (U.S. Census Bureau 2000:Table 70). These mothers and their children are the new poor in the United States. In 1998, 32.8 percent of all births in the United States were to unmarried mothers, up sharply from 18 percent in 1980 and 26.6 percent in 1990 (Preston 1984; U.S. Census Bureau 2000:Table 78). In addition, about half the children born to married women experience parental separation before they reach adulthood (Avison 1999). Indeed, as of 1998, 32 percent of American children under the age of eighteen live in households with one or both parents absent (U.S. Census Bureau 2000:Table 69). Many of those are female-headed households with incomes below or not far above the federal poverty line. *If* these mothers can find work, it tends to be poorly paid, and they must struggle to find and pay for child care. Both the children and their mothers are in extremely disadvantaged positions. For the mothers this disadvantage produces much depression and anxiety.

Single and divorced mothers are poorer, on average, than married mothers. But many intact families also feel economic hardships. The chronically unemployed obviously feel economic strain. But they are not the only ones. Many families just up from poverty do, too. In these families the husband is employed (unless temporarily laid off or sick). The wife may be employed, too, just to make ends meet. Many persons in the working and lower middle-class live with their resources pushed to the breaking point. Furthermore, parents with low levels of education (and thus insecure jobs that do not pay well) tend to have the most children. Compared to women with college degrees, those with high school degrees average twice the number of children and those with less than a high school degree average three times the number. Individuals and families that can least afford to have children generally have the most children, multiplying the economic hardships.

Strained Relationships

Children in the home also erode the quality of marital relationships. Satisfaction with one's marriage decreases with the birth of the first child, and does not return to prechildren levels until all the children have left home. Both husbands and wives are most satisfied with their marriage when there are no children at home, either because they are childless or because the children have left home. As the number of children, especially young children, increases, marital satisfaction decreases (Campbell et al. 1976; Pleck 1983; Rollins and Feldman 1970; Glenn and Weaver 1978; Veroff, Douvan, and Kulka 1981; Renne 1970). The quality of one's marriage has a large effect on psychological well-being. People who are satisfied with their marriage; who feel that the marriage is characterized by support, consideration, caring, love, and equity; and feel that they can really talk to their spouse about things they feel are important to them are much less depressed and anxious than those in marriages characterized by conflict, inequity, and a lack of consideration and caring.

Children worsen the quality of the marriage in part through economic strain. A couple with economic difficulties lives in a stressful environment in which failures tend to get blamed on the other spouse. Furthermore, many marital conflicts are about money. These conflicts are more likely to occur when there isn't enough. Children affect the quality of the marriage directly, too. Husbands and wives spend less time together when they have young children, and the time they do spend together is spent with (and focused on) the young child. Husbands feel they are getting less emotional support from their wives, whose energies now go into caring for the child. And wives, too, feel they get less support from husbands, who often distance themselves (sometimes literally) from the difficult care of young children. Women, especially those in the working class, report that their husbands are less likely to be "confidants"—to be there to talk to when needed—after the birth of the first child (Brown and Harris 1978).

Life Course Discords

Raising children can improve emotional well-being, but only in ideal circumstances. In societies such as ours, organized as a competition for status and wealth, a built-in discordance between social and biological timing works against adequate preparation for parenthood. Americans mature sexually in their teens, and get full adult status in their early twenties, but reach full occupational and economic maturity much later in their forties or fifties. Most parents begin their families in early adulthood—a time in life when jobs are insecure, incomes are low, and wealth is nonexistent or even negative as a result of school loans and other debt. Parenthood becomes somewhat beneficial to well-being after the children are grown and living on their own (Ross et al. 1990). At that point parents can enjoy the relationship without the economic burdens and marital strains of raising the children. Even that benefit, though, may depend on having delayed the first birth until after the age of twenty-two, as discussed in Chapter 5. Americans who begin parenthood earlier than that may never fully recover from the distressing consequences.

In sum, children greatly increase economic and interpersonal strains, even in married couples with good incomes and relationships. People generally have children at a time in life when jobs are insecure, incomes are low, and relationships are unseasoned. In addition, the adults least prepared for parenthood tend to have the most children. Affection for children does not eliminate the distress associated with raising them. Indeed, the emotional bond may simply heighten the distress felt when economic or interpersonal problems threaten the children's well-being. In ideal circumstances, raising children can improve emotional well-being, but relatively few parents enjoy ideal circumstances.

GENDER

Women carry a greater burden of total housework and paid work hours, pay greater costs of caring for the problems of family and friends, face greater practical constraints on personal employment and advancement, and get less autonomy, authority, recognition, and pay when employed (Kessler and McLeod 1984; Reskin and Padavic 1994; Ross and Mirowsky 1992, 1996; Turner, Wheaton, and Lloyd 1995). Women find themselves in stressful circumstances more often than men (Turner et al. 1995). Many of the stresses result from women's family responsibilities, which are emotionally demanding in themselves and often limit or conflict with full-time employment. Middle-aged women often work part-time but middle-aged men rarely do. Middle-aged women often keep house but middle-aged men almost never do. The middle-age gender gap in employment and earnings reflects a lifetime of past tradeoffs and tensions between work and family for women, and reproduces and reinforces those tradeoffs and tensions in the present. Many women find themselves in dire circumstances when family needs first disrupt employment and then later require employment doing menial work for low wages on an inflexible schedule. Many husbands, and even many wives, then feel the wife's lower earnings justify her greater burden of housework and child care. Even the ones who do not feel that way must face the economic logic of favoring the husband's higher paid job over the wife's when one of them has to make a sacrifice. These differences between women and men amount to unequal socio-economic status, with women in the disadvantaged position (Mirowsky 1996; Ross and Mirowsky 1996, 2002; Ross and Wright 1998).

Surveys consistently find that women report higher average levels of depression and anxiety than men (Aneshensel 1992; Mirowsky and Ross 1995). To us, the evidence that women are more distressed than men is compelling, yet the pattern has been questioned since the 1970s, when it was first uncovered by Walt Gove and his colleagues, and it continues to

be questioned today (Clancy and Gove 1974; Dohrenwend and Dohrenwend 1976, 1977; Gove and Clancy 1975; Rieker and Bird 2000; Ritchey, La
Gory, and Mullis 1991; Seiler 1975). Because of the ongoing controversy,
we will review in detail the evidence that women genuinely suffer greater
distress than men, and that the difference in distress reflects and reveals
women's relative disadvantage in American society. No one doubts that
women report more frequent and intense depression and anxiety than
men do. Many independent studies confirm that basic fact. Women do not
simply express their emotions more freely than men, thus appearing more
distressed. Women do not simply respond to stressors with depression
and anxiety while men respond with other emotions ignored in most surveys. A real gender difference in distress exists because women are socially
and economically disadvantaged relative to men.

Two perspectives question whether women really are more distressed
than men. We call them the response-bias view and the gendered-response
view. According to the response-bias view, women are more aware of their
emotions, more likely to talk about emotions to others, to be open and
expressive, and to think that discussing personal well-being is acceptable
rather than stigmatizing. Thus, when women and men are questioned
about depression and anxiety, the women report it more. According to the
gendered-response theory, women respond to the ubiquitous stress of life
with somewhat different emotions than men. In particular, women might
feel anxious and depressed where men feel agitated and angry. As detailed
later, we find that women express emotions more freely than men, and
women express distress somewhat differently than men. However, expression does not explain the difference in distress. In fact, the more our analyses adjust for differences in expression, the *greater* the gap in distress found
between women and men. Perhaps most surprising, women feel more
angry *more* often than men, not less (Mirowsky and Ross 1995).

Wife and Mother as Stressful Statuses

Measured as sadness, demoralization, hopelessness, anxiety, worry,
malaise, and anger, women experience distress about 30 percent more frequently than men. It is not simply that they are more likely to express their
feelings. It is not simply that men and women respond differently to the
ubiquitous stress of life. Women's and men's lives differ, and this difference puts women at higher risk of distress. Theories of gender inequality
or gender-based exposure to social stressors explain women's elevated
distress as the consequence of inequality and disadvantage (e.g., Gove and
Tudor 1977; Pearlin 1989, Ross and Huber 1985; Ross and Van Willigen
1996). In this view, first proposed by Gove and his colleagues, different
positions in the social structure expose individuals to different character-

istic amounts of hardship and constraint. Women's positions at work and in the family disadvantage them compared to men. Their greater burden of demands and limitations creates stress and frustration, manifest in higher levels of distress.

Stressfulness of the Traditional Female Status.

Gove and his colleagues were among the first sociologists to examine why women are more distressed than men. But where would they look? Biologists might think of hormones or ancestral patterns of sex-typed behavior among the apes, but sociologists have a different perspective. For heuristic purposes sociologists think of people as essentially interchangeable at birth. It is clear that by adulthood there are many important differences in the things people prefer, value, believe, and do. Many of these differences are shaped by situations and personal histories. Perhaps the same is true of differences in emotions. Perhaps women are more distressed than men because of differences in the lives that men and women live.

Thirty years ago the majority of adult women were exclusively housewives and men were the breadwinners and jobholders. Gove reasoned that if women are more distressed than men because of something different in their lives, then women who are employed will be less distressed than women who are exclusively housewives. This is exactly what he found in his sample of 2,248 respondents (chosen by stratified random sampling) throughout the United States. A number of follow-up studies replicated the finding (Gove and Tudor 1973; Gove and Geerken 1977; Rosenfield 1980; Ross, Mirowsky, and Ulbrich 1983; Kessler and McRae 1982). It was an important discovery. Freud had argued that women are born to be housewives and mothers and cannot be happy in the competitive world outside the home. Parsons (1949), an influential social theorist of the 1950s and 1960s, had argued that society and the people in it function most smoothly when women specialize in the loving, nurturing, family realm and men specialize in the competitive, acquisitive, jobholding realm. The discovery that women with jobs are less distressed than women without them overturned a century of armchair theorizing.

Gove's research shook preconceptions about women, but did not explain everything. Although employed women are less distressed than housewives, employed women are *more* distressed than employed men. This difference is found even when comparing men and women in jobs with roughly equal pay and prestige. Having a job is not the whole story. What explains the difference in distress between employed men and women in comparable jobs? A clue turned up in a study by Kessler and McRae (1982), who interviewed 2,440 randomly sampled adults in a national survey. They found that employment is associated with less distress among women whose husbands help with housework and child care, but there is little advantage to employment among women whose husbands do not help (ibid.). Surprisingly, they also found that the extra housework and child care done by husbands of employed women does not increase the husband's distress. Researchers had been comparing different types of women; perhaps it was time to compare different types of couples.

Lagged Adaptation to Women's Employment.

American marriages mostly have changed from ones in which the husband has a job and the wife stays home caring for the children and doing housework to ones in which the husband and wife both have jobs and share the housework and child care (Oppenheimer 1982). Although many today may believe this a positive change, not many would have believed it in 1900. The change did not happen because of preferences and values. It happened because the logic of social arrangements in 1900 undermined itself as the economy grew and changed from manufacturing to services.

At the beginning of the twentieth century, women only took jobs during the period between leaving school and getting married. A married woman worked outside the home only if her husband could not support the family. Women could be paid much less than men with equivalent education and skills because the women's jobs were temporary or supplemental. Many jobs quickly became "women's work," particularly services such as waiting on tables, operating telephone switchboards, elementary school teaching, nursing, and secretarial work. The economic incentive for employers to hire women, combined with economic growth and the shift from manufacturing to services, increased the demand for female employees. Eventually there were not enough unmarried or childless women to fill the demand, and employers began reducing the barriers to employment for married women and encouraging those whose children were grown to return to work. Still the demand for labor in female occupations continued to grow faster than the supply of women in accepted social categories, and by the 1950s growth in female employment reached the sanctum sanctorum—married women with young children (Oppenheimer 1973). Throughout the twentieth century individual women were drawn into the labor force by contingencies: economic need, the availability of work, and the freedom to work (Waite 1976). Despite the low pay and limited opportunities, many women came to prefer working and earning money, and many husbands began to realize the benefits of two paychecks instead of one. But who was taking care of the house and children? This brings us back to the question of why employed women are more distressed than employed men.

We compared the husband's and wife's depression levels in four types of marriages (see Figure 4.7) using data collected in 1978 around the peak of the transition to female employment (Ross, Mirowsky, and Huber 1983). In the first type of marriage the wife does not have a job; she and her husband believe her place is in the home, and she does all the housework and child care. This is the traditional marriage. In 1978 it included roughly 44 percent of the couples. This type of marriage is internally consistent—preferences match behavior. For this reason it may be psychologically beneficial, but more so for the husband. He is head of the household and has the power and prestige associated with economic resources. The wife, on the other hand, is typically dependent and subordinate. We found that the wife in this type of marriage has a higher level of depression than her husband.

In the second type of marriage the wife has a job but neither she nor her husband wants her to, and she does all the housework and child care. This is roughly 19 percent of the couples. Both of them believe that he should provide for the family while she cares for the home and children, but she has taken a job because they need the money. Psychologically, this is the worst type of marriage for both of them, and their distress is greater than in any other. The wife may feel that it is not right that she has to work, that her choice of husband was a poor one, that she cannot do all the things a "good" mother should; and she carries a double burden of paid and unpaid work. To the extent that the husband has internalized the role of breadwinner, his wife's employment reflects unfavorably on him, indicating that he is not able to support his family. He may feel guilty and ashamed that she has a job, worry about his loss of authority, and suffer self-doubt and low self-esteem. This is the only type of marriage in which the husband is more distressed than his wife.

Although adjustment may come slowly, people do not long bear a tension between the way they live and the way they think they should live. As economic, demographic, and historical changes nudge lives into new patterns, husbands and wives come to view wives' employment more positively. This is particularly true as more of their friends and neighbors become two-paycheck families. Thus, in the third type of marriage the wife has a job and she and her husband favor her employment, but she remains responsible for the home. About 27 percent of the couples are in this category. The husband is better off than ever before. He has adjusted psychologically, his standard of living is higher, and the flow of family income is more secure. He has even lower distress than men in the first type of marriage. Things are not quite as good for his wife. She is better off than in the second type of marriage, but still carries a double burden. In a system in which the wife stays home and the husband goes out to work it makes sense for her to do the most time-consuming household chores. When she also goes out to work, and particularly when she stops thinking

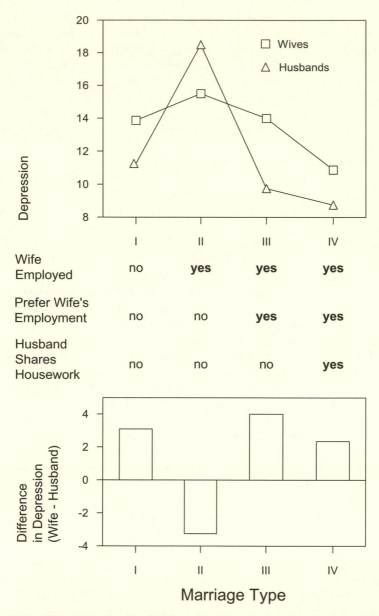

Figure 4.7. Depression levels of wife and husband in four types of marriage (top) and the differences in depression levels between wife and husband in each type (bottom). Data are from the Women and Work Study. Marriage types are based on the wife's employment status, preferences for her employment, and the household division of labor. The results are shown adjusting for education, income, age, religion, and race.

of her job as temporary, it becomes clear to her that the traditional division of the chores is no longer sensible or fair. Typically she assigns tasks to the children, mechanizes tasks like dishwashing, uses frozen foods and eats out more often, cuts down on optional events like dinner parties, and does not clean as often. Even so, the demands on her time are likely to be much greater than those on her husband's (Robinson 1980). The wife's level of distress in this type of marriage is about the same as in the first type, and the gap between her distress and her husband's is greater than in any other type of marriage.

Once the wife accepts the permanence of her new role as employed worker she may begin pressing for greater equality in the division of household labor. Although the husband may initially resist, once he has grown accustomed to the economic benefits of two paychecks he is likely to be open to negotiation. If his wife presses the issue, he often makes concessions rather than lose her earnings. In the fourth type of marriage the wife has a job, she and her husband approve of her employment, and they share housework and child care *equally*. This is about 11 percent of the couples in 1978. Both the husband and the wife are less distressed in this type of marriage than in any other, and the gap between them is smaller than in any other type of marriage.

The gap that remains is probably due to two things. First, the large majority of wives in type IV marriages still earn less than their husbands. Second, the category contains a small minority of wives who are very distressed because they are employed mothers of young children who have difficulty arranging child care.

In adapting to the wife's employment, the central problem for husbands seems to be one of self-esteem—of getting over any embarrassment, guilt, or apprehension associated with the wife's employment. For wives the central problem is getting the husband to share the housework.

We began with the discovery that women are more distressed than men, and housewives are more distressed than women with jobs. In the end we found that couples who share both the economic responsibilities and the household responsibilities also share much the same level of psychological well-being, and are less distressed than other couples. The difference in distress between men and women does not appear to be innate. The difference is there because men and women lead different lives, and as their lives converge the difference begins to disappear.

An analysis of the factors that increase the husband's housework shows that husbands with higher levels of education do more. Husbands also do more the higher the wife's earnings, and they do *less* the more their own earnings exceed their wife's. Thus, equality in the division of labor at home, which provides psychological benefits to the husband and wife, depends on their economic equality in the workplace.

There is a postscript to this research. In 1978 about 20 percent of the employed wives were in marriages where the couple shared the housework and child care equally. In the 1995 ASOC data almost 50 percent of employed wives share the housework and child care about equally with their husbands. (Actually, according to the wives' reports it is somewhat less than half the couples, and according to the husbands' reports it is somewhat more than half of them.) That represents a substantial move toward equality. Even so, about 38 percent of the employed wives in 1995 were in marriages where the husband did less than a third of the housework and child care. (Again, it is a smaller fraction according to the wives and a larger one according to the husbands.) The sharing of work in the household still lags considerably behind the sharing of work in the marketplace.

Conflict between Work and Family.

Many wives are employed yet are solely or largely responsible for child care. That produces role strain: overload from the sheer amount of effort it takes to perform in both arenas, and conflict from meeting the expectations of people who do not take each other into account (i.e., one's boss and one's children). Staying home with the children generally does not make things better. It cuts household income dramatically, greatly increasing the risk of economic hardship. Also, young children put constant demands on mothers who stay home to care for them. Children separate mothers from other adults and make them feel they are "stuck" in the house, at the same time decreasing their privacy and time alone (Gove and Geerken 1977). Paid employment outside the house generally improves women's emotional well-being. Even so, many women face incompatibilities between their responsibilities as mothers and as employees because the institutional and family support necessary to fulfill both roles often does not exist. Readily available, affordable child care can ease the strain on employed mothers, particularly those getting little help with child care from their husbands.

To examine some of these issues, we used the data from the Women and Work Study on 680 husbands and wives throughout the United States. We examined depression levels of husbands and wives depending on whether or not there are young children (under the age of twelve) at home, whether or not the wife is employed, whether the husband shares child care responsibilities with his wife or whether the wife has the major responsibility for child care, and whether child care arrangements for working parents are readily available and easy to arrange or whether arranging child care while the parents are at work is difficult.

Figure 4.8 shows the deviations from the overall mean depression level for wives. We focus on wives because regression analyses indicated that

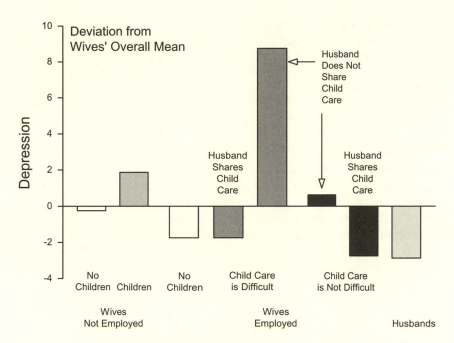

Figure 4.8. Deviations from the mean depression level for all wives, depending on employment status, children, difficulty of child care, and the husband's participation in child care. Data are from the Women and Work Study.

children had a larger effect on women than on men. The figure shows mean differences, which the regression analyses indicated are not merely spurious consequences of differences in age, education, income, or number of children.

Nonemployed wives with young children have significantly higher levels of depression than those without children. For employed wives, it is not children per se, but the difficulty in arranging child care and the husband's participation in the child care that affects psychological well-being. Employed wives with no children have lower than average depression levels. Many employed wives with children also have lower than average depression, most notably employed mothers whose husbands share the child care responsibilities with them and for whom arranging child care while the parents are at work presents no difficulties. These wives have depression levels as low as husbands. On the other hand, employed mothers whose husbands do not share the child care responsibilities with them and who have difficulty arranging child care have much higher than average depression levels.

In terms of the wives' mental health, the best arrangement appears to be employment and motherhood, coupled with easily arranged child care for the young children, and with shared participation by the husband in child care. The next best arrangement is employment and no children. The third best is employment, motherhood, and shared participation by the husband in child care, even if the couple has difficulty arranging child care. (The husband's participation in child care has more of an impact on wives than does the difficulty of arranging child care, possibly because it indicates two things: actual help with child care, and an equitable and fair relationship). Women in these three situations have lower than average depression levels. In the best case, the average depression is as low as that of husbands, and in all three cases the difference in average depression compared to husbands is small enough to be explained by chance. Staying home with the children is significantly more stressful. However, the most stressful situation for wives is one in which they are employed, have young children, have difficulty arranging child care, and have sole responsibility for child care.

When husbands and wives social roles are similar, their depression levels are similar. The gender gap in psychological well-being closes due to lower depression among wives and not due to greater depression among husbands. Some have argued that employment among wives puts a strain on husbands because of added responsibility for child care. We find no evidence that this is the case. *If* the wife's employment increases her husband's depression *at all* when he helps with child care, the increase in his depression is very small compared to the decrease in hers.

What we now think of as a "traditional" family pattern, in which the husband is employed and the wife stays home and cares for the household and children, is actually a consequence of the industrial revolution (Tilly 1983). Parsons (1949) claimed it is functionally imperative that the husband be the provider and the wife be the homemaker and child rearer. Becker (1976) claimed that, from the perspective of maximizing household utilities, it was economically rational for the wife to stay home caring for children because her market wages were typically lower than her husband's. Parsons's and Becker's theories of marital roles seem time bound. The massive labor force entry of married women with children has reduced the credibility of both theories. A pattern that appeared with industrial society may disappear in a postindustrial period. It is understandable, however, that scholars writing in a transitional period should see a shift away from the complementary marriage pattern in which the husband is employed and the wife stays home as stressful, disturbing, and threatening to the marriage. What is stressful is the transition in which one aspect of family roles has changed (such as employment of mothers of young children), but other family roles (such as the husband's participation in child care) or the family's links to other institutions (such as the availability of child care) have not caught up.

A return to the "traditional" family of the 1950s would put wives and mothers in a psychologically disadvantaged position in which husbands have much better mental health than wives. A shared family pattern in which both spouses are employed and both are responsible for child care, and in which there are supportive institutions for child care outside the nuclear family, is one in which both husbands and wives have low levels of depression. The well-being of husbands is not taxed by these changes. In fact, increased responsibilities for child care on the part of husbands may strengthen families by bringing fathers closer to their children.

Since 1970, the greatest labor force increases have occurred among young married women with young children, and there is no reason to think the trend will be reversed. It is unrealistic to think that Americans can care for their children by going back to a time when mothers were not engaged in productive labor and when child care and homemaking were full-time jobs (a short period of time historically, anyway). As the number of working couples increases, the need for child care policy increases.

Society can follow three strategies regarding the depression of employed mothers facing child care difficulties. The first strategy is to do nothing. This is unacceptable because it ignores the suffering and demoralization. It also ignores the fact that depression may interfere with the ability to work and to care for the children, creating secondary problems. The second strategy is to treat the depression and leave the social problem unsolved. If an employed mother seeks treatment for her depression, the doctor might prescribe medication, monitor her for side effects, listen to her talk, interpret her dreams, hypnotize her, send her to a hospital, and so on. The one thing a doctor cannot do is solve her child care problem. How much money would we have to spend on doctors, drugs, therapies, and hospitals to get such women's depressive symptoms down to tolerable and humane levels? The cheapest medical solution is a year's prescription for antidepressive medication renewed annually with a telephone call. This may now be the usual response. Drugs may ease the pain, but they have serious side effects and they leave the real problem unsolved (Glenmullen 2000). The third strategy is to urge fathers and husbands to share child care, and to provide child care services for everyone who needs them. Available and affordable child care can prevent depression in the first place. It can save women from the stress, frustration, and demoralization that creates the depression and save women from the dependency and risks of drug treatment.

The twentieth century was characterized by three trends: increases in educational levels, increases in women's labor force participation, and decreases in the number of children women have. There is no indication that these trends will be reversed. The three are closely related, because better-educated women are more likely to be in the labor force and tend to have fewer children. The association between women's employment and smaller families is in part due to the fact that the institutional and family arrangements necessary to be employed and to be a mother often do not exist. Providing this support reduces the strain on employed mothers and is associated with very high levels of psychological well-being on their part, higher than that of mothers who are not employed. There is nothing necessarily "antifamily" or "antinatalist" about the employment of women. It is the lack of readily available child care and the lack of shared responsibility for children within the couple that puts stress on the mothers and their families.

Expressiveness and Response Bias

According to the response-bias theory, men and women differ in the likelihood of expressing emotions or feelings to an interviewer (Ritchey, La Gory and Mullis 1993; Seiler 1975). Historically, women specialized in the emotionally supportive and expressive activities; men in the competitive ones (Rosenfield 1999). To women, emotions carry the signals between connected beings; to men they reveal stigmatizing weaknesses. Thus women express emotions more freely; men keep emotions more hidden, perhaps even from themselves. The response-bias theory claims that women's greater apparent distress flows largely from differences in reporting.

In order to determine whether a response tendency like expressiveness actually accounts for women's higher levels of distress, research must answer three empirical questions (Clancy and Gove 1974; Ross and Mirowsky 1984). First, does expressiveness significantly increase reports of distress? If not, then it cannot account for any differences in reported distress. Second, are women more likely to express their feelings than men? If not, then it cannot account for differences between women and men. And third, does adjusting for expressiveness substantially decrease the estimated effect of gender on distress? If not, then it accounts for only a small part of gender's effect on reported distress.

Using our survey of Work, Family, and Well-being, we find that women are more likely to express their feelings than men, according to two measures (Mirowsky and Ross 1995). First, we asked people a direct question about how much they agreed with the statement, "I keep my emotions to myself." Men were more likely to agree than women that they keep their emotions to themselves. Second, we used an unobtrusive measure, the tendency to report both positive emotions (happiness) and negative emotions (sadness), using a method that adjusts for the actual content of happiness and sadness. Women are more likely to express emotions regardless of content. The unobtrusive measure of expressiveness is associated with reports of various types of distress, including depressed mood (sadness), absence of positive mood (happiness), anxiety, anger, and malaise. However, to our surprise, people who say they keep their emotions to themselves actually report more distress of all types, not less. Maybe keeping one's emotions to oneself is distressing in the long run because it precludes supportive responses from the people close to you.

The most important finding is that adjustment for two measures of expressiveness does not account for sex differences in distress. On the contrary, adjustment for the tendency to express emotions leaves the gender gap intact. In most cases, the gap in distress favoring men increases. Even though women are more expressive than men, their expressiveness does not account for their high reported levels of distress.

Gendered Response

According to the gendered-response theory, men and women experience the same amount of stress but differ in the nature of their emotional responses to stress (Aneshensel, Rutter, and Lachenbruch 1991; Dohrenwend and Dohrenwend 1976, 1977; Rosenfield 1999; Horowitz and White 1987). Where men get angry and hostile, women get sad and depressed. According to gendered-response theory, depression emerges from the frustration of wants and aspirations. Frustration generates rage and hostility. Depression results when a person turns that anger inward, punishing the self for failure and inadequacy. Men are socialized for competitive and combative roles that allow, and even encourage, the outward expression of anger and hostility. Women are socialized for nurturing and supportive roles that discourage it (Rosenfield 1980, 1999). According to the gendered-response theory, women may appear more distressed than men simply because the standard indexes of distress ask more questions about depression and anxiety than about anger and hostility. Men and women may experience similar levels of frustration, but men take it out on others and women get upset with themselves.

Anger Does Not Displace Depression.

Evidence for the gendered-response perspective requires that women have higher levels of depression while men have higher levels of anger, and it requires that people with high levels of anger have low levels of depression. Neither requirement is met. Findings do not support gendered-response theory. First, women are more angry than men, not less. Even though most people wouldn't expect it, our findings conform to previous ones. Studies consistently find that women have equal or higher frequency of anger than men, in addition to higher frequency of depression (Conger et al. 1993; Frank, Carpenter, and Kupfer 1988; Ross and Van Willigen 1996; Schieman 1999; Weissman and Paykel 1974). Women especially get angry with family members, think about the anger more, talk to the person they feel angry with more, and take longer to stop feeling angry (Schieman 2000). Second, people with high levels of depression are more angry, not less angry. Depression and anger are positively correlated. If men avoided depression by becoming angry, anger and depression would be negatively correlated. In fact, the average level of depression increases with the frequency of anger reported, for both sexes. Anger does not substitute for depression. Anger accompanies depression.

In fact, all types of distress go together. Depression, anger, anxiety, unhappiness, and malaise all correlate positively. Different types of distress do not substitute for one another. Women and men do not face equal levels of frustration, stress, and disadvantage, but simply respond to ubiquitous stress in different ways. Women have more of all types of distress. In the ASOC survey of a representative sample of American adults, women report more depression, anxiety, and anger, and they report more of the aches and pains, headaches, and backaches that accompany psychological distress, as shown in Figure 4.9.

Troublesome Behavior Does Not Displace Distress.

Thus far we have talked about distress. Distress is an unpleasant subjective state consisting of emotions and feelings that cause pain and misery. A focus on misery and suffering seems justified on its own, without reference to other values. People would rather not be distressed. It is worse to feel sad, demoralized, lonely, worried, tense, anxious, angry, annoyed, run down, tired, and unable to concentrate or to sleep than to feel happy, hopeful about the future, and to enjoy life. Women are more distressed than men. But what about behaviors like heavy drinking, illegal drug use, and antisocial behavior? Are they substitutes for depression, anxiety, anger, unhappiness, and malaise that women experience? Do men avoid depression by these behaviors?

The distinction between emotional (or affective) problems like depression and anxiety, and behavioral problems, like heavy drinking, raises the possibility that gendered response may occur across realms of disorder, even though it does not occur within the emotional realm. In other words, women and men may experience equal levels of stress and hardship that produce emotional problems in women and behavioral problems in men. In particular, women qualify for psychiatric diagnoses of affective disorders more frequently than men, whereas men qualify for diagnoses of alcoholism, drug abuse, and antisocial behavior more frequently than

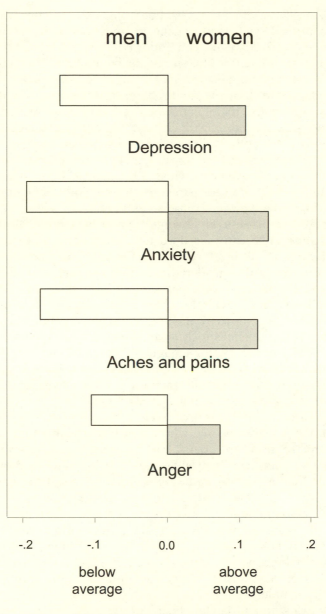

men   women

Depression

Anxiety

Aches and pains

Anger

| -.2 | -.1 | 0.0 | .1 | .2 |

below
average

above
average

Deviation from the grand mean

Figure 4.9. Difference in average levels of distress between women and men. Data are from the ASOC survey.

women (Aneshensel et al. 1991). Without diagnosing anyone, we also find that men drink heavily and engage in antisocial activities more than women do (Ross 2000). Gove and Tudor (1977) argued that symptoms or diagnoses from different realms should *not* be combined—that they represent inherently distinct phenomena that may be interrelated but should not be confounded. Distress is a problem for the person who suffers it. Antisocial behavior, drinking, and drug use may be correlated with distress (either positively or negatively), but are not themselves distress. In some cases such as antisocial behavior or alcoholism, the behaviors may be at least as much a problem for other people as for the person himself. However, the question remains whether women feel more distressed than men because the men transform their frustrations into behavioral disorder.

Two things must be true for transrealm gendered response to explain women's greater distress. First, some type of behavioral disorder must reduce distress. If a disorder does not lower distress, then it cannot account for lower male levels of distress. On this count, there is little or no support for transrealm gendered response. Studies find that distress *in*creases with the level of antisocial behavior, alcoholism, and drug abuse, which are the main behavioral problems found more commonly in men than in women (e.g., Boyd et al. 1984; Dohrenwend et al. 1980; Endicott and Spitzer 1972). Alcoholism, drug abuse, and antisocial personality multiply the odds of qualifying for a diagnosis of major depression by 4.1, 4.2, and 5.1, respectively (Boyd et al. 1984). One study finds that men who drink heavily, use opiates, and smoke cigarettes have higher levels of depression than those who do not, although marijuana use only correlated with depression when it was used to cope with problems (Green and Ritter 2000). We find that people who drink heavily have higher levels of depression than those who do not. We also find that people who engage in behavior that gets them in trouble with the law have higher levels of depression than more law-abiding individuals (Ross 2000). In our Community, Crime, and Health data set, we assessed antisocial and illegal behavior by summing "yes" responses to four questions: "In the past twelve months, have you (1) done anything that would have gotten you in trouble if the police had been around? (2) been caught in a minor violation of the law? (3) been arrested? and (4) been in jail for more than 24 hours?" These behaviors are positively associated depression in our representative community sample.

Heavy drinking and lawless behavior are not substitutes for depression. Engaging in these behaviors doesn't protect men from turning stress and frustration inward upon themselves. On the contrary, people who drink heavily or engage in antisocial activities have higher levels of depression than those who do not. Figure 4.10 illustrates. It shows that heavy drinkers (four or more drinks a day) are more depressed than other

Figure 4.10.   Mean depression score among moderate and heavy drinkers, by sex, adjusting for age and education. Data are from the ASOC survey.

drinkers, not less. That is especially true of the men, who are about three times more likely than women to drink heavily. Were it not for heavy drinking and lawless behavior, men would have even lower levels of depression than they already do. When we adjust for heavy drinking and lawless behavior the gender gap in depression does not *de*crease. Instead it *in*creases by about 40 percent. This means that heavy drinking and lawless behavior do not explain why men have lower levels of depression than women. On the contrary, if women drank and engaged in illegal activities as much as men do, women's depression levels would be even higher than they are now.

Some other behavior that might reduce distress might be more common in men than in women. One candidate is the use of psychoactive drugs. Men use illegal drugs more frequently than women, but there is no reason to think it reduces their distress. Furthermore, women may actually turn to drugs for relief more frequently than men. Women use *prescribed* psychoactive drugs far more than men—over *one woman in five* compared to less than one man in ten (Verbrugge 1985). Women are more likely than men to use psychoactive drugs to cope with personal problems. The fact that women use psychoactive drugs on the advice of their doctors, whereas men use psychoactive drugs on their own authority, is a legal distinction. At one time cocaine, opium, amphetamines, and barbiturates were prescribed by doctors. Historical accounts suggest that women were prescribed these drugs more than men. Men engage in more illegal activity of most kinds, but women use psychoactive drugs more than men. Men's use of drugs that are not prescribed by doctors makes it appear that men have more *problems* with psychoactive drugs even if women use them more often. In no case do men's destructive behaviors account for their low levels of depression. In fact the men who drink heavily, use illegal drugs, and engage in antisocial behavior have higher levels of depression than the men who don't. Women certainly would not protect themselves from getting depressed if they turned their stress and frustration outward; it would lead to even more depression. Depression accompanies anger, hostility, violence, illegal activity, use of drugs and heavy drinking; it does not displace them.

UNDESIRABLE LIFE EVENTS

So far we have been discussing the amount of distress people feel in different ongoing situations, such as being married, divorced, or widowed. Distress may also be associated with *changing* from one situation to another. This brings us to the fifth major fact: undesirable changes are distressing. Twenty years ago many researchers believed that *all* major changes are distressing, whether good or bad. Evidence gathered since then indicates that only the undesirable changes are distressing, as detailed in Chapter 6. Undesirable events are changes into situations with fewer resources (Pearlin 1989). The loss might involve income, wealth, economic security, time, autonomy, fulfilling work, social support, affection, family or household safety, physical functioning, health, or other resources that nourish emotional well-being (Turner et al. 1995). These ominous losses provoke anxiety. They also suggest a demoralizing and depressing helplessness or powerlessness, because of having happened despite being unwanted. More importantly, undesirable events leave individuals in worse situations that present more reasons for worry and fewer for hope. All too often, the more worrisome and depressing the situation the more it spawns additional undesirable events. The cumulative history of loss and failure adds to the burden of distress (Turner and Lloyd 1999).

AGE

What time of life is best? Many believe that youth is the best time of life. We live in a youth-oriented society, one in which beauty, vigor, health, and

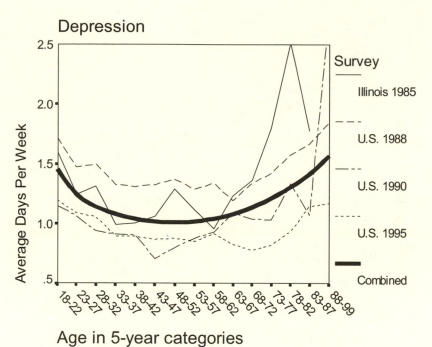

Depression

Age in 5-year categories

Figure 4.11. The frequency of depression by age in four surveys described in the Appendix, with a total of 18,450 respondents. A nonlinear regression line fit is shown for the combined sample.

well-being are considered practically synonymous with youth. Many assume the young are happy and carefree. Research shows that this is not the case. Young adults experience high levels of depression and anxiety associated with getting established and raising families. Measured in terms of depression, middle age is the best time of life. Figure 4.11 shows the results of four surveys taken over the past ten years. The four surveys together combine the reports of 18,450 American adults selected at random. (A description of the samples in the Appendix gives details.) Each jagged line traces the average level of depression across five-year age groups in one of the surveys. The smooth line summarizes the overall pattern. (It shows the curve fit by statistical regression.) The figure shows that middle-aged Americans report a lower average frequency of depression than younger and older adults do. Depression starts relatively high in early adulthood, drops to a lifetime low somewhere in the range of forty to sixty years old, and then rises in old age.

Although middle-aged adults are the least depressed, older adults are the least anxious and angry, as shown in Figure 4.12. This is one of the rare instances where the social patterns of depression and anxiety differ, so we

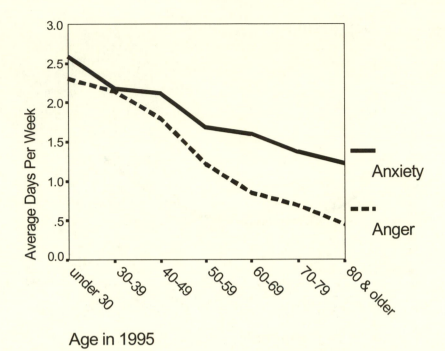

Figure 4.12. The frequency of anxiety and anger by age. Data are from the ASOC survey.

show them separately. Anxiety and anger are fairly common among young adults and about 20 to 30 percent less common among middle-aged adults. Unlike depression, though, anxiety and anger do not rise again in old age (Mirowsky and Ross 1999; Drentea 2000; Schieman 1999). Adults in their seventies report about 40 percent less anxiety than those under thirty, and about 70 percent less anger. Although groups with high levels of depression usually have high levels of anxiety and anger too (as among the young), this is not the case among seniors.

What accounts for the differences in depression and anxiety between age groups? Explaining the pattern requires that we understand the five aspects of age, the age-related conditions and beliefs that influence distress, and the circumstances that characterize each part of life.

The Five Views of Age

The time elapsed since birth defines a person's age. This simple physical measure marks five distinct aspects of age: maturity, decline, life cycle, generation, and survival (Mirowsky and Ross 1992). Each aspect contributes its part to the differences in depression between age groups. This section describes each view of age.

Age as Maturity.

People become more experienced, accomplished, and seasoned as they age. In a word, they mature. Each human sums a lifetime of experience, composing a self of elements arranged to function efficiently and successfully. Personal growth and development require time. Aging increases practice with living and the extent of self-composition. With growing insight and skill, social and psychological traits merge into an increasingly harmonious and effective whole.

Several developments suggest that maturity comes with age: lower crime rates, safer habits, a more orderly lifestyle, greater satisfaction, and a more positive self-image. Rates of crime decline steeply in early adulthood and continue to decline throughout subsequent ages (Hirschi and Gottfredson 1983; Ross and Mirowsky 1987). People in older age groups lead a more routine and orderly life, take fewer risks, avoid fights and arguments, drink more moderately and carefully, and refrain from the recreational use of illegal drugs (Umberson 1987). Workers in successively older age groups report greater satisfaction with their jobs beyond that due to their higher rank and pay (Kalleberg and Loscocco 1983). People in successively older age groups rate themselves more helpful, supportive, disciplined, able, and satisfied with life, and less emotional, nervous, and frustrated; they report greater self-esteem and, until age seventy-five, less of a sense that life is empty and meaningless (Campbell et al. 1976; Gove, Ortega, and Style 1989).

Age as Decline.

Just as humans sum and integrate experience they also sum and integrate failures, faults, injuries, and errors. Often the slow and steady deterioration produces little apparent effect at first. Many defects accrue too slowly to notice the changes from year to year. Eventually, though, the accumulation becomes apparent, like the wrinkling of skin or the graying of hair. Many physical problems that accumulate also compound. For example, weight gained in body fat reduces physical activity and then lower physical activity increases the rate of weight gain. Accumulating and compounding decline may affect behavior and emotions too, as a consequence of physiological decline or as an independent process (Aneshensel, Frerichs, and Huba 1984).

Several facts point to accelerating decline with advancing age. Many physical and mental abilities hold roughly stable throughout most of the adult years but erode at a slowly accelerating rate to produce substantial declines beyond age seventy (Schaie 1983). The incidence and prevalence of chronic disease increase at an accelerating rate with age (Collins 1988; Hartunian, Smart, and Thompson 1981). So does the average level of dysfunctions such as trouble seeing, hearing, walking, lifting, climbing stairs, grasping, and manipulating (Waldron 1983; Waldron and Jacobs 1988). Those dysfunctions interfere with the performance of daily activities such as shopping, cooking, cleaning, gardening, bathing, grooming, dressing, and eating (Berkman and Breslow 1983; Guralnik and Kaplan 1989). The peak performance of athletes and the typical levels of physical activity among nonathletes both decline (Shephard 1987). So does carbohydrate metabolism (the process that fuels the muscles), lung capacity, and bone density (Rowe and Kahn 1987). Mental functions also decline, including orientation to time and space, recall, attention, simple calculation, language comprehension, and the speed of perceptual, motor, and cognitive processes (Holzer et al. 1986; House and Robbins 1983; Rowe and Kahn 1987; Schaie 1983).

Age as Life-Cycle Stage.

Age marks a person's stage in the life cycle. Human life progresses through common sequences of roles: from school to job to retirement, from single to married to widowed (Hogan 1978). Over the lifetime adult status and prospects rise and fall. The phased roles interlock with a flow and ebb of freedoms, prerogatives, privileges, options, opportunities, scope, and resources. The achievements and acquisitions of early adulthood build the rank and prosperity of middle age that eventually erodes in the retrenchment and loss of old age.

Changes in marital, job, and economic status index the social life cycle. Most Americans begin their eighteenth year single, in school or recently graduated, and with little wealth or personal earnings. The progression to middle age increases the prevalence of marriage, parenthood, and employment. It generally increases the earnings of the employed and the total household income (Mirowsky and Ross 1989). Beginning around age sixty the progression into old age sharply increases the prevalence of retirement and widowhood, thus decreasing personal earnings and total household income.

Age as Generation.

Age marks a person's place in the major trends of recent history. At any given stage in their lives the members of younger generations benefit from material, economic, and cultural progress. In the United States twentieth-century trends increased average education, income, female employment, and life expectancy, and decreased family size and rural residence (Bianchi and Spain 1986; Sagan 1987). In the past fifty years alone median family income (adjusted for inflation) more than doubled, life expectancy at birth increased 20 percent, age-adjusted annual mortality rates dropped 60 percent, the proportion living in rural areas dropped from 45 to 25 percent, total fertility rates dropped 20 percent, and the proportion of women in the labor force more than doubled, from 25 percent to more than 50 percent (Bianchi and Spain 1986; Hoffman 1991; Sagan 1987). Fifty years ago 6 percent of Americans aged twenty-five through twenty-nine had less than five years of formal education and only 6 percent had completed four years of college (Hoffman 1991). Today, under 1 percent has less than five years of education, and 25 percent have four years of college. In 1900 one American in ten could not read. In 1940 it was one in twenty-five. Today it is less than one in one hundred. Aggregate increases in education may have generated the favorable trends in income, life expectancy, family size, and female employment (Sagan 1987).

Age as Survival.

Age indirectly indexes traits associated with differences in survival. Other things being equal, traits that confer a selective advantage become more common with age and those that confer a selective disadvantage become scarce. Being older increases the likelihood of having the traits associated with survival, particularly after age seventy. Those traits may create a false impression of aging's effect, perhaps making it appear beneficial or benign when it is actually destructive. Lower survival among the most depressed groups can make aging seem less depressing than it is.

Depression and the things that cause it tend to reduce survival. Severely depressed people die at two to four times the rate of others who are similar in terms of age, sex, socioeconomic status, preexisting chronic health problems such as hypertension, heart disease, stroke, cancer, and signs of fitness such as blood pressure, blood cholesterol, lung capacity, weight for height, and smoking habits (Bruce and Leaf 1989; Somervell et al. 1989). Many of the same statuses and conditions that produce depression also reduce survival. Life expectancy at birth is 4.4 years lower for minorities than for others (and 6.4 years lower for blacks than for others) (Kessler and Neighbors 1986; Mirowsky and Ross 1990; NCHS 1990). Unemployment, low education, and poverty all increase the age-specific rates of mortality (Antonovsky 1967; Berkman and Breslow 1983; Comstock and Tonascia 1977; Kitagawa and Hauser 1973; Kotler and Wingard 1989; Leigh 1983; Sagan 1987). So does being divorced, separated, or widowed (Berkman and Breslow 1983; Bowling 1987; Kaprio, Koskenuo, and Rita 1987; Kotler and Wingard 1989; Litwack and Messeri 1989).

Although most traits that increase depression also reduce survival there is one major exception: being female. Women are more depressed than men but they live an average of five to seven years longer (Gove 1984; Radloff 1975; NCHS 1990; U.S. Census Bureau 2000; Waldron 1983).

Conditions, Beliefs, and Age

Depression emerges from a process in which of objective conditions of life shape beliefs and, in turn, emotional distress. Conditions define the hard realities of status and circumstance that enable or restrain action (Aneshensel 1992). Beliefs form the mental bridge between external conditions and emotional response. Beliefs crystallize around the hard realities, forming interpretations and mental maps that blend observation, judgment, and prediction. Emotions arise from those beliefs. For example: poverty is a condition, perceived powerlessness a belief, and despair an emotion. Maturity, decline, life cycle, generation, and survival define the conditions that shape beliefs and emotions.

This section describes the conditions and beliefs that differ across age groups and affect well-being. It returns us to the facts about marriage, parenthood, education, work, and economic resources; and it takes us forward to the explanations for the social patterns of distress, anticipating the importance of controlling one's own life. The facts and figures come from our 1995 U.S. ASOC survey. (The Appendix on data and measures gives details about the survey.)

People of different ages live under very different conditions. Age is itself one of the most powerful ascribed social statuses. Society assigns many rights, obligations, and opportunities based on age. These include the right to drive, drink alcohol, get married, or vote, the obligation to serve in the military, hold a job, and raise a family, and the opportunity to go to college, run for congress, or head a corporation. Law prescribes the ages for some rights, obligations, and opportunities, but tradition prescribes the ages for most. In sociological terms, society is stratified by age. The different age groups form the graduated layers in a system of responsibility and privilege.

Economic Well-Being.

The list of conditions that affect emotional well-being begins with economic prosperity. Average personal earnings and household income are low among young people, peak in the fifty- to fifty-nine-year-old bracket—about the same time of life when depression reaches its lowest levels—and then decline. Many studies conducted since the 1960s find that higher earnings and income reduce an individual's probable level of

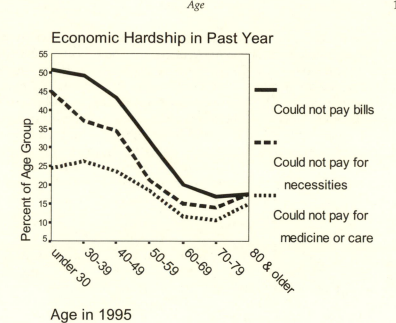

Figure 4.13. Economic hardship by age. Data are from the ASOC survey.

depression (Kessler 1979, 1982; Kessler and Cleary 1980; Mirowsky and Ross 1989; Wheaton 1978, 1980). Why? Two possibilities stand out. One is that earnings and income mark one's worth and status in the eyes of others. People judge themselves partly by seeing how others judge them. Thus low earnings or income can feel inadequate whereas higher earnings and income can feel honorable. Americans do harbor these feelings to some extent, but the main connection between economic and emotional well-being lies elsewhere. Higher earnings and income reduce depression mostly by reducing economic hardship (Ross and Huber 1985). People find it distressing to have difficulty paying the bills or buying household necessities such as food, clothing, or medicine. Economic hardship threatens one's personal security. Worse than that, it threatens the security of children, partners, and others whom one loves and sustains.

Economic hardship generally decreases with older age, as shown in Figure 4.13. Young adults have by far the highest levels of economic hardship. Half say they had difficulty paying bills in the past year. Forty percent report at least one period when they did not have the money to buy food, clothes, or other household necessities. Twenty-five percent report a time when they did not have the money for needed medicine or medical care. The levels of economic hardship drop sharply between the ages of forty and sixty. Hardship remains relatively low among those aged sixty and older. (Even then, one person in five reports a period of economic hardship during the previous year.) Clearly, earnings and income are not the only things that determine the risk of economic hardship. The elderly have relatively low rates of hardship despite low earnings and household income for two reasons. Mostly it is because older adults have fewer dependent children in the home (Mirowsky and Ross 1999). The amount of income per person in the household stays level above the age of sixty even though earnings and total income drop. Second, accumulated wealth, home ownership, and government programs such as social security, Medicare, and Medicaid meet many needs.

Employment.

The life cycle of employment generates the rise and fall of earnings and household income. Middle-aged adults are the most likely to be employed. Employment also improves emotional well-being apart from its impact on household economics. Adults employed full-time enjoy the lowest average frequency of depression (Gove and Geerken 1977; Kessler and McRae 1982; Kessler, Turner, and House 1989; Pearlin et al. 1981; Ross, Mirowsky, and Huber 1983). (Full-time employment improves physical health, too [Ross and Mirowsky 1995].) With the exception of full-time students, adults who are not employed full-time suffer from depression more frequently than those with full-time jobs. Adults who are unemployed, laid off, or unable to work because of disability carry the highest burden of depression. They experience depression two to four times more often than people with full time jobs. Luckily they comprise less than 10 percent of the typical random sample. Retirees and part-time employees make up much larger fractions: about 16 and 9 percent, respectively. Both of these groups have slightly more depression than the full-time employees, but not a lot more (around 10 to 20 percent). Women keeping house make up the second largest group not employed full-time (after the retirees): about 12 percent of adults. Women keeping house feel depressed about 37 percent more often than the women and 75 percent more often than the men who hold full-time paying jobs. The fact that women often keep house rather than hold a full-time paying job accounts for part of the difference between men and women in frequency of depression.

The quality of a job can affect well-being too. Many aspects of paid jobs improve with age for those who remain employed. In addition to earnings these include deciding what to do or how to do it, influence over work group goals, more autonomy, a higher management level, greater prestige and recognition, freedom to disagree with one's supervisor, and getting to do work that is less routine or unpleasant and more interesting and enjoyable in itself.

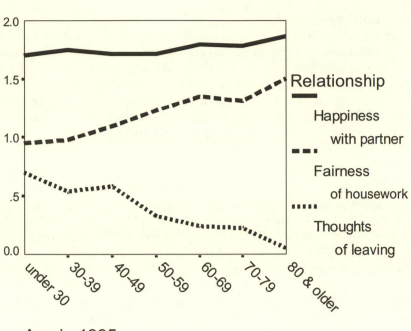

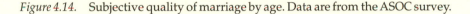

Age in 1995

Figure 4.14.   Subjective quality of marriage by age. Data are from the ASOC survey.

Marriage.

Marriage and family form another major aspect of the adult life cycle that affects well-being (Hughes and Gove 1981). Middle-aged adults are the ones most likely to be married. Young people are often single or cohabiting and older people are often widowed. Married people feel depressed about one-third less often than others. People who are recently divorced or widowed feel depressed the most often, with two or three times the frequency of symptoms as married persons. The level of depression drops with time for the divorced or widowed, but it remains about 40 to 50 percent higher than among married persons. Adults who never have been married also experience more symptoms than those who are married. People living together with someone as if married are between the married persons and others in their frequency of symptoms.

As we said earlier, marriage reduces depression for two main reasons: social support and economic resources. Marriage improves well-being by improving emotional and economic security. Adults benefit from a partnership that provides mutual intimacy and reliance (Gove et al. 1983; Mirowsky 1985; Pearlin and Johnson 1977; Ross et al. 1990). Of course some marriages meet these needs better than others. The quality of one's marriage affects well-being. A bad marriage can be worse than none. The quality of marriages improves with age for the ones that stay intact. Older married persons feel happier with their partners, divide housework more fairly, and think of separating less often, as shown in Figure 4.14. The quality of marriage improves with age for two reasons. First, people become more adept at managing their relationships as they mature. Second, the worst marriages break up. Learning by trial and error leads to improvement over time.

Children.

Young adults often have young children in the home. Adults in their twenties and thirties are most likely to have children at home. Few adults over the age of fifty have children in the household. Younger parents bear the greatest child care strains because they have lower income and younger children who need most care. Child care introduces the major strain associated with marriage (Ross and Huber 1985; Ross and Mirowsky 1988). Children improve the well-being of parents in conducive circumstances: adequate household income and a stable, supportive partnership with fair sharing of chores and sacrifices. Ready availability of affordable child care also helps. Unfortunately many parents find themselves in circumstances far from this ideal. Some lack the money. Some lack a partner or a helpful partner. Some mothers find themselves in extremely depressing circumstances: a failed or unsupportive marriage, a poorly paid job that does not accommodate family responsibilities, and no ready source of affordable child care.

Children also increase the need for money often while decreasing the household income. That income is greatest when both parents remain employed full-time with no prolonged absence from employment. Many mothers suspend full-time employment to care for young children, which reduces the income available for supporting the children. In addition to creating economic strains, children engage parents in conflict over behavior and instigate conflict between parents over housework and child care. Older adults have the low levels of economic hardship and conflict with their partners in large part because they do not have dependent children.

Education.

Most of the conditions discussed so far define the economic and family life cycle that accounts for much of the relationship between age and depression. The changes between generations account for some of the pattern too. Increasing education leads as the most important of those changes for well-being.

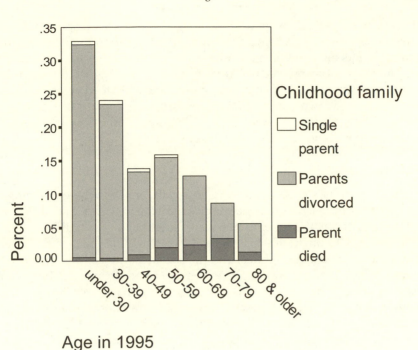

Age in 1995

Figure 4.15. Disruption of respondent's childhood family by age at interview. Data are from the ASOC survey.

Younger generations have higher levels of education than people from older cohorts. The frequency of depression drops with each additional year of education (Mirowsky and Ross 1990, 1992; Ross and Huber 1985). It takes an especially big step down with the high school degree. For the most part, though, the years of education rather than the degrees make the difference. The effect of education on depression does not fade with time as people grow old. In fact, the effect of education gets larger in successively older age groups (Miech and Shanahan 2000). Increasing education–based differences in the prevalence of physical health problems account for the diverging levels of depression (see below). Likewise, the effect does not fade in successive generations with rising educational standards. Each additional year of education reduces the average level of depression by the same amount as does an additional $40,000 in household income.

Remarkably, the education of one's parents has a similar although smaller lifelong effect. Each additional year of one's parents' education reduces the average depression by the same amount as an additional

$10,000 in household income. Middle-aged and older respondents finished about three or four years of education more than their parents did (young adults are sometimes still in school so their eventual educational attainment is not completed). If Americans under the age of thirty eventually do the same they will complete an average of sixteen years of education. That will do two things. It will help bring their depression down from current levels, and it will help keep their depression below the levels of previous generations at each stage in life.

Childhood Family.

The main trends of recent history generally improve the well-being of Americans with each new generation. Unfortunately one harmful trend works against the helpful ones: the increasing breakup of childhood families. Figure 4.15 illustrates that trend. Less than 10 percent of the adults now in their seventies, eighties, and nineties experienced the breakup of their childhood family. Almost 33 percent of the adults now in their twenties did. The death of a parent became less common in succeeding generations, but the divorce of parents increased dramatically. As with the education of one's parents, the breakup of their marriage has a lifelong effect on the frequency of depression. As we will elaborate in Chapter 5, adults from divorced childhood families feel depressed more often than adults from families that remained intact. The effect does not vanish as people get older and does not abate as parental divorce becomes more common. The effect remains the same among the young adults with a high prevalence of parental divorce as among the old adults with a low prevalence. A single parent or the death of a parent have even worse effects (Brown and Harris 1978).

Health and Physical Functioning.

As people get old they feel less healthy, have more impairments and medical conditions, and expect to live fewer additional years (Mirowsky and Hu 1996; Ross and Bird 1994). A large majority of Americans over the age of sixty have a serious chronic disease such as hypertension, heart disease, diabetes, cancer, osteoporosis, or arthritis. About 70 percent report some difficulty with common activities such as carrying a bag of groceries, and almost a fourth report a severe impairment of some type. Most physical problems increase in prevalence and severity with age. (There are a few welcome exceptions: older people report fewer headaches and allergies.) The problems take many forms: discomforting aches and pains, threatening diagnoses, disabling impairments, and a shortening future. People find all of these depressing, but impairments are the worst by far. Serious impairment can triple the frequency of depression, as shown in

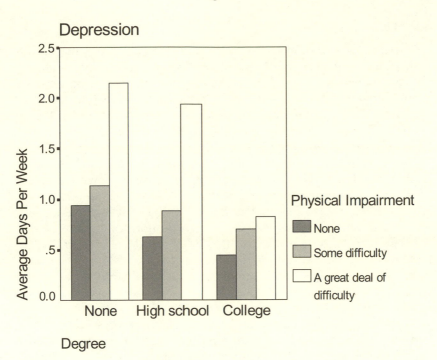

Figure 4.16. Average depression by physical impairment for respondents at three levels of education (less than high school degree, high school degree, or college degree). Data are from the ASOC survey.

Figure 4.16. Even moderate difficulty climbing stairs, kneeling, carrying, walking, hearing, seeing, or the like increases depression as much as not having finished high school. A major disability produces the same effect as that, marital breakup, and economic hardship put together. The total burden of impairment lies heaviest on the oldest adults.

There is some good news about physical impairment. Rising levels of education reduce both the amount of impairment and its impact on well-being. Figure 4.16 shows the impact of impairment on depression among people who have not finished high school, among those with a high school degree, and among those with a college degree. People with college degrees appear to cope with impairment much better than others, as Figure 4.13 suggests. Furthermore, education slows the rise of impairment with age (Ross and Wu 1996). People with college degrees have about the same level of impairment in their seventies as high school graduates in their sixties and as high school dropouts in their forties. Rising levels of education may help today's younger generations delay impairment longer and manage it better.

Sense Of Control.

The members of different age groups live under different conditions that influence their beliefs and emotions. The various conditions described above combine to produce the fall and rise of depression across age groups. Together those external conditions shape beliefs that produce the age group differences in depression. Mostly they work through the sense of controlling one's own life. As detailed below, old adults often feel they have little control over their lives.

The perception of directing and regulating one's own life varies by degree, ranging from fatalism and a deep sense of powerlessness and helplessness to instrumentalism and a firm sense of mastery and self-efficacy. Some people feel that any good things that happen are mostly luck—fortunate outcomes they desire but do not design. They feel personal problems mostly result from bad breaks, and feel little ability to regulate or avoid the bad things that happen. Others feel they can do just about anything they set their minds to. They see themselves as responsible for their own successes and failures, and view misfortunes as the results of personal mistakes they can avoid in the future.

The sense of control links the socioeconomic, interpersonal, behavioral, and physiological systems. A firm sense of control averts the tendency to become helpless in frustrating and aversive situations (Hiroto 1974). It also decreases autonomic reactivity. A low sense of control correlates with higher circulating catecholamines and corticosteroids in humans, as does learned helplessness in both humans and animals (Gold, Goodwin and Chrousos 1988; Rodin 1986). The catecholamine norepinephrine (noradrenaline) is implicated in depression and anxiety. The anti-inflammatory corticosteroid cortisol (hydrocortisone) may produce the sleep disorders related to depression, particularly those involving agitation and early morning rising (Greden et al. 1983). Cortisol regulates the metabolism of cholesterol (its parent compound), mobilizing energy to resist stress (Steward 1986). Improving the sense of control of nursing home patients lowers their odds of dying by a factor of 2.5 (eighteen-month follow-up) (Rodin 1986).

The average sense of control declines sharply among American's over fifty, as shown in Figure 4.17 (Mirowsky 1995; Mirowsky and Ross 1990, 1991). Adults younger than fifty typically report a firm sense of directing and regulating their own lives. They see themselves as responsible for their own successes and failures, and view their misfortunes as the results of personal mistakes they can avoid in the future. In older age groups the balance of perceived control shifts from a sense of mastery toward one of helplessness, from instrumentalism toward fatalism.

A number of things come together to produce the low sense of control observed among old Americans. They represent many aspects of age,

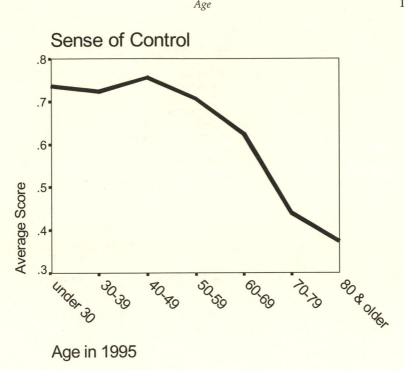

Figure 4.17. The sense of personal control by age. Data are from the ASOC survey.

including physical decline, the life cycle of employment, earnings, and marriage, and the generational trends in education and women's' employment. Health problems account for much of it. Subjective life expectancy has a large effect on the sense of control. The shorter someone expects to live, the less they feel in control of their own lives and outcomes. People find it hard to plan for a future that looks short, hard to manage a life that might end soon. Physical impairments also have big effects. Difficulty performing common daily tasks puts real limits on personal control. A general feeling of health and fitness bolsters the sense of control, but sickness and disease undermine that feeling. Specific diagnoses such as heart disease, cancer, or arthritis reduce the sense of control by making people feel sick, impaired, or near the end of life. Social and economic losses undermine the sense of control too. Widows feel less in control of their own lives than do married people of the same age. A full-time job and substantial personal earnings increase the sense of control, but they become scarcer as people get old. Retirees have a lower sense of control than people who are employed, in part because the daily activities of retirees are more isolated and routine (Ross and Drentea 1998).

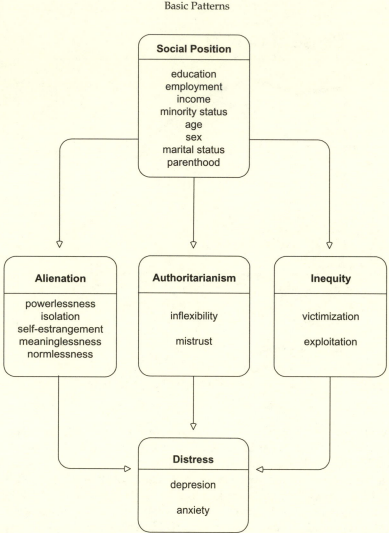

Figure 4.18. Theoretical model showing alienation, authoritarianism, and inequity as the links between social position and psychological distress

A large fraction of the fatalism and powerlessness that characterizes the elderly comes from having lived in harder times (Mirowsky 1995). Members of older generations had lower education than common today. Education accounts for about a third of the association between old age and low sense of control. For women the history of employment contributes too. Retirees who held full-time paying jobs most of their lives feel more in control than those who did not. Women who are over the age of seventy lived in a period when few women held full-time jobs over most of the years before retirement. By old age they feel little control over their own lives.

DISCUSSION

Patterns of psychological distress tell us about the quality of life in various social positions. Misery is an inherently meaningful yardstick in social research, serving much the same function as mortality in medical research. Although community surveys of the social patterns of distress only began in the 1960s, they have already corrected some erroneous preconceptions. In particular, the observed patterns of distress challenge the idea that emotional well-being results from a placid life of dependency, protection, and freedom from responsibility. Instead, the surveys show that responsibility, commitment, achievement, and control in one's own life, and reciprocity, consideration, and equity in personal relationships are the sources of well-being.

Socioeconomic status, sex, age, marriage, parenthood, and other sociodemographic variables mark the objective conditions of social life; based on socially patterned experiences, people develop beliefs, interpretations, and assumptions about the nature of society, human relations, themselves, and their relationship to others and to society; the level of distress depends on the nature of these beliefs. Three themes in the individual's understanding of self and society have been developed as explanations of the known social patterns of distress: subjective alienation, authoritarianism, and inequity (see Figure 4.18). Of these beliefs, a sense of controlling one's own life stands out. It is a main link between the external reality of objective social conditions and the internal reality of subjective distress.

The United States is in the middle of far-reaching historical changes. As forms of production become outmoded, the skills associated with them become obsolete. As families get smaller and more women are employed, traditional household arrangements also become obsolete. In the aggregate, people make these changes. As individuals, people are made over by them. They adapt in one of two ways. Individuals can be overwhelmed, demoralized, discouraged, and distressed, or they can be creative, curious, open-minded, active, and inventive.

5

New Patterns

Over the past decade our research developed in two new directions. Both take the established patterns as a starting point, but look at how those patterns relate to larger aspects of social structure. This chapter describes the new social patterns of distress emerging from those expanded avenues of research. The first set of new patterns relates distress to life course disruptions and unfavorable developments. Current distress often has social origins that lie far in the past. The competitive and cumulative nature of our stratification system means that early problems often have life-long distressing socioeconomic consequences. A bad break or a poor choice early on may produce a cascade of problems that creates distress anew at every subsequent point in life. Likewise, a small but cumulative disadvantage may grow throughout adulthood. The first section of this chapter describes three studies of life course disruption and development: the adulthood impact of childhood parental divorce, the effect of age at first birth on emotional well-being throughout the rest of life, and the expansion of the gender gap in depression in adulthood as women and men enter and live out their unequal social statuses. The second set of new patterns relates distress to qualities of the residential neighborhood. Most of our research looks at how individual social and economic disadvantages create distress. Some of our new research looks at the impact on well-being of the residential concentration of disadvantaged individuals. A special data set provides a new look at how the prevalence of poor and mother-only households in the neighborhood affects distress, and how neighborhood disorder links the two. We find that the childhood divorce of one's parents correlates with later depression as an adult, that becoming a parent too early in life correlates with greater depression thereafter, that the gender gap in depression appears small to nonexistent in early adulthood but grows until old age, and that residents find life in disadvantaged neighborhoods rife with signs of social disorder to be depressing.

130

LIFE COURSE DISRUPTIONS AND DEVELOPMENTS

Parental Divorce

Over the twentieth century the percentage of adults whose childhood families broke up in divorce rose sharply. Almost a third of adults under age thirty in 1995 experienced a childhood parental breakup, compared to less than 10 percent of those over the age of sixty-five. The century's upward trend in divorce generated much controversy at the time, and still does. The relaxing of laws and norms restricting divorce seems consistent with American ideals of individual liberty, and lets many individuals escape untenable situations. Even so, the adults and their children generally find the process and consequences of divorce very distressing (Booth and Amato 1991; Cherlin, Chase-Lansdale, and McRae 1998; Gerstel et al. 1985; Hines 1997). The best one can say for divorce is that an adult can wind up better off emotionally in the long run if the relationship lacked affection, companionship, and caring (Wheaton 1990). Even that depends on how things go subsequently, which for women depends on the number of dependent children (ibid.). Clearly the children suffer emotionally from the conflict, turmoil, loss, and deprivation associated with divorce, but that distress dissipates within a few years (Aseltine 1996). Children find marital conflict so distressing that those living with a parent who left a high-conflict relationship several years earlier are less distressed than those who continue to live in a conflict-ridden home (Jekielek 1998). Even so, they still may face long-run consequences of the new family and household circumstances. Two questions stand out. First, does childhood parental divorce produce lifelong detrimental effects on emotional well-being? Are adults who experienced childhood breakups more distressed than those whose parents remained together when they were children? Second, if they are, why are they? Are the lasting effects socioeconomic, interpersonal, or both?

Enduring Consequences.

Recent evidence shows an enduring negative effect of childhood parental divorce on adults' mental health (Amato, 1991; Amato and Sobolewski 2001; Cherlin et al. 1998; McLeod, 1991; Ross and Mirowsky 1999). The 386 adults in our ASOC survey who experienced childhood parental divorce range in age from 18 through 86, with a mean of 42 and a median of 37. In that sample, parental divorce increases the average frequency of depression by around 20 percent compared to persons whose parents remained together. To put it in perspective, that is about half the lasting effect of having experienced the death of a parent in childhood, and a little more than the impact of one's parents having had high school rather than college degrees. Lower parental education and higher parental conflict do not account for the correlation between adulthood distress and childhood parental divorce, although they do predispose the parents to divorce and also have enduring emotional consequences (Amato and Sobolewski 2001; Cherlin et al. 1998). So far, the studies consistently find that the parental divorce itself seems to have lasting detrimental effects on emotional well-being, apart from the conditions that predispose parents to divorce. Those effects apparently do not diminish with the passing of decades and do not diminish as divorce becomes more common (Ross and Mirowsky 1999).

How can an experience in a childhood long past persistently under-mine well-being throughout adulthood? Somehow the parental divorce must have had consequences in childhood that set the individual's life on a different and more distressing track. The life course disruption hypoth-esis focuses on two possible links between adult mental health and the divorce of one's parents in childhood: impaired status attainment and primed interpersonal difficulties. As detailed below, the children of divorce receive less formal education, which in turn reduces occupational status and income and increases the likelihood of unemployment and economic hardship. The children of divorce also experience disrupted interpersonal relationships: They tend to marry early, have unhappy mar-riages, divorce repeatedly, and mistrust people in general. Lowered socioeconomic status and problems in interpersonal relationships, in turn, affect depression in adulthood.

Impaired Status Attainment.

Parental divorce has negative socioeconomic consequences for adult children. It interferes with educational attainment, which shapes opportu-nities for the rest of life. Children of divorced parents achieve relatively less education than those from intact families: they are less likely to finish high school, less likely to go on to college if they finish high school, and less likely to finish college if they go (Amato and Bruce 1991; Astone and McLanahan 1991; Coleman 1988; Greenberg and Wolf 1982; Keith and Fin-lay 1988; McLanahan 1985; McLanahan and Sandefur 1994; Shaw 1982; Steelman and Powell 1991; Wojtkiewicz 1993). Adult children of divorce have lower occupational status and earnings, largely as a result of lower education (Biblarz and Raftery 1993; Powell and Parcel 1997). As in other studies, the adults in our ASOC sample whose parents divorced before they were eighteen years old have significantly lower educational attain-ment, occupational status, and household income. In addition, we find that they have more current difficulties paying bills or buying necessities, and more of a history of similar economic hardship. These associations are not simply due to background characteristics. All the associations with parental divorce remain significant with adjustment for parental education, minority status, sex, and age.

Our analyses indicate that lower education and more frequent and persistent economic hardship form the main socioeconomic links between childhood parental divorce and adulthood depression. Lower education increases depression directly, but also because it reduces economic hardship, as detailed in Chapter 4. Childhood parental divorce leads to economic hardship because of lower education. Interestingly, it also predisposes individuals to a history of hardship by predisposing them to early family formation and to divorce, as discussed in the next section. Lower education and greater economic hardship both contribute a partially independent component to the effect of childhood parental divorce on depression. Lower occupational status and lower household income do not. They influence depression only through their impact on the likelihood of economic hardship past and present. Considered by themselves, less education and more economic hardship account for about two-thirds to three-quarters of the effect of childhood parental divorce on adulthood depression. Because education decreases depression directly, and indirectly by way of improving one's economic circumstances, restricted educational attainment forms a major path linking childhood parental divorce to adult depression.

Primed Interpersonal Difficulties.

Childhood parental divorce undermines the quality and stability of adult relationships. Adult children of divorce marry earlier, divorce more often (Amato 1996; Glenn and Kramer 1987; Glenn and Shelton 1983; McLanahan and Bumpass 1988; Mueller and Pope 1977), and report greater problems, conflict, mistrust, and thoughts of divorce in their marriages (Amato 1996; Amato and Bruce 1991; McLeod 1991; Webster, Orbuch, and House 1995). In a representative sample of U.S. adults, people whose parents got divorced when they were children exhibited jealous, critical, domineering, angry, and uncommunicative behaviors that contributed to difficulties in sustaining long-term intimate relationships (Amato 1996).

We find that adults whose parents divorced when they were children are significantly more likely to have married early, to have a history of divorce and remarriage, and to have no current intimate relationship or an unhappy one. They also mistrust people in general more. Oddly, they do not report lower levels of social support, which implies that they get their support outside marriage. Having married as a teenager significantly increases depression, even adjusting for the presence and quality of a current intimate relationship. Individuals currently unhappy with a spouse or partner and thinking of leaving feel depressed more than those in a happy relationship. Individuals who have no one they consider a significant other or intimate partner also feel depressed more than those in a happy relationship. Thus, compared with persons in satisfying relationships, those in an unhappy relationship or not in a relationship are more distressed. Most previous research had compared married people to unmarried people, or satisfying relationships to unsatisfying ones, but not both. We find no psychological benefit to being in an unhappy marriage or partnership over being alone, but we find a large psychological benefit to having a satisfying intimate relationship. A history of divorce and remarriage in itself does not directly affect depression, but correlates with having no current relationship or an unhappy one. A general mistrust of others does increase depression directly. Thus, our analyses imply that childhood parental divorce increases depression throughout adulthood partly by leading to early marriages, unhappy or nonexistent intimate relationships, and a general mistrust of others. By themselves, these indicators of interpersonal difficulties account for about half of the effect of childhood parental divorce on adulthood depression.

Unfolding Problems.

The sections above treat the socioeconomic and interpersonal consequences of childhood parental breakup as analytically distinct links to adulthood depression. In reality they develop and influence depression together. Low education predisposes individuals to mistrust while leaving them without communication skills that might help resolve interpersonal tensions. Economic hardships strain marital relations, contributing to divorce, which generally makes economic hardship even worse. Developing and operating together, the impaired status attainment and primed interpersonal difficulties account for all of the adulthood depression produced by childhood parental divorce.

In many ways, life course disruptions are like stories that, once begun, write themselves. One thing leads to the next, with a grim self-fulfillment. A teenager, feeling unfairly punished by unwanted events and circumstances, looks for a way out. The mother, impoverished by single parenthood or trying to ease strains in a new marriage, seeks relief in the child's early exit. Circumstances limit the resources for continued education, while undermining parental authority that would keep the child in school. The child's father loses influence and interest. The mother's new partner, if she gets one, may never acquire much influence or interest. The mother alone lacks sufficient influence. So the child leaves school, and leaves home. Low education leads to unstable employment in unpleasant, low-paying jobs.

Together the low education and low pay result in frequent economic hardship. Feeling abandoned and insecure, the child looks to early marriage to fill a void. The marriage at first seems good, and eases the economic hardship by pooling earnings and effort. When children start to arrive, that period of economic relief ends. As the romance fades, the realities harden. Marital tensions increase. Lacking the communication skills one develops in college, efforts to address child care and money issues explode into arguments. Lacking trust, the parent suspects the partner of selfish and abusive motivations. The marriage spirals to an end. What follows is, at best, no better. More likely it intensifies the anger, loneliness, and economic hardship. Add to that the guilt from now having done the same terrible thing one's own parents did. A new and better marriage seems the best solution, and is desperately sought. And on the story goes.

Many individuals who experience childhood parental breakup manage to avoid sliding into economic and interpersonal problems. Even so, the childhood breakup of parents makes the slope steeper and slipperier for them. It is not clear yet what might help the children of divorced parents avoid the descent. Certainly efforts to counteract the effects of parental divorce on education seem like a good place to start. Longer schooling leads to later first marriages, greater trust and communication skills, and fewer episodes of economic hardship. Perhaps the most disturbing aspect of childhood parental divorce is its insidious self-replication across generations. We see no sign of a self-limiting prevalence, and no sign of consequences getting better as parental breakups become more common.

Age at First Birth

Whether being a parent erodes or improves emotional well-being depends partly on when in life a person becomes a parent (Mirowsky and Ross 2002). Having a child at a young age disrupts the transition from adolescence into adulthood, with persistent distressing consequences. People who become parents with undeveloped resources and unseasoned relationships often are overwhelmed by the strains of parenthood. Those strains further disrupt the needed relationships and attainments, creating a self-reinforcing accumulation of disadvantage. In societies organized around individual competition for status, a conflict exists between social and biological realities. Individuals come out of childhood lacking personal wealth, power, and prestige. They compete for status and reward through the educational and occupational system. Success brings a higher rate of attainment with self-reinforcing benefits akin to compounding interest. Whatever one thinks about the desirability of this system or the validity of its operating assumptions, it creates a likely conflict between biological and social realities. Humans in such a society mature reproductively a decade or more before maturing socially.

Consequences of Early Parenthood.

Early parenthood indicates a poor start in life. It reflects a disordered transition from adolescence into adulthood and itself disrupts that transition, with lifelong consequences that influence emotional well-being. Early births often delay or deter the completion of high school, discourage entry into college, or prevent the completion of college. The demands of caring for children often interfere with women's employment. The combination of added household needs, lowered educational attainment, and disrupted employment increase the risk of not having the money to pay for things such as food, clothing, and shelter. The resulting low education, interrupted employment, low household income, and economic hardship increase depression throughout life. Early first birth also creates family problems, such as premarital parenthood, early and unstable marriage, or large family size, that create persistent and depressing difficulties. Conditions like being a single or divorced parent or being locked in a strained and unsupportive marriage are distressing themselves and they often lead to further difficulties in the form of disrupted education or employment and periods of material or economic hardship. For women, health problems created by early pregnancy can add to this list of woes. Incomplete reproductive development and poor preparation for motherhood create risks for both mother and child. The closer a mother is to puberty the more likely she will have a serious complication of pregnancy or childbirth and the more likely her infant will be premature, unhealthy, or malformed. Her own persistent health problems and her child's can have long-term emotional consequences.

Fathers Included.

Most research on the consequences of early first birth focuses on the mother. Partly that's because pregnancy, nursing, and the mother's role limit her options more. Partly it's because only the mother risks direct health consequences of childbearing. However, the social complications of early parenthood have lifelong effects that apply to men as well as women, although not as strongly. First births that disrupt education and status attainment create depressing health problems throughout life for men as well as for women (Mirowsky 2002). In addition, adolescent parenthood slows the development of a sense of control over one's own life for men, as well as for women, largely because of its association with dropping out of school (Lewis, Ross, and Mirowsky 1999). Adolescent parenthood predicts higher levels of depression later on for men, adjusting for factors that predispose to early parenthood. Men who delay the first birth longer avoid problems such as marrying early, curtailing education, needing a job but not being able to find one, and not having enough money for food, clothes, rent, and other household needs (Mirowsky and Ross 2002). For men there seems to be no limit to the benefits of delaying. The later fathers became parents the greater their current emotional well-being. This suggests that consolidating socioeconomic status acts as a prerequisite to beneficial parenthood for men. Emotional problems associated with early parenthood are worse for women, but they exist for men as well.

Delay Makes Parenthood Beneficial.

Older age at first birth switches the long-run emotional impact of parenthood from unfavorable to favorable. Under the right conditions, parenthood can be emotionally beneficial. It encourages adults to adopt a sensible and responsible lifestyle, develops mature attitudes and interpersonal skills, provides affection and a sense of accomplishment, and creates supportive personal relationships. Whether parenthood diminishes well-being or enhances it depends on the parent's ability to meet the demands, avoid or manage the problems, and recognize and cultivate the benefits. Clearly, the emotional advantages of raising the children depend on the economic prosperity of the household, the mother's paid employment, the availability of affordable child care services, and the spouse's emotional support and shared participation in child care, as described in Chapter 4. Parenthood can provide emotional gratification after the children have grown and left the household too. When the children become independent the main burdens of parenthood are lifted. What remains are the qualities in the parents developed by the experience, and the qualities of the continuing relationships between the parents and their adult offspring. Individuals who take longer to prepare for parenthood benefit more from it emotionally throughout their remaining lives.

Risks of Long Delay.

Although social factors generally favor delaying the first birth, the physical demands of bearing and raising children also limit the benefits of delay for women (Mirowsky 2002). Pregnancy and childbirth put enormous stress on the body. Physical fitness and health generally decline as people age. A late first birth can precipitate developing health problems, with consequences for emotional well-being. Older women face higher than average risk of having a preexisting chronic condition during the pregnancy and birth. They also face higher than average risk of many complications of pregnancy or birth. For example, in the United States, pregnancy-related hypertension and eclampsia rates are highest in the forty-and-older bracket (next highest in the under-twenty bracket). Eclampsia is coma and convulsions during or immediately after pregnancy, related to high blood pressure, accumulation of fluid in body tissues, and large amounts of protein in

the urine, signifying kidney problems. The infant's risk of congenital mal-
formation also increases along with the risks to the mother. Women who
delay the first birth too long may not have the physical capacity to meet the
challenges. Chronic conditions and childbearing complications can initiate
or exacerbate each other. Tending and supporting children also can be
physically challenging, while limiting the time available for exercise (Bird
and Fremont 1991). Chronic disease, physical impairment, frequent aches
and pains, poor subjective health, and low energy and fitness are depressing. They discourage the afflicted and also indicate problems in the physiological systems that sustain emotional well-being. Although delaying
parenthood generally improves well-being, biological factors limit the
emotional benefits of delay for women.

Pivotal and Optimal Ages at First Birth.

In our research we looked for evidence of the best age to have begun
parenthood, in terms of its association with current depression. We asked
two questions. First, is there an age at first birth that acts as a dividing line
in the association between parenthood and emotional well-being? Individuals who became parents before that age are more depressed on average than nonparents who are otherwise similar to themselves in sex, age,
race/ethnicity, and status of origin (as measured by their own parents'
education). Individuals who became parents after the pivotal age are less
depressed than nonparents of similar background. We call that dividing
line the *pivotal* age at first birth. Second, is there an age at first birth associated with a minimum average level of depression for women? Mothers
who had a first birth at that age are less depressed on average than those
who had a first birth earlier or later. We call that age associated with the
lowest depression the *optimal* age at first birth for women.

Figure 5.1 illustrates the core results of our statistical models, based on
the ASOC survey sample of persons ages eighteen through ninety-five.
The figure graphs the ratio of depression predicted for each parent to that
predicted for nonparents who are similar to them. Each circle or line
through a circle represents one parent. No mothers and only a handful of
fathers had a first child after age forty-five. The upper panel shows the
results for men and the lower panel shows those for women. For both
sexes, the individuals who became parents before a pivotal age around
twenty-three are more frequently depressed than the nonparents who are
from similar backgrounds. For men the predicted parent-to-nonparent
depression ratio gets progressively more favorable to parenthood with
longer delay of the first birth. For women the ratio becomes somewhat
favorable to parenthood with delay beyond the pivotal age, reaching its
most favorable level at an optimal age around thirty.

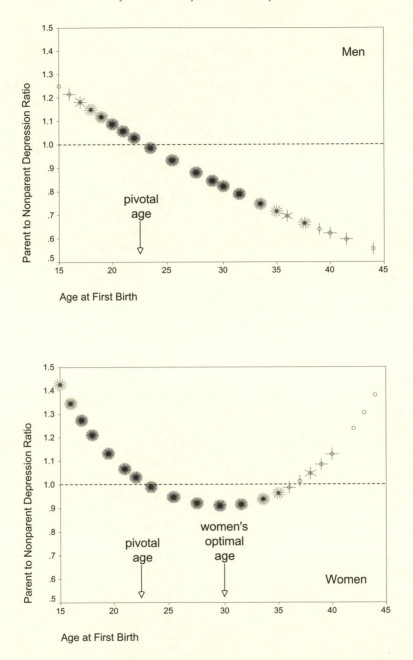

Figure 5.1.   The ratio of depression predicted for parents to that predicted for non-parents of similar age, sex, race/ethnicity, and status of origin, by age at first birth and sex. Data are from the 1995 U.S. ASOC survey.

Parenthood Better for Fathers Than for Mothers.

The relationship between parenthood and depression favors the fathers more than the mothers in several ways. Only about 35 percent of the fathers in the sample had a first child before the pivotal age, compared to about 60 percent of the mothers. Fathers also have smaller depression ratios associated with teenage first births than mothers do. There is no detectable limit to benefits of delay for the fathers, but the mothers do not gain additional benefit from delaying beyond age thirty, and actually have increasing average levels of depression associated with longer delay. About 90 percent of the mothers had a first birth before the optimal age. Overall, a larger fraction of mothers than fathers had first births at an age associated with greater depression compared to nonparents. Among the parents who had a first birth at an age associated with emotional benefits compared to nonparents, the ratios do not get as favorable for the mothers as for the fathers. Women do not get as much psychological benefit from long delay as do men. Overall, women can expect greater emotional burdens of early parenthood than men, but cannot expect the same emotional benefits of long delayed parenthood.

The Trend toward Later Parenthood.

If one takes our results at face value, then the trend toward older age at first birth in the United States and many other countries may be a good thing, despite the concerns expressed by obstetricians and reproductive biologists. In the United States the median age of mothers giving birth for the first time rose from 21.3 in 1969 up to 24.3 in 1998. The U.S. trend is driven by a sharp increase in the age at first birth of women with college degrees, along with an increase in the fraction of women getting college degrees. In 1994 almost half (45.5 percent) of the college graduate women having first births were age thirty or older, putting their median just short of the optimal age at first birth estimated in this study. Women planning careers may worry about the consequences of delaying the first birth beyond their early twenties. These results show no cause for worry. They imply that women can delay until their late twenties or early thirties with no general risk to future emotional well-being. Indeed, the results imply that such delay may improve well-being throughout life.

Age and the Gender Gap in Depression

The higher levels of depression among women than among men remains one of the oldest and most robust findings in community surveys of mental health. Much of the gap exists because women experience greater trade-offs and tensions from work and family than do men. Women carry a greater burden of total housework and paid work hours, pay greater costs of caring for the problems of family and friends, face greater practical constraints on personal employment and advancement, and get less autonomy, authority, recognition, and pay when employed. These differences between women and men amount to unequal socioeconomic status. The extent of that inequality grows in adulthood. For example, women ages sixteen to twenty-four earn about 90 percent of the weekly wage of men in that age bracket. Women over forty-four earn only 61 percent of the weekly wage of men their age (Reskin and Padavic 1994). The wage gap grows in adulthood because men's pay rises faster and for a longer period. That growing inequality in pay signifies and typifies a pervasive gender stratification that emerges in adulthood, increasing the gender gap in depression as women and men move into full adult status.

Age-Related Differences in Adult Statuses.

The life course of work and family circumstances differs for women and men in a manner that creates a growing disparity in standing during adulthood. The interacting marital and employment cycles form the core of a larger set of age-specific sex differences with implications for well-being. The employment cycle differs substantially by sex because it embodies the traditional division of labor. Young women and men at the start of adulthood have similar rates of full-time and part-time employment, but middle-aged men and women differ greatly. Middle-aged women often work part-time but middle-aged men rarely do. Middle-aged women often keep house but middle-aged men almost never do.

Psychologically speaking, the sex differences in adult statuses generally favor men. Women find themselves in stressful circumstances more often than men. Many of the stresses result from women's family responsibilities, which are emotionally demanding in themselves and often limit or conflict with full-time employment. The middle-age gender gap in employment and earnings reflects a lifetime of past trade-offs and tensions between work and family for women, and reproduces and reinforces those trade-offs and tensions in the present. Many women find themselves in dire circumstances when family needs first disrupt employment and then later require employment doing menial work for low wages on an inflexible schedule.

Just at the time in life when sex differences in child care and employment subside, the differences in the probability of widowhood rise sharply. That has two effects. First, it makes grief and loneliness more common among older women than among men of the same age. More women than men are adjusting to a recent loss, and fewer can find another partner. Second, it makes economic hardship more common among older

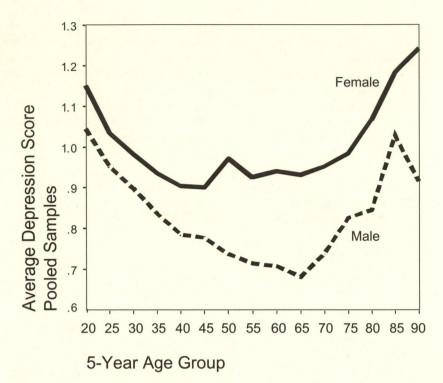

Figure 5.2.   Mean depression scores of men and women by age. Data are from three pooled samples (collected in 1985, 1988, and 1990) totaling 15,634 American adults.

women than among men of the same age. Widowhood sharply increases the financial difficulties of women but not those of men. The differences in financial strain account for much of the gender gap in distress observed among older adults.

Depression by Age for Women and Men.

The gender gap in depression grows in adulthood as women and men enter and undergo their unequal adult statuses (Mirowsky 1996). Figure 5.2 shows the mean depression for men and women by five-year age group. The data come from three samples with a total of over 15,000 Americans ages eighteen and up. Because the gender gap in depression exists largely due to status differences between men and women, much of it develops in adulthood. There is a comparatively small sex difference in depression among eighteen-year-olds. At that age the majority of the women and men remain in school. Only a small fraction of either sex is married or raising children. Jobs pay relatively little for both sexes. Work histories are too short to make much difference. This is not to say that women and men are equal at age eighteen. Girls are more depressed than boys in high school and perhaps earlier. The inequalities at age eighteen foreshadow even greater inequalities to come in employment, earnings, household duties, and family responsibilities. Moving up in age, the mean depression drops faster and longer for men than for women. Sex differences in employment status, housework, or child care as primary activities, difficulty arranging child care if employed, and trouble paying bills or buying necessities for the household and family account for much of the growing difference in depression.

Hormones, Sex Roles, and Gendered Response.

For the most part the adulthood growth of the gender gap in depression does not appear to arise from sexual differentiation in itself, whether biological or social. Rather, it results from emerging sex stratification—from the growing disparity of demands, sacrifices, resources, and benefits. Several things about the observed patterns seem worth mentioning. To begin with, hormonal changes undergone at puberty probably do not account for the growing sex difference in depression between the ages of 18 and 65. American girls begin to go through puberty around age 9 or 10, when their levels of estrogen and progesterone increase dramatically. The average age of menarche is 12.8, with a normal range of 10 to 15. Boys lag girls in development by a few years, but most of the significant changes happen between ages 11 and 16. Whatever impact those changes have at the time, they seem unlikely to account for the later growth of the gender gap in depression. Likewise, menopause cannot account for the growing difference in depression across adulthood, although it does seem to create a spike in women's depression. Menopause generally happens between the ages of 45 and 55, with a peak around age 50. Figure 5.2 shows a bump up in women's depression in that age range, followed by a return to the pre-existing age trend. The age-related growth in the gender gap exists well before age 45 and continues well after age 55. Likewise, differential socialization for adult sex roles in itself seems unlikely to account for the growing adult gender gap for similar reasons. Differential socialization begins in infancy and is in full force by puberty, well before the start of adulthood.

Some critics argue that depression is the feminine response to strains born equally by both sexes but expressed differently by them. They claim that women and men experience similar levels of frustration and hardship that produce emotional problems such as depression in women and behavioral problems such as violence, alcoholism, drug abuse, and antisocial behavior in men. Clearly men present behavioral problems more frequently than women do. Sex differences in response to stress cannot account for the growth of the gender gap in depression during adulthood, for two reasons. First, the gender gap in behavioral problems does not rise in adulthood in a manner that mirrors the rising gender gap in depression. In fact, men's behavior gets more like women's as men mature. Men's crime rates, substance abuse, and risk-taking decline as they become middle-aged. Second, behavioral problems do not protect men against depression. Behavioral problems increase depression. As men give up abusive and destructive behaviors that have emotionally distressing consequences they increasingly enjoy the full emotional benefits of their advantaged adult status.

Life Course Increases or Historical Decreases?

The historical changes in women's lives suggest that the gender gap in depression might be getting smaller in younger generations. As women have higher levels of education, fewer children, and more continuous full-time employment, their lives become more like men's (Oppenheimer 1982). That should make their levels of depression more like men's too. That raises an issue. Perhaps younger adults show a smaller difference in depression between women and men because they embody a new level of equality between the sexes. If they maintain that new level of equality throughout life, then the gender gap might not grow as they move through adulthood. Perhaps what looks like a growing difference in depression as men and women age actually reflects a greater inequality in older generations that is vanishing among the young. On the other hand, the generational changes for women may be "two steps forward, one step back." Women's full-time employment often creates distressing conflict between work and family—particularly difficulty in arranging child care. Changes in family and household responsibilities appear to lag behind those in employment, as discussed in Chapter 4. Women working full-time continue to have most of the responsibility for child care and housework. Also, women generally get paid less than men. Taken together these facts suggest that the move into full adult status continues to benefit men psychologically more than it does women.

Following women and men of the same age as they get five or six years older shows that their difference in depression does increase (Mirowsky 1996). The size of the increase is essentially the same as the difference compared to age groups five or six years older at the beginning. For example, as thirty-year-olds in 1989 became thirty-six-year-olds in 1995 their depression levels became like those of the thirty-six-year-olds in 1989. Data from the mid-1980s to the mid-1990s shows that the gender gap in depression grows over time as people age, with the growth essentially the same as implied by comparing age groups in Figure 5.2.

Surprisingly, the data do not show a clear trend toward smaller gender gaps at any given age in the newer cohorts. Earlier data from the nineteen-year period between 1957 and 1976 showed that the gender gap decreased by about a third (Kessler and McRae 1981; McLanahan and Glass 1985). It may be that a ten-year follow-up is not long enough to detect the generational changes. Or it may be that those changes slowed down. The earlier period (1957–1976) was when American women went from mostly homemakers to mostly full-time employees. Also, the end of that period was a severe recession with increased male unemployment.

Long-term trends toward smaller gender gaps in depression at any given age seem likely. Those trends mostly do not account for the age group differences in the gap shown in Figure 5.2. The gender gap in depression rises in adulthood as men and women enter and live out their unequal adult statuses. As long as that inequality remains, its cumulative effect across the adult lifetime will remain, increasing the gender gap in depression as women and men go through life.

NEIGHBORHOOD DISADVANTAGE AND DISORDER

Demographers and criminologists say that many ills in American society result from the concentration of disadvantaged households into separate neighborhoods. Sociologists working in the late nineteenth and early twentieth centuries often blamed those problems on urbanization. The early sociologists noticed that cities seemed to have high levels of social problems such as crime, violence, and alcoholism. They speculated that cities eroded social order by crowding large numbers of people together. The early sociologists thought the massing of population had three effects that combined to break down social controls on behavior: lots of people constantly in each others' presence and getting on each others' nerves, sheer numbers making each person anonymous to almost all of the others, and contact among various ethnic groups with contradictory norms and values that tended to invalidate each other. Not surprisingly, those early sociologists viewed the urbanization of society with alarm. They pictured cities as caldrons of tension boiling away the traditional restraints on behavior. No doubt their views encouraged the great suburban migration in the last half of the twentieth century. Most people who could leave the cities did, progressively concentrating the residue of poverty, social pathology, and physical decay. Once this process got going, the internal logic kept it going.

Concentrated Disadvantage

By the 1970s some researchers studying American cities began to argue against the old ideas, despite the ample evidence of urban disorder and decay. Contrary to popular ideas and the old theories, research finds vibrant, well-ordered, and satisfying communities in many urban neighborhoods (Fischer 1976). Few urbanites fit the old image of the atomized and alienated denizen. Most live firmly embedded in formal associations, informal social networks, and traditional activities centered in residential neighborhoods that typically have names, rough boundaries, and distinct identities. This fact led demographers and criminologists to take a second look at why cities seem to have so many problems. They found that urbanization itself—the scale, complexity, and density of the population—does not generate the problems. Rather, they found that the concentration of socially and economically disadvantaged individuals into separate neighborhoods generates the social problems associated with city life (Massey 1996; Sampson and Groves 1989; Sampson, Raudenbush, and Earls 1997). Ecological processes of differentiation create neighborhoods typically segmented along ethnic and economic lines. The neighborhoods of concentrated disadvantage become centers of despair, desperation, and social disorder.

Breakdown of Social Order.

Concentrated poverty breaks down public order (Massey 1996). Disadvantaged neighborhoods engender disorder because of limited opportunity (Wilson 1987, 1996), low social integration and cohesion (Sampson and Groves 1989), lack of formal services (LeClere, Rogers, and Peters 1997; Robert 1998), and normative climates conducive to nonconventional behavior (Brewster, Billy, and Grady 1993; Elliott et al. 1996; Jencks and Mayer 1990). Poor, isolated places often have few jobs, so that residents see little opportunity for employment (Wilson 1996). Young people who see little chance to succeed through normal, legitimate means tend to drop out of school and to engage in illegitimate activities, thus increasing the level of disorder in the neighborhood. Disadvantaged neighborhoods also have fewer or weaker informal social ties that bind neighbors together and help maintain social order (Sampson and Groves 1989). They also have fewer resources like good schools, parks, and medical services, which may suggest to residents that mainstream society has abandoned them (LaGrange et al. 1992; Taylor and Hale 1986; Robert 1998; Wilson 1987).

The concentration of single-parent families also contributes to the breakdown of public order in a neighborhood. Poverty seems not to have undermined social order as much when poor households were stable two-parent families with employed fathers (Wilson 1996). The chronic, widespread unemployment in neighborhoods where the disadvantaged concentrate undermines the role of father and breadwinner. As a result, many households with dependent children are headed by mothers, with no father present. Many have no adult male present. Some have men present at times, but the men often contribute little to the household in terms of money, house-work, childcare, or parental oversight. Breakdown of male participation in the family contributes to neighborhood disorder in three ways. First, many adult males lack the restraining influence of family responsibilities. Their activities and interests center on peer groups of males competing for status, rather than on wives and children depending on them for affection, guidance, and support. Second, the children in many families lack the restraining and guiding influence of a father. In some households a grandmother partially makes up for the absence of a second parent. Even so, the absence of a father makes it more difficult to control the behavior and activities of the children, particularly the adolescent males. Finally, the first two effects interact. Adult males recruit adolescents and sometimes younger children into the culture and economy of the street. Together these forces magnify the association between neighborhood disadvantage and neighborhood disorder.

Most research on neighborhood disadvantage looks at how it comes about and how it generates crime, deviance, and social disorder. We wanted to know if disadvantaged neighborhoods create psychological distress in their residents, perhaps because of the social disorder they generate. Many previous studies by us and others find that personal disadvantages such as low education or single parenthood make individuals distressed, as detailed in Chapter 4. We wanted to know if disadvantage concentrated in one's residential *neighborhood* creates distress. Based on the ideas of criminologists and urban sociologists, we thought it might perhaps be because of threatening and demoralizing exposure to neighborhood disorder.

Neighborhood Disadvantage

Our analyses focused on two related sets of issues and hypotheses. The first set explores the hypothesis that neighborhoods with characteristics that make life in them unfavorable to success produce distress. First we correlated measures of neighborhood disadvantage and individual psychological distress. We looked for the unfavorable aggregate qualities of neighborhoods most strongly and consistently related to distress, and used them to index the level of neighborhood disadvantage. Next we explored the possibility that disadvantaged neighborhoods only *seem* distressing because individuals distressed by their own personal disadvantages live in them. We adjusted the correlation of distress with neighborhood disadvantage for the individual's own disadvantages or advantages. We also explored the possibility that disadvantaged neighborhoods actually attract disadvantaged individuals by *reducing* the distress they would feel living in more advantaged neighborhoods.

Measuring Neighborhood Aggregations.

In order to look at the effects of neighborhoods, we developed a special "multilevel" data set called the Community, Crime, and Health (CCH) data. The CCH data links information from a telephone survey of individuals to census information about the neighborhoods in which they live. The survey asked our usual questions about emotional well-being, education, income, economic hardship, marital status, dependent children in the household, and so on. It also asked new questions about criminal victimization, trouble with the law, and signs of neighborhood disorder and decay. The CCH survey used computerized random-digit dialing to select households throughout the state of Illinois. We chose Illinois for several reasons: it includes communities ranging from sparsely populated rural counties to a major metropolis; it has neighborhoods in small cities, towns, and rural areas with social and economic disadvantages that rival those in big-city neighborhoods; it includes Chicago, where much of American urban sociology was and is done; it has a social and economic profile similar to that of the United States as a whole; and we once lived there, did an earlier survey there, and knew many of the places.

We used computer files from the U.S. Census Bureau to look up the aggregate statistics on each survey respondent's census tract. The tracts are the census geographic units that most closely approximate neighborhoods. Tracts are drawn within counties along visible boundaries that contain 1,500 to 8,000 persons, with the ideal about 4,000. They are designed to cover the same geographic area over many decades, so researchers can measure changes in the local populations over time. The aggregate statistics describe the prevalence of various individual or household traits. For example, they report the percentage of adults age twenty-five or older with a four-year college degree or higher and the percentage of households with incomes below the federal poverty line. Those aggregate statistics describe the general social and economic conditions surrounding each survey respondent's residence.

Measuring Neighborhood Disadvantage.

We looked at a number of aggregate statistics about the residents and households in a vicinity that indicate conditions more or less favorable to success. We concentrated on neighborhood measures parallel to ones for the individuals and households in our sample: the percentage of adults with a high school degree, the percentage of adults over age twenty-four with a college degree, the mean household income, the unemployment rate, the percentage of residences that are owner occupied, the percentage of households headed by females, the percentage of households headed by females raising dependent children, the percentage black, and the percentage minority. All of these correlated with individual levels of depression as might be expected. We looked at the size of each correlation, and whether it vanished with adjustment for the corresponding measure of individual disadvantage. (For example, adjusting for the respondent's own income eliminates the correlation between distress and the neighborhood's average household income.)

Of all the potential indicators of neighborhood disadvantage that we examined, the percentages of poor and mother-only households stood out as the most strongly, directly, and consistently related to individual distress. A poor household has an income lower than the amount estimated by the federal government as needed for basic sustenance. A mother-only household is headed by a woman raising dependent children with no male spouse or partner present. We created an index of neighborhood disadvantage by averaging the two percentages. That index provides the best single measure of distressing neighborhood disadvantage. Adjusting for it eliminates the correlations with distress of the other aggregate measures. That does not mean the other aggregate characteristics are unimportant. Some of them, like education, influence the prevalence of poverty and mother-only households. It means that the prevalence of those two disadvantages most strongly relate to whatever it is about neighborhoods that correlates with depression among the residents.

We also looked at two statistics that might indicate challenges for social control: the prevalence of young males (15–19 and 20–24), and residential instability (the percentage in the current residence less than five years). They do not directly indicate neighborhood disadvantage, although they might be related to it. However, demographers and criminologists find them important predictors of trends in crime and delinquency. We found they are not strongly or consistently related to psychological distress. The prevalence of young males among the residents does tend to be high in many disadvantaged neighborhoods, but it also tends to be high in suburban or middle-class neighborhoods dominated by families raising children and in neighborhoods near colleges. On the other hand, it tends to be low in disadvantaged rural or small-town neighborhoods, where many young men leave as soon as they can. The prevalence of young males in the neighborhood does not correlate with individual distress much. Residential instability does correlate with distress, but differently in poor neighborhoods than in well-to-do ones. It actually *de*creases the distress of residents in poor neighborhoods (Ross, Reynolds, and Geis 2000). Apparently individuals in poor neighborhoods with low turnover get demoralized about their prospects of getting out (ibid.). High turnover in a poor neighborhood may indicate some hope of better prospects.

More Than Just Individual Disadvantage.

Disadvantaged individuals tend to live in disadvantaged neighbor-hoods. That raises an issue. Does neighborhood disadvantage produce distress beyond that from the individual disadvantages that constrain choice of residence? The answer is "yes." The prevalence of poverty and single-mother households in the neighborhood correlates with higher dis-tress adjusting for the individual's own economic status and household composition. Individuals in more disadvantaged neighborhoods are more distressed than others similar to themselves in age, sex, race/ethnicity, education, employment status, household income, marital-by-parental status, household crowding, and residence in Chicago versus elsewhere but living in more advantaged neighborhoods. All those individual char-acteristics correlate with depression adjusting for each other, except for race/ethnicity, household crowding, and Chicago-versus-elsewhere, and they correlate with neighborhood disadvantage. We did find that about 60 percent of the apparent contextual effect was really due to the characteris-tics of the individuals who lived in the neighborhood, and we found that individual characteristics have a bigger impact on mental health than do neighborhood characteristics. Even so, individual disadvantages do not account for all of the elevated depression among residents of disadvan-taged neighborhoods. Some of that elevated depression comes from a dis-tinctive and distressing quality of life in disadvantaged neighborhoods.

Modifying Individual Disadvantage

If individuals find living in a disadvantaged neighborhood distressing, then why do they live there? The obvious answer is that they lack alterna-tives. Another possibility is that, in some backhanded way, it is better for them than living in a more advantaged neighborhood. Poor persons living among more prosperous others might feel shamed and ostracized. Like-wise, living among the poor might be distressing to others but not to the poor themselves. It could be the relatively advantaged persons living in the disadvantaged neighborhoods who account for the elevated distress. Even if disadvantaged individuals find disadvantaged neighborhoods distressing, they might not find them as distressing as more advantaged individuals do. As result they might feel less compelled to move out. We tested interactions of neighborhood by individual disadvantage to see if the match of person to context altered the association with distress. We found no significant interaction. Apparently disadvantaged neighbor-hoods are just as distressing to the kinds of people who normally find themselves in such places as to others. Likewise, advantaged neighbor-hoods are just as comforting to those who are socioeconomic aliens in them as to their usual kinds of inhabitants. This suggests that disadvantaged individuals live in disadvantaged neighborhoods because they have little choice.

Neighborhood Disorder

A second set of analyses explored the hypothesis that neighborhood disorder makes people distressed and accounts for the disturbing impact of neighborhood disadvantage. We correlated neighborhood disorder with individual distress adjusting for the individual traits that influence residential options. We also looked at whether disorderly neighborhoods might attract disadvantaged individuals by making them less distressed than they would be in more orderly neighborhoods. On the other hand, having to live in a threatening neighborhood might sharpen the distress associated with personal disadvantages that leave no other residential options.

Order is a state of peace, safety, and observance of the law. Neighborhood order and disorder are indicated by visible cues that residents perceive (Skogan 1986, 1990). Neighborhoods characterized by order are clean and safe; houses, apartments, and other buildings are well-maintained; and residents are respectful of one another and of each other's property. At the other end of the continuum, neighborhoods characterized by disorder present residents with observable signs that social control has broken down. In these neighborhoods, residents report noise, litter, vandalism, graffiti, drug use, trouble with neighbors, and other incivilities associated with a breakdown of social control (Ross 2000). Even if residents are not directly victimized, these signs of disorder indicate a potential for harm. Moreover, such signs indicate that the people who live around them are not concerned with public order, that the local agents of social control are either unable or unwilling to cope with local problems, and that those in power have probably abandoned the neighborhood.

Resident Observations of Neighborhood Disorder.

To measure neighborhood disorder we developed a set of questions for survey respondents, based on the theories and observations of criminologists and urban social scientists (Ross and Mirowsky 1999). Neighborhood disorder refers to conditions and activities, both major and minor, criminal and noncriminal, that residents perceive to be signs of the breakdown of social order. The index measures physical signs of disorder such as graffiti, vandalism, and abandoned buildings as well as social signs such as crime, people hanging out, drinking, and using drugs. It also includes reverse-coded signs of neighborhood order, such as people taking care of their houses and apartments and watching out for each other. Figure 5.3 lists the items in the index. The neighborhood disorder score averages the

Ross-Mirowsky Perceived Neighborhood Disorder Scale (1999).

Physical Disorder and Order
  There is a lot of graffiti in my neighborhood
  My neighborhood is noisy
  Vandalism is common in my neighborhood
  There are lot of abandoned buildings in my neighborhood
  My neighborhood is clean
  People in my neighborhood take good care of their houses and
    apartments

Social Disorder and Order
  There are too many people hanging around on the streets near my
    home
  There is a lot of crime in my neighborhood
  There is too much drug use in my neighborhood
  There is too much alcohol use in my neighborhood
  I'm always having trouble with my neighbors
  My neighborhood is safe
  In my neighborhood, people watch out for each other

To create a mean score disorder scale, disorder items scored strongly
disagree (1), disagree (2), agree (3), strongly agree (4); and order items
scored strongly agree (1), agree (2), disagree (3), strongly disagree (4).
(alpha reliability = .92, mean = 1.81).

Figure 5.3.   Signs of neighborhood disorder.

responses across items. Our measure differs from those used by some
other researchers in some important ways. Some researchers prefer to send
outsiders around to neighborhoods to rate the observable signs of disorder. Those ratings focus on things anyone on the street can see, such as
graffiti, broken windows and groups of young males hanging out. The
indexes based on those ratings represent the view of each neighborhood
that middle-class outsiders would have. Our index measures the views of
residents themselves. It includes some things only they would see, such as
neighbors helping each other. It also includes observations with an element of judgment, such as "too much drug use in my neighborhood." The
residents' own perceptions seemed more relevant to distress. Using them

also allowed us to include a representative sample of neighborhoods throughout the state and not just in metropolitan Chicago.

Disorder and Distress.

Our results show a substantial correlation between neighborhood disorder and average levels of depression. Figure 5.4 illustrates the relationship. It divides the sample into ten groups with roughly equal numbers of individuals, ordered from those reporting the least neighborhood disorder to those reporting the most. The figure shows that the frequency of depression generally increases with the level of neighborhood disorder. The biggest differences are at the top and bottom thirds of the scale. Average levels of depression do not change across the middle third of differences in neighborhood disorder. The frequency of depression drops by about 25 percent from those common neighborhoods near the middle to those where residents see the least disorder. It increases by more than 100 percent from the places scored near the middle to those where the residents see the most disorder. Adjusting for individual disadvantages reduces the association considerably, but still leaves most of it intact. Individual disadvantages associated with neighborhood disorder account for about a third of the differences in depression associated with neighborhood disorder. That leaves about two-thirds apparently resulting from the disorder itself.

People who live in a context of neighborhood disorder may be at risk of adopting distressing behaviors such as heavy drinking or illegal activities. That raises a question. Is it the neighborhood disorder itself that people find distressing, or just their own troublesome behavior arising from or consistent with the local culture? To address this question we adjusted for measures of heavy drinking and illegal activities. We asked individuals how often and how much they drink, and coded heavy drinking as more than fourteen drinks a week (the top 5 percent). To measure illegal activity we summed the number of "yes" responses to four questions about the past twelve months:

—Have you done anything that would have gotten you in trouble if the police had been around?
—Have you been caught in a minor violation of the law?
—Have you been arrested?
—Have you been in jail more than twenty-four hours?

People who drink heavily and engage in illegal activities have significantly higher levels of depression than those who do not. However those individual problem behaviors do not account for the association of neighborhood problems with depression. They account for less than 2 percent of

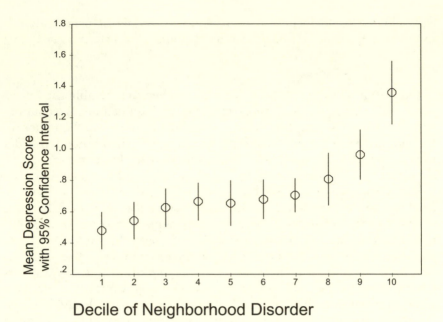

Decile of Neighborhood Disorder

Figure 5.4.   Mean depression scores by level of neighborhood disorder. Data are
from the 1995 CCH survey

neighborhood disorder's association with depression that is not already
explained by individual disadvantages. Neighborhood disorder either
attracts individuals with depressing behavioral problems or creates those
problems, but that accounts for little of the depression associated with
neighborhood disorder.

Disorder Linking Neighborhood Disadvantage to Distress.

   Neighborhoods with a lot of poor or mother-headed households have
high levels of neighborhood disorder. Disadvantaged neighborhoods
present residents with observable signs that social control has broken
down. The streets are dirty and noisy. Buildings are rundown and abandoned. Graffiti and vandalism are common. People hang out on the
streets, drinking, using drugs, and creating a sense of danger. Neighbors
seem indifferent or hostile. Residents in disadvantaged neighborhoods
face a threatening environment characterized by crime, incivility, and
harassment, which they find depressing.

   There is nothing inherently distressing about living in a neighborhood
with a lot of poor people or single mothers. It is the disorder common in

such neighborhoods that distresses residents. When we adjust for neighborhood disorder, the association of neighborhood disadvantage with depression vanishes. Among neighborhoods with similar levels of disorder, differences in the prevalence of poor or mother-headed households have no effect on distress. The stress of living in a poor neighborhood where many families are headed by women makes residents feel run-down, demoralized, and hopeless. That stress comes from the neighborhood disorder.

Affinity or Vulnerability?

If residents get depressed by neighborhood disorder, then why live there? As with neighborhood disadvantage, the simple answer is that they have little or no choice. But it might not be that simple. Perhaps disadvantaged individuals choose neighborhoods with evident disorder because they feel more comfortable with that than with the constraints of more orderly neighborhoods. It might be the relatively advantaged residents of disordered neighborhoods who find them distressing. Even if disadvantaged individuals would feel better in more orderly neighborhoods, they might not find the disorder as depressing as do the more advantaged individuals. A greater affinity or tolerance for disorder might make disadvantaged individuals less likely to avoid or leave disorderly neighborhoods. What we found is just the opposite, as detailed in Chapter 8. Individual disadvantages make people feel powerless. They also lead people to live in disadvantaged neighborhoods with a lot of apparent disorder. That sense of powerlessness makes the emotional consequences of the disorder even worse. The sense of powerlessness multiplies the mistrust generated by neighborhood disorder. Together, the powerlessness, disorder, and mistrust produce distress. We see no sign that disadvantaged individuals find life in disorderly neighborhoods more tolerable than others would. On the contrary, the more disadvantaged the individual, the more distress associated with neighborhood disorder. Apparently, the disadvantaged live in such neighborhoods because they have little or no choice.

Urban Concentrations, Disadvantage, Disorder, and Distress

People find life depressing in disadvantaged neighborhoods, characterized by high rates of poverty and mother-only households, because of the neighborhood disorder. They do not find urban residence depressing in itself. People living in the more orderly neighborhoods of Chicago are no more depressed than others similar to themselves living in equally orderly suburbs, small cities, towns, and rural areas of Illinois. The distress resulting from life in the big city comes from the high levels of neighborhood disorder produced by concentrated disadvantage. The residents of those neighborhoods are the ones who suffer the emotional burden. Clearly, the ecological and historical forces have concentrated disorder in Chicago neighborhoods. In the CCH survey, 58 percent of all the Illinois citizens with neighborhood disorder scores in the top 10 percent live in Chicago. Putting it the other way, 34 percent of the Chicago citizens report neighborhood disorder in the top 10 percent. The odds of living in a very disorderly neighborhood are ten times greater in Chicago than elsewhere in the state. Other places are not immune, though. Thirty-one percent of the Illinois citizens with neighborhood disorder scores in the top 10 percent live in suburbs (15 percent), small towns (12 percent), and rural areas (4 percent). Wherever disadvantage gets concentrated, the disorder grows, adding to the distress of the individual disadvantages that limit residential options.

In psychological terms, two processes probably account for the distress associated with neighborhood disorder. First, neighborhood disorder probably creates frequent activation of the fight-or-flight response, which is an unconditioned neuroendocrine response to perceived danger. Although the research described above looks at depression as an outcome, anxiety, anger, and fear follow a similar pattern. The graphs of their means across levels of neighborhood disorder look similar to the one for depression in Figure 5.4. Of these four emotions, fear and anger are the most concentrated in the most disorderly neighborhoods. Frequent activation of the fight-or-flight response sensitizes some individuals and desensitizes others. In the first case, it creates hair-trigger reactions and anxious malaise (autonomic symptoms such as heart palpitations, faintness, and sweaty palms). In the second it creates depressed malaise (lethargy, sleep problems, trouble concentrating). Neighborhood disorder probably also contributes to learned helplessness. Individuals exposed to uncontrollable and inescapable aversive stimuli become helpless, as described in Chapter 7. We see no indication that disadvantaged individuals might prefer to live is disorderly neighborhoods. On the contrary, our results suggest that disadvantaged individuals have no choice but to live in neighborhoods they find terrifying and threatening. The perceived inability to escape an aversive situation is depressing in itself. It also robs disadvantaged residents of disordered neighborhoods of the sense of control, with the consequences detailed in Chapter 7.

IV

Explaining the Patterns

6

Life Change: An Abandoned Explanation

Once researchers became convinced that the basic social patterns of distress are real, they began looking for explanations. As in science generally, they hoped to find a single underlying explanation for the various patterns. Almost all of the explanations offered over the years draw on the general concept stress: a mentally or emotionally disruptive or upsetting condition occurring in response to adverse external influences and capable of affecting physical health, usually characterized by increased heart rate, a rise in blood pressure, muscular tension, irritability, and depression. Despite that common theme, explanations can differ greatly, depending on what they portray as the most important and universal quality distinguishing stressful experiences. Not long after the results of the first community mental health surveys were published, life change became widely accepted as the main explanation of the social patterns of distress. The popularity of life change as an explanation was phenomenal, despite weak supporting evidence. It was so well accepted that, for years, researchers used "life change" and "stress" as synonyms. It took a decade or more of accumulating counterevidence to put the explanation to rest in scientific circles. No doubt many persons in the general public still believe it.

Life-change events mark major alterations in a person's daily activities. They include transitions such as the death of a spouse, birth of a child, move to a new home, loss of a job, getting married, and finishing school. Each event is relatively uncommon in any one person's life, but likely within the lifetime and common in the community as a whole. Life-change events require adaptation and readjustment of a person's habitual activities and social relations. They typically require a renegotiation or redefinition of the individual's social identity, because of the loss or gain of social roles and networks. Big changes in daily life force a person to use mental and physical energy developing habits and an identity that are suited to the new situation.

CONCEPTUAL HISTORY OF LIFE CHANGE AND STRESS

In the 1960s medical researchers noticed that major changes in a person's life seemed to increase susceptibility to disease. How could changes have this effect? Reasoning from laboratory experiments on regulatory mechanisms, they concluded that every person's behavior tends to settle into an optimal pattern that minimizes the energy and resources expended meeting daily needs. Habits are easy, efficient solutions to everyday problems. Big changes in a person's life, such as getting married or taking a new job, disrupt habits and force the person to use mental and physical energy adapting—that is, developing a new way of life optimized for the new situation.

To study the impact of change on health, two physician researchers asked a group of people to judge the amount of change demanded by each of forty-three major life events (Holmes and Rahe 1967). The researchers used methods from a branch of psychology, called psychophysics, that studies the proportionality between the objective and the subjective magnitude of stimuli, such as the decibel level and apparent loudness of a sound. Holmes and Rahe assigned each event a value, called a life-change unit, representing the average subjective magnitude of such a change as imagined by the raters. Then the researchers asked a different group what changes had happened in the past year and counted up the life-change units of each person's events. The researchers found that people with more units of change suffered more illness and psychological distress. This finding set off a wave of research that spilled across scientific and national boundaries. Researchers around the world began counting life-change units and correlating them with all kinds of physical and mental problems. Wherever they looked they seemed to find a devastating effect of change.

Although it was never the intent of the researchers involved, an image of the healthy, happy life emerged: a placid life of undisturbed routines. Should we each withdraw to an asylum of our own making? The studies correlating change with sickness and distress seemed to say we should. For years the change theory of distress was so well accepted that researchers defined stress as life change, and used the terms interchangeably.

The General Adaptation Syndrome

To a large extent, life change became the paramount explanation by working backward, from the symptoms of distress, to the endocrine and autonomic activity that produce such symptoms, to the environmental conditions that seemed likely to produce such biologic activity. Much of the inspiration came from Hans Selye's earlier discovery of the general adaptation syndrome, and related studies in psychosomatic medicine. Selye was a physician studying the endocrine system, particularly the hormones of the adrenal cortex, in the period from the 1940s through the

1960s. Almost all medical research prior to Selye's concentrated on the body's specific response to a specific organism, toxin, or injury. Each unique agent produces a unique set of bodily responses that reflect its specific chemical and physical effects. Breaking with that tradition, Selye got interested in the body's general response to a broad array of assaults and injuries. He began by exposing rats to a range of distinct toxins. Although each toxin produces unique and distinctive types of damage, Selye discovered a nonspecific response to all of them: enlargement of the adrenal cortex, indicating hyperactivation; shrinking of the thymus, spleen, lymph nodes, and all other lymphatic structures in the body, plus the disappearance of eosinophil cells in the blood, indicating compromised immune function; and deep ulcers in the stomach and duodenum (Selye 1976). The instigation of these changes eventually was traced to secretions of the pituitary gland, which in turn is stimulated by secretions of the hypothalamus—a small structure in the brain that is a bridge between it and the endocrine system. In a remarkable series of studies, Selye and his colleagues discovered that the same changes produced by the injection of toxins are produced by the injection of hormones such as adrenaline, insulin, and cortisone, by physical stressors such as extreme heat or cold, by behavioral stressors such as forced exercise or restriction of movement, and by psychological stressors such as noise or crowding.

Selye and other physicians were interested in the somatic response to stressors, rather than the emotional response. Their research focused on diseases that result directly from the body's response to stressors, such as stomach or duodenal ulcers, and on increased susceptibility to infections, toxins, and autoimmune problems resulting from overtaxed adaptive mechanisms. It was believed that the body's adaptive mechanisms could be triggered by mental and emotional states, which were the link to external stressors such as noise or crowding. For example, the brain can stimulate the adrenal medulla, which releases adrenaline (epinephrine) into the blood, which in turn can produce Selye's general adaptation syndrome. In theory, the chronic stimulation of this "fight or flight" mechanism results from prolonged or repeated fear and anxiety, which in turn results from threatening conditions such as life in dangerous neighborhoods, from tense jobs such as air traffic control, or from conflict-ridden relationships such as a bad marriage. Although some mental or emotional connection between social conditions and somatic response was assumed, the initial focus was on the somatic response and the ways it produces or allows disease.

From Rat Pathology to Human Distress

Holmes and Rahe, the two physician researchers mentioned earlier, set out to demonstrate the connection between social-psychological stressors and somatic illness in humans. To do so, they needed to adapt the concepts and methods of laboratory rat studies to research on live, whole humans out in the world. To do that, they made three big changes, described below.

Noxious Stimuli to Significant Events.

Generalizing from the somatic concepts of homeostasis and adaptation, and from Adolf Meyer's clinical "life chart," they decided to look for things that disrupt habitual activities and that demand adjustment to a new state (Holmes and Rahe 1967; Holmes and Masuda 1974). This was the first step away from the laboratory rat studies. Nothing in the actual methods or results of the rat studies indicated that events and changes were the culprit. The rat studies used repeated or chronic exposure to noxious stimuli to produce the General Adaptation Syndrome.

Biological Homeostasis to Social Readjustment.

The concepts of homeostasis and adaptation suggest a system temporarily destabilized and expending its energy to regain equilibrium, much like a spinning top righting itself. Holmes and Rahe needed a general and universal measure of each person's exposure to demand for readjustment. To get it, they developed the Social Readjustment Rating Scale described earlier (Holmes and Rahe 1967). They published an easy-to-use checklist of events a person might have experienced in the past year, along with the magnitude of change demanded by each as judged by their raters. Holmes, Rahe, and their colleagues found that subsequent physical illness increased with the sum readjustment weight of a person's events in the previous year (Holmes and Masuda 1974). It was not long before popular magazines published do-it-yourself checklists for assessing one's own Social Readjustment Units (SRUs). If you experienced a lot of changes last year, magazines warned, you might need help to deal with the stress.

Holmes, Rahe, and their colleagues asserted the importance of change itself. They specifically rejected the importance of the psychological and social desirability of events. Speaking of the events listed in the Social Readjustment Rating Scale, Holmes and Masuda note the following:

> Only some of the events are negative or "stressful" in the conventional sense, that is, are socially undesirable. Many are socially desirable and consonant with the American values of achievement, success, materialism, practicality, efficiency, future orientation, conformism, and self-reliance. . . . The emphasis is on change from the existing steady state and not on psychological meaning, emotion, or social desirability. (1974:46)

The emphasis on change per se, apart from its meaning and valence, was purely theoretical. The Social Readjustment Rating Scale was constructed on the assumption that change is the stressful aspect of events. In all their research constructing and using the scale, Holmes and Rahe never tested this assumption. They simply proceeded as if it were true. Many other researchers in psychosomatic medicine, epidemiology, psychiatry, sociology, and psychology did the same.

Somatic Disease to Emotional Distress.

Another step away from Selye's rat studies was the switch from somatic disease to emotional distress as the outcome of interest. Selye, Holmes, and Rahe were interested in somatic disease. Whatever strengths or weaknesses their ideas might have as explanations of somatic disease, those ideas were not meant to explain emotional distress. Nevertheless, most researchers studying distress were quick to see a connection. If things such as noise, crowding, or the death of a spouse can produce somatic illness, there must be a mental or nervous system link. The clear involvement of psychoactive hormones, such as adrenaline, imply a connection to emotional state. Probably the most suggestive fact, though, is the strong and consistent correlation between depressed or anxious mood and physiological malaise, such as headaches, sour stomach, palpitations, breathlessness, trouble sleeping, loss of appetite, and lethargy. Anything that causes psychosomatic illness can be suspected of also causing emotional distress.

The change theory of distress was so well accepted that for years researchers never examined the impact of negative and positive events separately. When they did, the evidence was clear: study after study found that undesirable events, not desirable ones, cause distress (Gersten et al. 1974; Mueller, Edwards, and Yarvis 1977; Myers, Lindenthal, and Pepper 1971; Vinokur and Selzer 1975; Ross and Mirowsky 1979; Williams, Ware, and Donald 1981).

CONTRADICTORY EVIDENCE

Despite the impressive rationales based on endocrinology and biological equilibrium, there never was much evidence that life change, itself, is emotionally distressing. On the contrary, there were always good reasons to suspect that the valence of an event, more than just the amount of change it demands, is emotionally salient. Even rats distinguish between rewards and punishments. Research by Osgood and his colleagues (Snider and Osgood 1969) shows that a good-bad, desirable-undesirable evaluation is the most powerful semantic dimension in human thought. Strong-weak is the second most powerful semantic dimension, and static-active is a distant third. Judgments of the change demanded by events are highly influenced by their desirability or undesirability (Ruch 1977). For example, Hough, Fairbank, and Garcia (1976) found that Anglos in Texas rate the change demanded by abortion on a level with that demanded by marriage, retirement, and birth of the first child. Although the latter three events mark substantial changes in ongoing, everyday habits and behavior, abortion does not. Many persons see it as an undesirable event with disturbing connotations, but it does not demand a major rearrangement of daily life. The desirability or undesirability of events is far more salient than the readjustment required.

Undesirability Rather Than Change

Once studies began to look, they found that undesirability, not change, is the distressing characteristic of life events (Gersten et al. 1974; Mueller et al. 1977; Ross and Mirowsky 1979; Vinokur and Selzer 1975). Holmes and Rahe published their Social Readjustment Rating Scale in 1967 (Holmes and Rahe 1967). As early as 1969 there were indications from clinical studies that only undesirable events are distressing. Patients admitted to treatment for depression, attempted suicide, and schizophrenia all reported higher rates of undesirable events than a comparison group of normal controls, but there was no difference in the rate of desirable events (Paykel 1974). A decade later, we systematically compared the impact of various aspects of life events in a random community sample. We found that distress increases with the number of a person's undesirable events. Events weighted by Holmes and Rahe's Social Readjustment Units were not associated with distress once their undesirability was taken into account (Ross and Mirowsky 1979). When we compared undesirable events with high change scores, undesirable events with low change scores, and desirable events with high change scores, only the undesirable events were associated with greater distress (whether or not they had high change scores). Even the desirable events that require a lot of readjustment, such as getting married, starting school, graduating, getting one's first job, and getting promoted, do not increase psychological distress. Not only that, but people who view change as a challenge, who are instrumental, who set new goals and struggle to achieve them, have *low* levels of psychological distress (Kobassa, Maddi, and Courington 1981). Change per se is not distressing.

The more negative events individuals experience the greater their distress. Subsequent research further refined this conclusion. Undesirable events over which a person has no control are most detrimental to psychological well-being (McFarlane et al. 1983). Controllable events, for which the person shares some responsibility, are less distressing. Some people had speculated that uncontrollable negative events might be less distressing than controllable ones because fate, rather than oneself, can be blamed. Events outside the person's control suggest less personal inadequacy and thus protect self-esteem. This argument seems plausible, but is not supported. Negative events over which a person has no control are more distressing than ones the person played a part in. Uncontrollable negative events increase feelings of helplessness and powerlessness. They leave people with the demoralizing sense that they are at the mercy of the environment, that no action will be effective in preventing bad things from happening in the future, and that they are not in control of their lives. Apparently, controllable undesirable events are not as distressing because the individual can hope to avoid them in the future.

Outcome Rather Than Change

Undesirability is highly salient to respondents because it is an evaluation of consequences. *Undesirable events generally mark transitions to worse positions.* Dohrenwend (1973) called undesirable events "status loss" events, which may be a better term. Undesirable, or status loss, events mark transitions to positions of lower status: from employed to unemployed, from married to divorced, from wife to widow. Many status losses are losses of income, power, or prestige. Compared to an employed head of household, an unemployed head receives less money and esteem and has less authority. Nevertheless, the demands of other statuses such as parenthood remain constant, resulting in a gap between means and obligations. The result is a higher level of distress. Some status losses are losses of emotional support. After divorce or death of a spouse the person is left without anyone to come home to, talk to, or provide support and comfort. The result is a higher level of distress. In each case, it is not the event, per se, that is important, but what the event signifies in terms of ongoing social position. Undesirable events mark transitions to social positions associated with higher levels of distress, such as unemployment, poverty, role overload, single parenthood, and widowed.

The context in which events occur can also be looked at more broadly. Context may modify the effects of events on distress. Wheaton (1990) looked at the context of negative events such as getting fired or divorced. He found that the emotional consequences of negative events depended on the prior stressfulness of the role. Job loss was less distressing if the job had been boring, exhausting, highly supervised, insecure, poorly paid, the hours were unpredictable, and the physical environment was unpleasant. Divorce was less distressing if the marriage was not characterized by caring, affection, equity, love, respect, and sharing. Even the death of one's spouse was less distressing if the marriage had problems. Similarly, Umberson and Chen (1994) found that, among adults, a parent's death increased distress more or less depending on circumstances. Women whose fathers had mental health problems when they were growing up experienced much less distress at their father's death than did women whose fathers had fewer problems.

VARIANTS OF THE LIFE CHANGE INDEX

One of the problems with life events indexes is that they add together things that may be quite different in their origins or their links to distress. This is true even if the index contains only undesirable events. Information on the characteristic causes and consequences of a specific event get lost when they are all lumped together in one index. For example, getting divorced and getting fired or laid off both involve status loss. They have some causes in common, such as low education or weak interpersonal skills, and both increase the distress of most individuals who experience them. Even so, they differ in many important aspects of their origins and effects. A high risk of divorce often flows from a personal history that undermined trust and commitment, whereas a high risk of job loss often flows from one that undermined the development of marketable skills or interest in productive self-expression. Even the seemingly shared precursors of the two events can have distinctive aspects. For example, low education generally limits marriage prospects to partners with low education too. That increases the risk of divorce, but not of job loss. The distressing aspects of events might differ somewhat too. Divorce might generate greater loneliness and anger, whereas job loss generates greater worry and self-doubt. For years, social and behavioral scientists studied stress by summing up the number of recent life events, perhaps weighted by imputed readjustment units. While summary indexes have their uses, they average out much of the information on the social and psychological processes that produce distress.

Social and behavioral scientists have taken a number of approaches to improving indexes of social stress. All of them now concentrate on undesirable or noxious situations, rather than on change. The best new stress indexes also concentrate on chronic situations that wear away at a person or on the accumulation over a lifetime of traumatic events. While the best of the new indexes embody important conceptual advances, all of them share one shortcoming with the earlier indexes of recent events: averaging out the distinctions.

Indexing Daily Hassles

Just as sociologists were abandoning life change indexes, Lazarus and other psychologists developed a similar inventory of "daily hassles" (Lazarus and Folkman 1984; DeLongis et al. 1982). Daily hassles are common and frequent irritants, such as missing a bus, getting stuck in traffic, or being served by a rude clerk. The daily-hassles index has some of the same problems as life events indexes, in that it equates exposures to things with distinct causes and reasons for being distressing. The daily-hassles index adds another problem. It confounds cause and effect. Instead of asking people if they get stuck in traffic a lot, the index asks people if being stuck in traffic is a problem for them (Dohrenwend and Shrout 1985). That confuses the occurrence (stuck in traffic) with the emotional response (irritated, annoyed, frustrated). People distressed for other reasons get high daily-hassle scores because they are distressed.

Worse than confounding cause and effect, the daily-hassles approach trivializes the social causes of distress. Being stuck in traffic, losing something, having unexpected company, or missing your bus is a hassle. Poverty is more than a hassle. Having a job that does not pay well, being told what to do instead of making decisions, and being economically dependent are more than hassles. Inequity and conflict in marriage are more than hassles. Living alone, without friends or support, is more than a hassle. Ongoing social positions that increase feelings of powerlessness, dependency, inequity, and isolation are not hassles. They are serious problems.

Both the idea of daily hassles and that of life change trivialize the social causes of psychological distress. Both implicitly deny stratification as a cause of distress. They divert attention from things like inequality, poverty, injustice, and lack of opportunity. Just as everyone has daily hassles to put up with, everyone's life changes. Life change is not disproportionately associated with lack of education, poverty, minority status, being female, or being unmarried. Change per se cannot explain the social patterns of distress because it is not linked to social position or to distress. The link is the undesirable events, losses, failures, and ongoing stressors that flow from inequality, inequity, and lack of opportunity.

Indexing Chronic Stress

Many life events begin or end an episode that lasts for months or years, that develops out of a lifetime of experiences, and that delivers the individual to a new phase in life. Take death of a spouse as an example. Sometimes it happened as a pure event, as when the spouse left for work in the morning and was killed in a car accident. Far more often it happened as part of a prolonged episode with a long history leading up to it. Often a widowed person was caring for an ill husband or wife for a long time. They knew the spouse was dying. The spouse had been sick and in and out of the hospital for a long time. The disease may have been diagnosed years before the spouse got really sick. What might be interpreted as an event, a death that requires adjustment, is actually a lot more. It reflects the ongoing stress of caring for a loved one, of having resources depleted by expensive medical care, of not being able to get out of the house to do things you enjoy, of adjusting psychologically over weeks and months to the fact that your spouse is dying while you are helpless to stop it. It also marks the transition to a new situation with difficulties of its own: being unmarried and perhaps living alone or with greatly diminished income. An event reflects something more than a mere occurrence. It represents the conditions and episodes that produce it and that follow from it.

The relationship of life events to chronic strains, and the wearing effects of those chronic strains, led sociologists to develop new checklists. The term "chronic" comes from medicine, where it refers to a condition or disease lasting a long period of time or marked by frequent recurrence over a long period. Wheaton, Turner, and Lloyd developed indexes of chronic stressors similar to indexes of undesirable life events but enumerating persistent or recurrent difficulties (Wheaton 1999; Turner, Wheaton, and Lloyd 1995; Turner and Lloyd 1999). They hoped that ongoing stressors would explain social patterns of distress. Like indexes of life events, the chronic stress indexes combine a variety of conditions. One index contains fifty-one items: five refer to economic hardship, such as not having enough money to buy the things you or your kids need; eight refer to negative work conditions such as excessive monitoring, not enough pay, and boring or repetitive work; nine refer to problems with one's marriage, such as a partner who does not understand you, doesn't show you enough affection, or expects too much of you; another five refer to the absence of a stable relationship, such as wondering if you will ever get married and feeling you are alone too much; other items relate to problems with children, living in a bad neighborhood, having others expect too much, or having someone close with a serious health problem (Turner and Lloyd 1999).

Indexes of chronic stress represent a major improvement over indexes of recent life events because they enumerate the persistent and corrosive problems that seriously demoralize a person. As summary indexes, though, they have strengths and weaknesses similar to those of undesirable event indexes. The number of chronic stressors measures well the current overall level of persistent difficulties. That lets researchers measure the overall contribution of chronic stress to individual or status-group differences in distress. However, counting the number of problems does not show how each problem develops, how the different problems interrelate, and whether they might produce distress in somewhat different ways. For example, persistent difficulties forming or maintaining gratifying intimate relationships and persistent money problems might have very different origins in personal history, and might be distressing in distinctive ways. On the other hand, money problems can sour intimate relationships, and a failure to form or maintain a relationship can create economic hardship. By their nature, indexes of chronic stress sum over the distinctions and interconnections, hiding all the details. Some research problems call for that broad, summary measure, but more require the details.

Indexing Lifetime Trauma and Cumulative Adversity

Indexes of chronic stressors and of recent life events share another trait that can be both strength and weakness. Both measure current or recent stress with little reference to long past events or episodes that might have persistent or cumulative effects on emotional well-being. Things that happened as a child or teenager, such as repeating a year of school or being physically abused, might shape persistent views of oneself or others with lifelong consequences for emotional well-being. Some shocking or traumatizing events, such as seeing someone killed or surviving a major accident, might have persistent emotional consequences no matter how long past. Indexes of lifetime trauma and cumulative adversity count up the disturbing experiences of a lifetime (Turner and Lloyd 1995). That can be useful for research measuring the overall contribution of such past experiences to current differences in distress among individuals or status groups. As with the indexes of undesirable events and chronic stress, though, the summing obscures sequences, interactions, and other details. The effect of a long-past disturbing event or episode might depend in important ways on what led up to it, how it was handled, and what followed. Isolated shocks might have little long-run impact, but several together might create persistent changes in worldview with lifelong consequences for well-being. And as with recent events, the apparent effects of past events might actually result from the situation that spawned the event or the redirection of life that followed. In addition, past events may have their effects by determining the emotional impact of recent events and current conditions. More often than not, progress lies in learning those details.

ALTERNATIVE CONCEPTS AND FUTURE RESEARCH

The concept of life change as stress implies that the distress associated with any transition will fade with time as the individual adapts to the situation. Currently there is no reason to think this is true of situations such as repetitive and unexpressive work, low wages, unemployment, low income, economic hardship, neighborhood disorder, material deprivation, bad marriages, single parenthood, keeping house while raising children, incompatible job and family situations, bad marriages, and physical impairment. Many stressful situations persistently elevate distress as long as individuals remain in them, and some may produce increasing levels of distress the longer an individual remains in them. There are good reasons, both biological and social psychological, to think that the effects of stressors on emotional well-being are cumulative and perhaps even multiplicative. Chronic or frequent stress may produce a compounding rise in distress, as individuals come to feel they will never escape or overcome their problems. Also, the same traits or strategies that help individuals avoid undesirable events can help them resolve a distressing episode sooner (Harnish, Aseltine, and Gore 2000). They also might help individuals manage the emotional strains of a threatening or disturbing episode better while in it. These too imply a greater amount of distress associated with a longer period of time in a stressful situation.

It may be the defining characteristic of an undesirable event that it usually marks a transition into a situation that persistently elevates distress as long as an individual remains in it. Perhaps only distress associated with positive or neutral transitions fades with time as individuals adapt. Bereavement may be the one exception. Even though widowhood is persistently distressing, the amount of distress following the loss subsides with time. Other than that kind of personal loss, though, the distress associated with a transition into an undesirable situation may generally increase with time in the situation. Think of unemployment, or economic hardship. They do not get easier with time. If anything, the threat and hopelessness implied increases with time.

Ongoing social positions and all that they indicate in terms of hardships versus successes, helplessness and powerlessness versus mastery and control, role overload and conflict versus compatibility of roles, etc., are most important to psychological well-being (Belle 1982). Events should be viewed as transitions with effects on distress largely determined by the contrast between origin and destination. Wheaton calls this the contextual approach to life transitions: "The potential for impact of an event is defined by the person's accumulated experience in the role that is altered by the transition" (1990:209). For example, among employed women, Wheaton finds that the increase in distress a year or two later associated with getting divorced gets larger the more children in the family but gets smaller the worse the marriage was near the end. He also finds that divorce does not generally increase the distress of women who were homemakers while married. Why? Because most of them get full-time jobs after divorce. The emotional gain from employment balances out the emotional loss from the divorce itself. As Wheaton's findings illustrate, stressfulness is not necessarily inherent in events themselves. The distress associated with an event depends on the situation that spawned it, the context of personal history and present conditions in which it occurs, and the new conditions to which it leads. The future of research on life events lies in viewing them as transitions that redirect life rather than as changes that destabilize it.

7

Alienation

Currently, most explanations of the social patterns of distress refer to alienation in one or more of its forms. On the most general level, alienation is any form of social dissociation, detachment, or separation. Although some theorists define alienation in terms of objective social conditions, studies of distress more commonly follow Seeman's (1959, 1983) classic definition of alienation in terms of expectations and beliefs. He described five major types of alienation: powerlessness, self-estrangement, isolation, meaninglessness, and normlessness. Seeman expressed his hope that subsequent research would uncover their consequences and the social conditions that produce them. As the material that follows will show, distress is one of the major consequences of alienation. We will describe each type of alienation, its social causes, and its emotional consequences.

Although Seeman's definitions of the five types of alienation provide a core set of concepts, forty years of research has broadened the topics being considered. We will discuss five issues that incorporate Seeman's original ideas, their variations, and related concepts: control, commitment, support, meaning, and normality (see Figure 7.1).

CONTROL

Of all the beliefs about self and society that might increase or reduce distress, belief in control over one's own life may be the most important. Seeman placed the sense of powerlessness at the top of his list of types of alienation, defining it as "the expectancy or probability, held by the individual, that his own behavior cannot determine the occurrence of the outcomes, or reinforcements, he seeks" (Seeman 1959:784). Alienation is any form of detachment or separation from oneself or from others. Powerlessness is the separation from important outcomes in one's own life, or an inability to achieve desired ends. Perceived powerlessness is the cognitive awareness of this reality. Seeman was careful to point out that powerlessness, as a social-psychological variable, is distinct from the objective

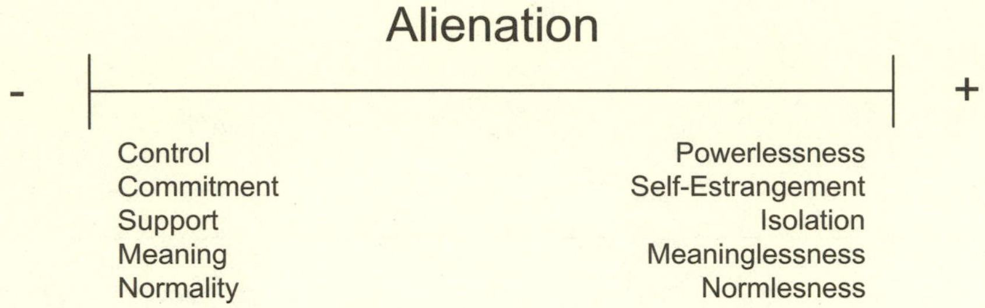

Alienation

Figure 7.1. Five types of subjective alienation, each scored from low (–) to high (+).

conditions that may produce it and the distress an individual may feel as a consequence of it. Thus, Seeman clearly stated the central position of powerlessness in a three-part model of conditions, beliefs and understandings, and feelings, while calling for an end to the practice that was common at the time of measuring alienation as a jumble of causes and effects.

Perceived control occupies the central position in a three-part model in which social conditions shape perceptions and beliefs, which, in turn, affect emotional well-being. In this section we describe the social causes and emotional consequences of perceived control. Perceived powerlessness is generated by objective conditions of powerlessness and leads to distress. Compared to the belief that outcomes are determined by forces external to oneself, belief in personal control is associated with low levels of psychological distress (Wheaton 1980, 1983; Pearlin et al. 1981; Kohn and Schooler 1982; Mirowsky and Ross 1983, 1984; Benassi, Sweeney, and Dufour 1988).

The Faces and Names of Powerlessness and Control

The importance of perceived control is recognized in a number of social and behavioral sciences, where it appears in several forms with various names. In sociology researchers build on themes of perceived powerlessness versus control. As a result, many of the constructs used by sociologists overlap, and they are not seen as very distinct. Concepts related to personal control appear under a number of different names in addition to perceived powerlessness and control, notably mastery (Pearlin et al. 1981), personal autonomy (Seeman 1983), the sense of personal efficacy (Downey and Moen 1987; Gecas 1989), and instrumentalism (Mirowsky et al. 1996; Wheaton, 1980), and at the other end of the continuum, fatalism (Wheaton 1980) and perceived helplessness (Elder and Liker 1982). In psychology concepts closely related to the sense of personal control include internal locus of control, self-efficacy, and helplessness. Psychologists are more likely than sociologists to focus on differences among related concepts. We briefly define the psychological concepts, saying how the sense of personal control is similar to and how it is different from locus of control, self-efficacy, and helplessness.

Locus of Control.

In cognitive psychology, perceived control appears as "locus of control" (Rotter 1966). Belief in an external locus of control is a *learned*, generalized expectation that outcomes of situations are determined by forces external to oneself such as powerful others, luck, fate, or chance. The individual believes that he or she is powerless and at the mercy of the environment. Belief in an internal locus of control (the opposite) is a learned, generalized expectation that outcomes are contingent on one's own choices and actions. Compared to persons with an external locus of control, those with an internal locus of control attribute outcomes to themselves rather than to forces outside themselves.

Both Rotter (1966) and Seeman (1959) recognized that perceived powerlessness—the major form of subjective alienation—and external locus of control were related concepts. In fact, Rotter derived the concept of locus of control from the sociological concept of alienation, stating "the alienated individual feels unable to control his own destiny" (1966:263). Our concept of the sense of personal control has its roots in the work of Seeman and Rotter.

Self-Efficacy.

The concept of perceived control overlaps to a large extent with that of self-efficacy, despite Bandura's (1986) claim that the two are distinct. Self-efficacy is the belief in one's own power or ability to produce a specific desired effect, such as staying healthy, quitting smoking, or doing well in school. Bandura refers to concepts of locus of control as outcome-expectancy theory. Self-efficacy, according to Bandura, focuses upon the individual's belief that he or she can (or cannot) effectively perform a specific action, whereas the sense of control focuses on the belief that one will achieve desired goals. According to Bandura, self-efficacy is specific to particular contexts. For example, "If I study hard I can get good grades." Researchers studying outcomes such as school performance often find that specific self-efficacy beliefs help to predict outcomes. However, emotional well-being reflects the general sense of control. Also, the sense of control is a more parsimonious concept than self-efficacy, with more universal application. The degree to which people think they can or cannot achieve their goals, despite the specific nature of the actions required, has applicability to almost all circumstances. More importantly, the sense of personal control may be the root of self-efficacy. A person with a high sense of personal control will try other actions if their current repertoire of behaviors isn't working. New behaviors may successfully obtain desired goals, which would in turn increase the perceived ability to shape other events and circumstances in life. Therefore, for all intents and purposes, the sense of control acts as the foundation of self-efficacy.

Learned Helplessness.

Learned helplessness is a concept similar to sense of control but from animal studies of reinforcement and learned behavior. Learned helplessness results from exposure to inescapable, uncontrollable negative stimuli. The behavior pattern is characterized by a low rate of voluntary response and low ability to learn successful behaviors (Seligman 1975). Although intended as an analog of human depression, it is important to remember that learned helplessness refers to the behavior, not to any cognitive attribution that reinforcements are outside one's control, and not to the imputed emotion of depression. In humans, however, there is a link between an external locus of control (a cognitive orientation) and learned helplessness (a conditioned response): the perception that reinforcement is not contingent on action. Hiroto (1974) found that, compared to subjects with an internal locus of control, those with an external locus of control were less likely to see a connection between behavior and reinforcement, and as a result, learned more slowly.

Personal Control.

The sense of personal control is a learned, generalized expectation that outcomes are contingent on one's own choices and actions (Mirowsky and Ross 1989; Rotter 1966; Ross, Mirowsky, and Cockerham 1983; Seeman 1983). People with a high sense of control report being effective agents in their own lives. They believe that they can master, control, and effectively alter the environment. Perceived control is the cognitive awareness of a link between efforts and outcomes. On the other end of the continuum, perceived powerlessness is the belief that one's actions do not affect outcomes. It is the belief that outcomes of situations are determined by forces external to oneself such as powerful others, luck, fate, or chance. People with a sense of powerlessness think that they have little control over meaningful events and circumstances in their lives. As such, perceived powerlessness is the cognitive awareness of a discrepancy between one's goals and the means to achieve them. Perceived control and powerlessness represent two ends of a continuum, with the belief that one can shape conditions and events in one's life on one end of the continuum, and the belief that one's actions cannot influence events and circumstances at the other.

Measuring Perceived Control

For our research we designed a set of questions about the general sense of personal control. We chose questions similar to those in the personal component of Rotter's classic locus-of-control scale, which includes questions like "When I make plans I can make them work" or "I have little influence over the things that happen to me." Many of our questions are similar to those in Pearlin's mastery scale, which sociologists often use (Pearlin et al. 1981; Turner and Lloyd 1999). The main difference is that our index uses a 2 × 2 design that has the same number of statements claiming control as claiming powerlessness, and the same number about good outcomes as about bad ones, as detailed below. That lets us eliminate any risk of bias from agreement tendencies and from self-defense or self-blame (Mirowsky and Ross 1991, 1996).

Personal Rather Than Universal, Global Rather Than Specific.

The concept of personal control refers to oneself rather than to others. Perceptions about the amount of control *others* have over their lives can influence mental health, as summarized in a later section, but they are distinct from the sense of personal control. Belief about the amount of control that other people have has been termed ideological control (Gurin, Gurin, and Morrison 1978), universal control, or American instrumentalism (Mirowsky et al. 1996) and should be distinguished from personal control or individual instrumentalism. Ideological, or universal, control refers to the degree one feels that others' successes or failures are their own doing; personal control refers to one's own life outcomes. Beliefs about people in general are not necessarily the same as beliefs about oneself. For example, many who would agree that "people get paid what their work is worth" would not agree that "I get paid what my work is worth." Beliefs about oneself are the most directly and strongly relevant to distress, as detailed later.

The sense of personal control refers to a global judgment about overall self-direction and mastery of one's own life, rather than about control in specific realms such as politics or specific endeavors like quitting cigarettes. Rotter's classic locus-of-control scale includes statements that refer to other people in addition to oneself. Many of them also refer to specific realms of action. For example: "The average citizen can have an influence in government decisions," "Getting people to do the right thing depends on ability; luck has nothing to do with it," "No matter how hard you try, some people just don't like you," and "Most students don't realize the extent to which their grades are determined by accidental happenings." Those statements refer to people in general rather than to oneself, and they are specific to the realms of politics, leadership, friendship, and school. Such beliefs may have implications for outcomes such as voter behavior,

membership in community action groups, networking, and school performance. They have no direct connection to mental health. They relate to
mental health only indirectly, because they tend to correlate with the general sense of control over one's own life (Mirowsky and Ross 1991). A large
collection of beliefs about specific realms of control can indicate the overall sense of control. It is more efficient and more accurate to ask direct
questions about the global sense of personal control. Unlike Rotter and
others, we exclude beliefs about the control others have over their lives
and realm-specific control, like political control, from our measure.

Averaging Out Cross-Cutting Factors: The 2 × 2 Structure.

Responses to questions about personal control capture the concept of
interest, and two other cross-cutting concepts—the tendency to agree and
the tendency toward self-defense or self-blame. Some people are inclined
to agree with most statements, but others are inclined to disagree with most.
In addition, some people are more likely to take responsibility for good outcomes in their lives than for bad ones (self-defense), whereas others take
more responsibility for their failures than for their successes (self-blame).
Tendencies toward agreement or disagreement and toward self-defense or
self-blame cross-cut the concept of perceived control. Measures of personal
control ideally should average out defensiveness and agreement tendencies to achieve unbiased measures. The Mirowsky-Ross (1991) measure of
the sense of control is a 2 × 2 index that balances statements about control
with those about lack of control, and statements about success (good outcomes) with those about failure (bad outcomes). It is shown in Figure 7.2.
The balanced 2 × 2 design lets us calculate an index of perceived control free
of any potential bias from self-defense, self-blame, and agreement tendencies. It also lets us calculate measures of those cross-cutting factors. Because
of our balanced 2 × 2 design, none of these cross-cutting tendencies biases
our measure of personal control, as detailed below.

Agreement tendency.   Agreement bias is the tendency to agree or to disagree with all statements, apart from the relative endorsement of each statement's distinctive content. Some people tend to agree with any statement
unless they feel quite differently about things. Others tend to disagree
unless they feel quite certain about endorsing what the statement voices.
These tendencies can bias the scores on indexes if all or most of the statements make similar claims. For example, take the statements "Most of my
problems are due to bad breaks" and "I have little control over the bad
things that happen to me." Some persons might agree with both because
they feel powerless in their own lives, but others might agree with both
because they generally acquiesce to most statements. Likewise, some might

Control Over Good:
  "I am responsible for my own successes"
  "I can do just about anything I really set my mind to"
Control Over Bad:
  "My misfortunes are the result of mistakes I have made"
  "I am responsible for my failures"
Powerless Over Good:
  "The really good things that happen to me are mostly luck"
  "There's no sense planning a lot – if something good is going to happen it will"
Powerless Over Bad:
  "Most of my problems are due to bad breaks"
  "I have little control over the bad things that happen to me"

The index takes the average score across the eight items. Responses to statements claiming control are coded strongly agree = 2, agree = 1, neutral = 0, disagree = -1, and strongly disagree = -2. Responses to statements claiming powerlessness are coded the opposite way: strongly agree -2, agree = -1, neutral = 0, disagree = 1, and strongly disagree = 2 (Mirowsky and Ross 1991).

Figure 7.2. Questions in the Mirowsky-Ross index of perceived control versus powerlessness, balanced for good and bad outcomes and for statements claiming control and those claiming powerlessness.

disagree with both because they feel in control, but others might disagree simply because they do not want to endorse any statement lightly.

Averaging out agreement tendencies can be important in social surveys of perceived control. Older Americans and those with lower levels of education tend to agree with statements whereas younger or better-educated ones tend to disagree, other things being equal (Mirowsky and Ross 1991, 1996). Many indexes of perceived control use mostly statements of powerlessness, such as "I have little control over the things that happen to me." That can make it look like older persons or those with lower levels of education feel more powerless than they really do.

Interestingly, Rotter's classic locus-of-control scale used a forced-choice format to solve the problem of agreement tendencies. Each statement expressing a sense of control was paired with another expressing a sense of powerlessness. Rotter asked his student respondents to choose the one statement in each pair closest to their own belief. That eliminates the potential bias from agreement tendencies, because agreeing with one statement requires disagreeing with the other. Unfortunately, it often annoys individuals who feel they cannot choose because the two statements are not exact opposites. It also requires long lists of paired statements, because each pair provides only one "bit" of data (a single yes or no). Social surveys need greater efficiency, so they unpair the statements and let individuals rate the level of agreement or disagreement.

One result of unpairing statements often confuses researchers who are unaware of the impact of agreement tendencies on responses. The level of agreement between two statements expressing the same belief (i.e., two expressing control or two expressing powerlessness) is greater than the level of *dis*agreement between two expressing opposite beliefs (i.e., one expressing control and one expressing powerlessness). That is because a pair expressing opposite beliefs requires that the individual agree with one and disagree with the other. Agreement tendencies work against that, reducing the level of disagreement. On the other hand, some part of the agreement with two statements expressing the same belief just reflects the agreement tendency, and not the belief in question. Some researchers mistakenly think that the sense of control and the sense of powerlessness are unrelated or independent beliefs rather than opposite ends of the same continuum. That error comes from misinterpreting the effects of agreement tendencies.

Self-defense and self-blame.   Self-defense is the tendency to claim responsibility for the good outcomes in one's life but deny responsibility for the bad ones. Self-blame, the opposite, is the tendency to claim responsibility for the bad outcomes but not the good ones. Like agreement tendencies, self-defense versus self-blame cross-cuts the sense of control. Some researchers focus on self-blame as a cause of depression, because of the self-derogatory sense of guilt or inadequacy common among the depressed. Many of those same researchers also think that self-defense protects against depression, by protecting the ego. Others, though, think that ego defensiveness carries an emotional cost. Our research finds that both self-defense and self-blame correlate with elevated depression (Mirowsky and Ross 1990). Both seem to be as depressing as feeling equally powerless over good *and* bad outcomes. Our balanced 2×2 measure averages out self-defense and self-blame, to give a pure measure of the general sense of control.

Belief Shaped by Experience

The most useful research on the links between social structure, perceptions of control, and emotional outcomes synthesize the strengths of psychology and sociology, as did that of Rotter and Seeman. Each discipline has working assumptions that greatly simplify reality to provide a base from which to proceed with research. In the extreme, psychology often assumes that beliefs come out of people's heads, unconstrained by social conditions. Sociology often assumes that social conditions determine outcomes regardless of the beliefs individuals hold. Psychologists too often discount the influence of social structure on perceptions. Sociologists too often discount the ways in which perceptions mediate or even change the effects of social position on well-being. To understand the processes by which social position affects psychological well-being, one must learn how social positions shape individual beliefs, and how beliefs determine the emotional consequences of social positions.

Perceptions, Not Just Conditions.

Sociologists sometimes imply that social structure has consequences for individual behavior or well-being regardless of individual beliefs or perceptions (Braverman, 1974). In those purely structural views, alienation exists in solely objective terms, as when the product of a peasant's labor belongs to his lord because of traditional and legal class relationships. The structural purist would say that the individual in this case is alienated from his labor, regardless of whether he is conscious of or disaffected by the separation. Erikson (1986) critiques sociologists who think that bringing in social psychological mediating variables somehow makes theory less structural. "There are those," says Erikson,

> who argue that one ought to be able to determine when a person is alienated by taking a look at the objective conditions in which she works. The worker exposed to estranging conditions is alienated almost by definition, no matter what she says she thinks or even what she thinks she thinks. That view . . . has the effect of closing off sociological investigation rather than the effect of inviting it. Alienation, in order to make empirical sense, has to reside somewhere in or around the persons who are said to experience it. (1986:6)

The association between the objective condition and the subjective perception is an important empirical question, one that must be investigated, not assumed (Seeman 1983).

Shaped by Reality, Not Just Imagined.

Some psychologists, on the other hand, discount the effects of social position, instead claiming that perceptions of control are as likely to be illusory as to be based on reality. For example, Levenson says that a sense of controlling important outcomes in one's life is *unrelated* to a sense that others, chance, fate, or luck control the outcomes [Levenson (1973); see Lachman (1986) for a review]. Brewin and Shapiro (1984) say that a perceived ability to achieve desirable outcomes is unrelated to a perceived ability to avoid undesirable ones. In both cases, the researchers think that people fail to see a connection, and that the realities of life do not suggest one. Implicitly, these views deny the effects of social status on the sense of control. Levenson's view suggests that education, prestige, wealth, and power do not shift the real balance of control from others and chance to one's self, or that individuals fail to perceive that balance in their own lives. Brewin and Shapiro's view suggests that the real social resources available for achieving success are useless for avoiding failure, or that individuals fail to see the relevance of wealth, income, status, education, and the like to both good and bad outcomes. Levinson's error comes from failing to recognize and correct for the effect of agreement tendencies on responses to statements about control. Brewin and Shapiro's comes from using a measure that encourages self-defensive or self-blaming responses.

Even when using measures biased by agreement tendencies and self-defense or self-blame, results generally show realistic correlations with measures of social status (Mirowsky and Ross 1990, 1991; Mirowsky et al. 1996). Both agreement with statements expressing a sense of control *and* *dis*agreement with those expressing a sense of powerlessness generally increase with higher socioeconomic status. So do claiming responsibility for good outcomes and claiming responsibility for bad ones.

Objective Power and Perceived Control

Beliefs about personal control typically represent realistic perceptions of objective conditions. An individual learns through social interaction and personal experience that his or her choices and efforts are usually likely or unlikely to affect the outcome of a situation (Rotter 1966; Seeman 1983; Wheaton 1980). Belief in external control is the learned and generalized expectation that one has little control over meaningful events and circumstances in one's life. As such, it is the cognitive awareness of a discrepancy between one's goals and the means to achieve them. Theoretically, social structural positions indicative of objective powerlessness, such as dependency, structural inconsistency, role stress, and alienated labor, increase the probability of this discrepancy and thus increase perceived powerlessness (Mirowsky and Ross 1989; Rosenfield 1989). Failure in the face of effort leads to a sense of powerlessness, fatalism, or belief in external control, beliefs that can increase passivity and result in giving up. Through continued experience with objective conditions of powerlessness and lack of control, individuals come to learn that their own actions cannot produce desired outcomes. In contrast, success leads to a sense of mastery, efficacy or belief in internal control, characterized by an active, problem-solving approach to life (Wheaton 1980, 1983; Mirowsky and Ross 1983, 1984).

Theoretical Conditions Undermining the Sense of Control.

Sociological theory points to several conditions likely to produce a belief in external control. First and foremost is objective powerlessness. Defined as an objective condition rather than a belief, it is the inability to achieve one's ends or, alternatively, the inability to achieve one's ends when in opposition to others. The second is structural inconsistency, which is a situation in which society defines certain goals, purposes, and interests as legitimate and desirable and also defines the proper procedures for moving toward the objectives but does not provide adequate resources and opportunities for achieving the objectives through legitimate means. The third is alienated labor, a condition under which the worker does not decide what to produce, does not design and schedule the production process, and does not own the product. The fourth is dependency, a situation in which one partner in an exchange has fewer alternative sources of sustenance and gratification than the other. The fifth is role overload, a situation in which legitimate expectations of others imply demands that overwhelm the resources and capabilities of the individual. Although these conditions are not exhaustive, they all point to the generative force of various forms of social power. In looking for the sources of perceived powerlessness researchers look for variables associated with conditions of powerlessness, structural inconsistency, alienated labor, dependency, and role overload.

Sociodemographic Correlates of Control and Powerlessness

In the United States, average levels of perceived control are high, and they vary systematically with positions of objective power. The large majority of Americans report that they control their own lives. We find that more than 90 percent of a representative national sample agree with the statements "I am responsible for my own successes" and "I can do just about anything I really set my mind to" (Mirowsky et al. 1996). A smaller percentage, but still more than two-thirds, agrees with statements claiming responsibility for personal misfortunes and failures. These levels of agreement are impressive, but they are inflated by the tendency of some respondents to agree with statements regardless of what they express (Mirowsky and Ross, 1991). That same tendency deflates the level of disagreement with fatalistic statements. Even so, disagreement with the fatalistic statements ranges from 54 to 79 percent. Averaging the percentage of instrumental responses across the eight personal control items shown in Figure 7.2 yields a mean of 77 percent. As a generalization, then, about three-fourths of Americans feel in control of their own lives and responsible for their own outcomes.

Despite high mean levels of personal control in the United States, considerable variation exists, too. The sense of personal control has four major social correlates: (1) socioeconomic status, including education, employment, and income, (2) race and ethnicity, (3) age and cohort, and (4) gender, work, and family. We describe those correlations below.

Socioeconomic Status.

Most research on the social structural correlates of perceived control looks at socioeconomic status: education, income, employment status, and jobs. A composite index of socioeconomic status, based on family income, occupational prestige of the respondent or breadwinner, and interviewer ratings of the social class of the neighborhood, home, and respondent, correlates negatively with the sense of powerlessness and, thus, positively with the sense of mastery and control (Mirowsky and Ross 1983). Looking at specific components of SES separately, income, education, employment, and autonomous and nonroutine work each decrease the sense of powerlessness, adjusting for the other components (Downey and Moen 1987; Mirowsky and Ross 1983; Ross and Mirowsky 1989, 1992; Ross, Mirowsky, and Cockerham 1983; Wheaton 1980).

Education.   Education develops capacities on many levels that increase the sense of control throughout life. Those learned abilities help people successfully prevent problems, solve problems if prevention fails, design their own lives, and achieve personal goals whatever those may be (Mirowsky and Ross 1989; Pearlin et al. 1981; Ross and Mirowsky 1992; Wheaton 1980). Through education, individuals develop capacities on many levels that increase the sense of personal control. Schooling builds human capital—skills, abilities, and human resources. Education develops the habits and skills of communication: reading, writing, inquiring, discussing, looking things ups, and figuring things out. It develops basic analytic skills such as observing, experimenting, summarizing, synthesizing, interpreting, and classifying. Because education develops the ability to gather and interpret information and to solve problems on many levels, it increases control over events and outcomes in life (Ross and Mirowsky 1989). Moreover, in education, one encounters and solves problems that are progressively more difficult, complex, and subtle. The process of learning builds problem-solving skills and confidence in the ability to solve problems. Education instills the habit of meeting problems with attention, thought, action, and persistence. Thus, education increases effort and ability, the fundamental components of problem-solving (Wheaton 1980).

Education also is key to a person's place in the stratification system. It increases the likelihood of employment at a good job with a high income. It also decreases the likelihood of experiencing economic hardship. This is partly because education increases household income by increasing pay, increases the probability of being married, and increases the likely earnings of one's partner (because most married people have similar levels of education). Thus education provides the ability to achieve the social and economic status that reinforces the sense of control over one's own life (Mirowsky 1995; Ross and Wu 1995).

Research by us and others consistently finds a substantial correlation between having a higher level of education and a greater sense of personal control. Figure 7.3 shows the association between education and the sense of personal control among adults in our 1995 ASOC survey. We find a similar association in our other data sets, too (e.g., Mirowsky 1995; Ross and Mirowsky 1992; Ross, Mirowsky, and Pribesh 2001). Statistical analyses of the association consistently show three things. First, it is not spurious. It does not vanish with adjustment for age, sex, race, ethnicity, and status of origin. Second, a large part of the association results from the effect of educational attainment on other aspects of socioeconomic status, such as employment, autonomy on the job, earnings, household income, and low risk of economic hardship. Third, the association remains significant even with adjustment for other aspects of socioeconomic status. In other words, the sense of control increases with level of education even when comparing individuals otherwise similar in terms of employment, job autonomy, earnings, household income, and economic hardship.

That third fact listed above suggests that something about education itself develops the sense of control over one's own life. Our research on the life course trajectory of perceived control (detailed later) also suggests that education directly builds the sense of control. In particular, we find that the sense of control generally increases from age fourteen through twenty-two, but only for those who stay in school (Lewis et al. 1999). Dropping out stops the increase in sense of control. Similarly, adults (ages eighteen and up) in school have a higher sense of control than others of the same age working full-time who have completed the same number of years of schooling (Ross and Drentea 1998). Taken together, the observations suggest that schooling continuously builds the sense of control, with the expected lifetime peak largely reflecting the total amount of training.

Employment, Jobs, and Work.

Productive labor generally reinforces the sense of control, maintaining it at the peak levels built up through formal education. Unlike education, though, jobs can detract from the sense of control when the pay is very low and workers have little or no say in what they do and how they do it (Ross and Mirowsky 1992). Even so, full-time employees in the United States typically feel more in control of their own lives than others do (e.g., Ross and Mirowsky 1992). Adults with full-time jobs report a greater sense of

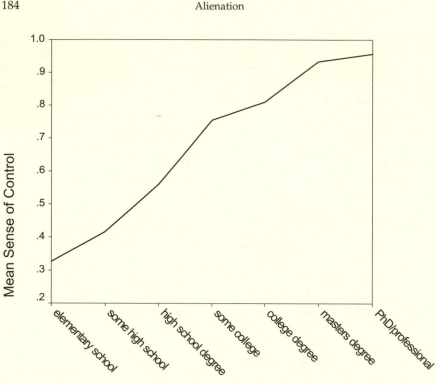

Figure 7.3.   Mean sense of control by level of education (1995 U.S. ASOC data).

control on average than do those who are unemployed, unable to work due to a disability or illness, retired, homemaking, or employed part-time, adjusting for age, sex, race, education, and marital status (Ross and Drentea 1998). Only students have a higher sense of control than full-time employees who are otherwise similar to themselves in age, sex, and so on. Being unable to work is clearly the worst for the sense of control. All the other categories except being in school are about the same.

Jobs are important for a number of reasons. Low-status jobs produce a sense of powerlessness because the job, and the opportunities and income it provides, are seen as barriers to the achievement of life goals (Wheaton 1980). Jobs that are substantively complex (especially in work primarily with information and people rather than with things) increase the sense of personal control and psychological self-directedness (Kohn 1976; Kohn and Schooler 1982; Ross 2000). Jobs that provide autonomy—freedom from close supervision and participation in decision-making—increase the sense of personal control (Bird and Ross 1993; Kohn and Schooler 1982; Ross and Mirowsky 1992). Substantively complex, nonroutine, autonomous work signals control over one's own work, which Kohn and his colleagues call occupational self-direction. Among the employed, occupational self-direction—rather than ownership or control over the labor of others—increases psychological self-direction, which is similar to the sense of personal control (Kohn 1976; Kohn and Schooler 1982; Kohn et al. 1990). Job latitude, like occupational self-direction, includes autonomous decision-making and nonroutine work, and it significantly increases perceived control (Seeman, Seeman, and Budros 1988).

Job disruptions such as being laid off, downgraded, fired, or leaving work because of illness decrease the worker's sense of mastery, partly by lowering income and increasing difficulties in acquiring necessities such as food, clothing, housing, and medical care, or optional but useful items such as furniture, automobiles, and recreation (Pearlin et al. 1981). A prolonged episode of being out of work and wanting or needing a job can reduce the sense of control years later. Compared to others who share the same current circumstances, individuals with a history of prolonged unemployment feel less in control of their own lives (Ross and Drentea 1998).

Taken together, studies imply that steady full-time employment in a job that pays adequately and allows a measure of autonomy reinforces the sense of control over one's own life. The inability to get or keep a job undermines the sense of control, whether it results from low skills, few opportunities, or limiting impairments. While jobs with poor pay and low autonomy can create a sense of wage slavery, full-time employment generally sustains the sense of control over one's life better than the alternatives.

Race and Ethnicity.

Research generally finds that minority group members, particularly blacks and Mexican Americans, have lower average sense of control than the majority whites. Most of that difference results from the lower average socioeconomic status of minorities. Lower levels of education, employment, and income mediate much of the impact of race on perceived control (Gurin, Lao, and Beattie 1969; Porter and Washington 1979; Hughes and Demo 1989; Wade, Thompson, Tashakori, and Valente 1989).

Data also show direct effects of race and ethnicity, even adjusting for education and income, indicating that blacks and Mexican Americans have a lower sense of control over their lives that is not entirely due to socioeconomic disadvantage. For blacks this seems likely to reflect the history of discrimination and restricted opportunities. Barriers based on race limit aspirations and may create a perceived disconnection between efforts and outcomes.

Mexican Americans apparently have an additional, cultural factor lowering their average sense of control compared to other Americans. Most of the lower sense of control among Mexican Americans results from restricted opportunities in an Anglo-dominated economic system. However, Mexican Americans also place an emphasis on subordination to the family that apparently decreases perceived control (Mirowsky and Ross 1984, 1987). Compared to Anglos, persons of Mexican ethnic heritage and identity have more of an orientation to family and pseudofamily, whereas Anglos place less emphasis on the mutual obligations of family and friends and more on the individual's personal responsibility for his or her own life. This appears to generate lower levels of personal control among Mexican Americans, but higher levels of social support. A later section details the trade-off between personal control and social support in their effects on distress. To some extent they represent alternative approaches to maximizing well-being. Anglo-American culture leans toward maximizing personal control, whereas Mexican culture leans toward maximizing social support.

Age and Cohort.

Our surveys using large representative samples of persons across the full range of adult ages, from eighteen to over ninety, show that older adults have a lower sense of control than do young or middle-aged adults (Mirowsky 1995, 1997). Figure 7.4 shows the means by five-year age groups for the 1995 U.S. ASOC survey. Our 1990 U.S. survey and our 1985 and 1995 Illinois surveys show much the same pattern. Generally speaking, the average sense of control rises somewhat in early adulthood as people finish college. Levels remain high across the middle-aged groups, but then begin to drop substantially in successively older groups. Other researchers find the same old-age dropoff in a large sample of senior patients in a general medical clinic at a large urban teaching hospital (Wolinsky and Stump 1996).

Studies prior to our series begun in 1985 had produced inconsistent and often contradictory results regarding age and the sense of control. In a review, Lachman (1986) concluded that about one-third of studies found low levels of control among the elderly, one-third found high levels, and one-third found no association between age and the sense of control. Rodin (1986) also concluded that there was little evidence that perceived control decreased with age. Many of those early inconsistencies resulted from the use of truncated, noncomparable, unrepresentative, and small samples. Many samples contained only elderly, so the comparative data showing higher levels of control among the young and middle-aged were unavailable. Samples with both old and young often used noncomparable, unrepresentative groups, such as comparing young college students to retired health plan members. Bias in the measures of perceived control

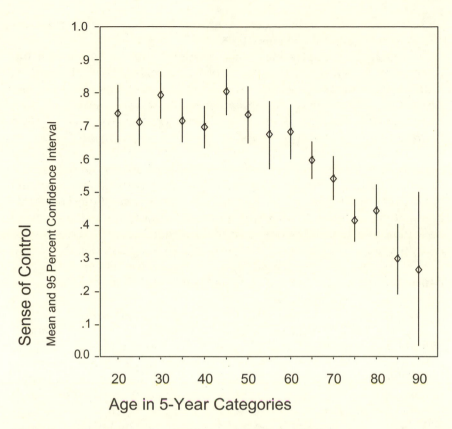

Figure 7.4. Mean sense of control by age (1995 U.S. ASOC data).

also produced some inconsistencies. Sometimes questions about planning, orderliness, perseverance, self-discipline, achievement, and the like were used to measure perceived control. Although perceived control may be correlated with these things, it is not the same. Many orientations such as regularity and orderliness increase with age, but that does not imply a corresponding increase in perceived control.

Why would older persons feel less control over their lives than younger? Rodin (1986) suggests three possible explanations for a negative association between age and the sense of control: loss of meaningful relationships, a deterioration of health and physical functioning, and dependency created and enforced through contact with health professionals that prefer compliant patients. In support of that view, we find that the increasing prevalence of widowhood, physical impairment, inability to work, and isolated and routine daily activities create much of the dropoff in sense of control seen in the older age groups (Mirowsky 1995; Mirowsky and Ross 1999; Ross and Drentea 1998).

Although aging and the life cycle account for much of the relationship between old age and low sense of control, historical factors are at work too. Individuals in older age groups lived their lives in times that were less prosperous. Technologies that extend personal control were less developed, and jobs allowed less autonomy. Rising average levels of education drove corresponding upward trends in prosperity and job quality. Lower levels of education, and all that implies across the life course, account for a substantial fraction of the lower sense of control seen among senior Americans. Although no one can predict the future with total certainty, the sense of control in old age should improve considerably if present trends and patterns continue to hold. Much of that follows from rising levels of education, which have two effects, as illustrated in Figure 7.5. First, higher education increases the sense of control at each age. Second, it delays the start of declines in sense of control to older ages. The higher the level of education, the longer that individuals manage to preserve the sense of control built up in school.

Many people probably see the decline in sense of control with advancing age as essentially biological. The contribution of physical impairment, inability to work, and widowhood to that decline reinforces a biological view. It is important to recognize, though, that those correlates of aging are themselves heavily influenced by social factors such as education. In particular, higher education lowers the level of physical impairment at each age and delays the rise of impairment until later ages (Mirowsky and Ross 1999:343). It also increases life expectancy, including that of one's spouse. Delaying impairment and widowhood helps preserve the sense of control into older ages. All of this implies that the life course trajectories in sense of control for today's young and middle-aged adults will be more favorable than implied by current differences among age groups. As college education becomes more the norm, the overall pattern may come to look more like the top curve in Figure 7.5.

Gender, Work, and Family.

Theory suggests that women have a lower sense of control over their lives than men as a result of economic dependency, restricted opportunities, role overload, and the routine nature of housework and women's jobs. Past evidence indicates that women have a lower sense of control than men (Mirowsky and Ross 1983, 1984; Thoits 1987), but that often the difference is insignificant (Ross and Bird 1994; Ross and Mirowsky 1989). Recent findings indicate that the difference between women and men in average sense of control depends on age, with greater equality in younger age groups (Ross and Mirowsky 2002). The following sections examine the

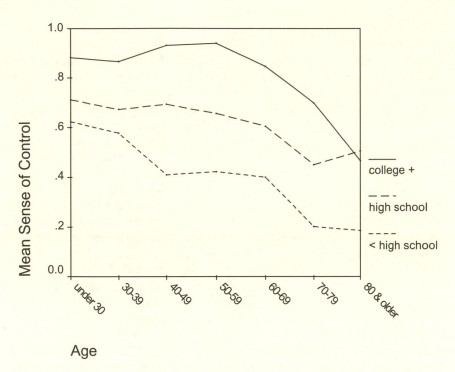

Age

Figure 7.5. Mean sense of control by age and education (1995 U.S. ASOC data).

empirical evidence for expecting women to feel less in control of their own lives than men do. Then we return to age-related differences between the sexes, and the circumstances under which women feel less in control than do men.

Paid and unpaid work. Women are more likely to do unpaid domestic work; men are more likely to work for pay. Compared to not working for pay, employment is associated with status, power, economic independence, and noneconomic rewards, for both men and women (Bird and Ross 1993; Gove and Tudor 1973). For women who are exclusively housewives, domestic work is done without economic rewards, without the opportunity for advancement or promotion for work well done, and because it is often invisible, devalued, and taken for granted, without psychological rewards (Bergmann 1986; Gove and Tudor 1973). Theory predicts that people employed for pay have a greater sense of control over their lives than homemakers. Perceived control over one's life is the expectation that one's behavior affects outcomes, and working for pay likely produces a mental connection between efforts and outcomes. In contrast, work done without pay or other rewards produces a sense of disconnection between efforts and outcomes. Effort and skill at housework have few consequences; one does not receive a raise, and one's standard of living is determined by someone else, not by one's abilities at the job. Furthermore, homemakers are economically dependent, which may decrease one's sense of control and increase the perception that powerful others shape one's life.

Both economic dependency and the disconnection between work and rewards theoretically decrease perceived control among unpaid domestic workers compared to paid workers. Empirical evidence indicates that employed persons have a higher sense of control than the nonemployed overall (Ross and Mirowsky 1992), that the employed have a higher sense of control than homemakers specifically (Bird and Ross 1993; Ross and Wright 1998; Ross and Drentea 1998), and that the employed have a greater sense of self-determination than housewives (Ferree 1976). Elder and Liker (1982) found that elderly women who had taken jobs forty years earlier, during the Great Depression, had a higher sense of self-efficacy and lower sense of helplessness than women who remained homemakers.

What explains the association between full-time homemaking and low personal control? Compared to paid work, homemaking is more routine, provides less intrinsic gratification, offers fewer extrinsic symbolic rewards, and is unpaid (Bird and Ross 1993). These differences account for homemakers' lower sense of control over their lives. Although homemakers are thanked for their work more often than male paid workers, being thanked for work does not significantly affect one's sense of control. However, housework offers one important advantage over the average paid job: higher levels of autonomy. Work autonomy significantly increases the sense of control. Were it not for their autonomy, homemakers would experience an even lower sense of control than is observed.

Work and family interactions.   Overall, the employed have significantly higher average perceived control than do homemakers. Not all jobs are alike, however; nor are all household contexts of employment. Critical combinations of low pay, no autonomous working conditions, and heavy family demands (conditions faced disproportionately by women) may negate the positive influence of employment on control (Ross and Mirowsky 1992). First, the difference in perceived control between employed and nonemployed depends on job conditions, including job autonomy and earnings. (Job authority, promotion opportunities, and job prestige are not significant.) As job autonomy and earnings increase among the employed, their sense of control relative to that of the nonemployed increases. Second, household labor modifies the effect of employment on the sense of control. The higher one's responsibility for household work, the less the association between employment and control (Ross and

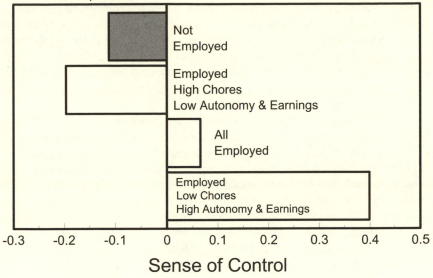

True-Score Standard Deviations
From the Sample Mean

Not
Employed

Employed
High Chores
Low Autonomy & Earnings

All
Employed

Employed
Low Chores
High Autonomy & Earnings

-0.3   -0.2   -0.1   0   0.1   0.2   0.3   0.4   0.5

Sense of Control

Figure 7.6. Mean sense of control by job and household circumstances (1985 Illinois data).

Mirowsky 1992). Responsibility for household work greatly decreases the sense of control associated with employment. (Household work does not decrease perceived control in itself; among people who are not employed, household work slightly increases the sense of control.) Similarly, Rosenfield (1989) finds that the role overload of mothers who are employed at full-time jobs increases their sense of powerlessness. Third, the greater the household income from sources other than one's own earnings, the less the association between employment and perceived control (Ross and Mirowsky 1992). The lower the household income available from other sources, the greater the sense of control associated with having a job compared to not having one. Although other household income increases the sense of control, it decreases the positive effect of one's own employment on the sense of control.

Qualities of the job combine with household circumstances to give some employees a lower sense of control than found among those who are not employed. Figure 7.6 illustrates that, depending on circumstances, employment can be associated with either a lower or a higher sense of control. The gray bar represents the adjusted mean sense of control among persons who are not employed. The bar just below represents the sense of control predicted for the employed who have low earnings and autonomy (a standard deviation below average) and major responsibility for household chores (a standard deviation above average). Under these circumstances, employment is associated with a lower average sense of control than among people who are not employed. At the other extreme, the large bar on the bottom represents the sense of control predicted for the employed with high earnings and autonomy and low responsibility for household chores. Under those circumstances, employment is associated with a much higher sense of control.

Job autonomy, earnings, responsibility for household work, and other family income combine to make the association between employment and the sense of control greater for most men than for most women. Men have higher autonomy and earnings, less responsibility for household work, and lower amounts of other household income. Because of the differences in these factors, employment increases the expected sense of control most for married males, followed by nonmarried males, then nonmarried females, and finally married females. For married women, the typical combination of low pay, low autonomy, high responsibility for household chores, and high family income other than personal earnings nearly negates the positive association between employment and the sense of control.

Gender, marriage, and children. Marriage has different effects on the sense of control for women than it does for men, and among women being married increases the expected sense of control in some ways but decreases it in other ways (Ross 1991). Adjusting for household income, nonmarried women have a significantly greater sense of control than both men and married women: ordered from lowest to highest sense of control are married females, nonmarried males, married males, and nonmarried females. Everything else being equal, marriage decreases perceived control among women, but not among men. However, everything else is not really equal. Married women have much higher household incomes than do nonmarried women ($33,680 compared to $20,380 in 1985, when the survey was taken). Thus marriage represents a tradeoff for women: it increases household income, which increases perceived control, but it decreases personal control in other ways. The reverse, of course, is true for nonmarried women, who have low household incomes, but otherwise have something (perhaps independence or a lack of subordination) that increases their sense of control. "The economic well-being of married women carries a price, paid in personal control" (Ross 1991:837). The cost of marriage could be due to direct negative effects on women's autonomy, but some of the negative effect of marriage is due to the circumstances of married women's employment, which is usually combined with heavy responsibilities for household work, as described above.

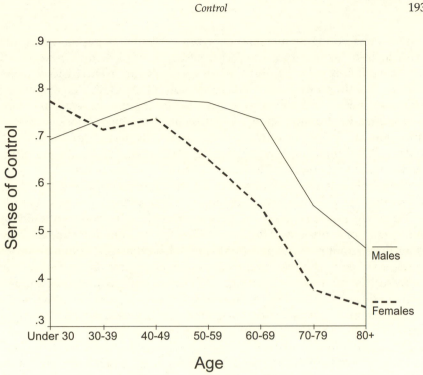

Figure 7.7. Mean sense of control by sex and age (1995 U.S. ASOC data).

Theory suggests that the presence of children in the household might lower the sense of personal control among parents, especially mothers, because children limit freedom, impose constraints, and decrease the ability to maintain an ordered, predictable, and controlled world (Gove and Geerken 1977). However, little evidence shows a detrimental effect of children on perceptions of control among women. Overall, the number of children in the household has no significant effect on women's sense of control (Ross 1991), and have no effect on the sense of control among middle-aged black mothers (Coleman, Antonucci, Adelmann, and Crohan 1987). Children born to mothers under the age of nineteen decrease self-efficacy, but children born to women over the age of nineteen do not (McLaughlin and Micklin 1983).

Gender and age. The theory and research described above strongly imply that women should feel less in control of their own lives than men do. Research does not always show an overall difference though. Our current research indicates that sex differences in sense of control depend on age (Ross and Mirowsky 2002). Little or no sex difference in perceived control exists among young women and men, but a substantial gap favoring men exists in the older age groups, as illustrated in Figure 7.7. Our analyses indicate that differences by sex and age in level of education and history of continuous full-time employment account for much of the emerging sex difference in the older age groups. Analyses of changes in sense of control over a three-year period show similar results. Men have more consistent employment histories prior to the beginning of the period, and more likely and stable full-time employment during the period. Both of those produce more favorable changes in the sense of control over the period.

While this is a new area of analysis, the overall pattern suggests an interaction between life course trajectories and historical trends. Women and men with the same level of education begin adulthood with similar perceptions of control over their own lives. Continuous full-time employment in jobs that provide good pay and substantial autonomy preserves the sense of control developed through formal education, and may even increase it somewhat as earnings and autonomy grow with seniority. Higher education increases the likelihood of securing that ideal work history, but more so for men than for women. As a result, the gender gap in sense of control emerges in adulthood, because of the accumulated differences in employment history and job quality. In older generations men had higher levels of education than women, and much more consistent full-time employment. That partly accounts for the greater sex difference in sense of control observed in the older age groups. The difference in education between men and women has disappeared in recent generations. Women's employment histories have gotten more like men's, too, but a substantial difference remains. Oddly, this may interact with the rising levels of education to preserve the life course emergence of a gender gap in sense of control. College educations may give men the opportunities for pay, autonomy, and productive creativity that continue to build the sense of control throughout the employment years. College-educated women face disadvantages in employment and pay and tradeoffs between work and family that often limit or negate such gains.

Powerlessness and Distress: Demoralization versus Instrumental Coping

Experiences that convey a message about the ability to achieve desired outcomes and avoid undesired ones develop and reinforce the sense of control or its opposite, the sense of powerlessness. Social stratification assures that the apparent control implied by personal experience is not random. As detailed in the previous section, aspects of socioeconomic status such as higher education, income and earnings, stable full-time employment, and autonomous, creative work imply a favorable balance of real control. That reality shapes beliefs about personal control, which in turn shapes emotional well-being. In this section we summarize the theoretical and empirical observations about the relationship of distress to perceptions of control, and about the importance of those beliefs as the link between socioeconomic status and distress.

Morale and Effective Action: The Theory.

Theoretically speaking, the sense of control has two important effects on emotional well-being. First, a greater sense of control implies greater self-assurance and hope. Individuals who believe they can achieve desired outcomes and avoid undesired ones feel confident. They see the undesirable events and outcomes in their own lives as unusual for them, and probably as something they can correct now and avoid in the future. As a result, they do not ruminate an unpleasant experience into a generally gloomy, discouraged, and hopeless state of mind. In contrast, those who feel powerless to achieve good outcomes and avoid bad ones see each new failure, loss, or burden as another punishing confirmation of inadequacy, disadvantage, or universal chaos. These interpretive frames influence emotional tone even in neutral circumstances. The sense of control represents the accumulated experience of a lifetime. The totality of that experience leaves some individuals with a heartening confidence, and others with a forlorn despair. Long experience forges the beliefs, and current belief prompts the emotions.

In addition to its direct, demoralizing impact, the sense of not being in control of the outcomes in one's life diminishes the will and motivation to solve and avoid problems. Wheaton (1983) argues that fatalism decreases coping effort. Belief in the efficacy of environmental rather than personal forces makes active attempts to solve problems seem pointless: What's the use? The result is less motivation and less persistence in coping and, thus, less success in solving problems and adapting. Taking Wheaton's arguments a step further, the fatalist has a reactive, passive orientation whereas the instrumentalist has a proactive one. Instrumental persons are likely to search the environment for potentially distressing events and conditions, to take preventive steps, and to accumulate resources or develop skills and habits that will reduce the impact of unavoidable problems. (For example, an instrumental person will drive carefully, wear a seatbelt, and carry accident insurance.) When undesired events and situations occur, the instrumental person is better prepared and less threatened. In contrast, the reactive, passive person ignores potential problems until they actually happen, making problems more likely to occur and leaving the person unprepared when they do. Furthermore, passive coping, such as trying to ignore the problem until it goes away, fails to limit the consequences of the problems. Thus, the instrumentalist is constantly getting ahead of problems, whereas the fatalist is inevitably falling behind. The theoretical result is a magnification of differences: fatalists suffer more and more problems, reinforcing their perceived powerlessness and thus producing escalating passivity in the face of difficulties, and more and more distress.

Low Sense of Control, High Distress: The Observations.

Individuals who believe they have little or no control over their own lives generally feel more distressed than others. That statement summarizes one of the best-established, most often reproduced findings in all of social psychology. Many elusive phenomena require careful sampling and measurement to be observed, but the correlation between distress and low sense of control is not at all subtle. It shows up with any of a number of indexes measuring distress and perceived control. It shows up in just about any sample a study takes, regardless of population segments the individuals come from or the manner in which they are found and recruited. Back in 1988 three psychologists looked up all ninety-seven studies published in psychology journals up to then that correlated an index of depression with an index of perceived control (Benassi et al. 1988). Every one of the studies reported a negative correlation between depression and the sense of control (mean $r = -.31$). That is remarkable. Psychology studies usually have qualities that work against finding a measurable correlation. Most psychology studies draw individuals from a relatively narrow range of backgrounds, such as sophomores at one college or patients with the same diagnosis at one clinic. That greatly limits the range of perceived control. Even so, psychologists find the correlation repeatedly. So do the sociologists who take large samples of respondents drawn from broad, general populations (e.g., Aneshensel 1992; Gecas 1989; Mirowsky and Ross 1986, 1989; Pearlin et al. 1981; Ross and Mirowsky 1989; Wheaton 1980, 1983). All the large-sample community surveys we know about that measure both distress and the sense of control find the same thing. Individuals with little or no sense of control over their own lives feel more distressed than others (Ross and Sastry 1999).

A sense of powerlessness correlates most strongly with depression, but also with anxiety and other unpleasant emotions such as anger and fear and with cognitive problems such as mistrust, paranoia, and schizophrenia (Mirowsky and Ross 1983, 1984; Ross and Van Willigen 1997; Wheaton 1985). Individuals who believe they have little or no control over their own lives generally have the most psychological problems. However, the "dose response" for greater levels of perceived control depends on a number of factors, including the specific type of distress. Low levels of perceived control correlate more strongly with depression than with anxiety and anger. Apparently that difference results from the attentive and active problem-solving characteristic of individuals with a greater sense of control. Individuals with a higher sense of control try to figure out the causes of their problems and take action to solve them (Ross and Mirowsky 1989). Individuals who see themselves as powerless try to ignore problems and just hope they will go away. The habitually attentive and active approach combats the hopelessness and lethargy characteristic of depression. However, it can temporarily raise anxieties, and also produce frustrations and conflicts when others seem unhelpful or refractory. Some individuals try to exert control well beyond the level most comfortable given their achieved and ascribed social statuses, as detailed in a later section. These trade-offs can limit the decrease in distress associated with an increment in sense of control. Even so, individuals who feel little or no control over their own lives feel the most anxious, as well as the most depressed. They also suffer much fear, anger, and mistrust.

The correlation of distress with a low sense of control mostly reflects the demoralizing impact of being powerless to direct one's own life. However, some of the correlation may reflect the corrosive effects of prolonged depression on the sense of control. Turner and Noh (1983) found a small but statistically significant effect of earlier depression on subsequent change in personal control (beta = −.11) in addition to the larger effect of earlier personal control on subsequent change in depression (beta = −.26). Depression may somewhat reduce the sense of control, but the lag time required for the effect appears to be much longer and the feedback only boosts the association between personal control and depression by a very small amount (Golin, Sweeney, and Schaeffer, 1981; Kohn and Schooler, 1982). Even small feedback loops between personal control and distress can amplify the effect of social disadvantages on distress over the lifetime. On the whole, though, the low sense of control creates the depression, rather than the other way around. Follow-up studies find that both higher initial sense of control and increases in the sense of control predict greater decreases in depression over time (Kohn and Schooler 1982; Pearlin et al. 1981).

Low Sense of Control Linking Disadvantaged Status to Distress.

A low sense of control over one's own life creates the primary link between psychological distress and disadvantaged social statuses such as low education, low income, economic hardship, unstable employment, and poorly paid, tedious, and oppressive jobs (Ross and Mirowsky 1989; Ross and Van Willigen 1997; Turner and Lloyd 1999). Perceived powerlessness over one's own life accounts for almost all of the distress associated with low socioeconomic position. Higher status individuals also tend to have greater social support, largely because education improves social skills and freedom from economic hardship reduces strains on partnerships. Greater social support also improves the emotional well-being associated with higher status. Mostly, though, the emotional benefits of higher socioeconomic status come from the increased sense of control over one's own life. The observed patterns imply that if low-status individuals did not feel relatively powerless over their own lives, they would not be substantially more distressed than others of higher status.

Contingent and Moderating Effects

Clearly, high distress goes with a low sense of control. Having established that generality, researchers next looked for specific contingencies that might determine the strength of the association. In this section we summarize the ideas and observations regarding contingencies that might alter the association between distress and the sense of control over one's own life. Theory and research address six main questions:

—Is a sense of responsibility for the bad outcomes in one's life as comforting as a sense of responsibility for the good ones?

—If individuals feel powerless, does it make them feel better or worse to think that most others are powerless too?

—Does it make any difference whether fatalistic individuals ascribe control over their lives to chance, powerful others, or God?

—Is a sense of control most important to well-being when in stressful circumstances, or is it most comforting in the absence of burdens and threats that challenge the belief itself?

—Does having someone who cares and will help in crises multiply the emotional benefits of perceived control, or does it limit the benefits because of mutual obligations?

—Is there a realistic limit to the level of perceived control that improves well-being, or can greatly unrealistic perceptions of control eliminate the emotional burden of social disadvantage?

As the following parts of this section detail, many contingencies do exist. The sense of control can have different effects on distress depending on specifics. Situations exist in which an increase in sense of control would not improve emotional well-being, and probably would make it a little worse. Even so, the lowest sense of control is always the most distressing state. There is no known situation in which it would be better to be among those with the lowest sense of control than among those with the highest.

Control over Good and Bad Outcomes.

It seems obvious that feeling responsible for the good things that happen would improve emotional well-being. Does belief in responsibility for the bad things that happen also reduce distress? Some concepts and observations suggest that it might not, at least not as much. The concept of ego defensiveness suggests that individuals protect self-esteem by accepting more credit for the good than discredit for the bad. Depressed persons often feel inadequate, ashamed, or guilty. Persons trying to avoid depression might dodge responsibility for failures and misfortunes. Indeed, Americans claim more responsibility for the good things in their own lives than for the bad (Mirowsky et al. 1996). For example, 93 percent agree that "I am responsible for my own successes" and 90 percent agree that "I can do just about anything I set my mind to." In contrast, only 83 percent agree that "I am responsible for my failures" and only 67 percent agree that "My misfortunes are the result of mistakes I have made."

While a large majority of Americans agree with most statements claiming control over their own lives, they clearly see more control over the good than over the bad. Does that tilt result from ego defensiveness? Not necessarily. Americans generally try to achieve success and avoid mistakes and failures. That makes good things more likely to seem the result of choices and efforts, and makes bad things seem less likely to result from them. The clear tilt toward claiming responsibility for good outcomes might reflect this commonsense slant to interpretations, rather than an ego-defensive one. A commonsense origin does not imply any emotional benefit from the slant. The concept of ego defense implies that slanted interpretations make individuals feel better, and thus motivate individuals to adopt a slanted view. Is that really happening? Apparently not.

We and others consistently find that greater perceived control over bad outcomes correlates with *lower* levels of depression, not higher (Bulman and Wortman 1977; Krause and Stryker 1984; Mirowsky and Ross 1990). Denying responsibility for problems, failures, and misfortunes shows no sign of protecting well-being. Furthermore, claiming responsibility for bad events and outcomes correlates just as negatively with depression as does claiming responsibility for good ones. Our 2 × 2 index allows us to test the hypothesis that both perceptions reduce depression equally. Analyses of data from our surveys consistently imply that perceived responsibility for bad outcomes and for good ones decreases depression equally (e.g., Mirowsky and Ross 1990, 1991, 1998; Mirowsky et al. 1996). We find no emotional benefit from a slant toward claiming more responsibility for good than for bad. Ego defensiveness does not work. Individuals benefit from a sense of responsibility for the bad events and outcomes, because it implies that they can correct and avoid such problems, and it motivates actions to do so. That is just as important to emotional well-being as taking credit for successes, feeling able to achieve the things you want in life, and going after them.

Personal and Universal Control.

A theory popular in psychology argues that people feel better about their own powerlessness if they regard it as systemic and universal rather than as a personal failing (Abramson, Seligman, and Teasdale 1978; Peterson and Seligman 1984). According to the "revised learned-helplessness theory," viewing helplessness as shared by all excuses individuals from a depressing sense of personal responsibility for undesirable events and outcomes. In order to test this idea, we asked a nationwide sample of American adults their beliefs about the amount of control most Americans have as well as the amount of control they themselves have. The belief that most Americans control their own lives, which we call universal control, affirms a belief in the dominant American ideology of a meritocratic system providing ample opportunity for people to succeed if they work hard, in contrast to a belief that the system is unfair and biased.

We find just the opposite of what the revised learned-helplessness theory predicts (Mirowsky et al. 1996). Believing that "in the United States, good things that happen to people are mostly just luck," "most people's problems are just bad luck," or "most people's problems are caused by others who are selfish, greedy, or mean" correlates with greater distress, adjusting for one's personal sense of control. Believing that "in the United States, most people can achieve anything they really set their minds to," "most people's problems result from their bad decisions and lack of effort," and "most people who have good things deserve them" correlates with lower distress, adjusting for one's personal sense of control. Furthermore, beliefs about personal and universal control interact in a manner opposite the way predicted by the theory. The more powerless individuals consider themselves, the more that a perception of control among Americans in general protects their emotional well-being. Thinking that everyone is as powerless as oneself makes personal powerlessness *more* depressing, not less. In fact, believing that others control their own lives reduces depression most among the Americans who see themselves as most powerless.

Belief that structural barriers and powerful others hinder achievement for other Americans does not mitigate the depressive effect of personal powerlessness. On the contrary, it exacerbates the effect. Americans who feel powerless find no comfort in the apparent powerlessness of others. Blaming fate or the system does not make people feel better, nor does blaming the successful. This underscores a generalization implied by other results too: the possibility of control in principle is better than no possibility of control at all. Theorists often speak of fatalism and resentment as the victim's refuge from blame, but fatalism and resentment provide no relief from poverty and failure. They represent a dispiriting pessimism that brings weariness rather than serenity and apprehension rather than aspiration.

Powerful Others, Chance, and God.

Individuals can attribute control of their own lives to a variety of outside forces. People can attribute the outcomes in their lives to luck, chance, family background, other people, God, and so on. All these external attributions act as logical opposites of internal control: either I control my life or control rests elsewhere. If perceived control rests elsewhere, it could be in the hands of other people, or luck and chance, or God. Studies have looked at the correlations with distress of these different external attributions.

Attributing control to powerful others or to chance correlates with higher levels of depression, as found in studies of psychiatric patients (Levenson 1973), alcoholics in treatment (Caster and Parsons 1977), clinically depressed and nondepressed subjects (Rosenbaum and Hadari 1985), and a variety of psychology samples (Benassi et al. 1988), as well as the general population (Ross 1990). Overall, the attribution of outcomes to powerful others is slightly more distressing than the attribution to chance (overall mean correlation = .38 compared to .31) (Benassi et al. 1988). Attributing one's successes to luck or connections correlates with higher distress, whereas attributing it to hard work, perseverance, and ability correlates with lower distress (Ross 1990). Believing that "trust and belief in God contribute to success," and that "God will reward those who try their best" does not correlate with distress one way or the other (ibid.). The same is true of believing that "success depends on the family you come from." Those beliefs may have no correlation with distress overall because to some individuals they imply fatalistic beliefs but to others they describe the source of the abilities that allow personal control of achievement.

Attributing control to powerful others or luck is distressing. Of the two, perceived control by powerful others has the worst impact. Feeling dependent on connections for good outcomes or at the mercy of selfish and exploitative powers generates the greatest distress. Even so, attributing outcomes to luck and chance provides no comfort. Those attributions imply a world that is unpredictable, uncertain, random, and unmanageable. The belief that anything could happen at any time implies a distressing helplessness.

Moderating the Effects of Problems.

A sense of control can make undesirable events and situations less demoralizing. In all situations, a sense of powerlessness increases the level of depression and anxiety, as well as increasing other types of problems such as mistrust, paranoia, and even hallucination and delusion. However, a sense of control provides its greatest emotional benefit in adversity, by making the hardship less depressing. Wheaton (1983) examined whether perceptions of control lessen the impact of acute and chronic stressors. Acute stressors are the undesirable life events discussed in Chapter 6, such as divorce and job loss. Chronic stressors include barriers to the achievement of one's goals, stagnation in the improvement of one's condition, inadequate rewards relative to one's effort or qualifications, too much or too little demand in the environment compared to the capacity of the individual, frustration of role expectations, and the absence of necessary resources. Wheaton looked at three psychological consequences of acute and chronic stressors: depression, anxiety, and schizophrenia-like hallucinations and delusions. He found that a sense of control reduces or eliminates the impact of acute and chronic stressors on depression and schizophrenia, but does not modify the impact of stressors on anxiety. Stated another way, a general sense of powerlessness is a necessary condition for a depressed or schizophrenic response to stressful events and situations, but it is not necessary for an anxious response.

The interaction between the sense of control and the presence of stressful events or conditions illustrates two important phenomena. In particular, differences in the sense of control help create what we call structural amplification. Individuals who feel in control of their own lives tend to avoid stressful events and situations, get out of them faster, and suffer less depression as a consequence of being in them. In contrast, those who feel powerless and fatalistic fail to avoid stressful events and conditions, stay in them longer, and suffer greater depression as a consequence of being in them. Furthermore, the structural disadvantages and personal histories that create and reinforces fatalism and a sense of powerlessness also predispose individuals to undesirable events and situations. These forces combine to push individuals in different directions. Some move toward ever better situations, fewer problems, greater confidence, and more active and effective responses. Others move in the opposite direction. The section of Chapter 8 on mistrust illustrates the principle of structural amplification in detail.

The different effects of perceived control on depressed and anxious responses to problems point to a second important phenomenon. Anxiety seems to be a normal and somewhat functional response to threats. Too much anxiety can overwhelm a person, provoking a wave of depression, but too little suggests a failure to attend to the problems. A greater sense of control makes individuals feel less anxious in all situations, but it does not suppress the *increase* in anxiety when something threatening happens. For example, getting laid off increases anxiety by about the same amount regardless of control beliefs. The level of perceived control correlates with the amount of anxiety before and after layoffs, but not with the amount of *increase* in anxiety. The layoff creates as much new worry for those who feel in control of their lives as for those who feel powerless. In contrast, the layoff creates much more new depression for those who feel powerless than for those who feel in control. The threatening event generates new anxieties in everyone, but depresses mostly those who feel helpless. This illustrates once again the importance of problem-focused action. Anxiety can reinforce such action. Depression's lethargy and distraction work against it. The orientation toward practical action associated with a greater sense of control suppresses the increment in depression associated with adverse events and situations, but not the increment in anxiety. Overall, a greater sense of control lowers anxiety because it helps individuals avoid those situations, and also makes individuals more confident in all situations. It lowers depression for those reasons too, but also because it makes adverse events and situations less demoralizing.

Support and Control: Mutually Limiting Resources.

Social support is the individual's perception of having others who care and will help if needed. A later section of this chapter details the generally beneficial effect of social support on distress. However, social support grows out of networks of reciprocity. Pairs of individuals have long-standing or strong ties based on emotional bonds or traditional relationships. Those ties imply mutual obligations that reassure the individuals and thereby help reduce anxiety and depression. The reciprocity implies obligations as well as benefits. That raises a question. Do social support and the sense of control enhance each other's effects on distress, or do they interfere with each other? We analyzed three views of the relationship between control and support as sources of well-being: *displacement, facilitation,* and *functional substitution* (Ross and Mirowsky 1989).

According to the *displacement hypothesis,* social support detracts from control and displaces active problem solving. In this view, social support implies a network of reciprocity and mutual obligation that limits instrumental action and fosters dependence. People who solve their own problems have a greater sense of control and self-esteem and are more effective in solving problems than those who turn to others (Brown and Harris 1978). Pearlin and Schooler (1978) consider turning to others as the opposite of self-reliance, and they find that those who rely on themselves to solve their own problems have lower levels of distress than those who turn to others.

According to the *facilitation hypothesis,* social support facilitates problem-solving and instrumental action. The importance of support is not that one leans on others in times of trouble, but that perceptions of support give people the courage to act. This perspective would account for the finding that distress is reduced by the perception of available support if needed (perceived support), but not by the actual receipt of support (received support) (Wethington and Kessler 1986).

According to the *functional substitution hypothesis,* support and control can substitute for one another to reduce depression. They are alternative means of reducing perceived threat. Control provides confidence in one's ability; support provides confidence in one's worth. Each reduces distress, and each reduces the effect of otherwise stressful conditions (Turner and Noh 1983). Thus, control is most beneficial—reduces distress the most—

when support is low. Similarly, support is most beneficial when control is low. One resource fills the breach if the other is absent.

Our analyses support the idea of functional substitution. We find that a stronger sense of personal control improves emotional well-being the most when social support is low (Ross and Mirowsky 1989). Likewise, greater social support improves emotional well-being most when the sense of personal control is low. This is the opposite of what the facilitation hypothesis argues, because each belief diminishes the beneficial effect of the other rather than magnifying it. Control and support provide alternative ways to hold down distress, but a strong reliance on one reduces the need for and benefit from the other.

We do not find that social support displaces the sense of control. Individuals with good social support also tend to have a strong sense of control. Also, social support does not interfere with active problem solving. Control and support provide alternative ways to deal with threat. A person who feels very much in control of his or her life does not depend so strongly on supportive relationships with others to maintain emotional well-being. Control and support can substitute for one another, with one filling the gap if the other is absent.

The functional substitution of social support for personal control may explain some apparent differences between cultures in their relative emphasis on family and friendship ties versus individual achievement. When the infrastructure and economy furnish inadequate personal resources for consistently meeting needs, individuals must rely more on networks of mutual support. Societies differ in their levels of wealth and human capital, and so do social strata and individuals within a society. The wealthier and more capable societies, strata and individuals may have the luxury of developing personal control to a higher level, making social support less necessary to well-being. All of this makes it seem that wealth and ability might increase the sense of control and decrease social support, but it does not work that way. Wealth and ability increase both personal control and social support. They provide more of both resources, reducing the dependence on each one because the other is available too. The poor, powerless, and uneducated depend more on social support to maintain well-being. That does not mean they have more social support, just that they lack the alternative of a greater sense of personal control. If this is true, then it implies that the emotional benefits of a greater sense of control over one's own life are limited by the real means of achievement and control available. That is indeed the case, as detailed next.

The Tradeoff between Optimism and Realism.

Is there such a thing as too much perceived control? When social and behavioral scientists began thinking about the relationship between distress and the sense of control, they figured there must be some realistic limit (Mirowsky and Ross 1990). Most erroneously assumed that fatalism comforts those with few resources or opportunities. Sociologists began taking nationwide U.S. attitude surveys around the end of the Great Depression and the period of World War II. Those early studies consistently found that low-status respondents placed less emphasis on college as essential to advancement, preferred a secure job with low income over an insecure one with high income, and were less likely to believe that hard work could get them a promotion or that the quality, energy, and willingness of one's work are important for advancement. Sociologists of that time saw this as a self-imposed barrier to improvement.

Why would low-status persons hobble themselves with counterproductive fatalism? Social theorists argued that a belief in luck rather than effort and ability helped low-status individuals preserve their self-esteem in the face of failure, but discouraged sustained endeavor. Anthropologists saw the impact of fatalism versus instrumental activism as culturally relative: each is one element in a mutually sustaining set of beliefs and ways that allows a cultural group to survive, and each is genuinely desirable in a culture that presupposes its truth and undesirable in a culture that does not. Political scientists promoting democracy and economic development saw fatalism as a self-defeating belief that sustains and regenerates the conditions under which it seems realistic and comforting.

All of the early views assumed that fatalism reduces the distress of individuals with inadequate resources and few opportunities for real control over their own lives. That turned out to be false. Oddly, it took almost four decades for anyone to directly test the hypothesized emotional benefits of fatalism for low-status persons. Theorists and researchers adopted the idea without direct evidence because it seemed to explain the prevalence of fatalism among low-status individuals and in undeveloped societies. When several studies in the 1980s looked for the hypothetical emotional benefits, they found none (Kluegel and Smith 1986; Turner and Noh 1983; Mirowsky and Ross 1984, 1990). Fatalism and powerlessness increase distress among the lowest-status segments of the U.S. population, and they increase distress as much in Juarez, Mexico, where they are common, as in El Paso, Texas, where they are unusual. Although the samples and analyses differ, none finds a subgroup in which a low sense of control reduces depression or anxiety.

The failure to find any emotional benefits of fatalism and low sense of control among the objectively disadvantaged turned the issues on end. If low-status individuals would feel better adopting a greater sense of control, then why don't they? A number of psychologists endorse the idea that illusory control is an essential psychological defense. For example, Martin, Abramson, and Alloy (1984) portray the sense of personal control as an emotionally healthy delusion that lets individuals see themselves with a rosy glow. Some scientists consider illusory control a social problem—an ideological narcotic with insidious social consequences (e.g., Kluegel and Smith 1986). Others consider it a personal cure—an antidote to the existential terrors of life (e.g., Martin et al. 1984). Either way, why don't the most disadvantaged individuals soothe their anxieties and fire their wills with the most extreme belief in control over their own lives? The answer: an inherent tension exists between the need for realistic appraisal and the need for psychological defense.

Wheaton (1985) argued that effective action requires realistic appraisal *and* motivation to act. Motivation to act requires a sense of control over outcomes. The dilemma of low status is that realistic appraisal suggests that little can be done. Everyone is motivated to maintain a firm sense of control over personal outcomes. The assault of reality undermines the effort for those with low status, little wealth, and few resources or opportunities. If this is true, there may be diminishing incremental effects of larger and larger "doses" of illusory control, and a threshold beyond which increasing doses are more damaging than soothing. Diminishing returns and a threshold of dysfunction are particularly likely if effective action, rather than self-delusion, is the key to emotional well-being. If so, then the need for realistic appraisal limits, and at some point cancels, the value of greater optimism.

Diminishing returns and the optimum sense of control.   Is there such a thing as too much perceived control? The speculation began with Julian Rotter, the psychologist who developed the concept of "internal versus external locus-of-control." In introducing his classic locus-of-control index, Rotter (1966:84) briefly mentioned that "individuals at both extremes of the internal versus external control of reinforcement dimension are essentially unrealistic." Herbert Lefcourt subsequently elaborated:

> To maintain external control expectancies when opportunities are available to act in one's behest seems a tragic waste. . . . Equally inappropriate is the maintenance of internal control expectancies in a non-responsive or malevolent milieu. . . . In less extreme cases, such as work settings, homes, and marriages, there are many instances where given outcomes are simply not within one's sphere of competence. . . . A mistaken self-reliance when one's actual skills are limited could be as self-defeating as would be the helpless retreat of persons when opportunities for control are available. (Lefcourt 1976:252)

Suppose that the emotional benefits of a sense of control result largely from effective action (Wheaton 1985). Effectiveness requires a combination of motivation and realistic appraisal. A greater sense of control implies greater motivation, but an excessive sense of control implies an unrealistic self-appraisal. The higher one's sense of control, the more unrealistic an increase probably would be. As a result, the higher one's sense of control, the less emotional benefit from an increase. A threshold exists at the point where the problems caused by greater self-delusion cancel the benefits from greater motivation. That threshold defines the optimum sense of control. It represents the best tradeoff between the emotional gain from greater optimism and the emotional cost of less realism.

Wheaton (1985) found direct support for this idea of an optimum sense of control. Individuals with the lowest sense of control have the highest distress. As the level of perceived control increases, the average level of distress goes down, but only up to a point. The optimum sense of control, associated with the minimum distress, occurs when perceived control is around the 80th percentile. Beyond that point, the level of depression increases at higher levels of perceived control. Wheaton used data collected in El Paso and Juarez in 1975. We have confirmed the finding in all four of our surveys. Figure 7.8 shows the predicted mean depression by level of perceived control in the four samples combined.

The graph of the relationship between depression and the sense of control illustrates several important facts. First, differences in the sense of control have their biggest effect at the low end, below the mean and especially below the neutral point where fatalistic beliefs outweigh instrumental ones. Second, the optimum sense of control is well above the average. Wheaton's original analysis of 1975 data from El Paso and Juarez put the optimum around the 80th percentile. Our 1985 data from Illinois also showed an optimum around the 80th percentile. Our samples from Illinois and the United States in the 1990s put it higher, around the 95th percentile. This suggests that the large majority of Americans would feel depressed less often if they had a higher sense of control. The difference in depression between the mean and the optimum sense of control looks small compared to the bigger differences below the mean. Even so, it adds up to a lot of days of depression given the number of people who might benefit from a higher sense of control. Although it is not apparent from the graph, our statistical tests show that the optimum sense of control is significantly greater than the mean. They also show it is significantly lower than the maximum possible score on our index (2). When the sense of control goes beyond the optimum, the expected prevalence of depression goes up only a little bit, but it definitely goes up.

Status and the optimum sense of control. Wheaton's optimum describes a fixed threshold balancing the emotional benefits of greater optimism against the emotional costs of unrealistic self-assessment. Taken at face value, it implies that high-status persons are closer to the optimum

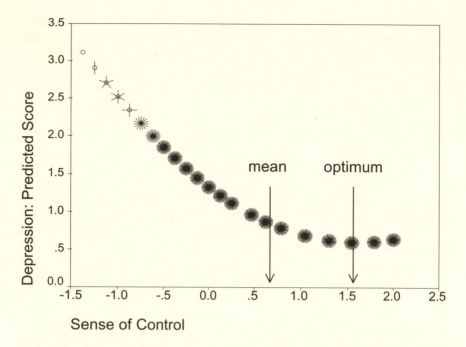

Figure 7.8. Depression predicted from sense of control, illustrating diminishing incremental effects and the optimum sense of control. Each circle or line through a circle represents one person. Data are combined from 1985 and 1995 Illinois surveys and 1990 and 1995 U.S. surveys, with a total of 7,905 persons.

because they have a higher sense of control, whereas low-status persons are further from the optimum because they have a low sense of control. It also implies that people of low status benefit from illusions of control up to the level of the optimum. These implications seem contrary to the basic theory behind the model, which emphasizes the constraints of realism. If the optimum is the point where the consequences of unrealistic self-assessment cancel the marginal benefits of increased motivation, then the optimum should increase with status.

We find that the optimum sense of control differs considerably depending on a person's socioeconomic status, as measured by things such as minority status, education, and household income (Mirowsky and Ross 1990). The higher the status, the higher the optimum sense of control. The optimum sense of control stays about .25 units (or roughly half a standard deviation) ahead of the sense of control predicted based on status. Because of the large status differences that exist, this adds up to a difference of .75 units (1.5 standard deviations) or more between the optimum sense of control at the bottom and top of the socioeconomic ladder. That represents a wide spread in the sense of control that minimizes depression. In addition, the prevalence of depression expected for persons with the optimum sense of control decreases as status increases. In other words, having an optimum sense of control reduces distress more the higher one's status. At their respective optimums, high-status persons have about half the prevalence of depression as low-status persons.

Our results are consistent with the idea that a low sense of control is more common in low-status groups because it is more realistic. The optimum sense of control increases with status. However, low-status people are not consoled by a low sense of control. A large majority of them would benefit psychologically from a higher sense of control, presumably because it would make them more effective within the constraints of their situations. The distress caused by low status can be reduced by a sense of control greater than average given one's status. However, the motivational benefits of optimism are limited at some point by the need for realistic appraisal. Even so, most Americans would benefit from erring on the optimistic side.

Our results have practical implications. The most important is that encouraging low-status persons to excuse themselves of responsibility for their situations is unlikely to help them feel better. Most people at all status levels would benefit from a greater sense of control over outcomes, whether the outcomes in their lives have been unusually good or unusually bad. Fatalism and a sense of powerlessness are the recognition of a painful reality, and in no way sooth its discomforts.

Support and the optimum sense of control. An earlier section noted the interaction between social support and a sense of control in their relationships to distress. Social support and the sense of control act as functional substitutes for each other. The more you have of one, the less important getting more of the other becomes. Although it may not be obvious, that interaction has an important implication. The higher one's social support, the lower the optimum sense of control. Apparently the opposite also holds. There is an optimum level of social support that decreases as the sense of control gets higher. Although our research on the linked optima remains preliminary, the results so far suggest two things. First, there seems to be an optimum combination of control and support. People can have too little of both, but the more you have of one the less of the other is best. At some point, the bonds of affection and mutual obligation may conflict with autonomy and self-development. Second, in the context of American society, optimizing control seems more effective at lowering distress than optimizing support. If this finding proves robust, it might be distinctive of countries such as the United States with democratic governments, high levels of education, income, and wealth, and cultures of individualism. Or it may be true everywhere. Theorists often speak of fatalism and strong family ties as a beneficial combination. That may only *seem* true when opportunity and resources are scarce. Even then, our results imply that most persons would benefit from claiming more control over their own lives. What appears to be a cultural difference in orientation toward family might be little more than making the best of a poor situation.

Perceived Control as Link Between Conditions and Emotions

Looking broadly at the ideas and findings, we see that instrumentalism and a sense of mastery are associated with achievement, status, education, employment, income, and work that is complex, variable, and unsupervised, whereas fatalism and a sense of powerlessness are associated with failure, stagnation, dependence, poverty, disadvantage, economic strain, poor health and physical impairment, heavy family demands, work overload, and work that is simple, routine, and closely supervised. People in higher socioeconomic positions tend to have a sense of personal control and people in lower socioeconomic positions a sense of personal powerlessness. This produces the socioeconomic differences in distress. The sense of powerlessness can be depressing and demoralizing in itself, but worse than that it can undermine the will to seek and take effective action. As a result, people in lower socioeconomic positions have a triple burden: First, they have more problems to deal with. Second, their personal histories are likely to have left them with a deep sense of powerlessness. Third, that sense of powerlessness discourages them from marshalling whatever energy and resources they do have in order to solve their problems. The result for many is a multiplication of despair.

COMMITMENT

It is impossible to find an English word that is an unambiguous label for the second concept of alienation. We have chosen to refer to the absence of this form of alienation as commitment, but words such as freedom, self-expression, involvement, identification, and pride each tap a part of the concept.

Self-Estrangement and Alienated Labor

The issue of commitment is probably best known from Marx's discussion of "alienated labor." Marx was concerned about the impact of wage labor and factories on the quality of life. He argued that in working for someone else the laborer belongs to another person and not to himself. The work is a means of satisfying other needs rather than providing satisfaction in itself; external rather than part of his or her nature; imposed rather than voluntary. Workers deny themselves in work rather than fulfill themselves. Marx argued that alienated labor makes the worker physically exhausted and mentally debased rather than developing his or her mental and physical energies. Thus, alienated labor produces a sense of misery rather than well-being (Kohn 1976). The set of ideas and orientations thought to result from alienated labor is called "self-estrangement" (Seeman 1959). Alienated labor is the condition in which the worker does not decide what to produce, does not design the production process, and does not own the product. Self-estrangement is the sense of being separate from that part of one's thoughts, actions, and experiences given over to the control of others; of work being foreign to oneself rather than an expression of oneself (Mirowsky and Ross 1983). Work is seen as drudgery. It has no intrinsic value. There is no pride in it. Any rewards lie outside the activity itself. At best one is compensated and at worst one is forced by circumstances to submit.

Although the idea of self-estrangement is quite clear, measures of it are often ambiguous or mixed with indicators of other concepts. Some researchers ask people if they are satisfied or dissatisfied with their work, and interpret the response as an indication of self-estrangement. However, many workers may think of satisfaction as a question of adequate compensation and good relations with coworkers and the boss. A worker could claim to be completely satisfied and yet find the idea of intrinsic gratification from work utterly incomprehensible and a contradiction in terms. To many, work seems to be, by definition, that which you would not do if no one were paying you to do it. To the alienated worker, pay is the only reason for working. To the committed worker, on the other hand, pay makes it possible to work and, beyond that, signifies recognition of the quality and value of one's work. Thus, measures of self-estrangement often include statements about intrinsic gratification and the meaning of pay at their core: "I can put up with a lot on my job as long as the pay is good" (Pearlin and Schooler 1978:21); "I find it difficult to imagine enthusiasm for my work," or "I find it hard to believe people who actually feel that the work they perform is of value to society" (Kobassa, Maddi, and Courington 1981:372). Our discussion of self-estrangement suggests several other items it might be useful to include in indexes: "I feel lucky because I get paid to do work I like to do anyway," "My job is like a hobby to me," "My job gives me a chance to do things I enjoy doing," "Work is a grind," "If it weren't for the pay, I'd never do the things I do at work."

The little existing research on occupational self-estrangement shows it is more common among workers who are older, have lower incomes, are less educated, and come from lower-status backgrounds (Schooler 1972; Pearlin and Schooler 1978). One study finds it is correlated with a sense of external control and powerlessness, and with a focus on the goals of security and freedom from want (Kobassa et al. 1981). We asked respondents how much they agreed with the statement, "My work gives me a chance to do things I enjoy." We found that enjoyable work was associated with low levels of perceived powerlessness (Ross and Wright 1998), and low levels of distress (Ross and Drentea 1998). On the other hand, some studies find no association between engaging, interesting, and challenging work and perceived powerlessness among mill workers (Greenberg and Grunberg 1995) or among a representative sample of employed white men (Seeman et al. 1988). Commitment to work may reduce perceived powerlessness and distress, but the evidence is equivocal. Furthermore, studies have not addressed the issue of whether self-estrangement is the mental link between the objective working conditions and distress. Overall, there are few studies that look at whether self-estrangement increases distress or explains the association of alienated labor with distress.

Voluntary Participation in Community Activities

Commitment is an issue in the wider social arena as well as in the workplace. Many people are deeply involved in churches, political parties, civic or charitable organizations, clubs, and hobbies. Because participation in these activities is voluntary and without pay, it is self-expressive rather than self-estranged. Mutran and Reitzes (1984) studied the social patterns and consequences of participation in voluntary organizations and cultural activities among persons sixty-five years old and over. They find that the amount of time spent in clubs, volunteer groups, political activities, or hobbies and the frequency of attendance at movies, museums, concerts, and sports increase with education and income and decrease with age and poor health. These community activities are, in turn, associated with greater feelings of being excited or interested in something, a greater sense of pride and pleasure in having accomplished something, and a feeling of being on top of the world with things going your way. Community activities are also associated with feeling less upset, lonely, bored, and depressed among the elderly, controlling for family social support. Using over-time data on adult heads of households in rural Illinois, Wheaton (1980) finds that the number of voluntary organizational memberships is increased by socioeconomic status and by the number of major changes in one's life in preceding years, and it is decreased by fatalism and by the sense that one's income, present job, and job opportunities are barriers to achievement. The number of memberships in voluntary organizations is negatively correlated with psychological and psychophysiological distress. However, when fatalism is controlled there is no significant association between the number of memberships and the level of distress. This could be because instrumental individuals join voluntary organizations more than do fatalistic ones, or that voluntary group participation increases a sense of instrumentalism and control, which in turn reduces distress. Rietschlin (1998) found that voluntary group association memberships decreased distress and that some, but not most of the association, was due to mastery and social support. Van Willigen (1996) found that participation in voluntary organizations increased the sense of personal control and social support, thereby decreasing depression.

SUPPORT

In all forms of alienation the individuals feel detached from themselves or society in some way. Powerlessness is a sense of detachment from effective influence over one's life, and self-estrangement is a sense of detachment from productive activities. Powerlessness and self-estrangement have to do with the individual's sense of place in the larger social order—the system of stratification, achievement, work, and production. A third type of alienation has to do with the individual's sense of detachment in the microsocial order of personal relationships. Social isolation is the sense of not having anyone who is someone to you and not being someone to anyone. The opposite of isolation is commonly called social support, which is the sense of being cared for and loved, esteemed and valued as a person, and part of a network of communication and obligation (Kaplan, Robbins, and Martin 1983). This concept of isolation and support differs radically from the classic definition of isolation as the individual's tendency to, "assign low reward value to goals or beliefs that are typically highly valued in the given society" (Seeman 1959:789), which is sometimes called "cultural estrangement" to distinguish it from social isolation of the sort discussed here. Although Seeman (ibid.) originally excluded "the warmth, security, or intensity of an individual's social contacts" from his definition of isolation, it is precisely this meaning that has greatest currency today, and that is most important in research on the social patterns of distress (Seeman 1983).

Social Embeddedness: Benefits and Costs

Studies of the relationship between distress and support fall into two categories: Those looking at objective social conditions indicative of more or less isolation, and those looking at the individual's sense of having fulfilling personal relationships. Those of the first type are actually studies of social integration rather than of social support. Presumably the structural density of a person's network, the number of relationships, the frequency of contact, and the number and types of social roles a person performs increase the probability of having fulfilling personal relationships, but they don't guarantee it. For example, marital status is generally considered an important indicator of social integration. As we noted earlier, studies consistently find that married persons are less distressed than people who are divorced, separated, widowed, or have never been married. It is an empirical question whether married persons have a greater sense of social support that accounts for their lower distress. Unmarried persons can have supportive relationships with their parents, children, other relatives, and friends. On the other side, marriage is no guarantee of a supportive relationship, and many married persons report a lack of reciprocity, affection, and communication that is strongly associated with distress (Pearlin 1975; Gove et al. 1983). On the whole, though, compared to those who are not married, married persons have higher levels of emotional support—a sense of being cared about, loved, esteemed, and valued as a person. They are more likely to report that they have someone they can turn to for support and understanding when things get rough, and that they have someone they can really talk to (Ross 1995).

Social integration has benefits and costs. The main benefit of social integration likely is that it increases the potential for supportive relationships. The costs of integration likely include constraints on freedom and autonomy, burdensome obligations, and dependency. The fact that integration has costs and benefits may account for the fact that the findings on integration and distress are mixed: some find positive effects on psychological well-being of network size or frequency of contact, while others find no effect (Lin, Ye, and Ensel 1999). Furthermore, the balance of costs and benefits probably depends on the nature of the social integration. Integration is a purely structural measure, like the number of friends or frequency of contact. Who it is you are connected to may determine the balance of benefits and costs. In some types of integration, like having a marriage partner, the benefits probably usually outweigh the costs; but other types of integration, like frequent contact with extended family members with health or money problems, the costs may outweigh the benefits.

Williams et al. (1981) found that increases in psychological well-being over time are associated with an index of social integration that includes contact with neighbors, friends, and relatives, as well as participation in religious and social groups. However, it was not clear whether integration into personal networks or participation in community groups was the active factor, or both.

Hughes and Gove (1981) looked at the impact of living alone on distress. They note that, according to theory, the density of social interaction strengthens common sentiments and fortifies social regulation and constraint. It is assumed that those who live alone typically experience less social interaction. Hours spent sleeping, cleaning house, preparing and eating meals, watching television, etc., are less likely to be spent with others. Relationships are less likely to build to the same level of closeness and intensity, and are less likely to be characterized by primary mutual obligations and mutual reinforcement. The person who lives alone is presumably isolated from a network of social and economic ties—the privileges, duties, and obligations centered on the dwelling place and typically associated with family. Counter to theoretical expectation, Hughes and Gove find that within categories of marital status (never married, separated or divorced, widowed) there is no difference in distress between those who live alone and those who live with relatives or friends. The difference in distress is between married persons and everyone else rather than between those who live alone and everyone else. Hughes and Gove speculate that social integration may involve a psychological tradeoff: "Just as persons may gain substantial satisfaction and personal gratification from family relations, they may also suffer frustration, aggravation, hostility, and repressed anger from being constrained to conform to the obligations necessary to meet socially legitimated demands of others in the household" (1981:71). This speculation is given credence by the results of other studies. In an analysis of data from the nationwide Health and Nutrition Examination survey, Eaton and Kessler (1981) find that depression is lower in two-person households than in households with only one person or with three or more persons (adjusting for marital status, age, sex, education, income, employment, race, and urban versus rural residence). This suggests that the tradeoff between social support and social demands is typically optimized in two-person households.

We find costs and benefits of social integration in Mexican culture, which emphasizes the mutual obligations of family and friends. Responsibility to the group places constraints on the individual, who must take into account the expectations, desires, and well-being of family and friends. These constraints produce a sense of not being in control of one's own destiny, which increases depression. However, the group is also responsible to the individual, which decreases anxiety (Mirowsky and Ross 1984). We also find that marriage has costs and benefits for women's sense of personal control. Marriage increases personal control by way of high household income but decreases it in other ways. Compared to being single, married women may face more constraints on their independence and autonomy (Ross 1995).

Integration into personal networks may have costs in terms of burdensome obligations as well (Rook 1984). Mutran and Reitzes (1984) find that among widowed persons sixty-five years old and over, receiving financial help, personal services, and practical advice from relatives is associated with lower distress, but giving similar forms of help to relatives is associated with greater distress. Belle (1982) found that getting help with child care from neighbors was a strategy of desperation among poor mothers, not choice; and Goldsteen and Ross (1989) found that mothers who got help with child care from friends and neighbors had specific obligations to provide care in return, while mothers who got help from relatives had diffuse obligations to family members that impinged on their ability to be by themselves when they wanted to.

Dependency may be another cost. Turner and Turner (1999) measure the potential psychological costs of reliance on interpersonal relationships. Reliance on others is measured by questions such as "I would feel completely lost if I did not have someone special" and "I would feel hopeless if I were deserted by someone I love." Women are much more reliant on others than are men, reliance on others increases depression, and this reliance explains some, but not much, of the fact that women have higher depression levels than men. Dependence on others may be the opposite of dependence on oneself—feeling responsible and in control of one's own destiny—and be distressing for that reason.

Links between Social Integration and Social Support

The benefits of social integration lie in the potential for supportive relationships, yet few studies look at whether integration is positively associated with support. Lin et al. (1999) are an exception. They explicitly examine the links between social integration and social support. They measure three types of integration: participation in community organizations, like church groups, civic and political organizations, and recreational groups; integration in social networks, measured as the frequency of contacts with friends, family, neighbors and so on; and the presence of a spouse or partner. These measure social integration at three levels of closeness—community, friends, and intimate partner. All three types of integration reduce depression. Next they ask, "Does perceived or actual social support reduce depression and mediate the effects of integration on depression?" Perceived emotional support is the only type of social support that significantly reduces depression. People who say that they have someone to talk to, someone who makes them feel good, loved, and cared for report lower levels of depression. Perceived emotional support is more important than instrumental support—the perception of having someone who would lend you money, give you a ride, watch your house, or help you out with cooking if you needed it. The actual receipt of emotional or instrumental support has no beneficial effect on psychological well-being. Finally, perceived emotional support mediates some of the impact of social integration on depression. People who belong to community organizations, have contacts with friends and family, and are married have low levels of depression in part because integration increases the perceived availability of social support.

Emotional Support

Embeddedness in a social network indicates the availability of social support, but it does not guarantee it. Pearlin et al. (1981) argue that support in times of trouble is not automatic simply because one has family, friends, and associates. "Support comes when people's engagement with one another extends to a level of involvement and concern, not when they merely touch at the surface of each other's lives. . . . The qualities that seem to be especially critical involve the exchange of intimate communications and the presence of solidarity and trust" (ibid.:340). Social support in this sense is emotional intimacy, which Pearlin et al. measure by asking if the respondent feels his or her spouse is someone "I can really talk with about things that are important to me," and by asking if the respondent has a friend or relative (other than the spouse) he or she can tell just about anything to and count on for understanding and advice. In an over-time study of the impact on men of job disruptions such as being laid off, fired, or put on sick leave, Pearlin and his colleagues find that emotional support indirectly reduces the impact of the disruption on depression. Job disruption typically decreases the sense of self-esteem and mastery, which in turn increases depression. However, emotional support reduces the impact of job disruption on self-esteem by as much as 30 percent and it reduces the impact of job disruption on the sense of mastery by as much as 50 percent.

In a study of job stress among employed men, LaRocco et al. (1980) find that overwork, conflicting demands, uncertainty, insecurity, lack of opportunity to use your skills, abilities, and training, and having little influence on the decisions that affect you increase depression, irritation, anxiety, and malaise. However, social support from one's supervisor, coworkers, wife, family, or friends tends to reduce the psychological impact of job pressures. Similarly, Turner and Noh (1983) find that the absence of emotional support is a necessary condition for the association of low socioeconomic status with distress among women who have recently given birth. The women who feel loved, wanted, valued, and esteemed, who feel that others in their network can be counted on, and who have a sense of mastery are not more distressed in lower-status positions than in higher-status ones, but women who lack either a sense of support or a sense of mastery are much more distressed in low socioeconomic positions.

Although some studies, such as the ones described above, find support acts as a buffer that reduces the impact of potentially stressful events and situations, many others do not find an interaction between stressors and support. For example, Kaplan et al. (1983) find that undesirable events increase distress among young adults regardless of whether they feel loved and esteemed by peers and family. The presence of social support reduces distress but it does not reduce the impact of undesirable events on distress. In a review of twenty-two studies that tested the possible interaction of stressors and social support, Wheaton (1985a) reports that seven find some evidence of interaction but the other fifteen do not. However, the types of stressors investigated and the definitions and measures of social support vary considerably across studies. In four of the seven that find interactions, the evidence pertains to job-related stressors, and in two of the other three studies the central indicator of support is marital status, which is an ambiguous indicator (as we discussed above). This is not strong evidence for a general interaction between social support and stressors, but neither is it strong evidence against an interaction. In a review of twenty-three studies, Kessler and McLeod (1985) find that the largest studies with the most reliable and valid measures of social support tend to find a significant buffering effect, presumably because the power of the significance test is better. Variation in the reliability or validity of support measures, as well as variation in sample size, can produce variation in the power of the signifi-cance test associated with the interaction term. Also, as Wheaton's com-parisons suggest, we may eventually find that only specific types of support reduce the impact of specific types of stressors in specific popula-tions. Finally, Thoits (1982) makes a convincing argument that the impor-tance of social support does not rest solely on whether it reduces the effect of stressors on well-being. Love, understanding, appreciation, mutual com-mitment, and clear expectations may reduce distress in and of themselves, aside from any value they may have as protection against stressful events and situations.

There is little doubt that perceived emotional support reduces distress, but it is not clear why. People who report that they have someone they can really talk to and someone they can turn to for support and understanding when things get rough have low levels of depression, but this is not due to actually talking to others when faced with a problem (Ross and Mirowsky 1989). In fact, talking to others about problems is associated with high lev-els of depression (ibid.); and seeking advice from others is associated with high levels of distress (Pearlin and Schooler 1978). Wethington and Kessler (1986) and Lin and his colleagues (1999) find no harm in talking to others about problems, but they find it does no good psychologically, either. Hav-ing emotionally supportive relationships reduces depression, but talking to others when faced with problems does not. This could be a method-ological artifact: turning to others when one has problems is confounded with the presence of problems (with children, marriages, jobs, etc.), and it may be those problems that are associated with distress. On the other hand, it could be that turning to others with problems is the opposite of self-reliance, the sense of being in control of one's own life (Ross and Mirowsky 1989). People who solve their own problems have a greater sense of control and are more effective than those who turn to friends and family for advice (Pearlin and Schooler 1978). Perhaps emotional support reduces distress simply by providing a sense of security and confidence in one's worth as a person, and thus functions as a general means of reducing perceived threat (Ross and Mirowsky 1989).

MEANING

In addition to a sense of control, commitment, and support, people may also require a sense of meaning in their lives. An unintelligible world can be disturbing for a number of reasons. Clearly, a world that cannot be understood also cannot be controlled (or, more precisely, a sense of mastery implies a sense of understanding how things work). If a person cannot choose among conflicting explanations or cannot predict with confidence the results of acting on a given belief, then the person cannot logically expect to act effectively unless it is by sheer luck or instinct. Thus, a sense of meaninglessness implies a sense of powerlessness, which increases distress. However, the importance of meaninglessness may go beyond its implications for the sense of control. People may require a sense of purpose in their lives—of knowing where they want to go as well as believing they know how to get there. Furthermore, people may require a sense of the inherent significance and value of their existence. This is what Thoits (1983) speaks of as "existential security." It is the self-assurance of believing that you know what is, that you know what is right, and that your life is a valid expression.

Although the concept of meaninglessness has a prominent place in some explanations of the social patterns of distress, this prominence is based on a respect for the thoughts of Durkheim and Mead, and on the convenience of meaninglessness as an interpretive concept, rather than on empirical validation.

Early studies simply counted up roles, or "identities," arguing that the more identities one has, the greater one's sense of meaningful existence (Thoits 1983). From a symbolic interaction perspective, Thoits argued that a normal personality and appropriate social conduct develop when the individual recognizes and adopts the roles associated with his or her social position. According to Thoits' identity-accumulation hypothesis, "Role requirements give purpose, meaning, direction, and guidance to one's life. The greater the number of identities held, the stronger one's sense of meaningful, guided existence. The more identities, the more 'existential security,' so to speak" (ibid.:175). Stated the other way, the fewer one's social roles the greater one's quandary and, thus, the greater one's distress. To test this hypothesis, Thoits counted the respondent's number of identities, adding one point if the person is married, has children, is employed, is in school, attends organizational meetings, attends church services, visits neighbors, and has two or more friends. In an over-time analysis she finds that the initial number of identities and increases in the number of identities are both associated with lower distress. She also finds an inter-action between the initial state and changes over time: The more identities lost the less good it does to have had them; the more identities gained the less damage it does not to have had them. This implies that one's present situation tends to abolish the impact of one's past situation. Thoits also finds some evidence of an equilibrating or floor-and-ceiling effect: the greater the initial number of identities the more one tends to lose identities over time, and the lower the initial number of identities the more one tends to gain identities over time. The results seemed to provide circumstantial support for the identity-accumulation hypothesis, but later conceptual and empirical critiques weakened this support.

First, the role accumulation hypothesis made the untenable claim that all roles are good for mental health, and second, it had a questionable opera-tionalization of "roles." Why is being employed counted as a role identity, whereas being a homemaker or a retired person is not? When roles were counted up, employed people received a score of one role and the nonem-ployed (like homemakers and the retired) received a score of zero, as if the statuses of homemaker or retired person implied the lack of a role. Being married was counted as a role, but being widowed or divorced was not. It is not clear how decisions were made about which employment status or marital status was a role and which was not, but it looks like the roles asso-ciated with psychological well-being were counted as roles and the roles associated with psychological distress were counted as the absence of a role. This makes the findings tautological. It leads to the second critique. Not all roles are equal. Many roles are probably associated with distress, like the roles of prisoner and disabled veteran, and some roles are known to be associated with distress, like the roles of widow and homemaker. These statuses seem to imply clear roles that carry certain identities. Prob-lems with simply counting up so-called "roles" led to a further refinement of the ideas and measures.

In this refinement, respondents were asked to answer the question, "Who am I?" with a list of answers, like mother, daughter, husband, worker, and student, and were then asked to list their answers in order of the importance of each identity (Thoits 1995). Thoits argues that important roles give meaning and purpose to life. However, she found no evidence that identity-relevant roles protect mental health. Simon's work also showed that sometimes salient, or important, roles can lead to distress. She found that fathers for whom the role was very important were more dis-tressed when their children had problems than were fathers for whom the role held less importance, whereas for mothers, the importance of the role of mother had no effect on mental health in the face of children's problems (Simon 1992).

Identity may also be an issue to racial and ethnic minorities. A meaningful identity may protect mental health. Noh and his colleagues (1999) measured the strength of ethnic identity among Southeast Asian refugees in Canada with a choice of responses like "my ethnicity is of central importance for my life," "without my ethnic background, the rest of my life would not have much meaning to it," and "I make decisions on the basis of ethnic background." Noh and his colleagues found that Asian refugees who felt that they had been discriminated against had higher distress levels than those who reported no discrimination, and the negative impact was much worse for those with strong ethnic identification. Ethnic identification did not decrease depression, and in the face of discrimination it made it worse. Minority ethnic identity could indicate alienation from mainstream society—a sense of being separate and isolated from the majority of people around you.

Having a meaningful identity appears neither good nor bad for mental health. Some research indicates that in the face of negative events and conditions relevant to the identity in question, a strong identification increases distress (Noh et al. 1999; Simon 1992). Theoretically, then, under positive circumstances relevant to the identity, distress should decrease, although Thoits (1995) found no evidence for this prediction.

A few other studies took a different approach. Instead of trying to get at the importance of a role or identity, they thought that a global sense of meaning in life might mediate the impact of statuses like being employed, being married, or being a parent on distress. Only two studies we know of (described later) actually developed or used an index of meaninglessness, although one other used an index that could be getting at meaninglessness. Kobassa et al. (1981) measured "alienation from self" as the belief that trying to know yourself is a waste of time, the belief that life is empty and meaningless, and a preference for a simple life with no decisions. The index is highly correlated with a sense that most of one's activities are determined by what society demands and that it doesn't matter if people work hard because only a few bosses profit. The index is also moderately correlated with belief in external control. Measures of self-esteem often contain items that might be considered indirect measures of meaninglessness, such as feeling you are a person of worth and not feeling useless. Measures of depression also may contain items that could be interpreted as indications of a sense of meaninglessness, such as wondering if anything is worthwhile. Several things are necessary to transform the concept of meaninglessness from a plausible explanation of distress to a valid one: a definition of meaninglessness that makes clear both its essence and its distinction from other concepts such as self-esteem, depression, and powerlessness; a reliable index of beliefs that have face validity as indicators of meaninglessness and are not indicators of self-esteem, depression, etc.

(this may require purging indicators of meaninglessness from indexes measuring other concepts); tested models showing that variations in the sense of meaninglessness account for social patterns of distress.

Umberson and Gove (1989) and Burton (1998) measured meaninglessness by asking respondents the amount they agreed with the following statements:

(1) I feel my life just isn't complete.
(2) My life often seems empty.
(3) I feel as if I have nothing to live for.
(4) I don't know what to do with my life.
(5) I feel as if I'm not interested in anything.

Burton eliminated two items from the meaninglessness scale used by Umberson and Gove that appear to be confounded with depression—feeling lonely and all alone in the world. The opposite of meaninglessness is meaning. Umberson and Gove (1989) found that parents reported more meaning in their lives than nonparents although they did not examine whether meaning mediated an impact of parenthood on distress. Burton (1998) went a step further. He showed that global meaning explained some of the impact of being a married, employed, parent on psychological well-being. Family statuses, especially marriage and parenthood, increased the sense of meaning in life. Positive effects of these family statuses on psychological well-being were mediated by the sense of meaning, but employment's benefits were only explained by meaning if the employed person was also a married parent.

In the end, everyone has meaningful identities, and they may always cut both ways. A threat or insult to a meaningful identity can create frustration, anxiety, guilt, anger, and other unpleasant emotions. Some meaningful identities may express and sharpen alienation, as when bikers flaunt their colors and flout the norms and laws. The mere presence, strength or number of meaningful identities seems unlikely to account for social differences in distress. Although it is too early to tell for certain, a global sense of meaning and purpose in life may be more to the point. The immersion of self in constructive social roles may contribute to that sense, thereby improving emotional well-being.

NORMALITY

Detachment from the rules and standards of social life constitutes the fifth and final type of alienation that links social conditions to distress. In addition to a sense of control, commitment, support, and meaning, people may also need a set of reliable expectations. Expectations can be disappointed or violated if actions do not follow normal, usual, discernible, or socially desirable patterns. The failure of others, society, or one's own life to conform to expectations can be distressing. Research on normality and distress has developed around four topics, each of which is discussed below: normlessness, labeling, role stress, and the life cycle.

Normlessness

Normlessness is the belief that socially unapproved behaviors are required to achieve one's goals (Seeman 1959). If the community fails to convince the individual of the legitimacy of its standards for behavior, the individual may choose the most efficient means toward ends, whether legitimate or not. The principle of efficiency displaces that of social desirability as a guide for behavior. A pattern that is related to normlessness, and that can be discussed under the same heading for our purposes, is the displacement of community values such as prestige and respect with elementary pleasures. Instead of wanting to own a pleasant home, earn a good pay from a respectable job, and raise a family that is liked and esteemed, the individual prefers to seek basic, personal pleasure in sex, drugs, and thrills. The essence of normlessness, as broadly defined, is the rejection of the community as a source of standards. Good advice and exemplary behavior are seen as invalid guides. In rejecting standards that arise from the expressed needs, preferences, and rights of others, the individual falls back on biologically intrinsic satisfactions and pragmatic efficiency as guides that do not require faith in others.

Measures of normlessness are fairly well developed. Some focus on insensitivity to anything but crude enforcement, as indicated by the belief that if something works it doesn't matter if it's right or wrong, that it is all right to do anything you want as long as you stay out of trouble, that it is all right to get around the law as long as you don't actually break it, and that nothing is wrong if it is legal (Kohn 1976). Others focus on somewhat more extreme antisocial attitudes and behaviors, such as believing that people are honest only out of fear of getting caught if they are dishonest, that you can get around the law, and that people should take everything they can get, and such as ignoring people who are upset by your behavior or scaring people just for fun (Ross and Mirowsky 1987).

Although excellent measures are available, the causes and consequences of normlessness have not been widely explored in research on social patterns of distress. Theory suggests that normlessness is most common under conditions of structural inconsistency, where access to effective legitimate means is limited. However, in a study of the effects of occupation, Kohn (1976) finds that normlessness actually increases with position in the organizational hierarchy or with ownership of the means of production, controlling for the level of occupational self-direction (complex, unsupervised, nonroutine work). Self-direction is negatively associated with normlessness, controlling for hierarchical position and ownership, but about half the correlation is attributable to higher education among self-directed workers. Because ownership and hierarchical position are highly correlated with education and self-direction, normlessness tends to be most common among nonowners in low-ranked positions even though ownership and rank may themselves create some pressure toward normlessness.

The theoretical cognitive and emotional consequences of normlessness are mistrust and anxiety. In the extreme, a person who is despised by the community and wanted by the law is one person against the world. Other people exist to be manipulated, cheated, robbed, or used. The normless person must disguise his or her actions and purposes, or otherwise protect against preemption and retaliation. As a result, normlessness is correlated with signs of mistrust and paranoia, such as believing you are being plotted against, feeling it is safer to trust no one, feeling alone or apart even among friends, hearing voices without knowing where they're coming from, and believing that people talk about you behind your back, as well as with symptoms of distress such as brooding, worrying, feeling nothing is worthwhile anymore, and being afraid of closed places (Mirowsky and Ross 1983). In rejecting the community as a source of guidance, the normless person sets himself or herself against everyone else. If all human contact is a potential invasion or infiltration, then others can provide gratification but not comfort.

One behavioral consequence of normlessness is trouble with the law. Normless individuals are much more likely to get in trouble with the law, but only if they are also instrumental (Ross and Mirowsky 1987). Normless individuals who also feel powerless to control their lives do not engage in illegal activities or get in trouble with the law. People who engage in illegal activities and get in trouble with the law, in turn, have high levels of depression (Ross 2000).

Labeling

The second link between normality and distress is the social process of labeling. People who are thought of as mentally ill, insane, disturbed, disordered, schizophrenic, psychotic, neurotic, depressed, manic, anxious, suicidal, obsessive-compulsive, paranoid, hysterical, demented, addicted, alcoholic, antisocial, maladjusted, psychosomatic, Type A, and so on, are being placed in a mental pigeonhole by the person thinking of them in these terms. Each word suggests an idea, and each idea represents a grouping of phenomena treated as if they have an existence and essence that transcends the individual being considered. Putting aside the philosophical question about whether this style of thought is logically defensible, it is widely used in both science and everyday life, and for practical purposes it may be a useful way of thinking. However, labeling theorists note that there are potential pitfalls associated with it. One of these is the possibility of "secondary deviance": If I think someone is mentally ill then I will tend to act as if they are mentally ill, and their reaction to being treated as mentally ill will be interpreted as a sign of mental illness because it is common among persons considered mentally ill. For our purposes, the question is whether psychiatric diagnosis and treatment might actually increase distress.

In a follow-up study of a group of mental patients mostly hospitalized with the diagnosis of schizophrenia, Greenley (1979) found that whether the family expected the patient to be better, the same, or worse after release did not affect the returned patient's actual level of symptoms. However, the family's expectation that the patient would not be able to help with household chores, dress and groom, manage finances, help with shopping, or perform the usual duties of breadwinner, housewife, or student actually decreased the returned patient's performance of these tasks, controlling for the patient's level of symptoms and level of performance before hospitalization. Greenley's data suggest that social functioning is influenced by expectations but symptoms are not. However, Greenley's subjects were mostly classified as schizophrenics, so their symptoms were mostly hallucinations, delusions, and bizarre behavior rather than sadness, anxiety, and malaise. The results might have been different if the patients were mostly classified as depressed. Also, the research on powerlessness strongly implies that poor social functioning and dependence on one's family among returned patients will increase their distress.

Later studies found much the same thing as the earlier study. The stigma associated with a label does not create or even reinforce the severe symptoms considered mental illness, but it does affect social functioning, self-conceptions, and quality of life (Link et al. 1997). Link and his colleagues call this view and the support for it "modified labeling theory." Ex-mental patients who expect rejection based on their status have lower levels of self-esteem and mastery, more distress and demoralization, less satisfaction with their lives, and they are less likely to be employed (Link 1987; Link et al. 1997; Rosenfield 1997; Wright, Gronfein, and Owens 2000).

Role Stress

The third link between normality and distress has to do with disjunctions in the system of roles. Each role involves a set of expectations concerning the behavior of the person in the role and of people in other articulating roles (e.g., husband and wife, mother and child, employee and employer). The expectations are standards or norms in two senses. First, they are understandings and assumptions about the usual behavior of people in particular social categories or situations. As such, they are like maps or guide books that represent the behavioral topography and provide handy information for the social traveler. The planning and coordination of action is greatly enhanced by knowing what to expect of others and knowing what others expect of you. Second, the expectations are also standards or norms in the sense that they are required and enforced. If sociology had a set of propositions akin to the laws of physics, one would surely be that the usual is required and the unusual is prohibited. By demanding the usual of each other and ourselves we simplify decisions and plans, minimize the amount of negotiation necessary to coordinate our lives, and create a workable order. Because the violation of expectations disturbs this order it carries an onus that threatens both self-evaluations and one's relationships with others.

Role stress arises when expectations are not met. Aside from the situation in which the individual chooses not to meet expectations, which we discussed above as normlessness, there are three types of role stress. Role conflict exists when two legitimate expectations produce incompatible or mutually exclusive demands, such as when a man's family expects him to be at his child's birthday party at the same time his boss expects him to be at work. Role ambiguity exists when it is not clear what is expected, such as when grandparents are planning a holiday family gathering and don't know whether to invite the father of their grandchildren who has divorced their daughter. Role overload exits when expectations imply demands that overwhelm the resources and capabilities of the individual, such as when an employee is expected to work double shifts to meet a crash order. Most studies of role stress have focused on jobs and the workplace. For example, LaRocco et al. (1980) find that the amount of work and conflicting demands on the job are associated with depression, irritation, anxiety, and somatic complaints. However, the impact of role conflict and overload on distress can be reduced by emotional and instrumental support from the worker's family, friends, coworkers, and supervisor. In other words, open-minded understanding and a willingness to adjust to the worker's plight can reduce the distress produced by conflicting or excessive demands. This makes perfect sense. If our expectations put somebody on the spot, readjustment of our expectations can ease the tension.

Although studies of the workplace tend to support the role-stress hypothesis, studies of employment among married women may appear to contradict it. Since the turn of the century there has been a trend toward greater rates of employment among married women. However, the trend toward approval of such employment tended to lag over much of the period, and the trend toward readjustment of household and family roles was even further behind—really only getting under way in the last thirty years. One would expect overwhelming role-stress among employed wives and their families, including conflict between the demands of the job versus those of home and family, ambiguity and uncertainty concerning the proper obligations and rights of an employed wife and mother, and overload among women struggling to do all the things a good mother and wife should do while simultaneously holding a job. Thus, one would expect sharply elevated distress among employed wives. However, the research results do not support this prediction. Studies comparing wives who were employed to those who were exclusively housewives either found no difference (e.g., Radloff 1975) or that the employed wives were actually less distressed than the housewives (e.g., Kessler and McRae 1982; Ross, Mirowsky, and Huber 1983). Furthermore, our research showed that the apparent inconsistencies are due to the fact that marital and family roles are in transition. Some couples are living according to the traditional norms, some according to new egalitarian norms, and many are in between. Husband and wife are both less distressed if the wife's (un)employment matches their role preferences and are both more distressed if her (un)employment contradicts their preferences. The pattern of differences in distress suggest that, in the transition from traditional to egalitarian roles, the central problem for husbands is one of self-esteem—of getting over any embarrassment, guilt, or apprehension associated with their wives' employment. For the wives the central problem is getting their husbands to share the housework (ibid.).

Life Cycle

The fourth and last link between normality and distress is the standard or normal sequence of roles, statuses, and transitions over the life cycle. For example, a man usually finishes school, gets a job, gets married, has children, raises his children and sends them off on their own, retires, and dies—in that order. Transitions that happen out of their usual sequence create practical and moral dilemmas, and may also threaten the sense of the meaningful, predictable, and secure social reality. For example, very early childbearing generates disapproval but so does childlessness over the age of thirty (Menaghan 1989). Even highly undesirable events, such as the death of a parent, can have very different effects depending on when in one's life they occur. For example, Brown and Harris (1978) find that the loss of her mother before age eleven greatly increases a woman's vulnerability to stressful events and situations in adulthood. The childhood loss of a mother disrupts the usual cultural and social arrangements for the child's training and care, puts the child's relationships with other relatives and the outside world in flux, and undermines the child's assumption that social support is secure and continuous. In contrast, the loss of one's mother in middle age may bring grief, but it is rarely a direct disruption of one's job, friendships, daily home and family life, or community ties.

Research on the life course of men provides indirect evidence that deviations from usual patterns are distressing. Hogan (1978) finds that men typically finish school first, then get a job, and then get married. Deviations from this order result in a 17 to 29 percent increase in the probability that the first marriage will end in divorce or separation, controlling for ethnicity, level of education, military service, age at marriage, and cohort. As noted earlier, being divorced or separated is associated with distress (e.g., Hughes and Gove 1981).

Many of the effects of expectation on distress can be thought of as *contextual effects*. Expectations are mental representations of normal social conditions. If we ask ourselves what qualities of social conditions will change expectations and thus modify the impact of events, one answer is the prevalence of the events or sequence of events among others in the same social category. The higher the prevalence the less unusual it is and, thus, the greater the cultural, social, and mental preparation for it. For example, Lennon (1982) looked at the impact of menopause on distress. Although it is commonly believed that menopause is a "natural" period of distress for women, Lennon argues that the appropriate timing of life course change is socially defined and that individuals are aware of these age expectations and evaluate their own experience against the normative standard. Life course changes are not ordinarily traumatic if they occur on time because they have been anticipated and rehearsed. Major distress is caused by events that upset the normal, expected sequence and rhythm of life. Menopause marks the beginning of "midlife"—the period between parenthood and old age. The median age at menopause is 49.7 years, and three-quarters of natural menopauses happen between ages 45 and 54. Using data from the Health and Nutrition Examination survey on 3,886 women, Lennon finds that women between the ages of 25 and 43 currently going through menopause have 72 percent more symptoms of depression than premenopausal women of the same age, and women between the ages of 54 and 74 currently going through menopause have 78 percent more depression than postmenopausal women of the same age, but among women ages 44 through 53 there is no difference in depression between those who are premenopausal, currently menopausal, and postmenopausal (controlling for race, marital status, education, income, and number of children). Thus, the impact of menopause on distress depends entirely on whether it happens inside or outside the usual age range. This illustrates the effect that the life course timing of prevalence may have on the emotional consequences of events.

ALIENATION: THE PRIME STRESSOR

Sociological theory about the forms, causes, and consequences of subjective alienation has inspired much research on social patterns of distress. Perceptions of control, commitment, support, meaning, and normality can reduce distress either by inherently meeting basic psychological needs or by reducing the impact of potentially threatening or disturbing events and situations. A sense of personal control forms a major link to distress from socioeconomic status, gender differences in the work and family nexus, and age. Social support forms a major link to distress from marriage and parenthood. Less is known about whether commitment, meaning, and normality link social conditions to distress, either because the research has not yet been done, or because the sense of control and social support are really the two main links. Although social variations in subjective alienation are a major source of social variations in distress, there are other factors that also play a part: authoritarianism and inequity. We discuss these next.

8

Authoritarianism and Inequity

Many social psychologists became interested in authoritarianism and inequity because of political upheavals surrounding the Great Depression, World War II, the cold war, and the social movements of the 1960s. Most of the theory and research about authoritarianism sought to explain mass support for totalitarian dictatorships. Most about inequity sought to explain the rise in democratic countries of social movements promoting the rights of labor, the poor, minorities, and women. Research focused on the political inclinations relevant to authoritarianism and inequity, and on their political consequences. Effects on distress were not the motivating concern. Certainly, few social and behavioral scientists seemed interested in whether supporters of fascism suffered distress as a consequence of their beliefs. Even so, social psychologists recognized that authoritarianism and inequity have emotional elements that provide the motivation behind sentiment and action. When social scientists began looking for explanations of the social patterns of distress, many naturally turned to the literature on authoritarianism and inequity for ideas. Although these avenues of research were distinct from those into alienation covered in the previous chapter, they led to much the same place: the sense of powerlessness creates the main link to distress.

AUTHORITARIANISM

Authoritarianism is a complex worldview with a number of thematically related elements. Chief among these is a sense that tradition and authority are compelling guides to behavior, and a belief that ethical conduct and compliance with the dictates of tradition and authority are identical. A number of other beliefs and habits of thought are associated with this:

(1) belief that there is only one legitimate perspective and only one right way to do things;

(2) belief that familiar social institutions, traditions, and roles are facts of nature, results of cosmic laws, or manifestations of divine will and not simply the aggregate product of human interactions over a period of time;

(3) belief that differences in opinions and behaviors arise either because others perversely refuse to acknowledge the truth and conform or because others are ignorant of the truth due to misfortune or the machinations of diabolical forces;

(4) rejection of negotiation and compromise and the glorification of righteous indignation, suspicion, hostility, and aggression as the proper response to opinions, preferences, and behaviors that are different from one's own;

(5) stereotyped ideas about people in other social categories, including a tendency to disregard variations among individuals within the stereotyped categories;

(6) belief that human suffering is the consequence of failure to comply and is therefore divine or natural punishment that cannot or should not be alleviated except by reforming the sufferers;

(7) belief that mankind's unrestrained nature is evil; and

(8) mistrust, especially of those who are different (Gabennesch 1972; Meissner 1978).

Authoritarianism as defined and described above is not a coherent theoretical concept with a clear definition. Instead it is a set of attitudes and beliefs that contribute to support for belligerent dictatorial regimes. Nonetheless, authoritarianism has two important elements that contribute to distress and help explain its social patterns: (1) inflexibility in dealing with practical and interpersonal problems, and (2) suspiciousness and mistrust. These two elements, rather than authoritarianism broadly speaking, form the main links to distress. Emotionally speaking, the problem lies not so much in the self-righteous narrow-mindedness itself as in the disability it engenders.

Inflexibility

Cognitive flexibility is an open-ended, open-minded approach to solving problems, characterized by the ability to elaborate and weigh arguments and evidence both for and against a proposition, by the ability to imagine a complex set of actions necessary to solve a practical problem, and by the ability to imagine and compare multiple solutions to a single problem. Inflexibility is characterized by a tendency to favor particular modes of coping in all stressful situations, by a dearth of strategies for solving problems, by reliance on conformity and obedience as coping strategies, by rigid application of rules and standards, by an inability to imagine contradictory views and complex solutions, and by dedication to tradition as a means of adaptation (e.g., Kohn and Schooler 1982; Wheaton 1983).

According to theory, inflexibility is learned as a habitual style of thought and action in social situations that limit the individual's horizons and demand conformity and obedience. Insular personal networks and a lack of exposure to the views of other cultures, historical periods, and sectors of society can create a sense that the familiar, traditional order has a universal and unique validity that transcends time, place, and situation. Low-status jobs often require unreflecting compliance with rules and plans the individual did not have a part in making. In contrast, education increases intellectual flexibility. It exposes people to different ways of looking at the world, and encourages open, creative, flexible ways of thinking. Furthermore, people with low levels of education have restricted job opportunities and often end up doing work that is routine, closely supervised, simple, and does not allow workers to solve problems, make decisions, use their creativity, or exercise initiative. Routine, closely supervised jobs reduce the individual's flexibility in solving cognitive and social problems. Furthermore, educational and occupational experiences shape the values and beliefs that parents pass on to their children (e.g., Kohn and Schooler 1982; Kohn 1972). The result is that inflexibility is associated with low current socioeconomic status and with a low status of origin.

Wheaton (1983) compares the theoretical effect of inflexibility on distress to that of fatalism. As discussed earlier, the belief that outcomes are determined by external forces beyond one's control implies a lack of coping effort. If luck, fate, chance, and powerful others are the controlling forces in your life then there is no point in trying. By comparison, inflexibility reduces coping ability. The individual who lacks the mental skill to imagine all aspects of a problem or multiple solutions to a problem, who cannot understand other points of view, and who thus finds it difficult to negotiate and compromise, will have trouble solving personal, interpersonal, and social problems.

Both theory and laboratory studies of animals suggest an intimate link between fatalism and inflexibility, with the two reinforcing each other. Recall that learned helplessness can be created by exposing animals to inescapable electric shock. It is characterized by subsequent failure to attempt escape when an avenue of escape is available and by a diminished ability to learn escape behaviors even when forcibly and repeatedly demonstrated (Seligman 1975). It is as if the animal learns inattention to the connections between signs, actions, and outcomes. Similarly, fatalism may produce inflexibility by reducing the individual's efforts to understand events and situations. Not only will this tend to produce a rigid, habitual response to any given problem, but it will also limit the development of intellectual problem-solving skills. This inflexibility in turn reduces the ability to cope with problems, and the consequent failures increase the sense of not being in control. Thus, there could be a "vicious circle," with low coping effort producing low coping ability, which in turn produces low coping effort.

Kohn and Schooler (1982) find evidence of this pattern in their study of the cognitive and emotional impact of job characteristics. Kohn and his colleagues measure both attitudinal and task flexibility (Kohn and Slomczynski 1993; Kohn et al. 1990, 2000). They ask whether respondents agree with statements such as "the most important thing to teach children is obedience," and "it is generally best to keep on doing things the traditional way." They also ask testlike questions such as: "You are going to open a fast food restaurant (or newspaper stand) and are trying to choose a location. List all the factors that go into your decision," and "List as many reasons as you can *for* and *against* banning cigarette ads on television." The researchers score the respondents' ability to solve complex problems and to see many sides of an issue. The researchers also judge the respondent's apparent intelligence, and judge the aesthetics in a "draw-a-person test" (Lilienfeld, Wood, and Garb 2001). They find two important things. First, cognitive flexibility increases "self-directedness" (instrumentalism), which in turn increases cognitive flexibility, so the two reinforce each other. Second, in the long run flexibility and self-directedness lead the individual into jobs that are less routine, less closely supervised, and more complex, and those feed back to increase flexibility and self-directedness. Kohn and Schooler did not find a direct effect of flexibility on distress. However, they did find that self-directedness decreases distress. Because flexibility reinforces self-directedness, boosts the impact of job characteristics on self-directedness, and leads to jobs with characteristics that produce self-directedness, problem-solving flexibility has an indirect impact on distress.

Wheaton (1983) looked at the effect of flexibility on distress in a different way. If flexibility increases coping ability, then the impact of acute and chronic stressors on distress will decrease as the level of flexibility increases. The concept he calls flexibility is really authoritarianism more broadly. His measure contains three components: authoritarian conservatism, normlessness, and mistrust. Authoritarian conservatism is essentially the same as Kohn's attitudinal inflexibility: a belief in reliance on tradition and authority, measured by agreement with statements about the need for rigid standards and the preeminent value of obedience and tradition. Normlessness is a type of alienation in which people believe that socially unapproved behaviors are necessary to get ahead, as we discussed in Chapter 7. It is measured by agreement with sentiments such as not blaming someone for trying to take everything he can get. Mistrust is a distinct aspect of authoritarianism we discuss in the next section, measured by beliefs such as that it is not safe to trust anyone. Wheaton looked at three outcomes: depression, anxiety, and schizophreniform hallucinations and delusions. He found that flexibility reduces the amount of depression associated with acute and chronic stressors and that flexibility eliminates the association between stressors and schizophrenic symptoms. He also found that flexibility decreases anxiety, although it does not reduce the impact of stressors on anxiety.

Although Kohn's group has published over fifty research articles on cognitive flexibility, researchers outside his circle generally have focused on other concepts. Partly that may reflect the difficulty of recording and scoring the flexibility tests. However, responses about attitudinal inflexibility and authoritarian conservatism are easy to record and score, and they also have not appeared in the literature much. Perhaps other researchers had the same experience we did. When we asked questions like Kohn's about obedience and tradition, we found the answers had little relationship to distress, particularly after adjusting for the sense of control. Cognitive flexibility may be important largely through its impact on job conditions and the sense of control, which directly influence distress. In recent years sociologists have turned their attention toward trust more than cognitive flexibility. That interest mostly comes from criminologists and others studying neighborhood differences in social cohesion. Not surprisingly, though, trust and mistrust have important consequences for emotional well-being. Recent discoveries suggest that low perceived control catalyzes the effect of neighborhood disadvantage and disorder on mistrust, with serious implications for emotional distress.

Mistrust

Trust is a belief in the integrity of other people. Trusting individuals expect that they can depend on others (Rotter 1980). They have faith and confidence in other people. Mistrust, its opposite, is the cognitive habit of interpreting the intentions and behavior of others as unsupportive, self-seeking, and dishonest (Mirowsky and Ross 1983). Mistrust is an absence of faith in other people based on a belief that they are out for their own good and will exploit or victimize you in pursuit of their goals. Mistrusting individuals believe it is safer to keep their distance from others, and suspicion of other people is the central cognitive component of mistrust (Kramer 1999). Trust and mistrust express inherently social beliefs about relationships with other people. Trust and mistrust embody learned, generalized expectations about other people's behaviors that transcend specific relationships and situations (Barber 1983; Garfinkel 1963; Gurtman 1992; Johnson-George and Swap 1982; Rotter 1971; Sorrentino et al. 1995).

Reliance, Collective Efficacy, and Social Capital.

The ability to form positive social relationships depends on trust. It allows pairs of individuals to establish cooperative relationships whenever doing so is mutually beneficial (Coleman 1988, 1990; Rotter 1980). Coleman emphasizes trust as an element of social capital, because trusting social relationships help produce desired outcomes. Sampson and his colleagues also emphasize trust in their definition of collective efficacy: the mutual trust and social bonds among neighbors that are likely to be effective in decreasing crime (Sampson et al. 1997). People who trust others form personal ties and participate in voluntary associations more often than do mistrusting individuals (Brehm and Rahn 1997; Paxton 1999). Trusting individuals are themselves more trustworthy and honest and are less likely to lie and harm others (Gurtman 1992; Rotter 1971, 1980) so that they create and maintain environments of trustworthiness, without which the social fabric cannot hold (Putnam 1995). Trusting people enter relationships with the presumption that others can be trusted until there is evidence to the contrary. (Given contrary evidence, though, they are not gullible [Rotter 1971, 1980].) Because trusting individuals can form effective associations with others, the presumption of trust can be an advantageous strategy, despite the fact that expecting people to be trustworthy is risky (Molm, Takahashi, and Peterson 2000; Orbell and Dawes 1991; Sullivan and Transue 1999).

In contrast, the consequences of mistrust can be far-reaching and severe. Mistrust can interfere with the development, maintenance, and use of social support networks. Mistrusting individuals may not seek social support when in need, may reject offers of such support, and may be uncomfortable with any support that is given. Furthermore, mistrusting individuals help create and maintain the very conditions that seem to justify their beliefs. Their preemptive actions may elicit hostile responses, and their diminished ability to participate in networks of reciprocity and mutual assistance may have several consequences (Mirowsky and Ross 1983). Without allies they are easy targets of crime and exploitation. When victimized or exploited they cannot share their economic or emotional burden with others. Finally, by not providing aid and assistance to others, mistrusting individuals weaken the community's power to forestall victimization and exploitation and to limit its consequences.

Zero-Sum Views.

Mistrust forms an integral part of a zero-sum worldview, which is part of an authoritarian outlook prevalent in poor peasant societies (Gabennesch 1972; Grabb 1979; Woolcock 1998). The zero-sum worldview regards the total amount of wealth, power, or prestige as limited, so that one person's gain implies another person's loss. In populations with few resources, everyone competes for a limited pool. People with power and wealth presumably got it by exploiting those without it. People generally seem selfish and willing to exploit others for personal gain. Victimization and exploitation appear inevitable and common, with dire consequences for the victims (ibid.). Mistrust is a logical corollary of the authoritarian belief that mankind's unrestrained nature is evil.

Michael Woolcock vividly describes a peasant village in India that illustrates the relationship between disadvantage and mistrust.

> The main problems, the villagers say, are that most people cannot be trusted, that local landlords exploit every opportunity to impose crushing rates of interest on loans, and pay wages so low that any personal advancement is rendered virtually impossible. There are schools and health clinics, but teachers and doctors regularly fail to show up for work. Funds allocated to well-intentioned government programs are siphoned off by local elites.... Why should we trust anyone? (1998:152–53)

The habit of interpreting the intentions and behavior of other people as unsupportive, self-seeking, and dishonest can develop into paranoia, especially under conditions of powerlessness and socioeconomic disadvantage (Mirowsky and Ross 1983). Paranoia is an even more profound rift with others than is mistrust. Individuals can go from a more general belief that people are manipulative and may harm them in pursuit of goals, to a more specific belief that they have been singled out as a target for persecution. "When other people in one's life have become a hostile army, social alienation is at its deepest" (ibid.:238).

A Distressing Alienation.

Mistrust represents a profound form of alienation that has gone beyond a perceived separation from others to a suspicion of them. Although social psychologists originally considered mistrust as an element of authoritarianism, its importance for psychological distress comes from the deep alienation it represents. The suspicion of others indicates a heightened sense of threat, and the lack of confidence in others is a form of demoralization. As a result, mistrust heightens both anxiety and depression. As social animals, all humans must live and work around others. Mistrust creates a dilemma. Engaging with others generates anxiety, because those others pose threats. Disengaging from others generates depression, because of the loneliness. The dilemma itself also generates depression, because of the inescapable punishment one way or the other. Mistrust is uncommon among U.S. adults, but distressing when it occurs. For example, we asked our 1995 Illinois respondents how often they felt it was not safe to trust anyone, felt suspicious, and felt sure everyone was against them. Only about 3 percent of adults report feeling those things most days of the past week, compared to about 75 percent who said they felt none of

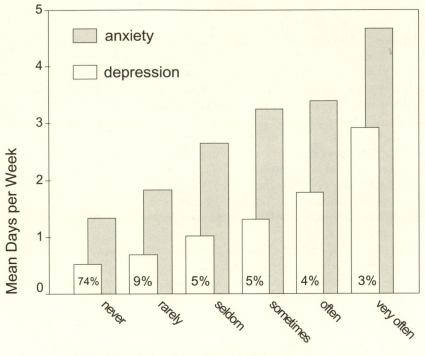

Mistrust in the Past Week

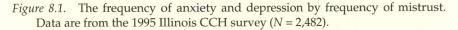

Figure 8.1. The frequency of anxiety and depression by frequency of mistrust. Data are from the 1995 Illinois CCH survey (*N* = 2,482).

them. Those groups differ enormously in levels of depression and anxiety, as illustrated in Figure 8.1. Anxiety is about 3.5 times more frequent and depression about five times more frequent among those who very often feel mistrusting, compared to those who say they never do. While that is a small group at the high end, the prevalence of anxiety and depression increases progressively with the frequency and intensity of mistrust. Mistrust may contribute substantially to the social difference in distress. Mistrust develops when social disadvantages decrease the sense of control over one's own life while restricting residential options to threatening neighborhoods. As described next, the low sense of control combines with high levels of neighborhood disorder to generate a deep sense of mistrust.

Disorder, Powerlessness, and Mistrust.

Mistrust and trust imply judgments about the likely risks and benefits posed by interaction. How do people make decisions about interaction when it is uncertain whether other people can be trusted? We think that three things influence the level of trust: scarce resources, threat, and powerlessness. Where the environment seems threatening, among those who feel powerless to avoid or manage the threats, and among those who have few resources with which to absorb losses, suspicion and mistrust seem well-founded. Mistrust makes sense where threats abound, particularly for those who feel powerless to prevent harm or cope with the consequences of being victimized or exploited. Furthermore, for people with few resources, the consequences of losing what little one has will be devastating. Those with little cannot afford to lose much, and need to be vigilant in defense of what little they have. If so, then mistrust will be more common among persons who live in threatening and dangerous environments, among individuals who feel powerless to prevent or deal with the consequences of harm, and among those who have few resources to make up for any losses.

In Chapter 5 we reported that neighborhood disadvantage and disorder are associated with depression. Why are they? Part of the reason may be that life in these neighborhoods generates mistrust and powerlessness. To examine some of these ideas we use our survey of Community, Crime, and Health (CCH). In order to assess levels of mistrust, respondents were asked the number of days in the past week they "felt it was not safe to trust anyone," "felt suspicious," and "felt sure everyone was against you." (Measurement of neighborhood disadvantage and disorder are described in Chapter 5 and perceived powerlessness in Chapter 7.)

Through daily exposure to a threatening environment, where signs of disorder are common, residents come to learn that other people cannot be trusted. Neighborhoods with high levels of disorder present residents with observable signs and cues that social control is weak (Skogan 1986, 1990). In these neighborhoods, residents report noise, litter, crime, vandalism, graffiti, people hanging out on the streets, public drinking, run-down and abandoned buildings, drug use, danger, trouble with neighbors, and other incivilities associated with a breakdown of social control. In neighborhoods with a lot of disorder, residents view those around them with suspicion, as enemies who will harm them rather than as allies who will help them. Mistrust makes sense in threatening environments.

The sense of powerlessness reinforced by a threatening environment amplifies the effect of that threat on mistrust, whereas a sense of control would moderate it. At heart, individuals who feel powerless feel awash in a sea of events generated by chance or by powerful others. They feel helpless to avoid undesirable events and outcomes, as well as powerless to bring about desirable ones. Individuals who feel powerless may feel unable to fend off attempts at exploitation, unable to distinguish dangerous persons and situations from benign ones, and unable to recover from

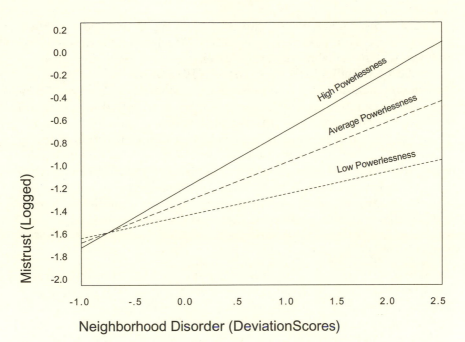

Figure 8.2. The interaction of powerlessness with neighborhood disorder in their effects on mistrust. Data are from the 1995 Illinois CCH survey.

mistaken complacency. Neighborhood disorder generates high levels of mistrust among those who feel powerless to control their lives. In contrast, those with a sense of personal control may feel that they can avoid victimization and harm and effectively cope with any consequences of errors in judgment. Neighborhood disorder signals the potential for harm. Some people feel they can avoid harm, or cope with it. Neighborhood disorder produces little mistrust among individuals who feel in control of their own lives, but a great deal among those who feel powerless. This is illustrated in Figure 8.2. Neighborhood disorder increases mistrust directly and indirectly by generating the powerlessness that amplifies disorder's effect on mistrust.

Mistrust emerges in disadvantaged neighborhoods with high levels of disorder, among individuals with few resources who feel powerless to avoid harm. Mistrust is the product of an interaction between person and place, but the place gathers those who are susceptible and intensifies their susceptibility. Specifically, disadvantaged individuals generally live in disadvantaged neighborhoods where they feel awash in threatening signs of disorder.

Because disadvantaged individuals live in disadvantaged neighborhoods, we needed to take into account individual characteristics in order
to know whether neighborhoods affect mistrust over and above the characteristics of the individuals who live there. We took into account age, race,
sex, employment status, income, education, and family status. Older people, whites, employed persons, those with high household incomes, and
the well-educated are more trusting than younger persons, nonwhites,
those with low incomes, and those with less education. In terms of family
status, single parents have the highest levels of mistrust, followed by single people without children, married parents, and married persons without children, respectively. Men are more mistrusting than women despite
their more advantaged status. With the one exception of gender, in general
individual socioeconomic disadvantage correlates with mistrust.

Structural Amplification.

Structural amplification exists when conditions undermine the personal
attributes that otherwise would moderate their undesirable consequences.
The situation erodes resistance to its own ill effect. More generally, it exists
when a mediator of the association between an objective condition and a
subjective belief or feeling also amplifies the association. The mediator of
an undesirable effect is also a magnifier of that effect.

Neighborhood disorder reinforces a sense of powerlessness that makes
the effect of disorder on mistrust even worse. Exposure to uncontrollable,
negative events and conditions in the neighborhood in the form of crime,
noise, vandalism, graffiti, garbage, fights, and danger promote and reinforce perceptions of powerlessness. In neighborhoods where social order
has broken down, residents particularly feel powerless to achieve a goal
most people desire—to live in a clean, safe environment free from threat,
harassment, and danger (Geis and Ross 1998). Among individuals who
feel in control of their own lives, neighborhood disadvantage and disorder
produce little mistrust. However, neighborhood disorder impairs residents' ability to cope with its own ill effect by also producing a sense of
powerlessness. Neighborhood disorder destroys the sense of control that
would otherwise insulate residents from the consequences of disorder.
Thus, the very thing needed to protect disadvantaged residents from the
negative effects of their environment—a sense of personal control—is
eroded by that environment. This is an instance of what we call structural
amplification, illustrated in Figure 8.3.

Mediators link objective social conditions to subjective beliefs and feelings. Mediators are a consequence of an exogenous (or independent)
variable and a "cause" of a dependent variable. They explain patterns.
Modifiers condition associations between objective conditions and subjec-

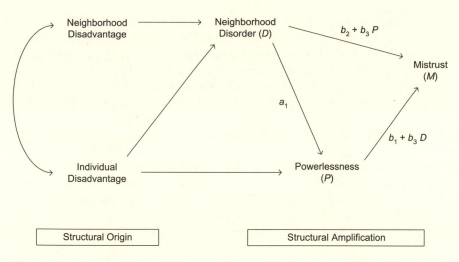

Figure 8.3. Theoretical path diagram illustrating the structural amplification of mistrust.

tive beliefs or feelings, making the associations between exogenous and dependent variables stronger or weaker, depending on their level. Modifiers sometimes moderate effects, lessening the ill effects of disadvantaged or threatening conditions, but in structural amplification, modifiers amplify ill effects, making them worse. Most importantly, in structural amplification, modifiers are also linked to social conditions. Here a sense of powerlessness amplifies the association between neighborhood disorder and mistrust, but the perception of powerlessness does not just come out of people's heads without reference to social conditions. A sense of powerlessness is also a consequence of neighborhood disorder. When modifiers of the association between a social condition and mistrust result from the condition itself, this produces structural amplification.

Disadvantage and Mistrust.

Neighborhood and individual disadvantage set in motion the structural amplification that magnifies mistrust among those with few resources. Neighborhood disorder, common in neighborhoods where disadvantaged individuals live, influences mistrust directly and indirectly by increasing perceptions of powerlessness among residents, thereby amplifying disorder's effect on mistrust. Individuals with low incomes and little education, the unemployed, minorities, young people, or single parents often lack the resources that encourage trust. When individuals have few resources the dire consequences of mistaken trust makes them wary. Those with few resources cannot afford to lose much, and need to be vigilant in defense of what little they have. In the United States, the impact of individual disadvantage is magnified by the residential concentration of disadvantaged individuals. Neighborhood disadvantage is indicated primarily by a high prevalence of poor and mother-only households, as well as by a low prevalence of adults with college degrees and home ownership, as detailed in Chapter 5. Neighborhood disadvantage produces neighborhood disorder, and individual disadvantage limits residential options to disadvantaged and disordered neighborhoods, as illustrated in Figure 8.3. The individual disadvantage also creates a sense of powerlessness that sharpens the mistrust associated with living in a disorderly neighborhood. Disadvantaged individuals are more mistrusting than others because they feel powerless as a consequence of their individual disadvantage and because they often must live in disadvantaged neighborhoods with high levels of disorder.

Concentrating Distress.

Structural amplification concentrates high levels of distress among the most disadvantaged individuals and in the most disadvantaged neighborhoods. The structural amplification of mistrust contributes substantially to that process. Other instances of structural amplification probably do too. Whenever a corrosive situation reduces the sense of control needed to motivate problem solving, it amplifies the distress associated with traits that steer individuals into that situation. Whenever a susceptibility predisposes individuals to stressful events and conditions, and also undermines the ability to cope, it amplifies distress. Structural amplification concentrates a disproportionate amount of distress in a minority of the population. In doing so, it puts the greatest burden of distress on society's most disadvantaged individuals and groups.

INEQUITY

The sense of right and wrong, feelings of guilt or grievance, and the relation of exploiter and victim are concerns as old as the earliest stories and writings. Emotions are deeply related to the sense of fairness. Indignation and guilt are the marks and consequences of unfairness. They are the types of distress attributed to the sense of being victim or exploiter.

Victims and Exploiters

People get angry when they see themselves giving more than they get (Walster, Walster, and Berscheid 1978). It may seem, at first, that anger and depression are incompatible emotions. They are not. Anger about relations with the family is far more common among severely depressed women than among women with similar social characteristics who are not distressed (Weissman and Paykel 1974). Anger and depression are both reactions to situations that are frustrating and unfair. In part, the depression results from the implicit lack of control. Some people choose to exploit, but few choose to be victims. The victim in an unfair relationship is constrained and directed in ways he or she does not desire, which produces depression. Outbursts of anger about the unfairness also lead to depression indirectly. Women often seek treatment for severe depression after finding themselves uncontrollably enraged at members of their family (ibid.). The explosions make them feel as powerless to control themselves as they are powerless to control the situation. The rage can leave a deep sense of remorse and guilt, especially if the anger is directed at an innocent but powerless child rather than at a powerful spouse who is the source of frustration.

If equity theory simply argued that the victim in an unfair relationship is distressed by the unfairness, then its predictions would not be unique. However, equity theory argues that the exploiter in an unfair relationship is also distressed. There are several reasons. The exploiter may feel guilty about taking advantage of someone. Guilt and depression are correlated among students, and guilt is far more common in depressed patients than in nondepressed controls (Peterson 1979; Prosen et al. 1983). Furthermore, flagrant unfairness is a violation of general norms and may meet with disapproval from others. A person's sense of self-worth reflects the approval or disapproval of others. Violating the norms of fairness can lower the sense of self-worth or self-esteem necessary for emotional well-being (e.g., Prosen et al. 1983; Weissman and Paykel 1974; Rosenberg, Schooler, and Schoenbach 1989). The exploiter also may dread retaliation and punishment by the victim, and by others who see the relationship as unjust (Walster et al. 1978). Symptoms of anxiety, such as nervousness, cold sweats, headaches, trembling hands, and acid stomach are correlated with depression to such a high extent that both are often combined in measures of general psychological distress (e.g., Wheaton 1982; Mirowsky and Ross 1983). Finally, flagrant unfairness elicits hostility from the victim. It is unpleasant to be a target of hostility, and a hostile victim may obstruct the exploiter's actions. The difference between willing and grudging compliance represents a tremendous loss of efficiency and effectiveness. The victim's resistance limits the exploiter's personal control.

Marriage: Cynical and Optimistic Views.

Most of the work on equity and distress is concerned with marriage. The relationship between husband and wife is a particularly good laboratory for studying equity. Marriages are long-term relationships that are meaningful to the couple and others in their social circle. The lives and fortunes of married partners are intertwined and they, their friends, and families have firm beliefs about proper conduct in the relationship (Schafer and Keith 1980; Pearlin 1975). Married people feel distressed if the other partner expects more than he or she is willing to give back, acts like the only important person in the family, and demands more compliance than he or she is willing to give (Pearlin 1975). How does the selfish partner feel?

The self-aggrandizement hypothesis is a cynical view of the balance of marital power: well-being is achieved at the partner's expense. The psychological benefits of domination are unmitigated by fairness, sympathy, or mutual interest. Each partner feels best when dominating as much as the other will tolerate submitting, and submitting as little as possible in return. In this cynical view, getting what you want, doing what you choose, and directing your own life and actions increases mental well-being. If it is better to dominate than to submit, better to control than to be controlled, and better to be the one who decides than the one who does not, then dominance in the family reduces depression. One partner's dominance is the other's submission. It follows that one partner's well-being is the other's depression, as illustrated in the left panel of Figure 8.4.

Equity theory presents an alternative and optimistic view of marital relations: In their hearts the husband and wife both know what is fair. If they do what is right they will both lead happier and more productive lives. There is no inherent conflict of interest. The basic equity implies that both partners are least depressed if they share marital power equally, as illustrated in the right panel of Figure 8.4.

The truth lies between the optimistic and cynical views (Mirowsky and Ross 1985). Husband and wife both find that sharing marital power is less depressing than usurping it. Married persons are more depressed if their partner's effort at cooking, housekeeping, earning income, companionship, and child care seems too small *or too great* compared to their own effort (Schafer and Keith 1980). Balanced marital relationships reinforce the sense of emotional support—of having someone to turn to for support and understanding when things get rough. Married people who share housework (doing between one-third and two-thirds of it) have better emotional support than those who do most of it themselves or who have a spouse who does most of it (Van Willigen and Drentea 2001). The same is true of those who share marital power rather than dominating or being dominated. However, we find that each partner is least depressed by a balance of power more in his or her own favor than the balance the other is least depressed by. We call this partial equity. It is partial in two senses of the word, as illustrated in Figure 8.5. First, an element of self-aggrandizement remains, so equity is incomplete. Second, each spouse is partial to his or her own influence.

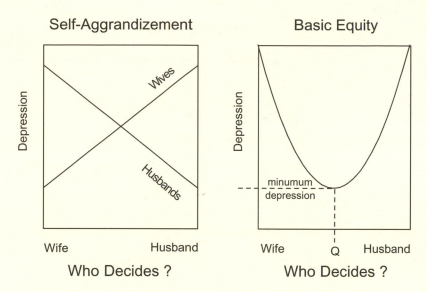

Figure 8.4. The self-aggrandizement hypothesis contrasted with the basic equity hypothesis. Each graph shows depression as a function of marital power. On the left side the wife makes all the important decisions and on the right side the husband makes them. According to the self-aggrandizement hypothesis, the husband's depression decreases and his wife's increases as his influence in the major decisions increases. According to the basic equity hypothesis, depression is high at the extremes, where one spouse makes all the decisions. Depression is lowest in the middle, where decisions are shared. The extent of the husband's predominance versus the wife's that is associated with the lowest depression is the equity point, labeled Q.

A sense of equity reduces the tension between husband and wife over marital power. The gap between their equity points allows some tension to remain. The existing balance of marital power cannot minimize both partners' depression if the two have different equity points. One can enjoy minimum depression at the other's expense, or they can compromise on a balance that is less than optimal for both. Compromise is typical, but it is usually a compromise that favors husbands. The actual balance of marital power in the average marriage is closer to one that minimizes husbands' depression than it is to one that minimizes wives'.

As Homans puts it, "Justice is a curious mixture of equality within inequality" (1961:244). Equal influence in major family decisions is not necessarily seen as fair. Not only are the equity points different for husbands and wives, but they also shift depending on the husband's earnings. The shift has more to do with norms than with the objective value of

Partial Equity

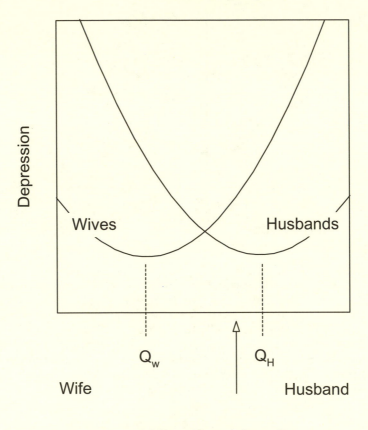

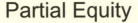

Who Decides ?

Figure 8.5.   Equity is partial. Based on the data from the Women and Work Study, there are separate equity points, Q_H and Q_W, for husbands and wives. The husband's depression is lowest when the balance of marital power is far more in his favor than the balance at which his wife's depression is lowest, and vice versa. The arrow points to the actual balance of marital power in the average couple. It is closer to the husband's equity point than to the wife's. Results shown are adjusted for age, education, earnings, religion, and sex-role beliefs.

contributions to the marriage. A dollar earned by the wife buys the same things as a dollar earned by the husband, but only the husband's earnings shift the equity points. The more he earns, the more his marital power is justified, in her eyes as well as his. The less he earns, the less it is justified. Her earnings, or the absence of them, do not justify more or less of her influence.

The wife's sense of a just division of marital power also depends on her acceptance of a social philosophy that supports the husband's dominance. The husband's does not. The more traditional the wife's sex-role beliefs, the greater the amount of her husband's marital power associated with her minimum depression. The husband's sex-role beliefs do not influence his equity point. Regardless of whether his beliefs are traditional or nontraditional, the more the husband earns the more he feels justified in making the major family decisions.

Income: Just Reward or Just Enough?

The sense of equity links the quality and nature of marital relationships to depression. Does equity also mediate the impact of larger, more impersonal social relationships? Are there people suffering from a sense of having far greater income and wealth than they deserve? The answer is simple: if there are such people, community social surveys have yet to find them. It appears that impersonal, competitive economic relationships free us, in our society, from any sense of economically exploiting others (e.g., Kluegel and Smith 1986). The essence of equity theory is the assertion that getting more than you deserve is worse psychologically than getting exactly what you deserve. It is very difficult to test this assertion in regard to income and wealth, let alone demonstrate its truth. The reason is that so few believe that they have or get more than they deserve—about 2 percent in the United States, compared to 30 to 40 percent who believe they get substantially less than they deserve (Robinson and Bell 1978; Kluegel and Smith 1986; Shepelak and Alwin 1986). The wealthiest and highest paid are not typically the ones who feel overbenefited. People who say the fair pay for their job is less than they earn tend to be in the middle-income brackets, and to be somewhat traditional wives whose earnings are approaching those of their husbands (Mirowsky 1987). On the whole, excessive economic benefit is something that happens to others (Alves and Rossi 1978; Jasso and Rossi 1977). Top executives, physicians, and government officials are considered overpaid by 70 percent of Americans (Ross and Lauritsen 1985). Very few consider themselves overpaid. Depression due to a sense of excessive income and wealth is a moot issue.

On the other side—the down side—there are plenty of people who feel their pay is unfairly low. This is what we find about depression and underpayment (using data from the Women and Work study). First, depression among husbands is proportional to the *percentage* raise needed to close the gap between what they get and what they feel they deserve. There is no association between depression and the dollar amount of the gap. Second, there was no association between depression and perceived underpayment among employed wives, although this may have changed. It may be that a sense of underpayment is depressing only if it implies inadequate performance as a spouse or parent. Third, economic hardship is depressing for both husbands and wives. Not having enough money to provide food, clothing, shelter, and medical care for one's family is profoundly depressing. Dismay over not meeting family needs is far worse than discontent with one's pay. It is the hardship, not the injustice, that is most depressing.

Powerlessness and Unfair Treatment.

Equity theory's distinction is the prediction of elevated distress among persons who are unfairly advantaged. That prediction comes true in close personal relationships such as marriage. It fails to be true in the larger and impersonal socioeconomic context. Apparently very few individuals, if any, see themselves as unfairly overpaid, wealthy, important, or powerful. On the other hand, many see themselves as having been unfairly mistreated because of race, ethnicity, gender, age, religion, physical appearance, sexual orientation, or other characteristics (Finch, Kolody, and Vega 2000; Kessler et al. 1999; Noh et al. 1999; Schulz et al. 2000). About a third of American adults say that at some time in their lives they have experienced major discrimination such as not getting hired or promoted, or being denied service, medical care, a bank loan, a scholarship, or an apartment (Kessler, Mickelson and Williams 1999). About 60 percent say they have been discriminated against in mundane ways, such as being called names or insulted, threatened or harassed, treated as inferior, stupid, dangerous, or dishonest, treated with discourtesy or disrespect, or given poor service because of race, ethnicity, sex, age, etc. The greater the frequency and variety of these experiences the greater the level of depression and anxiety.

People reporting exposure to discrimination feel unjustly treated. In American usage the word "discrimination" implies an unjust categorical treatment. Surveys that ask directly about "unfair" treatment (Finch et al. 2000; Schulz et al. 2000) get essentially the same results as those that ask about being "discriminated against" (Kessler et al. 1999; Noh et al. 1999). It is not yet clear why perceived discrimination and unfairness cause distress. They may often provoke indignation. Beyond that, discrimination and unfair treatment may create a distressing sense of powerlessness by restricting achievement, by making effort and ability seem less effective, and by demeaning the individual (often publicly). Humiliating experiences may teach individuals to see themselves as socially inferior and thus powerless compared to others. The reality of having to swallow insults or injustices may compel individuals to acknowledge subordinate status. In Chapter 7 we defined the sense of powerlessness as a learned and generalized belief that important outcomes in one's own life are determined by chance, fate, or powerful others. Discrimination speaks of chance and fate, and unfair treatment speaks of powerful others. Perhaps that demoralizing message comes through all too clearly all too often.

V

Conclusion

9

Why Some People Are More Distressed Than Others

CONTROL OF ONE'S OWN LIFE

Of all the things that might explain the social patterns of distress, one stands out: the sense of control over one's own life. Other things explain parts of the patterns, but the sense of control seems central. Many studies in many sciences find the sense of control associated with lower distress. The sense of control reflects the reality of the individual's experiences, opportunities, and resources. It motivates an attentive, active, and proactive approach to problems. The sense of control relates to most of the known social patterns of distress, and also to the other social-psychological explanations of distress. An emotionally beneficial sense of control comes from the power to get things done, rather than from the power to win conflicts. It comes from power over your own life, rather than from power over that of others. Because emotional benefits come from effective action, the optimum sense of control balances optimism and realism, as well as personal freedom and mutual support. Resources that give individuals real control over their own lives, such as education or income, increase the level of perceived control that minimizes depression. While reality puts the optimum sense of control lower for disadvantaged individuals, the vast majority of them would benefit from having a higher sense of control than they do. At all social levels, optimism helps. The greatest benefits, though, come from gaining real control over one's own life.

Control and the Patterns of Distress

All of the established and emerging social patterns of distress point to the sense of control as a critical link. The patterns of emotional well-being reflect the patterns of autonomy, opportunity, and achievement in America. The realities of class and status have a profound influence on the sense of control. Education, family income, unemployment, and economic

253

hardship all affect the sense of control and, through it, depressed and anxious mood and malaise, and even paranoia and schizophrenia.

Minority status—being black, Hispanic, Asian American, or Native American—is also associated with a lower sense of control. Partly it is because of lower education, income, and employment. Partly, though, it reflects an intrinsic fact about minority status. Any given level of achievement requires greater effort, and provides fewer opportunities, for members of minority groups. This fact is not lost on the people who must live with it. It is reflected in a lower sense of control, and consequent distress.

Undesirable events also decrease the sense of control. By their very nature, undesirable events are unwanted. Their occurrence implies the powerlessness to avoid them. Undesirable events also interact with a preexisting sense of powerlessness, magnifying each other's demoralizing impact. Many people are caught in a self-reproducing spiral of undesirable events that lead to difficult situations, both of which undermine the sense of control, which undermines attentive, active, and proactive problem solving, which leads to more undesirable events and difficult situations. Depression, and possibly schizophrenia, emerge from such spirals, and add to them.

Aging also decreases the sense of control. The early years of adulthood combine a moderate income with a strong sense of control, reflecting optimism about the future. Family income peaks in the mid-forties, and drops after the fifties. The sense of control drops with it, and depression rises. The elderly face a reality of difficult and often shocking losses. Only a few have jobs. Many have seen their lifelong friends and partners die. The future promises little more than sickness and death. As resources, networks, and powers decay, so does the sense of control.

The barriers of class and status, the misfortunes of life, and the losses of old age are impersonal oppressors. The personal world of family holds out the hope of an alternative source of power and support. That hope can be realized, but also can be undermined. Marriage is psychologically beneficial for both men and women, but more so for men. Women are more distressed than men, particularly in marriage. The effect of marriage on the sense of control is uniformly positive for men, but there are some contradictory effects for women. On the one hand, marriage increases the sense of control of both men and women by increasing the average household income and by creating a partnership of mutual effort. However, if we compare married and unmarried with similar incomes and social support, the men have a greater sense of control if they are married, and the women have a greater sense of control if they are not married. To the extent that marriage represents an alliance of two partners, it gives both of them greater strength and effectiveness in their own lives. To the extent that marriage represents an unequal alliance, with one partner dominating the other, it benefits one at the expense of the other. For 2 to 4 percent of married persons, an unfair and unsatisfying marriage makes them more distressed than the average person who is separated or divorced.

For married women, employment also shapes the sense of control. In general, employment increases wives' sense of control, but for some it decreases it: employed mothers whose husbands do not share the child care responsibilities with them and who have difficulty arranging child care are under a lot of strain. These women, who are not getting help they desperately need, may feel overwhelmed—powerless to influence their employers and husbands, and powerless to provide proper care for their children.

Control and Other Explanations of Distress

Control is not the only possible explanation of the social patterns of distress. Commitment, support, meaning, normality, flexibility, trust, and equity are other possibilities. Each of these other explanations may add something unique to the overall patterns, but much of what they imply is greater effectiveness, and thus a greater sense of control.

Commitment is seeing your actions and labors as expressions of your own will and identity. Commitment is the opposite of self-estrangement, which is the sense of being the instrument of someone else's will. A slave can perform a task with more or less energy, skill, and insight, but the task is still given rather than chosen. Almost everyone is happier putting as much energy, skill, and insight into a task as it will allow, but any task is better for a volunteer than for a slave. Even the simplest and most tedious task is transformed if it is chosen and performed as a means to one's own ends. People stuffing envelopes for a charitable or political campaign voluntarily and happily perform a task that many couldn't be paid to do. Every task and job is a component in a system of behavior assembled toward some end. If the goal expresses the will of the person performing the task or job, then doing it enhances the person's sense of control.

Support is the sense of being valued by others who are close, and being part of a network of communication and obligation. Support is the opposite of isolation, the sense of detachment from personal relationships. Support can enhance the sense of control by bolstering confidence. Close family and friends are allies, helpers, boosters, and comforters. They may increase a person's control directly by providing services, and indirectly by providing feedback and encouragement. Apparently, though, support can also undermine control. A person can be hemmed in by friends and family, overly constrained by a thicket of obligations. Helpers, boosters, and comforters may inadvertently foster dependency, defensive or unrealistic assessments, and emotional rather than instrumental responses.

While many Americans would benefit from a greater sense of support, a substantial minority would benefit from greater independence.

Meaning is the sense that life is intelligible, purposeful, and valid. Meaninglessness is the opposite sense, that life has no rhyme or reason, that it is "a tale told by an idiot, full of sound and fury and signifying nothing" (Macbeth v.i. 19). Logically, a sense of meaning is necessary for a sense of control. Without knowledge, control is impossible. Without purpose, control is moot. One must judge the value of events and outcomes, and the appropriateness of beliefs and actions. On some level, these judgments rest on conditioned intuition, like finding meaning in language or beauty in music.

Normality is the sense that things are going as expected—as normal. Normlessness is the opposite sense—that social rules and standards do not exist, apply, or fit. Normality enhances the sense of control by making the future seem orderly and predictable. The middle-class student who finishes high school and goes to college acts out of habit, convention, and the belief that going to college will have the same consequences in the future as it had it the past. The young couple intending to finish school, get married, and have a baby can expect things will go more smoothly if they do these things in the usual order than if they do not. Normality enhances the effectiveness of planning, and thus enhances active and proactive problem solving. If norms seem ambiguous, contradictory, or inapplicable, then the individual cannot count on standard means.

Flexibility is a capacity for open-ended, open-minded problem solving. It is characterized by the ability to elaborate and weigh arguments, to consider two or more sides of an issue, to imagine complex solutions to problems, and to imagine multiple or contingent solutions. Flexibility increases the sense of control by allowing the individual to find solutions to problems. In particular, flexibility allows the individual to negotiate with and among others. Flexibility also increases the psychological benefits of a sense of control. It increases the effectiveness of effort, and reduces the tradeoffs between personal control and social support.

Trust is the belief that people are basically benign, charitable, and sincere. It is the opposite of mistrust, which is the belief that others are unsupportive, self-seeking, and devious. Mistrust is highly distressing. A sense of control greatly increases trust, particularly in circumstances that would otherwise be quite threatening. A firm sense of control eliminates the mistrust otherwise associated with life in low socioeconomic positions and disadvantaged and dangerous neighborhoods.

Equity is a sense of proportionality between contributions and rewards, and of fair exchange in relations with others. For the victims, inequity erodes the sense of control. Victims feel caught in unfair situations not of their choosing. For the exploiters, inequity erodes the emotional value of a greater sense of control. Resistance undermines the exploiter's effectiveness. Victims cannot be trusted. Retaliation or rebellion must be feared. The exploiter's sense of personal control may be enhanced, but its emotional value is canceled by mistrust and suspicion.

THE IMPORTANCE OF SOCIAL FACTORS

How important are the social patterns of psychological distress? This question actually has two parts. First, how much of all distress is attributable to social factors? What fraction of the pool of misery would be drained if all social groups had things as good as those who have it best? Second, how serious is the distress that is socially patterned? Is it strictly minor psychological irritation, or does it include extreme states of profound distress? In this section we will show that, by both these standards, the social factors are very important sources of psychological distress.

The Proportion of Symptoms Attributable to Social Factors

Given what we know about the patterns, we can grade people according to their social risk of distress. We divided the 2,592 respondents in the 1995 U.S. ASOC survey into ten groups of roughly equal size, based on their sex, age, marital status, employment status, education, economic hardship, social support, trust, and sense of personal control. There are more social factors we could take into account, but these are the most important. We defined the groups in a way that maximizes the differences among them in average distress. The first group is the 10 percent of the sample (the decile) with the social traits that indicate the lowest risk of distress. The second decile has the second lowest risk, and so on.

The collective impact of the social factors on depression is illustrated in Figure 9.1. The average number of symptoms increases as we go from the decile with the best social traits to the one with the worst. The bars represent the average level of symptoms in each social decile. Each average has two parts. The base represents the symptoms we would find if all ten segments of the sample had the same level of symptoms as the best tenth. The excess represents the symptoms attributable to not having the best social traits. Of all the symptoms reported, 37.1 percent are in the base, and 62.9 percent are excess. In this sense, more than half of all the symptoms of depression are attributable to social factors. In the worst social decile, 85.0 percent of all symptoms are excess above the base—symptoms the people in the best social decile do not have.

Clearly, there is a substantial base of depression that is not attributable to social factors. Even in the best of social circumstances, people get sick, loved ones die, accidents happen, relationships break up, ventures fail,

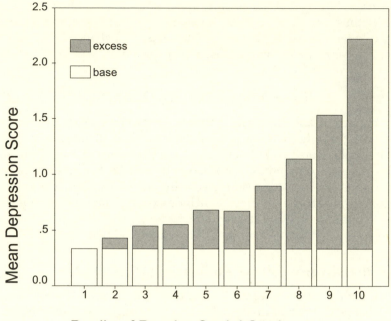

Decile of Psycho-Social Strain

Figure 9.1.   Base and excess depression in the best to worst social deciles. If the rest of society had as few symptoms as the best 10 percent, the total pool of symptoms would be reduced by 62.9 percent. Data are from the 1995 U.S. ASOC survey.

and there are bad weeks. Clearly, there is an equally substantial excess of depression that *is* attributable to social factors. If the most fortunate 10 percent of society avoids the excess depression suffered by others, then perhaps the others can avoid it too. The common strains of human life can be minimized, even if never entirely eliminated.

Social Factors and Severe Psychological Problems

Social factors account for a lot of distress, but do they account for severe psychological problems? Some people believe that serious psychiatric disorder is essentially genetic in origin, and has relatively little relationship to social factors, as discussed in a following section. According to this view, the really serious emotional problems are typically "endogenous" rather than "reactive." This means that they develop from a flaw in the organism, rather than from a normal response to environmental stress. The flaws are more or less random with respect to social traits, so severe psychological

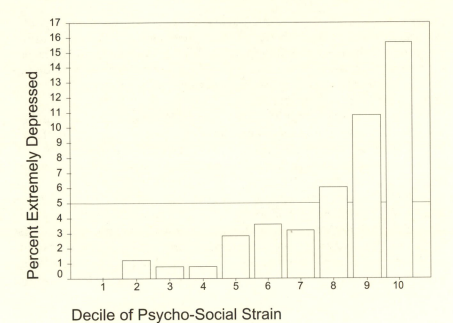

Decile of Psycho-Social Strain

Figure 9.2. The probability of having more symptoms of depression than 95 percent of the sample, by decile of psychosocial strain. Sixty-one percent of persons with scores this extreme qualify for a psychiatric diagnosis. Among
persons who do not qualify for a psychiatric diagnosis, only 3 percent have
symptoms this extreme. Data are from the 1995 U.S. ASOC survey.

problems are more or less random with respect to social traits, too. The
alternative point of view, which we endorse, is that severe psychological
problems are a normal response to very difficult situations. If this is the
case, then extreme distress is a function of social factors, too.

In order to explore this issue, we define extreme depression as having a
level of symptoms greater then 95 percent of the population. By this definition, the extremely depressed have at least four out of seven symptoms
every day. This level of symptoms typically indicates a problem severe
enough to get a psychiatric diagnosis, and it is unusual in people who
would not get a diagnosis. A community study shows that 61 percent of
people with this level of symptoms meet the criteria for a psychiatric diagnosis: Of the severely depressed, 35 percent are eligible for a diagnosis of
major depression, 4 percent for a diagnosis of minor depression, and 22
percent for other diagnoses such as anxiety, phobia, panic, somatization,
or drug abuse (Boyd et al. 1982). Another 37 percent qualify for a diagnosis, but they are grieving the death of someone close, they have a major

physical illness probably causing the depression, or they seem to be functioning normally despite the emotional distress (ibid.). Of people in the community who do not qualify for a psychiatric diagnosis, only 3 percent are severely depressed by our definition. Again, most of those who do not qualify for a diagnosis but are severely depressed are grieving, ill, or managing to function despite their mood.

Severe depression is highly related to social factors, as illustrated in Figure 9.2. The pattern of severe depression by social decile is similar to the pattern of mean depression. In fact, if we split society into two halves, better and worse, the worse half of society has 78.5 percent of all severe depression. The better half has only 21.5 percent of the severe depression. Stated another way, the odds of being severely depressed are 7.5 times greater in the worse half than in the better half. Severe depression is particularly concentrated in the worst 10 percent of society. In the worst decile, 15.7 percent are severely depressed (compared to 4.5 percent in the total sample). This means that the 10 percent of society with the worst social conditions has 35 percent of all the severely depressed in the entire population.

GENETICS AND BIOCHEMISTRY AS ALTERNATIVE EXPLANATIONS

The second half of the twentieth century saw the rise of an enormously wealthy industry marketing drugs for the treatment of depression, anxiety, and other psychological problems. In 1950 few psychiatrists, physicians, or researchers considered drug treatment effective for mental disorders (Glenmullen 2000; Valenstein 1988). By the end of the century the pharmaceutical industry was selling over $4 billion worth of Prozac, Zoloft, and Paxil a year in the U.S. To put it in perspective, that's enough money to buy roughly 27,000 new homes or 40,000 used ones at median prices, each year. Those are just the three top-selling antidepressants designed to boost serotonin levels in the synaptic gaps between neurons (called selective serotonin reuptake inhibitors, or SSRIs). It excludes sales of other SSRIs, antidepressants designed to work through other mechanisms, and a host of mood elevators and anxiety suppressors, not to mention drugs to suppress mania or hallucinations and delusions, drugs to manage behavioral problems such as hyperactivity, and drugs to manage dependency on other drugs.

In order to gain acceptance of drug treatment for psychological distress, the pharmaceutical industry promoted the idea that depression, anxiety, and other psychological problems result from abnormalities in the brain or endocrine system. The favored hypotheses evolve over time (Glenmullen 2000; Valenstein 1988). Currently, the favorite theories about depression argue that it results from (a) a shortage of serotonin in the synaptic gaps between brain neurons that use it to communicate, (b) a similar shortage of norepinephrine in the gaps between the brain neurons that use it to communicate, or (c) structural or functional abnormalities in a hormonal system called the hypothalamic-pituitary-adrenal axis and/or parts of the brain that seem to influence its activity (Glenmullen 2000; Nemeroff 1998; Schwartz 1999; Valenstein 1988). Currently most drug treatment claims to correct one or both of the supposed neurotransmitter deficiencies.

Many Americans, possibly most, now believe that severe, debilitating, or persistent depression and anxiety result from chemical imbalances determined by genetic inheritance. Americans are barraged with advertisements, informational brochures, public service announcements, and news stories promoting that theme. The plain facts are that

(1) the genetic connection is not overwhelming and its mechanisms are unspecified or unconfirmed,

(2) no one has yet demonstrated a correlation of depression or anxiety with a synaptic shortage or excess of serotonin, norepinephrine, or any other neurotransmitter,

(3) the drugs do not help the majority of patients for whom they are supposedly indicated,

(4) placebos produce benefits almost as often and almost as strong, but without the side-effects and withdrawal symptoms, and

(5) cognitive and behavioral therapies work as well as or better than drugs (Glenmullen 2000, Kirsch and Sapirstein 1998; Schwartz 1999; Valenstein 1988).

A full review of the science behind the above statements is beyond the scope of this book. For those who are interested, we recommend the critical reviews and comments by three researchers of very different backgrounds. Glenmullen (2000) is a practicing psychiatrist and clinical instructor in psychiatry at Harvard Medical School. Although he uses therapeutic drugs in his practice, he is alarmed by their indiscriminate, widespread prescription for problems with better and less dangerous treatments. Valenstein (1988) is a former chairman of the biopsychology program at the University of Michigan. He is appalled by the promotional mendacity that obscures the limits of current knowledge and theory, thereby misleading the public and derailing scientific advance. Schwartz (1999) is a sociologist at Columbia School of Public Health. She urges sociologists who study mental health to also study the bioscience of psychological disorders and take part in its debates and investigations, which we endorse.

The following sections briefly critique the evidence for a correlation of depression or anxiety with differences in genetic code, abnormal levels of neurotransmitters, and anomalies of the neuroendocrine system. None of the research demonstrates that any of the social patterns of distress can be explained, in whole or in part, by reference to biopathology. For example, no study demonstrates that differences in genetic code create a spurious association between low education and depression. No study demonstrates that a neurotransmitter shortage creates a spurious association between the sense of powerlessness over one's own life and depression. No study demonstrates that swollen or shrunken structures in the limbic system or in the hypothalamic-pituitary-adrenal (HPA) axis create a spurious association between economic hardship and anxiety. And so on. Similarly, no study demonstrates that biochemical or anatomical effects of alienation, authoritarianism, or inequity mediate their relationships to distress. Studies do show that extreme or chronic stress creates persistent abnormalities in the structure and function of the HPA axis for some individuals. For now, though, it is not clear how important such changes are overall as mediators. Biological research rarely takes representative samples. When it does, it rarely measures the hypothetical biological confounders or mediators. We do not know of any research showing that adjustment for a measured allele (genotype), neurotransmitter level, or HPA anomaly substantially reduces any socioeconomic or social-psychological correlation with distress in the general population. For now, biological explanations of the social patterns of distress rest on speculation from tenuous evidence.

Genetic Predispositions

The weakness of genetic explanations stems from the fact that geneticists have not isolated DNA profiles that distinguish depressed or anxious people from others (Horwitz 2002; National Institute of Mental Health 1997; U.S. Department of Health and Human Services 1999). They also have not isolated alleles (gene variants) that distinguish among the various diagnostic categories of depression and anxiety used by psychiatrists and others. Imagine sociologists trying to demonstrate and unravel the effects of income on depression without ever measuring income. That is the situation geneticists are in. They are only now becoming able to measure the variables they talk about. A gene is an ordered sequence of base pairs located at a particular position on a particular chromosome. The base pairs are chemical codes and the genes are code sequences used as blueprints when cells create molecules they need. Geneticists figure that humans have about three billion base pairs in their twenty-three pairs of chromosomes inherited from mother and father. Differences in genetic heritage come from distinct code sequences (alleles) in a location on a chromosome. Geneticists do not agree on the number of human genes. Textbooks put it around 100,000, but recent estimates are more like 30,000 to 40,000. Biologists generally do not know precisely which genes provide the codes for which proteins or other molecules. Proteins can act as parts of cells, enzymes, hormones, neurotransmitters, and so on. A few genes have been found that apparently code for the receptors where transmitters dock on a receiving neuron or for transporters that pump excess transmitters back into a sending neuron, but variations in those genes do not correlate consistently with emotional problems (National Institute of Mental Health 1997). After decades of looking, those who seek genetic connections to depression and anxiety have not established the specific genes or alleles involved, let alone a pathological structure or process they encode.

So far, the claim of a genetic contribution to depression and anxiety rests largely on studies showing that the odds of having the same or similar emotional problems increases with the degree of genetic relatedness (Horwitz 2002). The best of those studies compare monozygotic (identical) twins to dizygotic (fraternal) twins, or compare twins raised together to those raised apart. Twin studies produce statistics on concordance and heritability. For example, the concordance for unipolar depression (i.e., without manic episodes) is about 40 percent in monozygotic twins and 17 percent in dizygotic ones. In other words, if one twin qualifies for the diagnosis, the probability the other does too is 40 and 17 percent, respectively. Likewise, the probability the other does not qualify for the diagnosis is 60 and 83 percent, respectively. When put into standard equations, these numbers imply a heritability around 30 percent. That number supposedly represents the percentage of variance in major depression across individuals in the population that results from their differences in genetic makeup. Of the various emotional disorders, bipolar depression, obsessive-compulsive disorder, and panic disorder have the largest heritability numbers: about 60, 50, and 40 percent, respectively, although estimates vary greatly across studies (National Institute of Mental Health 1997).

Heritability numbers need to be interpreted with caution, for several reasons. First, the estimates vary widely across studies, possibly because of interactions discussed below. Second, heritability refers to differences in a phenotype (a measurable characteristic) among the individuals in a population at a point in time. It excludes changes in the prevalence or mean level of the trait over time. Heritability estimates can remain constant in a population over decades while environmental trends substantially change the phenotypic prevalence or mean. (This happens with measured IQ, which increases between generations although the heritability estimates remain around 70 percent.) Third, heritability estimates come from statistical models that require assumptions that probably are incorrect (Schwartz 1999). In particular, the models assume that the effects of genes do not depend on the environment. That may rarely be true. Mental health researchers who believe in genetic predisposition usually argue that genetic susceptibility lowers the threshold of a depressed or anxious response to environmental strains. When such an interaction exists, changing the environment changes the heritability. The value calculated then represents the average heritability across environmental conditions at a particular time and place in a population with a particular mix of relevant alleles.

The 1999 surgeon general's report on mental health succinctly states the implications of current scientific beliefs about the genetic inheritance of risk for mental illness:

> To our knowledge, all mental illnesses and all normal variants of behavior are genetically complex. What this means is that no single gene or even a combination of genes dictates whether someone will have an illness or a particular behavioral trait. Rather, mental illness appears to result from the interaction of multiple genes that confer risk, and this risk is converted into illness by the interaction of genes with environmental factors. The implications for science are, first, that no gene is equivalent to fate for mental illness. This gives us hope that modifiable environmental risk factors can eventually be identified and become targets for prevention efforts. (U.S. Department of Health and Human Services 1999:53)

The last caution about heritability estimates may be the most important. The equations for estimating heritability assume a null correlation between genetic and environmental components of variance. Put another way, they treat any differences in mental health that are correlated with differences in genetic makeup as a genetic effect. While logically correct, many individuals misinterpret genetic effects as completely anatomical or physiological in their mechanisms. Currently we have little reason to believe that is the case. For example, genes that encode for negroid features contribute to the estimated heritability of depression to the extent that negroid features correlate with depression. Clearly, genetic heritage influences the density of melanin pigment in skin, which in turn correlates with the risk of depression. Melanin (not to be confused with melatonin) has no known role in the brain or HPA, but it is a major part of why some individuals look black. Heritability estimates are totally blind to the reasons for a correlation. They could include beauty, height, muscularity, and other traits with largely conventional or culture-bound connections to depression and anxiety.

Biochemical Anomalies

The biochemical alternative to social explanations of distress has a weaker base of findings in community research, and more logical problems, than the genetic alternative. The links between nervous response, endocrine activity, and symptoms of distress are well established. We think that these systems, functioning normally, are the mechanism through which events, conditions, perceptions, and beliefs produce the subjective sensation of emotion. To extend the example used above, genetic heritage determines skin color, which heavily determines racial status, which influences opportunity, which influences achievement, which shapes the sense of control, which arouses nervous response and endocrine activity, which is manifest in symptoms of depression and anxiety. The presence of a biochemical link elaborates the causal chain but does not alter the basic story. The question is whether *defects* in the nervous and endocrine systems are a major reason some people are more distressed than others.

The pharmaceutical industry promotes the idea that depression and anxiety result from imbalances in neurotransmitters that their drugs correct. For example, the SSRIs such as Prozac, Zoloft, and Paxil increase the amount of serotonin that remains in synaptic gaps between the neurons that use it to communicate. To sell physicians on prescribing the drugs and patients on taking them the industry insinuates, and often outright says, that the drugs correct a shortage of serotonin that causes depression. Actually, decades of research have failed to demonstrate that low synaptic serotonin levels correlate with depression, let alone cause it (Glenmullen 2000; Valenstein 1988). So far no one can measure the levels of serotonin, or any other neurotransmitter, in the synapses of live humans. Tests exist to measure some byproducts of neurotransmitter chemical reaction that are found in cerebrospinal fluid, urine, or blood cells. Most of those metabolites come from the body's use of the same chemicals for processes other than signaling between brain neurons. So far, no biochemical test exists for depression and anxiety in any of their clinical manifestations, despite half a century of vigorous searching. One reasonable interpretation: chemical imbalances do not characterize the disorders, let alone cause them.

Current drug treatments for depression and anxiety alter the normal physiology and anatomy of the brain (Glenmullen 2000, Valenstein 1988) and liver (Preskorn and Magnus 1994). For example, the SSRIs used to treat depression interfere with processes and structures that clean up the excess serotonin that collects in synapses. Blocking "reuptake" raises the level of serotonin in the gaps. Theoretically that makes each neuron more sensitive to signals from the others. However, the chronic excess of serotonin over a period of a month or two forces compensatory changes in the neurons, to correct the excess sensitivity. Those changes amount to habituation. Once that happens, stopping the drug probably will produce abnormally low serotonin levels. Many patients who stop taking the drugs experience symptoms that they interpret as a sign of really needing the drugs (Glenmullen 2000). Tapering off over several months generally eliminates that need. Many patients simply stay on a drug permanently, long after the episode that led to its use.

Psychiatric drugs often have persistent and sometimes escalating effects. Prozac and other SSRIs inhibit liver enzymes that catalyze the formation of things the body needs such as steroids, prostaglandins, and fatty acids. Those same enzymes also speed the breakdown of foreign chemicals that include pollutants, plant and animal products, alcohols, and other drugs (Preskorn and Magnus 1994). For example, Prozac inhibits the liver's ability to clear Valium, making that drug more potent and more dangerous. Prozac also inhibits the liver enzyme that helps clear Prozac itself. That self-amplification of dose effect probably also amplifies the compensatory changes in neurons. Sometimes the excess serotonin may dominate, and sometimes the compensatory changes. That creates different responses among individuals and drifting or oscillating responses within individuals over time. Naive patients and physicians often misinterpret the effects of blocked liver enzymes, excess neurotransmitters, and compensatory changes in the brain as signs of a disease process that caused the depression, rather than as a consequence of the drug treatment (Glenmullen 2000).

Back in the 1960s social psychologists studying mental health often emphasized the self-fulfilling effects of labeling someone as mentally ill. People often interpret the behavior of those considered mentally ill as a sign of the mental illness, even when the behavior is perfectly normal (Rosenhan 1973). According to labeling theory, being treated as mentally ill elicits "secondary deviance," which is a reaction to being treated as mentally ill. Others see the reaction as distinctive of the mentally ill and thus as a sign of their mental illness. Labeling theory fell into disrepute when its proponents sought to interpret all emotional, mental, and behavioral problems as merely reactions to labeling. A recent revival focuses on labeling as a factor in adjustment to mental illness, rather than as a cause of the emotions, thoughts, and behaviors considered signs of mental illness (see Chapter 7). Perhaps it is time to revive the concept of secondary deviance too, but in a modern biochemical version. Call it "secondary mental disease." When a physician thinks a patient has a neurotransmitter imbalance, the physician prescribes medications that produce side effects, compensatory restructuring, and withdrawal symptoms, often interpreted by the physician and patient as caused by the purported neurotransmitter imbalance. The brain's processes and structures may have been perfectly normal to begin with. Unrelenting chronic exposure to drug-induced neurotransmitter excess produces abnormalities with signs and symptoms taken as confirmation of the purported imbalance supposedly being corrected. Psychiatric drug treatment might actually turn distress into disease, while seemingly justifying itself in the process.

Structural Anomalies

Research on animals shows that exposure to severe or chronic stress creates persistent anomalies in the structure and function of the endocrine system, and also in parts of the brain that regulate endocrine response (LeDoux 1996; Sapolsky 1998; Selye 1976). Research on humans suggests similar effects of severe or chronic stress (Gold et al. 1988; Nemeroff 1998; U.S. Department of Health and Human Services 1999). The organs involved activate and regulate the organism's response to threats, called the fight or flight syndrome. The system, functioning normally, plays a major role in anger, fear, and anxiety. Apparently the system also reshapes itself in response to chronic stress, somewhat like muscles getting larger and more efficient from exercise. Unlike greater strength and stamina, though, a beefed-up stress response produces undesirable effects, particularly in the context of modern society, where neither fighting nor fleeing are functional. Not surprisingly, the beefed-up stress response seems to play a major role in anxiety disorders such as panic, phobia, posttraumatic stress, and generalized anxiety. Oddly, it also seems to play a major role in depression, although the mechanisms are not clear. Some researchers speak of the changes as "permanent" (e.g., Nemeroff 1998), but "persistent" might be more accurate.

The structures involved in the stress response link the brain's perception of threat to the body's general state of alarm. A tiny structure in the brain called the hypothalamus has neurons that act like endocrine glands. They secrete a variety of hormones that travel down a tube to a gland called the pituitary, which in turn releases other hormones into the blood that circulate to remote organs where they stimulate chemical responses. In the stress response, the hypothalamus releases corticotropin-releasing hormone (CRH), which gets it name from the fact that it stimulates the pituitary to release adrenocorticotropic hormone (ACTH). When the ACTH reaches the adrenal glands, it stimulates the release of three other hormones. Epinephrine (adrenaline) stimulates heart rate, metabolic rate, and glucose concentration, which delivers energy to muscles for fight or flight. Norepinephrine (noradrenaline) is similar to epinephrine but also acts as a neurotransmitter in the sympathetic nervous system, which increases heart and respiration rate and sweating, shuts down digestive and sexual activity, and redirects blood flow to muscles. Cortisol (hydrocortisone) stimulates the creation of blood sugar and suppresses inflammatory and immune response.

Decades ago researchers discovered that exposure of laboratory animals to chronic psychosocial stressors such as crowding or unstable status hierarchies produces structural changes in several organs. The adrenal glands get enlarged, the stomach gets ulcerated, and the thymus and lymph nodes degenerate (Selye 1976). While interesting, these changes seem unlikely to greatly heighten susceptibility to anxiety and depression. Degeneration of the thymus and lymph nodes reduces immune response, which is more directly relevant to physical health than to emotional well-being. Gastric ulcers are unpleasant, but otherwise probably not a major link to distress. Enlarged adrenal glands can generate and pump more hormones, but that is more a result than a cause of heightened response. Current research suggests that stress-induced changes in a specific part of the brain may occur along with the well-known changes to endocrine glands, increasing susceptibility to both anxiety and depression.

Recall that a part of the brain called the pituitary initiates the stress response in the endocrine system by releasing CRH. According to current theory, that release is regulated by two other parts of the brain (LeDoux 1996; McEwen 1998; Nemeroff 1998; Sapolsky 1998; U.S. Department of Health and Human Services 1999). The amygdala signals the pituitary to release CRH, and the hippocampus signals it to stop releasing CRH. Together, the balance of "go" and "stop" signals regulates the phasing (rise and fall) and intensity of the stress response. The amygdala combines immediate sensory information with learned emotional meaning of events and objects. The hippocampus encodes and consolidates memories distinguishing persons, places, things, and events that have emotional undertones. The hippocampus also happens to have many receptors for cortisol, and thus serves a thermostat-like control function. When blood cortisol levels are high or rising rapidly, the hippocampus signals the pituitary to cut back on the release of CRH. Unfortunately, the high sensitivity to cortisol means that high levels of it can damage the hippocampal neurons. Under peak load a neuron can suffer a deficit of energy or oxygen and die. To protect themselves from frequent exposure to high cortisol, the neurons atrophy dendrites, which are their signal-receiving filaments. Over time the trimming of dendrites lowers the responsiveness of the hippocampus to high or rising cortisol. (It also impairs some memory functions.) While that protects the neurons in the short run, it reduces the ability of the hippocampus to counteract the "go" signals from the amygdala during exposure to stress. As a result the levels of epinephrine, norepinephrine, and cortisol rise faster with less provocation, peak higher, and stay high longer. That in turn puts the hippocampal neurons at even greater risk.

The theory of hippocampal atrophy is appealing for several reasons. In particular, it explains how chronic exposure to stressful events and conditions might produce cumulative, self-amplifying changes that begin as adaptive but eventually become pathological. Clearly, research needs to look for accumulators that sum the effects of experience. Accumulators allow the flow of past events to have effects in the present. They create current experience and also sometimes regulate response to it. It is important to recognize, though, that accumulators need not be pathological or even biological to account for the effects of past experience on current emotional state. Conditions and beliefs can be stable influences on behavior and emotion. Animals learn helplessness through perfectly normal conditioning. Likewise, humans learn to see themselves as powerless or in control through the same normal processes by which they learn to see themselves as attractive or not, smart or not, and so on. Learning restructures the brain. It raises or lowers response thresholds, grows or deletes synaptic connections, and perhaps even grows or deletes neurons. Those changes need not be pathological on the organic level, no matter how disturbing the associations and beliefs they encode. Chronic or recurring distress also can result from stable conditions such as racial or ethnic disadvantage. While those are fixed ascribed statuses, other stable conditions represent sums of past gains or losses, such as level of education, work history, job quality, accumulated wealth, marital history, and marital quality. Each person's habits, beliefs, and situation carry the past into the present, with consequences for emotional well-being.

The amygdala and hippocampus both seem to house or channel memories by which the need for alarm gets judged. Those memories, rather than hippocampal atrophy, may prove the real source of heightened reactivity, anxiety, and depression. The biological researchers say a correlation exists between some types of extreme anxiety and depression and measures of hippocampal pathology (Nemeroff 1998; U.S. Department of Health and Human Services 1999). As knowledge progresses, those correlations may prove spurious in part or in whole. The same memories and associations that evoke anxiety and depression may stimulate the alarm that eventually causes hippocampal pathology. That pathology may be nothing more than another consequence of those memories and associations, rather than a critical link in the causal chain. The memories that go unmeasured in pathology studies determine the balance of signals to the pituitary, thereby causing the hippocampal pathology. Adjustment for those memories might well eliminate the correlation between measures of the pathology and measures of mental health. Clearly, people with no signs of hippocampal pathology get anxious and depressed, sometimes severely. Currently there is no conclusive evidence that hippocampal pathology causes anxiety or depression in any of their forms. It might contribute to some types of problems more than others, but the correlation also might be completely spurious in every case. It is not even entirely clear that the correlations really exist.

The hypothetical correlations between measures of hippocampal pathology and diagnoses of depression and anxiety rest on uncertain ground, because of difficulty measuring the hypothetical pathology in live humans (Schwartz 1999). The hypothetical degeneration occurs in a part of a relatively small structure deep inside the brain. Brain scans have to measure the size or activity levels in tiny regions, and biochemical tests need to measure tiny amounts of byproducts or peculiar patterns of rise and fall in blood levels of the byproducts. It is easy to lose the signal in the noise, and just as easy to perceive a pattern where none exists. Researchers also take unrepresentative samples, because they must use patients who are available and willing. As a result, the kinds of people studied can vary greatly across studies. These difficulties create variance in results across studies, with some seeming to find the expected correlations and others not. Researchers also often select the mentally ill sample in a questionable manner designed to maximize the odds of finding the predicted correlation. For example, researchers sometimes select only depressed individuals who also show signs of agitation and restlessness. Comparing that group to a randomly selected group of nondepressed patients loads observations in favor of finding more signs among the depressed group of inability to shut down the stress response or of hippocampal atrophy. Even so, the correlations of depression and anxiety with brain scans and biochemical assays are too weak and inconsistent for reliable use in diagnosis, even for the subtypes considered most strongly based in biopathology.

No Biological Test Yet

Over a decade ago we reviewed the literature on the two hot-topic biological tests for depression: the dexamethasone nonsuppression test for hypercortisolism, and 3-methoxy-4-hydroxy-phenylglycol (MHPG) test for norepinephrine metabolism. Neither one panned out.

The dexamethasone nonsuppression test identifies individuals who fail to suppress cortisol output. Dexamethasone is a synthetic variant of cortisol. After an injection of dexamethasone, the hippocampus should detect the rapid increase and high level of what it sees as cortisol and signal the pituitary to cut down cortisol release from the adrenal glands. If the injection fails to suppress cortisol output, that suggests atrophy of the regulating neurons in the hippocampus. There is little reason to think cortisol dysregulation causes depression. For example, there are great differences in cortisol levels among nonsuppressors, but those differences are not associated with worse mood or worse personal and social functioning (Carroll et al. 1981). Depression and cortisol dysregulation probably both result from prolonged stress (Gold et al. 1988). Cortisol dysregulation appears to be an additional or secondary consequence of the same things that cause depressed mood: chronic personal, social, economic, and environmental stressors.

Other tests measure blood or urine concentrations of MHPG. The chemical is a product of the metabolism of norepinephrine (noradrenaline) in brain neurons mainly in a structure called the locus coeruleus and the pons (Gold et al. 1988). In the early 1980s, experts said low levels indicate depression (e.g., Baldessarini 1983), later they said it was high levels (Gold et al. 1988), and now they again say it is low levels (e.g., Nemeroff 1998). One theory said a shortage of norepinephrine at critical receptors causes depression (called the "catecholamine-depletion hypothesis"). Another theory said depression is marked by excess activity of neurons that synthesize norepinephrine and release it at the synapse. Some studies find relatively low levels of MHPG in the blood and urine of depressed people, and others find relatively high levels. Feelings of depression correlate with both agitation and exhaustion, as our results in an earlier chapter show. Whether MHPG is higher or lower in depressed patients compared to nondepressed controls may depend on whether the sampling bias favors the selection of patients in an agitated state or an exhausted one. The fact that the depressed mood is the same in either case contradicts the idea that the mood results from either arousal or depletion in nerves that synthesize norepinephrine. It suggests that the depressed mood, the agitation, and the exhaustion have the same causes: chronic personal, social, economic, and environmental stressors.

Unlike the glucose tolerance test for diabetes, there are no definitive biological tests for emotional disorders. When we wrote the first edition of this book we said something that remains true today: medicine is not about to require biological indications of underlying brain pathology for medical intervention. If biochemical or anatomical signs of pathology were required for treatment with psychotherapeutic drugs, the market for those drugs would be severely curtailed. The biochemical tests and brain-scanning technologies provide scientific window dressing. No one uses them to diagnose depression and anxiety because they do not distinguish the mentally ill from the mentally well, do not distinguish one type of mental illness from another, do not adequately predict who will get worse or better in the absence of drug treatment, and do not adequately predict which patients will get better given which treatments. At core, anxiety and depression are known today by what they always have been: someone feels worried, restless, afraid, sad, lonely, hopeless, worthless, and so on. As social scientists, we should be forgiven for pointing out one possibility. Maybe biological tests are not useful because the origin and essence of emotional problems does not lie in anatomical or physiological pathology.

Down-Regulating Iatrogenic Helplessness

Portraying anxiety and depression as essentially biological pathologies has damaging implications that need to be stated and criticized. Not all research into the biology of emotions argues for an anatomical or physiological pathology. Intense and even bizarre manifestations of anxiety can be explained in terms of essentially normal learning processes (LeDoux 1996), as can profound helplessness (Seligman 1975). Unfortunately, knowledge about brain, mind, and emotion too often serves an ideological and commercial purpose: justifying medical interventions. The message is clear: anxiety and depression are beyond control except by medical intervention. Even sociological correlations are harnessed to promote the myth of biopathology. For example, a correlation between childhood abuse or neglect with later overactive stress response is portrayed as indicating permanent damage to the brain (Nemeroff 1998). Where is that idea leading? Perhaps to lifelong drug treatment from childhood on of individuals born to poverty and strife. Drug treatments have many problems, as the previous sections suggest. Even if they create no side effects and no pathological changes in the brain, they still deliver a destructive message: anxiety and depression are the result of chance, fate, and luck, and correcting or avoiding them is in the hands of powerful others. An individual who believes this has no reason to seek causes in experiences of the past. A society that believes it has no reason to seek the social wellsprings of distress and correct them.

Breggin (1991) calls the physiological and ideological effects of psychotherapeutic drug treatment "iatrogenic helplessness." The adjective "iatrogenic" refers to something induced in a patient by a physician's activity, manner, or therapy, most often in reference to a complication.

> Even without the production of brain dysfunction, the giving of drugs or other physical interventions tends to reinforce the doctor's role as an authority and the patient's role as a helpless or sick person. The patient learns that he or she has a "disease," that the doctor has a "treatment," and that the patient must "listen to the doctor" in order to "get well again." The patient's learned helplessness and submissiveness is then vastly amplified by the brain damage. The patient becomes more dutiful to the doctor and to the demoralizing principles of biopsychiatry. . . . I have designated this unique combination of authoritarian suggestion and brain damage by the term *iatrogenic helplessness*. (Breggin 1991:59).

Breggin's views may seem extreme. As a practicing psychiatrist, he seems deeply frustrated from decades of trying to get his colleagues to view their patients as human beings with human problems. Glenmullen, another practicing psychiatrist, hides his irritation better, but expresses similar views (Glenmullen 2000). To him, a therapist's job is to help patients gain control of their own emotional well-being by helping them see how specifics of their past experience and present circumstance combine to make them anxious or depressed. In his view, drug therapy often clouds the issues and misleads the patient. As sociologists, we look for the ways that society again and again generates and reinforces distress, rather than for the specific distressing elements of an individual's history and situation. Even so, we share their alarm about the message of drug treatment, sometimes merely implied but all too often stated baldly as if it were true, that emotional problems are random bad luck that insight and action will never change.

We think that some people are more distressed than others primarily because they are in difficult circumstances that their personal histories have not prepared them to master. The social differences in misery are not just an epiphenomenon of genetics and biochemistry. Certainly, for anything to happen in a human being, there must be a genetic potential realized in biological structure and process. We are social. We think. We feel. These things come from the organism. The basic link between powerlessness and distress probably comes from the organism. But the man out of work, the employed woman wondering if her children are all right, the black facing discrimination, the divorcee alone and uncertain, the old person losing everything, the young family struggling to make ends meet—these things come from the world we create for ourselves and each other. They come from society.

WHAT CAN BE DONE

Social factors are important explanations of why some people are more distressed than others. They account for at least half of all symptoms, and for the large majority of serious distress. We think the evidence shows that distress, whether moderate or severe, is primarily a normal response to difficult circumstances, rather than a manifestation of unseen flaws in the organism. If we are correct, what does it mean? Is there anything people can do about it? A person can't stop growing old. A woman can't become a man. A black can't become white. The ascribed statuses are given, not chosen. Likewise, if people are miserable because they are poor, what good does it do to tell them they would be happier if they were rich? Chances are they already suspect this is true.

What can be done? Our answer to this question goes beyond what we have learned to what we think it implies. It is a judgment: an opinion based on consideration of the evidence and arguments. As researchers, rather than counselors, giving advice is out of our line. We feel a bit uncomfortable making judgments and giving advice about what to do. Like most researchers, we want you to think about what we have learned and about the other things you know, and make your own judgment. Still, it would be false to suggest that we have no opinion. To us it seems that our opinion was formed by the things we learned. To others is may seem that our opinion colors the things we learned. In the end, it seems best to say what we think can be done about distress, so you can consider it in making your own judgment.

We think that the informed individual and the informed community can do a great deal to prevent distress. We also think that strategies for preventing distress can be built on a few simple things: education, a fulfilling job, a supportive relationship, and a decent living are to mental health what exercise, diet, and not smoking are to physical health. Emotional well-being is founded on active, attentive, and effective problem-solving. Unpleasant emotions are not themselves the problems to be solved. They are signs that problems remain unsolved. Hiding from problems, hoping they'll go away on their own, and disowning responsibility for the things that happen in one's life are formulas for failure and distress. Focusing on the distress itself, rather than trying to understand and overcome its cause, is also a formula for continued failure and distress. Drugs that ease distress do not solve problems, whether they are self-administered or prescribed by a professional. Easing the emotional pain may be humane. It may help a person regain sufficient composure to address the problems. It is not itself a solution. Similarly, having someone else solve your current problems is not a long-run solution. As with drug-induced relief, it is temporary and counterproductive unless it merely lightens your burdens while building strength. Emotional well-being is not simply the luck of the draw. It does not come from telling yourself comforting lies, or from being told comforting lies. It does not come from salves and ointments. Emotional well-being comes from facing and solving problems.

Education: The Headwaters of Well-Being

The process of becoming educated is one of encountering and solving problems that are progressively more difficult, complex, and subtle. Even if the things learned had no practical value in life, the process of learning would build confidence and self-assurance. But the things learned do have practical value. The most general, and the one of greatest value, is the habit of meeting problems with attention, thought, action, and persistence. The next most general are the habits and skills of communication: reading, writing, inquiring, discussing, looking things up, asking around, and so on. These are important for two reasons: they build and provide access to the culture's store of solutions to standard problems, and they enhance the ability to negotiate and coordinate with others toward common ends. The next most general are analytic skills used in many different endeavors. These include the traditional mathematical skills, such as algebra, calculus, and statistics, and the newer skills, such as systems analysis, computer modeling, word processing, and the design and management of databases. Finally, there are the ideas and skills needed to practice a specific occupation, such as chemistry, carpentry, journalism, engineering, printing, agriculture, plumbing, social work, law, nursing, psychology, mechanics, business, and geology. This is where the general means of solving problems are tailored to a specific set of related problems. Education develops the ability to solve problems on all these levels. Solving problems is the way to emotional well-being.

Education is available to both the individual and the community as a means toward well-being. Every individual can improve his or her knowledge and skills. Many, perhaps most, could arrange additional formal training. It is true that there are large differences in educational opportunity. It is equally true that everyone can exploit the opportunities that are available. We think most would benefit by doing so.

The community can choose to improve the educational opportunities available to all individuals who want to learn. From preschool through postdoctoral training, the community can strive to improve quality and broaden opportunity. It is far better to give people the skills they need to solve the problems they encounter, than it is to let people be overwhelmed, and become problems for us all. The educated community is a prosperous one. Prosperity improves the emotional well-being of the entire community. When the level or quality of education available to a segment of the community improves, the benefit is enjoyed by all segments.

One important thing a community can do is to treat education as a lifelong process of development. Traditionally, our society has treated education as something like a booster rocket. Some people get a bigger boost than others, but everyone's educational fuel is spent by the mid-twenties. Historically it was convenient to organize education this way. These days, it makes less and less sense. Going to school is not just for kids anymore. There is the welfare mother who has decided that dropping out of school wasn't such a good idea after all, the assembly line worker whose plant closed, the woman returning to the labor force after years as a housewife, and the fifty-year-old chemist facing a company reorganization. If these people want to go to school, it should be possible. Making it possible will require new forms of organization and new support services. Whenever and wherever people realize that they need to learn more, the means should be available.

A Good Job: Adequate Income, a Measure of Autonomy, Accommodation to Family

Some of the reason education is important to emotional well-being is because of what it leads to. Foremost is a job. Study after study in the United States finds that employment reduces distress. There is something about having a job, in and of itself, that is good for people. Even if we compare employed women and housewives with the same levels of family income, the employed women are less distressed. There are conditions that counteract the emotional benefits of having a job, but employment benefits Americans in most circumstances.

Not all jobs are equally beneficial. It's good to have a job. It's better to have a good job. In terms of its impact on distress, a good job has three major attributes. First, it pays enough to eliminate the family's economic hardship. Being unable to pay for the food, clothing, shelter, transportation, or health care one's family needs is extremely distressing. Second, a good job allows a measure of autonomy. Jobs that give people a say in what they do and how they do it are much more gratifying than jobs that do not. Third, a good job minimizes conflict between the demands of work and family. Jobs that keep people from ever seeing their families, or make it difficult to manage child care, can be as distressing, and sometimes even more distressing, than unemployment.

Education increases the likelihood of having a good job, and helps to make jobs better. Education leads to jobs that pay more, that allow greater autonomy, and that provide the flexibility (and sometimes even direct services) that reduce conflicts between work and family. Education also helps people get more out of the job they have. It helps people to spend their earnings and family income more effectively. At any given level of income, people with higher education have fewer difficulties providing the things their families need. The association between low income and a sense of economic hardship is decreased by education. Education also helps people negotiate with their employers or supervisors, allowing greater autonomy and reducing tension between job and family demands. Education is not the only way to get a better job, or to make a job better, but it is a good way and an important one.

A Supportive Relationship: Fair and Caring

The final ingredient in well-being is a supportive relationship. Emotionally, it is good to have someone you care about and who cares about you. This appears to be an elementary human need. Supportive relationships reduce distress, whatever the conditions and events of life. To work, the relationship must be balanced and fair, with neither person exploiting the other. Education promotes supportive relationships. By increasing the likelihood of employment and the level of pay, education reduces economic strains on a relationship. Poverty makes it very difficult to build and maintain supportive and equitable relationships. Education also helps partners understand and negotiate with each other. Education develops cognitive flexibility, which includes the ability to see more than one side of an issue. Inflexible people respond to differences in preferences, opinions, and goals with anger, indignation, and punishment. Flexible people respond with attempts to understand the other's position and to arrange something that is mutually satisfactory. Flexibility improves the ability to build and maintain a supportive relationship.

"TAKE ARMS AGAINST A SEA OF TROUBLES"

Why are some people more distressed than others? Our answer is that some conditions rob people of control over their own lives. The insidious message of conditions such as joblessness, dependency, alienated labor, and victimization can ingrain a gut sense of futility and powerlessness that demoralizes and distresses. But, however threatening or constricting the situation, it is better to try to understand and solve the problems it poses then it is to avoid or meekly bear them as the inevitable burden of life. The most destructive situations hide from people in them the fact that everyone has a choice. As Shakespeare's Hamlet put it (Act III, scene i), the choice is to "suffer the slings and arrows of outrageous fortune," or to "take arms against a sea of troubles, and by opposing end them."

APPENDIX

Description of Data Sets and Measures

AGING, STATUS, AND THE SENSE OF CONTROL SURVEY

In 1995 we collected the first wave of the Aging, Status, and the Sense of Control (ASOC) Survey. It is a national telephone probability sample of U.S. households. Respondents were selected using a prescreened random-digit dialing method that decreased the probability of contacting a business or nonworking number and decreased standard errors compared with the standard Mitofsky-Waksberg method while producing a sample with the same demographic profile (Lund and Wright 1994; Waksberg 1978). The ASOC survey had two subsamples designed to produce an 80 percent oversample of persons aged 60 or older. The main sample drew from all households; the oversample drew only from households with one or more adults aged 60 years or older. In the main sample, the adult (18 years or older) with the most recent birthday was selected as respondent. In the oversample, the senior (60 years or older) with the most recent birthday was selected. The survey was limited to English-speaking adults. Up to 10 callbacks were made to select and contact a respondent, and up to 10 call-backs were used to complete the interview once contact was made. Interviews were completed with 71.6 percent of contacted and eligible persons: 73.0 percent for the main sample and 67.3 percent for the oversample. The final sample had 2,592 respondents ranging in age from 18 to 95. Fifty-eight percent of the sample was under age 60 ($N = 1,496$) and 42 percent of the sample was 60 years and older ($N = 1,096$).

The following statistics compare the demographic characteristics of the ASOC sample to those for the U.S. population as a whole (U.S. Bureau of the Census 1995). These statistics are weighted to compensate for the oversample of seniors. For the ASOC sample and the U.S. population, respectively, there were 56.2 and 51.2 percent women, 85.1 and 82.9 percent white, and 55.7 and 55 percent married (excluding cohabitors and the separated). The mean household size was 2.67 and 2.59. For people aged 25 or

278

older, the percentages with a high school diploma were 85.1 and 80.9 percent, and the percentages with a college degree were 25.6 and 22.2 percent. The mean household incomes were $43,949 and $41,285.

In 1998 we reinterviewed 56 percent of the respondents. Younger people, blacks, unmarried persons, those with lower levels of education, the unemployed, and older people with high levels of physical impairment and depression were less likely to be reinterviewed. We take this into account in all the analyses that follow respondents over time.

Depression is measured using a modified, seven-item version of the Center for Epidemiological Studies' Scale of Depression (CES-Dm; Ross and Mirowsky 1984). Respondents were asked, "On how many days during the past week (0–7) have you: felt you just couldn't get going? had trouble keeping your mind on what you were doing? had trouble getting to sleep or staying asleep? felt that everything was an effort? felt lonely? felt you couldn't shake the blues? felt sad?" The first four items measure the malaise component of depression and the second three measure mood. Level of depression is equal to the mean of all seven responses and can range from 0 to 7. Respondents averaged depressive symptoms about one day per week (mean = .93). Depression is a good overall indicator of poor mental health because it is correlated with other aspects of distress such as anxiety and anger (Mirowsky and Ross 1995) and with the clinical diagnosis of depression (Weissman, Scholomskas, Pottenger, Prusof, and Locke 1977), making it a sensitive psychological barometer of life strains (Pearlin and Johnson 1977). In this study, the scale had an alpha reliability of .85. CES-Dm correlates .92 with the full version of the scale.

Depression can also be divided into sadness (depressed mood), the absence of happiness (positive mood), and malaise. *Sadness* averages the frequency of feeling sad, lonely, and unable to shake the blues (α-reliability = .82). *Happiness* averages the frequency of feeling happy, feeling hopeful about the future, and enjoying life (α = .79). *Malaise* averages the frequency of feeling everything is an effort, feeling that you just can't get going, having trouble keeping your mind on what you are doing, and having trouble getting to sleep or staying asleep (α = .73).

Anxiety averages the frequency of worrying a lot about little things, feeling tense or anxious, and feeling restless (α = .82). *Anger* averages the frequency of feeling angry, feeling annoyed with things or people, and yelling at someone (α = .71). *Aches* averages the frequency of having aches and pains, having headaches, and feeling weak all over (α = .60).

Response tendencies are measured in two ways. The first measure is a *self-evident question* about agreement with the statement, "I keep my emotions to myself." The response categories are "strongly disagree" (coded –2), "disagree" (–1), "don't know" (0), "agree" (1), and "strongly agree" (2). The second is an *unobtrusive latent factor* implicit in the reports of positive mood and depressed mood. People who report more of both are considered more expressive.

Parental divorce was measured by asking respondents, "Thinking back to your childhood, were your parents divorced before you were 18 years old?" Seventeen percent of respondents experienced parental divorce before age 18.

Socioeconomic status includes education, lifetime occupational status, household income, current economic hardship, and a history of economic hardship.

We measure *education* as the number of years of formal education completed. On average, respondents had completed 13.40 years in 1995.

The survey asked all respondents who had ever been employed full-time about their *occupation*. We assigned all respondents a lifetime occupational status score as follows. Respondents currently working for pay were assigned NORC/GSS SEI scores based on their current occupation (Nakao, Hodge, and Treas 1990). For those not currently employed, we used the SEI score based on the respondent's most recent full-time job. Only 6.4 percent of the sample had never been employed. We scored these missing cases to the mean SEI score (44.59) and included a dummy variable scored 1 for persons missing on occupational prestige in initial regressions. By using lifetime occupational prestige, we did not exclude people who are not currently in the paid labor force.

We measured three aspects of *economic resources*: household income, economic hardship, and a history of economic hardship. Household income was coded in thousands of dollars per year. The mean household income was $43,949. Current economic hardship was measured by asking respondents, "During the past 12 months, how often did it happen that (1) you did not have enough money to pay for medical care; (2) you did not have enough money to buy food, clothes, or other things your household needed; and (3) you had trouble paying the bills?" Responses were coded never (0), not very often (1), fairly often (2), or very often (3). The three items were averaged (mean = 1.44). History of economic hardship was measured by asking respondents, "Was there ever a time when you didn't have enough money for clothes, food, rent, bills, or other necessary things like that?" Responses were coded no (0) or yes (1). At some time in their adult lives, 42.5 percent of respondents experienced economic hardship.

Interpersonal Relationships. Problems in interpersonal relationships take two forms: those relating to close relationships and those that are more general. The first includes a history of divorce and remarriage, an early marriage, a current unhappy relationship with a spouse or partner, or no current close relationship. General interpersonal problems include a lack of trust in other people and low social support.

A history of divorce and remarriage was measured by first asking respondents, "How many times have you been married?" Responses were initially coded from 0 (never been married) to 5 marriages. Persons who reported 3 or more marriages had 2 or more divorces. We coded people with 2 or more divorces (and 3 or more marriages) as having a history of divorce and remarriage (1) as compared with all others (0). Of all respondents, 4.4 percent had 2 or more divorces.

An early marriage was measured by first asking respondents, "How old were you when you were (first) married?" Respondents who were married before the age of 19 were coded 1 for an early marriage, compared with everyone else, who received a code of 0; 15.8 percent of respondents married before the age of 19.

Current relationship presence and quality compared people in a happy relationship with those in an unhappy relationship and no relationship. This set of comparisons allowed us to include the quality of relationships for those in them as well as people who were not currently in a relationship. People in a relationship reported that they were (a) married, (b) living together with someone as married, or (c) "had any one person they would consider their significant other or intimate partner." Thus we defined close relationships broadly to include marriage and other partnerships. Everyone who reported being married, cohabiting, or having a partner was asked, "How happy would you say you are with your partner?" Responses were coded as very happy (1), somewhat happy (2), somewhat unhappy (3), or very unhappy (4). They were also asked, "In the past 12 months how often would you say that the thought of leaving your partner crossed your mind?" Responses were coded never (1), rarely (2), sometimes (3), or often (4). Dissatisfaction with one's relationship was the mean response to these two questions coded so that high scores indicated unhappy relationships. In order to create a set of three contrasts, we dichotomized partner dissatisfaction at the mean, calling those with above-average dissatisfaction "unhappy" and those with below-average dissatisfaction "happy," and we created two dummy variables contrasting no relationship and an unhappy relationship with a happy relationship.

Social support includes emotional and instrumental support. To measure emotional support, respondents were asked about their agreement with the following statements: "I have someone I can turn to for support and understanding when things get rough" and "I have someone I can really talk to." For instrumental support, the statements were: "I have someone who would help me out with things, like give me a ride, watch the kids or house, or fix something" and "I have someone who would take care of me if I were sick." Responses were coded from 1 to 5, where 1 = strongly disagree, 2 = disagree, 3 = neutral or not sure, 4 = agree, and 5 = strongly agree. The responses were averaged (α = .85, mean = 3.312).

Mistrust is the generalized expectation that other people can or cannot be trusted (Rotter 1980). Interviewers asked respondents, "On how many of the past 7 days have you (1) felt it was safer to trust no one, (2) felt suspicious, and (3) felt sure everyone was against you?" Mistrust was the mean score on these three measures and ranged from a low of 0 to a high of 7 (α = .62). The average response is 0.52 (about half a day per week).

Age at first birth is measured by asking respondents, "How old were you when your first child was born?" *Parenthood* is coded 1 for people who report having had one or more children and 0 for others, in response to the question, "How many children have you had in total (whether or not they live in the household)?"

Sociodemographic Characteristics include parental education; age measured in years; minority status, coded 0 for whites and 1 for nonwhites and Hispanics; and sex, coded 0 for men and 1 for women. In terms of sociodemographics, the average age was 47.60 years, 57.5 percent of the respondents were women, and 17.5 percent were minorities. Parental education was measured as the average number of years of education attained by the respondent's parents, which had a mean score of 11.21. Mothers' and fathers' educations were correlated .574; mothers' educations correlated .876 with the average, and fathers' educations correlated .853 with the average. If data were missing for one parent, we used the value for the other parent. If data were missing for both parents, we assigned the mean. We included a dummy variable scored 1 for respondents who were missing on parental education in the regressions.

COMMUNITY, CRIME, AND HEALTH SURVEY

Community, Crime, and Health (CCH) is a probability sample of Illinois households with linked census tract information, based on addresses. Census tracts are the best approximation of neighborhoods. Where tract information was missing, we used zip codes. Respondents were interviewed by telephone and were selected into the sample by random-digit dialing. There are 2,470 respondents, age 18 and older, in wave 1, collected in 1995. We use the multilevel statistical modeling program MLn to analyze the data.

Mistrust is assessed by three questions. Respondents were asked the number of days in the past week they "felt it was not safe to trust anyone," "felt suspicious," and "felt sure everyone was against you."

Neighborhood disadvantage is an index of the percentage of tract households with children headed by women and the percentage of tract households below the federal poverty line.

Perceived neighborhood disorder refers to conditions and activities, both major and minor, criminal and noncriminal, that residents perceive to be signs of the breakdown of social order. The index measures physical signs of disorder such as graffiti, vandalism, noise, and abandoned buildings, and social signs such as crime, people hanging out on the street, people drinking, or using drugs (see Chapter 5).

The sense of personal powerlessness vs. control is a 2×2 index that balances statements claiming or denying control over good or bad outcomes, like "I can do just about anything I really set my mind to" on the one hand, or "There is no sense planning a lot—if something good is going to happen it will", on the other. The scale is also shown in chapter 7. The balanced 2×2 design eliminates defensiveness (the tendency to claim control over good outcomes but deny control over bad) and agreement bias from the measure of personal control.

Individual sociodemographic characteristics include individual education, household income, family status, age, sex, and race. Education is measured in years of formal education completed, and age is measured in years. Household income is measured in thousands of dollars. Race is a dummy variable coded 1 for whites and 0 for nonwhites. Marital status is coded 1 for people who are married or living together as married, and coded 0 for people who are single, divorced or separated, or widowed.

Urban residence is measured by a dummy variable contrasting residence in Chicago (coded 1) with suburbs, small cities, towns, and rural areas (coded 0). Sixteen percent of respondents lived in the city of Chicago.

Individual drinking and deviance is measured by heavy drinking and criminal activity. We measured heavy drinking by asking, "On average, how often do you drink any alcoholic beverages such as beer, wine, or liquor?" and "On the days that you drink, on average, how many alcoholic drinks do you have?" From these questions, we computed a drinking quantity/frequency score by multiplying the number of days per week a person drinks by the number of drinks reported for the average day. We then created a dummy variable for heavy drinking defined as more than 14 drinks a week (coded 1) and compared with everyone else (coded 0); 4.5 percent of the sample drank heavily. Finally, criminal activity in the last year was measured by summing "yes" responses to four questions: "In the past twelve months, have you done anything that would have gotten you in trouble if the police had been around?" "In the past 12 months, have you been caught in a minor violation of the law?" "In the past 12 months, have you been arrested?" and "In the past 12 months, have you been in jail for more than 24 hours?" These activities form a Guttman scale of increasing trouble with the law. On a scale scored from 0 to 4, the mean is 0.156.

ILLINOIS SURVEY OF WELL-BEING

The Illinois Survey of Well-Being is a telephone survey of a probability sample of Illinois residents. Data were collected in 1985. Random-digit dialing was used in Chicago and surrounding suburbs, and systematic random selection of numbers from current telephone directories was used in other areas of the state. Random-digit dialing ensures the inclusion of unlisted numbers (Waksberg 1978). However, the percentage of unpublished phone numbers outside the Chicago Metropolitan Statistical Area is sufficiently small that random-digit dialing is not necessary. For each household, respondents were selected on the criteria of being 18 years or older, and having had the most recent birthday among members of that household (a method for randomly choosing a respondent within the household). The adjusted response rate is 79 percent, for a total of 809 respondents. Respondents' ages range from 18 to 85. We are the principal investigators of this study, which was supported by the Research Board of the University of Illinois. Sampling, pretesting, and interviewing were conducted by the Survey Research Laboratory of the University of Illinois.

Depression levels are measured by a modified form of the Center for Epidemiological Studies' Depression scale (CES-Dm). Respondents were asked, "How many days during the past week (from 0 to 7) have you . . . (1) felt you just could not get going, (2) felt sad, (3) had trouble getting to sleep or staying asleep, (4) felt that everything was an effort, (5) felt lonely, (6) felt you couldn't shake the blues, (7) had trouble keeping you mind on what you were doing?" Responses were summed to produce an index of symptoms of depression. The alpha reliability is .76. This index is correlated .92 with the full CES-D.

Anxiety is measured by a two-item index. Respondents were asked, "How many days during the past week (from 0 to 7) have you . . . (1) felt tense or anxious and (2) worried a lot about little things?"

The sense of personal control is measured by the Mirowsky-Ross 2×2 index. Respondents were asked whether they agreed with the following statements, the first four indicating control and the second four indicating lack of control (or powerlessness): "(1) I am responsible for my own successes, (2) I can do just about anything I really set my mind to, (3) My misfortunes are the result of mistakes I have made, (4) I am responsible for my failures, (5) The really good things that happen to me are mostly luck, (6) There's no sense planning a lot—if something good is going to happen it will, (7) Most of my problems are due to bad breaks, (8) I have little control over the bad things that happen to me." Responses to the first four questions were coded strongly disagree (–2), disagree (–1), neutral (0), agree (+1), strongly agree (+2), and responses to the second four questions (5 through 8) were coded in reverse. The final index is the average response to the eight items, which runs from low perceived control (powerlessness) to high perceived control.

Social support is measured by the degree of agreement with the following statements: "I have someone I can really talk to, and I have someone I can turn to for support and understanding when things get rough." Responses were coded strongly disagree (1), disagree (2), neutral (3), agree (4) strongly agree (5). The items were summed to produce a scale coded from low to high levels of social support.

LIFE STRESS AND ILLNESS PROJECT

The Life Stress and Illness Project is a cross-cultural survey. Data were collected by means of a survey questionnaire administered in face-to-face home interviews in 1975 in El Paso, Texas, and Juarez, Mexico, companion cities on opposite sides of the border separating Mexico and the United States. The survey was a comparative study of Mexican and Anglo heritage adults. Blacks, Asians, American Indians, Jews, and persons not raised in the United States or Mexico were excluded. In El Paso, dwellings were randomly selected from the city directory, and one adult between the ages of 18 and 65 was then randomly selected from each household. The response rate was 73 percent. In Juarez, a multistage area sample based on aerial photographs was used because of the absence of accurate information on which to base a sampling frame. The response rate was 75 percent. The total number of cases is 463. The questionnaire was administered in Spanish or English, depending on the respondent's preference. Note that a sample based on telephones produces a representative sample in the United States where over 95 percent of the population has a telephone, but would have produced a biased sample in Mexico, so that face-to-face home interviews were necessary. The principal investigators on the project were Richard Hough and Dianne Timbers. Data collection was funded by the National Institute of Mental Health (NIMH-CER RO1-MH16108), the Hogg Foundation for Mental Health, and the University of Texas at El Paso. The 91 symptoms in this data set are listed in Chapter 2. For a focus on cross-cultural comparisons, see the article by Audrey Burnam, Dianne Timbers, and Richard Hough, "Two measures of psychological distress among Mexican Americans, Mexicans and Anglos" (1984).

WOMEN AND WORK STUDY

The Women and Work Study is a survey of a representative sample of adults in the United States. Data were collected by telephone in late 1978. Random-digit dialing was used to ensure a representative sample, including those with unlisted numbers (Waksberg 1978). The sample contains 2,000 adults between the ages of 18 and 65. It also contains a subsample of married persons in which both spouses were interviewed. After a married respondent was interviewed, the interviewer asked to speak to his or her spouse. There are 680 husbands and wives in which both spouses were interviewed. The spouses range in age from 18 to 75. The response rate is 76.5 percent. Joan Huber was the principal investigator. Data collection was supported by a grant from the National Science Foundation. Sampling, pretesting, and interviewing were conducted by the Survey Research Laboratory of the University of Illinois. Our focus in this study was on psychological well-being and distress. For a focus on women and work, see the book by Joan Huber and Glenna Spitze, *Sex Stratification* (1983).

Depression levels are measured by a modified form of the Center for Epidemiological Studies' Depression scale (CES-Dm). Respondents were asked, "On how many days during the past week (from 0 [never] to 7 [every day] . . . 1. Did you feel that you could not shake off the blues? 2. Did you have trouble keeping your mind on what you were doing? 3. Did you feel that everything was an effort? 4. Did you feel sad? 5. Did you feel you could not get going? 6. Did you not feel like eating? 7. Did you have trouble falling asleep or staying asleep? 8. Did you feel lonely? 9. Were you bothered by things that don't usually bother you? 10. Did you think your life had been a failure?" Items 1 through 10 were summed to calculate the total number of symptoms of depression. The alpha reliability of the depression index is .83. This modified form of the CES-D is correlated .93 with the modified form of the CES-D used in the Illinois Survey of Well-Being.

Household income is measured in thousands of dollars, translated into 1983 dollars. *Education* is measured in number of years of formal education completed.

Division of labor at home is an index composed of the average response to questions about who does the 5 most time-consuming household chores: "Who prepares meals on a daily basis?" "Who shops for food?" "Who does the daily chores?" "Who cleans up after meals?" If the couple had children living at home they were also asked, "who takes care of the children?" Responses were coded, the wife always (1), the wife usually (2), husband and wife share equally (3), the husband usually (4), the husband always (5). Only two husbands usually did the housework and none always did. Thus responses greater than or equal to 3 were coded as shared.

The husband's and wife's *preferences for the wife's employment* were measured in the following ways. Husbands were asked, "How do you (or would you) feel about your wife's working?" Responses were coded on a 5-point scale from strongly opposed to strongly in favor. Wives were asked whether they preferred homemaking or employment.

Marital power is measured by an index composed of four questions: "Who decides what house or apartment to live in, where to go on vacation, whether the wife should have a job, and whether to move if the husband gets a job offer in another city?" These are comparatively infrequent decisions that affect the entire household, and that a powerful spouse is unlikely to delegate. The response categories are the wife always (coded 1), the wife usually (2), both equally (3), the husband usually (4), the husband always (5). The answers are averaged so that 1 indicates the wife's dominance, 5 indicates the husband's, and 3 indicates equality in making major decisions.

WORK, FAMILY, AND WELL-BEING SURVEY

Work, Family and Well-being (WFW) is a 1990 telephone survey of a national probability sample of U.S. households. Random-digit dialing was used to ensure the inclusion of unlisted numbers (Waksberg 1978). Within each household, the person 18 years or older with the most recent birthday was selected as respondent. (This is an efficient method to randomly select a respondent within the household [O'Rourke and Blair 1983]). The response rate of 82.3 percent yielded a total of 2,031 respondents (1,282 females and 749 males), ranging in age from 18 to 90. Measures are identical to those in ASOC.

References

Abramson, L. Y., M. E. P. Seligman, and J. D. Teasdale. 1978. "Learned Helplessness in Humans: Critique and Reformulation." *Journal of Abnormal Psychology* 87: 49–74.

Alves, Wayne M. and Peter H. Rossi. 1978. "Who Should Get What? Fairness Judgments of the Distribution of Earnings." *American Journal of Sociology* 84:541–64.

Alwin, Duane F., Philip E. Converse, and S. S. Martin. 1984. "Living Arrangements, Social Integration and Psychological Well-Being." Paper presented at the Midwest Sociological Association annual meeting, Chicago.

Amato, Paul R. 1991. "Parental Absence During Childhood and Depression in Later Life." *Sociological Quarterly* 32:543–56.

Amato, Paul R. 1996. "Explaining the Intergenerational Transmission of Divorce." *Journal of Marriage and the Family* 58:628–40.

Amato, Paul R. and K. Bruce. 1991. "Parental Divorce and Adult Well-Being: A Meta-Analysis." *Journal of Marriage and the Family* 53:43–58.

Amato, Paul R. and Juliana M. Sobolewski. 2001. "The Effects of Divorce and Marital Discord on Adult Children's Psychological Well-Being." *American Sociological Review* 66:900–21.

American Psychiatric Association. 1980. *Diagnostic and Statistical Manual of Mental Disorders III.* Washington: American Psychiatric Association.

Aneshensel, Carol. 1992. "Social Stress: Theory and Research." *Annual Review of Sociology* 18:15–38.

Aneshensel, Carol S., Ralph R. Frerichs, and Virginia A. Clark. 1981. "Family Roles and Sex Differences in Depression." *Journal of Health and Social Behavior* 22: 379–93.

Aneshensel, Carol S., Ralph R. Frerichs, and George J. Huba. 1984. "Depression and Physical Illness: A Multiwave, Nonrecursive Causal Model." *Journal of Health and Social Behavior* 25:350–71.

Aneshensel, Carol S., Carolyn M. Rutter, and Peter A. Lachenbruch. 1991. "Social Structure, Stress, and Mental Health: Competing Conceptual and Analytic Models" *American Sociological Review* 56:166–78.

Antonovsky, Aaron. 1967. "Social Class, Life Expectancy and Overall Mortality." *Milbank Memorial Fund Quarterly* 45:31–73.

Aseltine, Robert H. 1996. "Pathways Linking Parental Divorce with Adolescent Depression." *Journal of Health and Social Behavior* 37:133–48.

Astone, N. M. and S. S. McLanahan. 1991. "Family Structure, Parental Practices and High School Completion." *American Sociological Review* 56:309–20.

Avison, William R. 1999. "Family Structure and Processes." Pp. 228–58 in *A Handbook for the Study of Mental Health: Social Contexts, Theories, and Systems,* edited by Allan V. Horwitz and Teresa L. Scheid. New York: Cambridge University Press

Baldessarini, R. J. 1983. *Biomedical Aspects of Depression and Its Treatment.* Washington, DC: American Psychiatric Press.

Bandura, Albert. 1986. *Social Foundations of Thought and Action.* Englewood Cliffs, NJ: Prentice-Hall.

Barber, B. 1983. *The Logic and Limits of Trust.* New Brunswick, NJ: Rutgers University Press.

Becker, Gary. 1976. *The Economic Approach to Human Behavior.* Chicago: University of Chicago Press.

Belle, Deborah. 1982. *Lives in Stress. Women and Depression.* Beverly Hills: Sage.

Benassi, Victor A., P. D. Sweeney, and C. L. Dufour. 1988. "Is There a Relationship between Locus of Control Orientation and Depression?" *Journal of Abnormal Psychology* 97:357–66.

Bergmann, B. 1986. *The Economic Emergence of Women.* New York: Basic Books.

Berkman, Lisa F. and Lester Breslow. 1983. *Health and Ways of Living: The Alameda County Study.* New York: Oxford.

Bianchi, Suzanne M. and Daphne Spain. 1986. *American Women in Transition.* New York: Russell Sage Foundation.

Biblarz, T. M. and A. E. Raftery. 1993. "The Effects of Family Disruption on Social Mobility." *American Sociological Review* 58:97–109.

Bird, Chloe E. and Allen M. Fremont. 1991. Gender, Time Use, and Health. *Journal of Health and Social Behavior* 32:114–29.

Bird, Chloe E. and Catherine E. Ross. 1993. "Houseworkers and Paid Workers: Qualities of the Work and Effects on Personal Control." *Journal of Marriage and the Family* 55:913–25.

Booth, Alan and P. Amato. 1991. "Divorce and Psychological Stress." *Journal of Health and Social Behavior* 32:396–407.

Bowling, Ann. 1987. "Mortality after Bereavement: A Review of the Literature on Survival Periods and Factors Affecting Survival." *Social Science and Medicine* 24:117–24.

Boyd, Jeffrey H., Jack D. Burke, Ernst Gruenberg, Charles E. Holzer, Donald S. Rae, Linda K. George, Marvin Karno, Roger Stolzman, Lary McEnvoy, and Gerald Nestadt. 1984. "Exclusion Criteria of DSM-III: A Study of Co-Occurrence of Hierarchy-Free Syndromes." *Archives of General Psychiatry* 41:983–89.

Boyd, Jeffrey H., Myran M. Weissman, Douglas Thompson, and Jerome K. Myers. 1982. "Screening for Depression in a Community Sample: Understanding the Discrepancies between Depression Symptom and Diagnostic Scales." *Archives of General Psychiatry* 39:1195–1200.

Bradburn, Norman M. 1969. *The Structure of Psychological Well-Being.* Chicago: Aldine.

Braverman, H. 1974. *Labor and Monopoly Capital: The Degradation of Work in the Twentieth Century.* New York: Monthly Review.

Breggin, Peter R. 1991. *Toxic Psychiatry*. New York: St. Martins.

Brehm, John and Wendy Rahn. 1997. "Individual-Level Evidence for the Causes and Consequences of Social Capital." *American Journal of Political Science* 41:999–1023.

Brewin, C. R. and D. A. Shapiro. 1984. "Beyond Locus of Control: Attribution of Responsibility for Positive and Negative Outcomes." *British Journal of Psychology* 75:43–49.

Brewster, Karin L., John O. G. Billy, and William R. Grady. 1993. "Social Context and Adolescent Behavior: The Impact of Community on the Transition to Sexual Activity" *Social Forces* 71:713–40.

Brown, George W. and Tirril Harris. 1978. *Social Origins of Depression*. New York: Free Press.

Bruce, Martha Livingstone and Philip K. Leaf. 1989. "Psychiatric Disorders and 15-Month Mortality in a Community Sample of Older Adults." *American Journal of Public Health* 79:727–30.

Bulman, R. J. and C. B. Wortman. 1977. "Attributions of Blame and Coping in the Real World: Severe Accident Victims React to Their Lot." *Journal of Personality and Social Psychology* 35:351–63.

Burnam, M. Audrey, Dianne M. Timbers, and Richard L. Hough. 1984. "Two Measures of Psychological Distress among Mexican Americans, Mexicans, and Anglos." *Journal of Health and Social Behavior* 25:24–33.

Burton, Russell P. D. 1998. "Global Integrative Meaning as a Mediating Factor in the Relationship between Social Roles and Psychological Distress." *Journal of Health and Social Behavior* 39:201–15.

Campbell, Angus, Philip E. Converse, and Willard L. Rodgers. 1976. *The Quality of American Life*. New York: Russell Sage.

Carroll, Bernard J., Michael Feinberg, John F. Greden, Janet Tarika, A. Ariav Albala, Roger F. Hasket, Norman McI. James, Ziad Kronfol, Naomi Lohr, Meir Steiner, Jean Paul de Vigne, and Elizabeth Young. 1981. "A Specific Laboratory Test for the Diagnosis of Melancholia: Standardization, Validation, and Clinical Utility." *Archives of General Psychiatry* 38:15–22.

Caster, D. U. and O. A. Parsons. 1977. "Locus of Control in Alcoholics and Treatment Outcome." *Journal of Studies on Alcohol* 38:2087–95.

Cherlin, A. J. 1981. *Marriage, Divorce, Remarriage*. Cambridge, MA: Harvard University Press.

Cherlin, A. J., P. L. Chase-Lansdale, and C. McRae. 1998. "Effects of Parental Divorce on Mental Health throughout the Life Course." *American Sociological Review* 63:239–49.

Clancy, Kevin and Walter R. Gove. 1974. "Sex Differences in Mental Illness: An Analysis of Response Bias in Self-Reports" *American Journal of Sociology* 80: 205–15.

Cleary, Paul D. and David Mechanic. 1983. "Sex Differences in Psychological Distress among Married People." *Journal of Health and Social Behavior* 24: 111–21.

Cobb, S. 1976. "Social Support as a Moderator of Life Stress." *Psychosomatic Medicine* 38:301–14.

Cole, Stephen. 1972. *The Sociological Method*. Chicago: Markham.

Coleman, James S. 1988. "Social Capital in the Creation of Human Capital." *American Journal of Sociology* 94:S95–S120.

Coleman, James S. 1990. *Foundations of Social Theory.* Cambridge, MA: Harvard University Press.

Coleman, L. M., Toni C. Antonucci, Pamela K. Adelmann, and Susan E. Crohan. 1987. "Social Roles in the Lives of Middle-Aged and Older Black Women." *Journal of Marriage and the Family* 49:761–71.

Collins, John Gary. 1988. "Prevalence of Selected Chronic Conditions, United States, 1983–85." *NCHS Advancedata* 155:1–16.

Comstock, George W. and James A. Tonascia. 1977. "Education and Mortality in Washington County, Maryland." *Journal of Health and Social Behavior* 18:54–60.

Conger, Rand D., Frederick O. Lorenz, Glen H. Elder, Ronald L. Simmons, and Xiaojia Ge. 1993. "Husband and Wife Differences in Response to Undesirable Life Events." *Journal of Health and Social Behavior* 34:71–88.

Davis, James A. 1985. *The Logic of Causal Order.* Beverly Hills: Sage.

DeLongis, Anita, James C. Coyne, Gayle Dakof, Susan Folkman, and Richard S. Lazarus. 1982. "Relationship of Daily Hassles, Uplifts, and Major Life Events to Health Status." *Health Psychology* 1:119–36.

Dohrenwend, Barbara S. 1973. "Life Events as Stressors: A Methodological Inquiry." *Journal of Health and Social Behavior* 14:167–75.

Dohrenwend, Bruce P. and Barbara S. Dohrenwend. 1969. *Social Status and Psychological Disorder: A Causal Inquiry.* New York: Wiley.

Dohrenwend, Bruce P. and Barbara S. Dohrenwend. 1976. "Sex Differences in Psychiatric Disorder." *American Journal of Sociology* 82:1447–59.

Dohrenwend, Bruce P. and Barbara S. Dohrenwend. 1977. "Reply to Gove and Tudor." *American Journal of Sociology* 82:1336–45.

Dohrenwend, Bruce P. and Patrick E. Shrout. 1985. "Hassles in the Conceptualization and Measurement of Life Stress Variables." *American Psychologist* 40:780–85.

Dohrenwend, Bruce P., Patrick E. Shrout, Gladys G. Egri, and Frederick S. Mendelson. 1980. "Nonspecific Psychological Distress and Other Dimensions of Psychopathology." *Archives of General Psychiatry* 37:1229–36.

Downey, G. and P. Moen. 1987. "Personal Efficacy, Income and Family Transitions: A Longitudinal Study of Women Heading Households." *Journal of Health and Social Behavior* 28:320–33.

Drentea, Patricia. 2000. "Age, Debt, and Anxiety." *Journal of Health and Social Behavior* 41:437–50.

Eaton, William W. and Larry G. Kessler. 1981. "Rates of Symptoms of Depression in a National Sample" *American Journal of Epidemiology* 114:528–38.

Elder, G. H. and J. K. Liker. 1982. "Hard Times in Women's Lives: Historical Influences across Forty Years." *American Journal of Sociology* 88:241–26.

Elliott, Debert S., William Julius Wilson, David Huizinga, Robert J. Sampson, Amanda Elliott, and Bruce Rankin. 1996. "The Effects of Neighborhood Disadvantage on Adolescent Development." *Journal of Research in Crime and Delinquency* 33:389–426.

Endicott, Jean and Robert L. Spitzer. 1972. "What! Another Rating Scale? The Psychiatric Evaluation Form." *The Journal of Nervous and Mental Disease* 154:88–104.

Erikson, Kai. 1986. "On Work and Alienation." *American Sociological Review* 51:1–8.

Ferree, M. M. 1976. "Working Class Jobs: Housework and Paid Work as Sources of Satisfaction." *Social Problems* 23:431–41.

Finch, Brian Karl, Bohdan Kolody, and William A. Vega. 2000. "Perceived Discrimination and Depression among Mexican-Origin Adults in California." *Journal of Health and Social Behavior* 41:295–13.

Fischer, Claude S. 1976. *The Urban Experience* New York: Harcourt Brace Jovanovich.

Frank, Ellen, Linda L. Carpenter, and David Kupfer. 1988. "Sex Differences in Recurrent Depression: Are There Any That Are Significant?" *American Journal of Psychiatry* 145:41–5.

Frerichs, Ralph R., Carol S. Aneshensel, and Virginia A. Clark. 1981. "Prevalence of Depression in Los Angeles County." *American Journal of Epidemiology* 113:691–99.

Gabennesch, Howard. 1972. "Authoritarianism as World View." *American Journal of Sociology* 77:857–75.

Garfinkel, H. 1963. "A Conception of, and Experiments with, Trust as a Condition of Stable Concerted Actions." Pp. 81–93 in *Motivation and Social Interaction: Cognitive Determinants,* edited by O. J. Harvey. New York: Ronald.

Gecas, Viktor. 1989. "The Social Psychology of Self-Efficacy." *Annual Review of Sociology* 15:291–316.

Geis, Karlyn J. and Catherine E. Ross. 1998. "A New Look at Urban Alienation: The Effect of Neighborhood Disorder on Perceived Powerlessness." *Social Psychology Quarterly* 61:232–46.

Gerstel, Naomi, Catherine Kohler Riessman, and Sarah Rosenfield. 1985. "Explaining the Symptomatology of Separated and Divorced Women and Men: The Role of Material Conditions and Social Networks." *Social Forces* 64:84–101.

Gersten, Joanne C., Thomas S. Langner, Jeanne G. Eisenberg, and Lida Orzek. 1974. "Child Behavior and Life Events: Undesirable Change or Change Per Se?" Pp. 159–70 in *Stressful Life Events,* edited by Barbara S. Dohrenwend and Bruce P. Dohrenwend. New York: Wiley.

Glenmullen, Joseph. 2000. *Prozac Backlash: Overcoming the Dangers of Prozac, Zoloft, Paxil, and Other Antidepressants with Safe, Effective Alternatives.* New York: Simon and Schuster.

Glenn, Norval D., and K. B. Kramer. 1987. "The Marriages and Divorces of the Children of Divorce." *Journal of Marriage and the Family* 49:811–25.

Glenn, Norval D., and B. A. Shelton. 1983. "Preadult Background Variables in Divorce." *Journal of Marriage and the Family* 45:405–10.

Glenn, Norval D. and Charles N. Weaver. 1978. "A Multivariate, Multisurvey Study of Marital Happiness." *Journal of Marriage and the Family* 40:269–82.

Glenn, Norval D. and Charles N. Weaver. 1981. "Education's Effects on Psychological Well-Being." *Public Opinion Quarterly* 45:22–39.

Gold, Philip W., Frederick K. Goodwin, and George P. Chrousos. 1988. "Clinical and Biochemical Manifestations of Depression: Relation to the Neurobiology of Stress (First of Two Parts)." *New England Journal of Medicine* 319(6, August 11):348–53.

Gold, Philip W., Frederick K. Goodwin, and George P. Chrousos. 1988. "Clinical and Biochemical Manifestations of Depression: Relation to the Neurobiology of Stress (Second of Two Parts)." *New England Journal of Medicine* 319(7, August 18):413–20.

Goldsteen, Karen and Catherine E. Ross. 1989. "The Perceived Burden of Children." *Journal of Family Issues* 10:504–26.

Golin, S., P. D. Sweeney, and D. E. Shaeffer. 1981. "The Causality of Causal Attributions in Depression: A Cross-Lagged Panel Correlational Analysis." *Journal of Abnormal Psychology* 90:14–22.

Gore, Susan and Thomas W. Mangione. 1983. "Social Roles, Sex Roles, and Psychological Distress." *Journal of Health and Social Behavior* 24:330–12.

Gove, Walter R. 1984. "Gender Differences in Mental and Physical Illness: The Effects of Fixed Roles and Nurturant Roles." *Social Science and Medicine* 19:77–84.

Gove, Walter R. and Kevin Clancy. 1975. "Response Bias, Sex Differences, and Mental Illness: A Reply." *American Journal of Sociology* 81:1463–72.

Gove, Walter R. and Michael R. Geerken. 1977. "Response Bias in Surveys of Mental Health: An Empirical Investigation." *American Journal of Sociology* 82:1289–1317.

Gove, Walter R. and Michael R. Geerken. 1977. "The Effect of Children and Employment on the Mental Health of Married Men and Women." *Social Forces* 56:66–76.

Gove, Walter R., Michael M. Hughes, and Carolyn B. Style. 1983. "Does Marriage Have Positive Effects on the Psychological Well-Being of the Individual?" *Journal of Health and Social Behavior* 24:122–31.

Gove, Walter R., James McCorkel, Terry Fain, and Michael D. Hughes. 1976. "Response Bias in Community Surveys of Mental Health: Systematic Bias or Random Noise?" *Social Science and Medicine* 10:497–502.

Gove, Walter R., Suzanne T. Ortega, and Carolyn Briggs Style. 1989. "The Maturational and Role Perspectives on Aging and Self through the Adult Years: An Empirical Evaluation." *American Journal of Sociology* 94:1117–45.

Gove, Walter R. and Jeannette F. Tudor. 1973. "Adult Sex Roles and Mental Illness." *American Journal of Sociology* 78:812–35.

Gove, Walter R. and Jeannette F. Tudor. 1977. "Sex Differences in Mental Illness: A Comment on Dohrenwend and Dohrenwend." *American Journal of Sociology* 82:1327–35.

Grabb, Edward G. 1979. "Working-Class Authoritarianism and Tolerance of Outgroups: A Reassessment." *Public Opinion Quarterly* 43:36–47.

Greden, John F., Robert Gardner, Doug King, Leon Grunhaus, Bernard Carroll, and Ziad Kronfol. 1983. "Dexamethasone Suppression Tests in Antidepressant Treatment of Melancholia: The Process of Normalization and Test-retest Reproducibility." *Archives of General Psychiatry* 40:493–500.

Green, Brian E. and Christian Ritter. 2000. "Marijuana Use and Depression." *Journal of Health and Social Behavior* 41:40–49.

Greenberg, D. and D. Wolf. 1982. "The Economic Consequences of Experiencing Parental Marital Disruptions." *Children and Youth Services Review* 4:141–62.

Greenberg, E. S. and L. Grunberg. 1995. "Work Alienation and Problem Alcohol Behavior." *Journal of Health and Social Behavior* 36:83–103.

Greenley, James R. 1979. "Familial Expectations, Posthospital Adjustment, and the

Societal Reaction Perspective on Mental Illness." *Journal of Health and Social Behavior* 20:217–27.

Guralnik, Jack M. and George A. Kaplan. 1989. "Predictors of Healthy Aging: Prospective Evidence from the Alameda County Study." *American Journal of Public Health* 79:703–8.

Gurin, Gerald G., Joseph Veroff, and Sheila Feld. 1960. *"Americans View Their Mental Health.* New York: Basic.

Gurin, P., G. Gurin, R. C. Lao, and M. Beattie. 1969. "Internal-External Control in the Motivational Dynamics of Negro Youth." *Journal of Social Issues* 25:29–53.

Gurin, P., G. Gurin, and B. M. Morrison. 1978. "Personal and Ideological Aspects of Internal and External Control." *Social Psychology* 41:275–96.

Gurtman, M. B. 1992. "Trust, Distrust, and Interpersonal Problems: A Circumplex Analysis." *Journal of Personality and Social Psychology* 62:989–1002.

Harnish, Jennifer D., Robert H. Aseltine, and Susan Gore. 2000. "Resolution of Stressful Experiences as an Indicator of Coping Effectiveness in Young Adults: An Event History Analysis." *Journal of Health and Social Behavior* 41:121–36.

Hartunian, Nelson S., Charles N. Smart, and Mark S. Thompson. 1981. *The Incidence and Economic Costs of Major Health Impairments: A Comparative Analysis of Cancer, Motor Vehicle Injuries, Coronary Heart Disease, and Stroke.* Lexington MA: Lexington.

Hiday, Virginia A. 1980. "View from the Front Line: Diagnosis and Treatment of Mental Health Problems among Primary Care Physicians." *Social Psychiatry* 15:131–36.

Hines, A. M. 1997. "Divorce-Related Transitions, Adolescent Development and the Role of the Parent-Child Relationships: A Review of the Literature." *Journal of Marriage and the Family* 59:375–88.

Hiroto, Donald S. 1974. "Locus of Control and Learned Helplessness." *Journal of Experimental Psychology* 102:187–93.

Hirschi, Travis and Michael Gottfredson. 1983. "Age and the Explanation of Crime." *American Journal of Sociology* 89:552–84.

Hirschi, Travis and Hanan C. Selvin. 1967. *Principles of Survey Analysis.* New York: Free Press.

Hoffman, Mark S. (Ed.). 1991. *The World Almanac and Book of Facts, 1991.* New York: Pharos.

Hogan, Dennis P. 1978. "The Variable Order of Events in the Life Course." *American Sociological Review* 43:573–86.

Holmes, Thomas H. and Minoru Masuda. 1974. "Life Change and Illness Susceptibility." Pp. 45–71 in *Stressful Life Events,* edited by Barbara S. Dohrenwend and Bruce P. Dohrenwend. New York: Wiley.

Holmes, Thomas H. and Richard H. Rahe. 1967. "The Social Readjustment Rating Scale." *Journal of Psychosomatic Research* 11:213–18.

Holzer, Charles E. III, Brent M. Shea, Jeffrey W. Swanson, Phillip J. Leaf, Jerome K. Myers, Linda George, Myrna M. Weissman, and Phillip Bednarski. 1986. "The Increased Risk for Specific Psychiatric Disorders among Persons of Low Socioeconomic Status: Evidence from the Epidemiologic Catchment Area Surveys." *American Journal of Social Psychiatry* VI (4, fall):259–71.

Homans, George. 1961. *Social Behavior: Its Elementary Forms*. New York: Harcourt Brace.

Horowitz, Allan and Helene Raskin White. 1987. "Gender Role Orientations and Styles of Pathology Among Adolescents." *Journal of Health and Social Behavior* 28:158–70.

Horwitz, Allan V. 2002. *Creating Mental Illness*. Chicago: University of Chicago Press

Horwitz, Allan V. and H. R. White. 1991. "Becoming Married, Depression, and Alcohol Problems among Young Adults." *Journal of Health and Social Behavior* 32:221–37.

Hough, Richard L, Dianne Timbers Fairbank, and A. M. Garcia. 1976. "Problems in the Ratio Measurement of Life Stress." *Journal of Health and Social Behavior* 17:70–82.

House, J. S., K. R. Landis, and D. Umberson. 1988. "Social Relationships and Health." *Science* 241:S40

House, James S. and Cynthia Robbins. 1983. "Age, Psychosocial Stress, and Health." Pp. 175–97 in *Aging and Society: Selected Reviews and Recent Research*, edited by Maltida White Riley, Beth B. Hess, and Kathleen Bond. Hillsdale, NJ: Erlbaum.

Huber, Joan and Glenna Spitze. 1983. *Sex Stratification: Children, Housework, and Jobs*. New York: Academic.

Hughes, M. and D. H. Demo. 1989. "Self-Perceptions of Black Americans: Self-Esteem and Personal Efficacy." *American Journal of Sociology* 95:132–59.

Hughes, Michael M. and Walter R. Gove. 1981. "Living Alone, Social Integration, and Mental Health." *American Journal of Sociology* 87:48–74.

Hyman, Herbert B. 1966. "The Value Systems of Different Classes: A Social Psychological Contribution to the Analysis of Stratification." Pp. 488–99 in *Class, Status and Power: Social Stratification in Comparative Perspective* (2nd ed.), edited by R. Bendix and S. M. Lipset. New York: Free Press.

Jasso, Guillermina and Peter H. Rossi. 1977. "Distributive Justice and Earned Income." *American Sociological Review* 42:639–51.

Jekielek, Susan. 1998. "Parental Conflict, Marital Disruption and Children's Emotional Well-being." *Social Forces* 76:905–35.

Jencks, Christopher and Susan E. Mayer. 1990. "The Social Consequences of Growing Up in a Poor Neighborhood." Pp. 111–84 in *Inner-City Poverty in the United States*, edited by Laurence E. Lynn and Michael G. H. McGeary. Washington, DC: National Academy Press.

Johnson, David Richard and Richard L. Meile. 1981. "Does Dimensionality Bias in Langner's 22-Item Index Affect the Validity of Social Status Comparisons?" *Journal of Health and Social Behavior* 22:415–33.

Johnson-George, Cynthia and Walter C. Swap. 1982. "Measurement of Specific Interpersonal Trust: Construction and Validation of a Scale to Assess Trust in Specific Other." *Journal of Personality and Social Psychology* 43:1306–17.

Kalleberg, Arne L. and Karyn A. Loscocco. 1983. "Aging, Values, and Rewards: Explaining Age Differences in Job Satisfaction." *American Sociological Review* 48:78–90.

Kandel, Denise B., Mark Davies, and Victoria H. Raveis. 1985. "The Stressfulness of Daily Social Roles for Women: Marital, Occupational, and Household Roles." *Journal of Health and Social Behavior* 26:64–78.

Kaplan, Howard B., Cynthia Robbins, and Steven S. Martin. 1983. "Antecedents of Psychological Distress in Young Adults: Self-Rejection, Deprivation of Social Support and Life Events." *Journal of Health and Social Behavior* 24:230–44.

Kaprio, Jaakko, Markku Koskenuo, and Heli Rita. 1987. "Mortality after Bereavement: A Prospective Study of 95,647 Widowed Persons." *American Journal of Public Health* 77:283–87.

Keith, V. M. and B. Finlay. 1988. "The Impact of Parental Divorce on Children's Education Attainment, Marital Timing, and the Likelihood of Divorce." *Journal of Marriage and the Family* 50:797–809.

Kessler, Ronald C. 1979. "Stress, Social Status, and Psychological Distress." *Journal of Health and Social Behavior* 20:259–72.

Kessler, Ronald C. 1982. "A Disaggregation of the Relationship between Socioeconomic Status and Psychological Distress." *American Sociological Review* 47: 752–64.

Kessler, Ronald C. 2000. "Psychiatric Epidemiology: Selected Recent Advances and Future Directions." *Bulletin of the World Health Organization* 78:464–74.

Kessler, Ronald C. and Paul D. Cleary. 1980. "Social Class and Psychological Distress." *American Sociological Review* 45:463–78.

Kessler, Ronald C. and M. Essex. 1982. "Marital Status and Depression: The Importance of Coping Resources." *Social Forces* 61:484–507.

Kessler, Ronald C. and Jane D. McLeod. 1984. "Sex Differences in Vulnerability to Undesirable Life Events." *American Sociological Review* 49:620–31.

Kessler, Ronald C. and Jane D. McLeod. 1985. "Social Support and Mental Health in Community Samples." Pp. 219–40 in *Social Support and Health*, edited by Sheldon Cohen and S. Leonard Syme. New York: Academic.

Kessler, Ronald C. and James A. McRae. 1981. "Trends in the Relationship between Sex and Psychological Distress: 1957–1976." *American Sociological Review* 46:443–52.

Kessler, Ronald C. and James A. McRae. 1982. "The Effect of Wives' Employment on the Mental Health of Married Men and Women." *American Sociological Review* 47:216–27.

Kessler, Ronald C., Kristin A. Mickelson, and David R. Williams. 1999. "The Prevalence, Distribution, and Mental Health Correlates of Perceived Discrimination in the United States." *Journal of Health and Social Behavior* 40:208–30.

Kessler, Ronald C. and Harold W. Neighbors. 1986. "A New Perspective on the Relationships among Race, Social Class, and Psychological Distress." *Journal of Health and Social Behavior* 27:107–15.

Kessler, Ronald C. and Shanyang Zhao. 1999. "The Prevalence of Mental Illness." Pp. 58–78 in *A Handbook for the Study of Mental Health: Social Contexts, Theories, and Systems*, edited by Allan V. Horwitz and Teresa L. Scheid. Cambridge: Cambridge University Press.

Kessler, Ronald C., J. Blake Turner, and James S. House. 1989. "Unemployment, Reemployment and Emotional Functioning in a Community Sample." *American Sociological Review* 54:648–57.

Kirsch, Irving and Guy Sapirstein. 1998. "Listening to Prozac but Hearing Placebo:

A Meta-Analysis of Antidepressant Medication." *Prevention and Treatment* 1:1–16.

Kitagawa, Elaine M. and P. M. Hauser. 1973. *Differential Mortality in the United States.* Cambridge, MA: Harvard University Press.

Kluegel, James R. and Eliot R. Smith. 1986. *Beliefs About Inequality.* Hawthorne, NY: Aldine de Gruyter.

Kobassa, Suzanne C., Salvatore R. Maddi, and Sheila Courington. 1981. "Personality and Constitution as Mediators in the Stress-Illness Relationship." *Journal of Health and Social Behavior* 22:368–78.

Kohn, Melvin. 1972. "Class, Family and Schizophrenia." *Social Forces* 50:295–302.

Kohn, Melvin. 1976. "Occupational Structure and Alienation." *American Journal of Sociology* 82:111–30.

Kohn, Melvin L., Atsuhi Naoi, Carrie Schoenbach, Carmi Schooler, and Kazimierz M. Slomczynski. 1990. "Position in the Class Structure and Psychological Functioning in the United States, Japan, and Poland." *American Journal of Sociology* 95:964–1008.

Kohn, Melvin and Carmi Schooler. 1982. "Job Conditions and Personality: A Longitudinal Assessment of Their Reciprocal Effects." *American Journal of Sociology* 87:1257–86.

Kohn, Melvin L. and Kazimierz M. Slomczynski. 1990. *Social Structure and Self-Direction: A Comparative Analysis of the United States and Poland.* Cambridge: Blackwell.

Kohn, Melvin, Wojciech Zaborowski, Krystyna Janicka, Bogdan W. Mach, Valeriy Khmelko, Kazimierz M. Slomczynski, Cory Heyman, and Bruce Podobnik. 2000. "Complexity of Activities and Personality under Conditions of Radical Social Change: A Comparative Analysis of Poland and Ukraine." *Social Psychology Quarterly* 63:187–208.

Kotler, Pamela and Deborah Lee Wingard. 1989. "The Effect of Occupational, Marital and Parental Roles on Mortality: The Alameda County Study." *American Journal of Public Health* 79:607–12.

Kramer, Roderick M. 1999. "Trust and Distrust in Organizations: Emerging Perspectives, Enduring Questions." *Annual Review of Psychology* 50:569–98.

Krause, N. and S. Stryker. 1984. "Stress and Well-Being: The Buffering Role of Locus of Control Beliefs." *Social Science and Medicine* 18:783–90.

Kruskal, Joseph B. and Myron Wish. 1978. *Multidimensional Scaling.* Beverly Hills: Sage.

Lachman, M. E. 1986. "Personal Control in Later Life: Stability, Change, and Cognitive Correlates." Pp. 207–36 in *The Psychology of Control and Aging,* edited by M. M. Baltes and P. B. Baltes. Hillsdale, NJ: Erlbaum.

LaGrange, Randy L., Kenneth F. Ferraro and Michael Supancic. 1992. "Perceived Risk and Fear of Crime: Role of Social and Physical Incivilities." *Journal of Research in Crime and Delinquency* 29:311-334.

Langner, Thomas S. 1962. "A Twenty-Two Item Screening Score of Psychiatric Symptoms Indicating Impairment." *Journal of Health and Human Behavior* 3:269–76.

LaRocco, James M., James S. House, and John R. P. French. 1980. "Social Support, Occupational Stress, and Health." *Journal of Health and Social Behavior* 3:202–18.

Lazarus, Richard S. and Susan Folkman. 1984. *Stress, Appraisal, and Coping.* New York: Springer.

LeClere, Felicia B., Richard G. Rogers, and Kimberley D. Peters. 1997. "Ethnicity and Mortality in the United States: Individual and Community Correlates" *Social Forces* 76:169–98.

LeDoux, Joseph. 1996. *The Emotional Brain: The Mysterious Underpinnings of Emotional Life.* New York: Touchstone.

Lefcourt, Herbert M. 1976. *Locus of Control. Current Trends in Theory and Research.* Hillsdale, NJ: Lawrence Erlbaum.

Leigh, J. Paul. 1983. "Direct and Indirect Effects of Education on Health." *Social Science and Medicine* 17:227–34.

Leighton, D. C., J. S. Harding, D. B. Macklin, A. M. MacMillan, and A. H. Leighton. 1963. *The Character of Danger: Stirling County Study,* Vol. 3. New York: Basic.

Lennon, Mary Clare. 1982. "The Psychological Consequences of Menopause: The Importance of Timing of a Life Stage Event." *Journal of Health and Social Behavior* 23:353–66.

Lennon, Mary Clare and Sarah Rosenfield. 1992. "Women and Mental Health: The Interaction of Job and Family Conditions." *Journal of Health and Social Behavior* 33:316–27.

Levenson, H. 1973. "Multidimensional Locus of Control in Psychiatric Patients." *Journal of Consulting and Clinical Psychology* 41:397–404.

Lewis, Susan K., Catherine E. Ross, and John Mirowsky. 1999. "Establishing a Sense of Personal Control in the Transition to Adulthood." *Social Forces* 77:1573–99.

Lilienfeld, Scott O., James M. Wood, and Howard N. Garb. 2001. "What's Wrong with This Picture?" *Scientific American* 284:81–87.

Lin, E. and S. V. Parikh. 1999. "Sociodemographic, Clinical and Attitudinal Characteristics of the Untreated Depressed in Ontario." *Journal of Affective Disorders* 53:153–62.

Lin, Nan, Xiaolan Ye, and Walter M. Ensel. 1999. "Social Support and Depressed Mood: A Structural Analysis." *Journal of Health and Social Behavior* 40:344–59.

Link, Bruce. 1987. "Understanding Labeling Effects in the Area of Mental Disorders: An Assessment of the Effects of Expectations of Rejection." *American Sociological Review* 52:96–112.

Link, Bruce G., Mary Clare Lennon, and Bruce P. Dohrenwend. 1993. "Socioeconomic Status and Depression: The Role of Occupations Involving Direction, Control, and Planning." *American Journal of Sociology* 98:1351–87.

Link, Bruce, Elmer L. Struening, Michael Rahav, Jo C. Phelan, and Larry Nuttrock. 1997. "On Sigma and Its Consequences: Evidence from a Longitudinal Study of Men with Dual Diagnoses of Mental Illness and Substance Abuse." *Journal of Health and Social Behavior* 38:177–90.

Litwack, Eugene and Peter Messeri. 1989. "Organizational Theory, Social Supports, and Mortality Rates: A Theoretical Convergence." *American Sociological Review* 54:49–66.

Locke, Ben A. and E. A. Gardner. 1969. "Psychiatric Disorders Among the Patients of General Practitioners and Internists." *Public Health Reports* 84:167–73.

Lovell-Troy, Lawrence. 1983. "Anomia among Employed Wives and Housewives." *Journal of Marriage and the Family* (May):301–10.

Lund, Laura and William E. Wright. 1994. "Mitofsky-Waksberg vs. Screened Random Digit Dial: Report on a Comparison of the Sample Characteristics of Two RDD Survey Designs." Presented at the Center for Disease Control's 11th Annual BRFSS Conference: Atlanta.

Martin, David J., Lyn Y. Abramson, and Lauren B. Alloy. 1984. "Illusion of Control for Self and Others in Depressed and Nondepressed College Students." *Journal of Personality and Social Psychology* 46:125–36.

Massey, Douglas S. 1996. "The Age of Extremes: Concentrated Affluence and Poverty in the Twenty-First Century." *Demography* 33:395–412.

Mausner, Judith S. and Anita K. Bahn. 1974. *Epidemiology: An Introductory Text.* Philadelphia: W. B. Saunders.

McEwen, B. S. 1998. "Protective and Damaging Effects of Stress Mediators." *New England Journal of Medicine* 338:171–79.

McFarlane, Allan H., Geoffrey R. Norman, David L. Streiner, and Ranjan G. Roy. 1983. "The Process of Social Stress: Stable, Reciprocal, and Mediating Relationships." *Journal of Health and Social Behavior* 24:160–73.

McLanahan, S. S. 1985. "Family Structure and the Reproduction of Poverty." *American Journal of Sociology* 90:873–901.

McLanahan, Sara and Julia Adams. 1987. "Parenthood and Psychological Well-Being." Pp. 237–57 in *Annual Review of Sociology* (volume 13), edited by W. Richard Scott and James F. Short. Palo Alto, CA: Annual Reviews.

McLanahan, Sara S. and Larry L. Bumpass. 1988. "Intergenerational Consequences of Family Disruption." *American Journal of Sociology* 94:130–52.

McLanahan, Sasa and Jennifer Glass. 1985. "A Note on the Trend in Sex Differences in Psychological Distress." *Journal of Health and Social Behavior* 26:328–35.

McLanahan, Sara S. and Gary Sandefur. 1994. *Growing Up with a Single Parent.* Cambridge, MA: Harvard University Press.

McLaughlin, S. D. and Michael Micklin. 1983. "The Timing of the First Birth and Changes in Personal Efficacy." *Journal of Marriage and the Family* 45:47–55.

McLeod, Jane D. 1991. "Childhood Parental Loss and Adult Depression." *Journal of Health and Social Behavior* 32:205–20.

Meisner, W. W. 1978. *The Paranoid Process.* New York: Jason Aronson.

Menaghan, Elizabeth G. 1985. "Depressive Affect and Subsequent Divorce." *Journal of Family Issues* 6:295–306.

Menaghan, Elizabeth G. 1989. "Psychological Well-Being among Parents and Nonparents." *Journal of Family Issues* 10:547–65.

Miech, Richard Allen and Michael J. Shanahan. 2000. "Socioeconomic Status and Depression over the Life Course." *Journal of Health and Social Behavior* 41: 162–76.

Mills, C. Wright. 1959. *The Sociological Imagination.* New York: Oxford University Press.

Mirowsky, John. 1985. "Depression and Marital Power: An Equity Model." *American Journal of Sociology* 91:557–92.

Mirowsky, John. 1987. "The Psycho-Economics of Feeling Underpaid: Distributive Justice and the Earnings of Husbands and Wives." *American Journal of Sociology* 92:1404–34.

Mirowsky, John. 1995. "Age and the Sense of Control." *Social Psychology Quarterly* 58:31–43.

Mirowsky, John. 1996. "Age and the Gender Gap in Depression." *Journal of Health and Social Behavior* 37:362–80.

Mirowsky, John. 1997. "Age, Subjective Life Expectancy, and the Sense of Control: The Horizon Hypothesis." *Journal of Gerontology: Social Sciences* 52B(3): S125–34.

Mirowsky, John. 2002. "Parenthood and Health: The Pivotal and Optimal Age at First Birth." *Social Forces* 81:315–48.

Mirowsky, John, and Paul Nongzhuang Hu. 1996. "Physical Impairment and the Diminishing Effects of Income." *Social Forces* 74:1073–96.

Mirowsky, John and Catherine E. Ross. 1980. "Minority Status, Ethnic Culture, and Distress: A Comparison of Blacks, Whites, Mexicans, and Mexican-Americans." *American Journal of Sociology* 86:479–95

Mirowsky, John and Catherine E. Ross. 1983. "Paranoia and the Structure of Powerlessness." *American Sociological Review* 48:228–39

Mirowsky, John and Catherine E. Ross. 1983. "The Multidimensionality of Psychopathology in a Community Sample." *American Journal of Community Psychology* 11:573–91.

Mirowsky, John and Catherine E. Ross. 1984. "Mexican Culture and its Emotional Contradictions." *Journal of Health and Social Behavior* 25:2–13.

Mirowsky, John and Catherine E. Ross. 1985. "Depression and Marital Power: An Equity Model." *American Journal of Sociology*. 91:557–92.

Mirowsky, John and Catherine E. Ross. 1986. "Social Patterns of Distress." *Annual Review of Sociology* 12:23–45.

Mirowsky, John and Catherine E. Ross. 1987. "Support and Control in Mexican and Anglo Cultures." Pp. 85–92 in *Health and Behavior: Research Agenda for Hispanics*, edited by Moises Gaviria and Jose D. Arana. Chicago: University of Illinois.

Mirowsky, John and Catherine E. Ross. 1989. *Social Causes of Psychological Distress*. Hawthorne, NY: Aldine de Gruyter.

Mirowsky, John and Catherine E. Ross. 1990. "The Consolation Prize Theory of Alienation." *American Journal of Sociology* 95:1505–35.

Mirowsky, John and Catherine E. Ross. 1990. "Control or Defense? Depression and the Sense of Control over Good and Bad Outcomes." *Journal of Health and Social Behavior* 31:71–86.

Mirowsky, John and Catherine E. Ross. 1991. "Eliminating Defense and Agreement Bias from Measures of the Sense of Control: A 2 x 2 Index." *Social Psychology Quarterly* 54:127–45.

Mirowsky, John and Catherine E. Ross. 1992. "Age and Depression." *Journal of Health and Social Behavior* 33:187–205

Mirowsky, John and Catherine E. Ross. 1995. "Sex Differences in Distress: Real or Artifact?" *American Sociological Review* 60:449–68.

Mirowsky, John and Catherine E. Ross. 1995. "Age and the Sense of Control." *Social Psychology Quarterly* 58(1):31–43.

Mirowsky, John and Catherine E. Ross. 1996. "Age and the Gender Gap in Depression." *Journal of Health and Social Behavior* 37:362–80.

Mirowsky, John and Catherine E. Ross. 1998. "Education, Personal Control,

Lifestyle and Health: A Human Capital Hypothesis." *Research on Aging* 20(4):415–49.

Mirowsky, John and Catherine E. Ross. 1999. "Economic Hardship across the Life Course." *American Sociological Review* 64:548–69.

Mirowsky, John and Catherine E. Ross. 1999. "Well-Being across the Life Course." Pp. 328–47 in *A Handbook for the Study of Mental Health: Social Contexts, Theories, and Systems,* edited by Allan V. Horwitz and Teresa L. Scheid. New York: Cambridge University Press.

Mirowsky, John and Catherine E. Ross. 2002. "Depression, Parenthood, and Age at First Birth." *Social Science and Medicine* 54:1281-98.

Mirowsky, John, Catherine E. Ross, and John R. Reynolds. 2000. "Links between Social Status and Health Status." Pp. 47–67 in *The Handbook of Medical Sociology* (5th edition), edited by Chloe E. Bird, Peter Conrad, and Allen M. Freemont. Upper Saddle River, NJ: Prentice Hall.

Mirowsky, John, Catherine E. Ross, and Marieke M. Van Willigen. 1996. "Instrumentalism in the Land of Opportunity: Socioeconomic Causes and Emotional Consequences." *Social Psychology Quarterly* 59:322–37.

Molm, Linda D., Nobuyuki Takahashi, and Gretchen Peterson. 2000. "Risk and Trust in Social Exchange: An Experimental Test of a Classical Proposition." *American Journal of Sociology* 105:1396–1427.

Mueller, C. W. and H. Pope. 1977. "Marital Instability: A Study of Its Transmission between Generations." *Journal of Marriage and the Family* 39:83–93.

Mueller, D. D., W. Edwards, and R. M. Yarvis. 1977. "Stressful Life Events and Psychiatric Symptomatology: Change or Undesirability?" *Journal of Health and Social Behavior* 18:307–16.

Mutran, Elizabeth and Donald G. Reitzes. 1984. "Intergenerational Support Activities and Well-Being among the Elderly: A Convergence of Exchange and Symbolic-Interaction Perspectives." *American Sociological Review* 49:117–30.

Myers, Jerome K., Jacob J. Lindenthal, and Max P. Pepper. 1971. "Life Events and Psychiatric Impairment." *Journal of Nervous and Mental Disease* 152:149–57.

Nakao, Keikeo, Robert W. Hodge, and Judith Treas. 1990. "On Revising Prestige Scores for all Occupations." GSS Methodological report no. 69. Chicago: NORC.

National Center for Health Statistics. 1990. "Advance Report of Final Mortality Statistics. 1988." *Monthly Vital Statistics Report* 39:1–47.

National Institute of Mental Health. 1997. *Report of the National Institute of Mental Health's Genetics Work Group.* http://www/nimh.nih.gov/research/genetics.gov downloaded 3/4/02.

Nemeroff, Charles B. 1998. "The Neurobiology of Depression." *Scientific American* 282:42–49.

Noh, Samuel, Morton Beiser, Violet Kaspar, Feng Hou, and Joanna Rummens. 1999. "Perceived Racial Discrimination, Depression, and Coping: A Study of Southeast Asian Refugees in Canada." *Journal of Health and Social Behavior* 40:193–207.

O'Rourke, Diane and Johnny Blair. 1983. "Improving Random Selection in Telephone Surveys." *Journal of Marketing Research* 20:428–32.

Oppenheimer, Valerie Kincade. 1973. "Demographic Influence on Female Employment and the Status of Women." Pp. 184–99 in *Changing Women in a Changing Society*, edited by Joan Huber. Chicago: University of Chicago Press.

Oppenheimer, Valerie Kincade. 1982. *Work and Family: A Study in Social Demography*. New York: Academic.

Orbell, John and Robyn M. Dawes. 1991. "A 'Cognitive Miser' Theory of Cooperators' Advantage." *American Political Science Review* 85:515–28.

Parsons, Talcott. 1949. "The Social Structure of the Family." Pp. 173–201 in *The Family: Its Function and Destiny*, edited by Ruth Anshen. New York: Harper.

Paxton, Pamela. 1999. "Is Social Capital Declining in the United States? A Multiple Indicator Assessment." *American Journal of Sociology* 105:88–127.

Paykel, Eugene S. 1974. "Life Stress and Psychiatric Disorder: Applications of the Clinical Approach." Pp. 135–50 in *Stressful Life Events: Their Nature and Effects*, edited by Barbara S. Dohrenwend and Bruce P. Dohrenwend. New York: Wiley.

Pearlin, Leonard I. 1975. "Sex Roles and Depression." Pp. 191–208 in *Life Span Developmental Psychology: Normative Life Crisis*, edited by Nancy Datan and Leon H. Ginsberg. New York: Academic.

Pearlin, Leonard I. 1975. "Status Inequality and Stress in Marriage." *American Sociological Review* 40:344–57.

Pearlin, Leonard I. 1989. "The Sociological Study of Stress." *Journal of Health and Social Behavior* 30:241–56.

Pearlin, Leonard I. and Joyce S. Johnson. 1977. "Marital Status, Life Strains and Depression." *American Sociological Review* 42:704–15.

Pearlin, Leonard I. and Morton A. Lieberman. 1979. "Social Sources of Emotional Distress." Pp. 217–48 in *Research in Community and Mental Health* (volume 1), edited by Roberta G. Simmons. Greenwich, CT: JAI.

Pearlin, Leonard I., Morton A. Lieberman, Elizabeth G. Menaghan, and Joseph T. Mullen. 1981. "The Stress Process." *Journal of Health and Social Behavior* 22:337–56.

Pearlin, Leonard I. and Carmi Schooler. 1978. "The Structure of Coping." *Journal of Health and Social Behavior* 19:2–21.

Pedhazur, Elazar J. 1982. *Multiple Regression in Behavioral Research* (2nd edition). New York: Holt, Rinehart, and Winston.

Peterson, Christopher. 1979. "Uncontrollability and Self-Blame in Depression: Investigation of the Paradox in a College Population." *Journal of Abnormal Psychology* 88:620–24.

Peterson, Christopher and Martin E. P. Seligman. 1984. "Causal Explanations as a Risk Factor for Depression: Theory and Evidence." *Psychological Review* 91:347–74.

Pleck, Joseph. 1983. "Husbands' Paid Work and Family Roles: Current Research Issues." Pp. 251–333 in *Research in the Interweave of Social Roles. 3: Families and Jobs*, edited by Helena Lopata and Joseph Pleck. Greenwich, CT: JAI.

Porter, J. R. and R. E. Washington. 1979. "Minority Identity and Self-Esteem." *Annual Review of Sociology*. 19:139–61.

Powell, M. A. and T. L. Parcel. 1997. "Effects of Family Structure on the Earnings Attainment Process: Differences by Gender." *Journal of Marriage and the Family* 59:419–33.

Preskorn, Sheldon H. and Ryan D. Magnus. 1994. "Inhibition of Hepatic P-450 Isoenzymes by Serotonin Selective Reuptake Inhibitors: In Vitro and In Vivo Findings and Their Implications for Patient Care." *Psychopharmacology Bulletin* 30:251–59.

Preston, Samuel H. 1984. "Children and the Elderly in the U.S." *Scientific American* 251:44–49.

Prosen, Mel, Davie C. Clark, Martin Harrow, and Jan Fawcett. 1983. "Guilt and Conscience in Major Depressive Disorders." *American Journal of Psychiatry* 140:839–44.

Putnam, Robert D. 1995. "Bowling Alone: America's Declining Social Capital." *Journal of Democracy* 6:65–78.

Radloff, Lenore. 1975. "Sex Differences in Depression: The Effects of Occupational and Marital Status." *Sex Roles* 1:249–65.

Radloff, Lenore. 1977. "The CES-D Scale: A Self-Report Depression Scale for Research in the General Population." *Applied Psychological Measurement* 1:385–401.

Renne, Karen. 1970. "Correlates of Dissatisfaction in Marriage." *Journal of Marriage and the Family* 32:54–67.

Reskin, Barbara and Irene Padavic. 1994. *Women and Men at Work*. Thousand Oaks, CA: Pine Forge.

Reynolds, John R. and Catherine E. Ross. 1998. "Social Stratification and Health: Education's Benefit beyond Economic Status and Social Origins." *Social Problems* 45:221–47.

Rieker, Patricia P. and Chloe E. Bird. 2000. "Sociological Explanations of Gender Differences in Mental and Physical Health." Pp. 98–113 in *Handbook of Medical Sociology* (5th edition), edited by Chloe E. Bird, Peter Conrad, and Allen M. Fremont. NJ: Prentice Hall.

Rietschlin, John. 1998. "Voluntary Association Membership and Psychological Distress." *Journal of Health and Social Behavior* 39:348–55.

Ritchey, Ferris J., Mark La Gory, and Jeffrey Mullis. 1991. "Gender Differences in Health Risks and Physical Symptoms among the Homeless." *Journal of Health and Social Behavior* 32:33–48.

Ritchey, Ferris J., Mark La Gory, and Jeffrey Mullis. 1993. "A Response to the Comments of Walter R. Gove on Gender Differences in Health Risks and Physical Symptoms among the Homeless." *Journal of Health and Social Behavior* 34:182–85.

Robert, Stephanie A. 1998. "Community-Level Socioeconomic Effects on Adult Health." *Journal of Health and Social Behavior* 39:18–37.

Robinson, John P. 1980. "Housework Technology and Household Work." Pp. 53–67 in *Women and Household Labor*, edited by Sarah Fenstermaker Berk. Beverly Hills: Sage.

Robinson, Robert V. and Wendell Bell. 1978. "Equality, Success, and Social Justice in England and the United States." *American Sociological Review* 43:125–43.

Rodin, Judith. 1986. "Aging and Health: Effects of the Sense of Control." *Science* 233:1271–76.

Rodin, Judith. 1986. "Health, Control, and Aging." Pp. 139–65 in *The Psychology of Control and Aging*, edited by Margaret M. Baltes and Paul B. Baltes. Hillsdale, NJ: Erlbaum.

Rollins, Boyd and Harold Feldman. 1970. "Marital Satisfaction over the Family Life Cycle." *Journal of Marriage and the Family* 32:11–28.

Rook, Karen S. 1984. "The Negative Side of Social Interaction: Impact on Psychological Well-Being." *Journal of Personality and Social Psychology* 46:1097–1108.

Rosenbaum, M. and D. Hadari. 1985. "Personal Efficacy, External Locus of Control, and Perceived Contingency of Parental Reinforcement among Depressed, Paranoid, and Normal Subjects." *Journal of Personality and Social Psychology* 49:539–47.

Rosenberg, Morris, Carmi Schooler, and Carrie Schoenbach. 1989. "Self-Esteem and Adolescent Problems: Modeling Reciprocal Effects." *American Sociological Review* 54:1004–18.

Rosenfield, Sarah. 1980. "Sex Differences in Depression: Do Women Always Have Higher Rates?" *Journal of Health and Social Behavior* 21:33–42.

Rosenfield, Sarah. 1989. "The Effects of Women's Employment: Personal Control and Sex Differences in Mental Health." *Journal of Health and Social Behavior* 30:77–91.

Rosenfield, Sarah. 1997. "Labeling Mental Illness: The Effects of Received Services and Perceived Stigma on Life Satisfaction." *American Sociological Review* 62:600–72.

Rosenfield, Sarah. 1999. "Splitting the Difference: Gender, the Self, and Mental Health." Pp. 209–24 in *Handbook of the Sociology of Mental Health*, edited by Carol S. Aneshensel and Jo C. Phelan. New York: Plenum.

Rosenfield, Sarah. 1999. "Gender and Mental Health: Do Women Have More Psychopathology, Men More, or Both the Same (and Why)?" Pp. 348–60 in *A Handbook for the Study of Mental Health*, edited by Allan V. Horwitz and Teresa L. Scheid. New York: Cambridge University Press.

Rosenhan, David L. 1973. "On Being Sane in Insane Places." *Science* 179:250–58.

Ross, Catherine E. 1990. "Emotional Consequences of Various Attributions of Success." *Sociological Focus* 23:101–13.

Ross, Catherine E. 1991. "Marriage and the Sense of Control." *Journal of Marriage and the Family* 53:831–38.

Ross, Catherine E. 1995. "Reconceptualizing Marital Status as a Continuum of Social Attachment." *Journal of Marriage and the Family* 57:129–140.

Ross, Catherine E. 2000. "Neighborhood Disadvantage and Adult Depression." *Journal of Health and Social Behavior* 41:177–87.

Ross, Catherine E. and Chloe E. Bird. 1994. "Sex Stratification and Health Lifestyle: Consequences for Men's and Women's Perceived Health." *Journal of Health and Social Behavior* 35:161–78.

Ross, Catherine E. and Patricia Drentea. 1998. "Consequences of Retirement Activities for Distress and the Sense of Personal Control." *Journal of Health and Social Behavior* 39:317–34.

Ross, Catherine E. and Joan Huber. 1985. "Hardship and Depression." *Journal of Health and Social Behavior* 26:312–27.

Ross, Catherine E. and Janet Lauritsen. 1985. "Public Opinion About Doctors' Pay." *American Journal of Public Health* 75:668–70.

Ross, Catherine E. and John Mirowsky. 1979. "A Comparison of Life Event Weighting Schemes: Change, Undesirability, and Effect-Proportional Indices." *Journal of Health and Social Behavior* 20:166–77.

Ross, Catherine E. and John Mirowsky. 1984. "Components of Depressed Mood in Married Men and Women: The Center for Epidemiologic Studies' Depression Scale." *American Journal of Epidemiology* 119:997–1004.

Ross, Catherine E. and John Mirowsky. 1984. "Socially Desirable Response and Acquiescence in a Cross-Cultural Survey of Mental Health." *Journal of Health and Social Behavior* 25:189–97.

Ross, Catherine E. and John Mirowsky. 1987. "Normlessness, Powerlessness, and Trouble with the Law." *Criminology* 25:257–78.

Ross, Catherine E. and John Mirowsky. 1988. "Child Care and Emotional Adjustment to Wives' Employment." *Journal of Health and Social Behavior* 29:127–38.

Ross, Catherine E. and John Mirowsky. 1989. "Explaining the Social Patterns of Depression: Control and Problem-Solving—or Support and Talking." *Journal of Health and Social Behavior* 30:206–19.

Ross, Catherine E. and John Mirowsky. 1992. "Households, Employment, and the Sense of Control." *Social Psychology Quarterly* 55:217–35.

Ross, Catherine E. and John Mirowsky. 1995. "Does Employment Affect Health?" *Journal of Health and Social Behavior* 36:230–43.

Ross, Catherine E. and John Mirowsky. 1996. "Economic and Interpersonal Work Rewards: Subjective Utilities of Men's and Women's Compensation." *Social Forces* 75(1):223–46.

Ross, Catherine E. and John Mirowsky. 1999. "Parental Divorce, Life Course Disruption, and Adult Depression." *Journal of Marriage and the Family* 61:1034–45.

Ross, Catherine E. and John Mirowsky. 1999. "Disorder and Decay: The Concept and Measurement of Perceived Neighborhood Disorder." *Urban Affairs Review* 34:412–32.

Ross, Catherine E. and John Mirowsky. 2002. "Age and the Gender Gap in the Sense of Personal Control." *Social Psychology Quarterly* 65:125–45.

Ross, Catherine E., John Mirowsky, and William C. Cockerham. 1983. "Social Class, Mexican Culture, and Fatalism: Their Effects on Psychological Distress." *American Journal of Community Psychology* 11:383–99.

Ross, Catherine E., John Mirowsky, and Karen Goldsteen. 1990. "The Impact of the Family on Health: The Decade in Review." *Journal of Marriage and the Family* 52:1059–78.

Ross, Catherine E., John Mirowsky, and Joan Huber. 1983. "Dividing Work, Sharing Work, and In-Between: Marriage Patterns and Depression." *American Sociological Review* 48:809–23.

Ross, Catherine E., John Mirowsky, and Shana Pribesh. 2001. "Powerlessness and The Amplification of Threat: Neighborhood Disadvantage, Disorder, and Mistrust" *American Sociological Review* 66:568–91.

Ross, Catherine E., John Mirowsky, and Patricia Ulbrich. 1983. "Distress and the Traditional Female Role: A Comparison of Mexicans and Anglos." *American Journal of Sociology* 89:670–82.

Ross, Catherine E., John R. Reynolds, and Karlyn J. Geis. 2000. "The Contingent Meaning of Neighborhood Stability for Residents' Psychological Well-Being." *American Sociological Review* 65:581–97.

Ross, Catherine E. and Jaya Sastry. 1999. "The Sense of Personal Control: Social Structural Causes and Emotional Consequences." Pp 369–94 in *The Handbook of the Sociology of Mental Health*, edited by Carol S. Aneshensel and Jo C. Phelan. New York: Plenum.

Ross, Catherine E. and Marieke Van Willigen. 1996. "Gender, Parenthood and Anger." *Journal of Marriage and the Family* 58:572–84.

Ross, Catherine E. and Marieke Van Willigen. 1997. "Education and the Subjective Quality of Life." *Journal of Health and Social Behavior* 38:275–97.

Ross, Catherine E. and Marylyn P. Wright. 1998. "Women's Work, Men's Work, and the Sense of Control." *Work and Occupations* 25:333–55.

Ross, Catherine E. and Chia-ling Wu. 1995. "The Links between Education and Health." *American Sociological Review* 60:719–45.

Ross, Catherine E. and Chia-ling Wu. 1996. "Education, Age, and the Cumulative Advantage in Health." *Journal of Health and Social Behavior* 37:104–20.

Rotter, Julian B. 1966. "Generalized Expectancies for Internal vs. External Control of Reinforcements." *Psychological Monographs* 80:1–28.

Rotter, Julian B. 1971. "Generalized Expectancies for Interpersonal Trust." *American Psychologist* 26:443–52.

Rotter, Julian B. 1980. "Interpersonal Trust, Trustworthiness, and Gullibility." *American Psychologist* 35:1–7.

Rowe, John W. and Robert J. Kahn. 1987. "Human Aging: Usual and Successful." *Science* 143:143–49.

Ruch, Libby O. 1977. "A Multidimensional Analysis of the Concept of Life Change." *Journal of Health and Social Behavior* 18:71–83.

Sagan, Leonard A. 1987. *The Health of Nations: True Causes of Sickness and Well-Being.* New York: Basic.

Sampson, Robert J. and W. Byron Groves. 1989. "Community Structure and Crime: Testing Social-Disorganization Theory." *American Journal of Sociology* 94: 774–802.

Sampson, Robert J., Stephen W. Raudenbush, and Felton Earls. 1997. "Neighborhoods and Violent Crime: A Multilevel Study of Collective Efficacy." *Science* 277:918–24.

Sapolsky, Robert M. 1998. *Why Zebras Don't Get Ulcers: An Updated Guide to Stress, Stress-Related Diseases, and Coping.* New York: W.H. Freeman.

Schafer, Robert B. and Patricia M. Keith. 1980. "Equity and Depression among Married Couples." *Social Psychology Quarterly* 43:430–35.

Schaie, K. Warner. 1983. "The Seattle Longitudinal Study: A 21-year Exploration of Psychometric Intelligence in Adulthood." Pp. 64–135 in *Longitudinal Studies of Adult Psychological Development*, edited by K. Warner Schaie. New York: Guilford.

Schieman, Scott. 1999. "Age and Anger." *Journal of Health and Social Behavior* 40: 273–89.

Schieman, Scott. 2000. "Education and the Activation, Course, and Management of Anger." *Journal of Health and Social Behavior* 41:20–39.

Schiffman, S. S., M. L. Reynolds, and F. W. Young. 1981. *Introduction to Multidimensional Scaling: Theory, Methods, and Applications.* New York: Academic.

Schooler, Carmi. 1972. "Social Antecedents of Adult Psychological Functioning." *American Journal of Sociology* 78:299–323.

Schulz, Amy, David Williams, Barbara Israel, Adam Becker, Edith Parker, Sherman

A. James, and James Jackson. 2000. "Unfair Treatment, Neighborhood Effects, and Mental Health in the Detroit Metropolitan Area." *Journal of Health and Social Behavior*. 41:314–32.

Schwartz, Sharon. 1999. "Biological Approaches to Psychiatric Disorders." Pp. 79–103 in *A Handbook for the Study of Mental Health: Social Contexts, Theories, and Systems*, edited by Allan V. Horwitz and Teresa L Scheid. Cambridge: Cambridge University Press.

Seeman, Melvin. 1959. "On the Meaning of Alienation." *American Sociological Review* 24:783–91.

Seeman, Melvin. 1983. "Alienation Motifs in Contemporary Theorizing: The Hidden Continuity of Classic Themes." *Social Psychology Quarterly* 46:171–84.

Seeman, Melvin, A. Z. Seeman, and A. Budros. 1988. "Powerlessness, Work, and Community: A Longitudinal Study of Alienation and Alcohol Use." *Journal of Health and Social Behavior* 29:185–98.

Seiler, Lauren H. 1975. "Sex Differences in Mental Illness: Comment on Clancy and Gove's Interpretations" *American Journal of Sociology* 81:1458–62.

Seligman, Martin E. P. 1975. *Helplessness*. San Francisco: Freeman.

Selye, Hans. 1976. *The Stress of Life* (revised edition). New York: McGraw-Hill.

Shaw, L. B. 1982. "High School Completion for Young Women: Effects of Low Income and Living with a Single Parent." *Journal of Family Issues* 3:147–63.

Shepelak, Norma J. and Duane F. Alwin. 1986. "Beliefs about Inequality and Perceptions of Distributive Justice." *American Sociological Review* 51:30–46.

Shephard, Roy L. 1987. *Physical Activity and Aging* (2nd edition). Rockville, MD: Aspen.

Simon, Robin W. 1992. "Parental Role Strains, Salience of Parental Identity and Gender Differences in Psychological Distress." *Journal of Health and Social Behavior* 33:25–35.

Skogan, Wesley G. 1986. "Fear of Crime and Neighborhood Change." Pp. 203–30 in *Communities and Crime*, edited by A. J. Reiss and M. Tonry. Chicago: University of Chicago Press.

Skogan, Wesley G. 1990. *Disorder and Decline*. Berkeley: University of California Press.

Snider, J. G. and Charles E. Osgood (Eds.). 1969. *Semantic Differential Technique*. Chicago: Aldine.

Somervell, Philip D, Berton H. Kaplan, Gerardo Heiss, Herman A. Tyroler, David G. Kleinbaum, and Paul A. Oberist. 1989. "Psychological Distress as a Predictor of Mortality." *American Journal of Epidemiology* 130:1013–23.

Sorrentino, R. M., J. G. Holmes, S. E. Hanna, and A. Sharp. 1995. "Uncertainty Orientation and Trust in Close Relationships: Individual Differences in Cognitive Styles." *Journal of Personality and Social Psychology* 68:314–27.

Srole, Leo and Anita Kassen Fischer. 1980. "To the Editor." *Archives of General Psychiatry* 37:1424–26.

Srole, Leo, Thomas S. Langner, S. T. Michael, M. D. Opler, and T. C. Rennie. 1962. *Mental Health in the Metropolis: The Midtown Manhattan Study* (volume 1). New York: McGraw-Hill.

Steelman, L. C. and B. Powell. 1991. "Sponsoring the Next Generation: Parental Willingness to Pay for Higher Education." *American Journal of Sociology* 96:1505–29.

Steward, Joseph. 1986. *Clinical Anatomy and Physiology*. Miami, FL: MedMaster.

Sullivan, J. L. and J. E. Transue. 1999. "The Psychological Underpinnings of Democracy: A Selective Review of Research on Political Tolerance, Interpersonal Trust, and Social Capital." *Annual Review of Psychology* 50:625–50.

Susser, Mervyn. 1973. *Causal Thinking in the Health Sciences: Concepts and Strategies of Epidemiology*. New York: Oxford University Press.

Tausig, Mark. 1982. "Measuring Life Events." *Journal of Health and Social Behavior* 23:52–64.

Taylor, Ralph B. and Margaret Hale. 1986. "Testing Alternative Models of Fear of Crime." *Journal of Criminal Law and Criminology* 77:151–189.

Thoits, Peggy A. 1981. "Undesirable Life Events and Psychological Distress: A Problem of Operational Confounding." *American Sociological Review* 46:97–109.

Thoits, Peggy A. 1982. "Conceptual, Methodological, and Theoretical Problems in Studying Social Support as a Buffer against Life Stress." *Journal of Health and Social Behavior* 23:145–59.

Thoits, Peggy A. 1983. "Multiple Identities and Psychological Well-Being: A Reformulation and Test of the Social Isolation Hypothesis." *American Sociological Review* 48:174–87.

Thoits, Peggy A. 1987. "Gender and Martial Status Differences in Control and Distress." *Journal of Health and Social Behavior* 28:7–22.

Thoits, Peggy A. 1995. "Identity-Relevant Events and Psychological Symptoms: A Cautionary Tale." *Journal of Health and Social Behavior* 36:72–82.

Tilly, Louise. 1983. "The World Turned Upside Down: Age and Gender in Europe, 1750–1950." Paper presented at the American Sociological Association annual meeting, Detroit.

Tufte, Edward R. 1974. *Data Analysis for Politics and Policy*. Englewood Cliffs, NJ: Prentice-Hall.

Turner, Heather A. and R. Jay Turner. 1999. "Gender, Social Status and Emotional Reliance." *Journal of Health and Social Behavior* 40:360–73.

Turner, R. Jay. 1981. "Social Support as a Contingency in Psychological Well-Being." *Journal of Health and Social Behavior* 22:357–67.

Turner, R. Jay and Donald A. Lloyd. 1995. "Lifetime Traumas and Mental Health: The Significance of Cumulative Adversity." *Journal of Health and Social Behavior* 36:360–76.

Turner, R. Jay and Donald A. Lloyd. 1999. "The Stress Process and the Social Distribution of Depression." *Journal of Health and Social Behavior* 40:374–404.

Turner, R. Jay and Samuel Noh. 1983. "Class and Psychological Vulnerability among Women: The Significance of Social Support and Personal Control." *Journal of Health and Social Behavior* 24:2–15.

Turner, R. Jay, Blair Wheaton, and Donald A. Lloyd. 1995. "The Epidemiology of Social Stress." *American Sociological Review* 60:104–25.

U.S. Census Bureau. 1995. *The Statistical Abstract of the United States, 1995*. Washington D.C.: U.S. Government Printing Office.

U.S. Census Bureau. 2000. *Statistical Abstract of the United States, 2000*. Washington, DC: U.S. Government Printing Office.

U.S. Department of Education. 1992. *Digest of Education Statistics* (92-097). Washington, DC: National Center for Education Statistics.

U.S. Department of Health and Human Services. 1999. *Mental Health: A Report of the*

Surgeon General. Rockville, MD: U.S. Department of Health and Human Services, Substance Abuse and Mental Health Services Administration, Center for Mental Health Services, National Institutes of Health, and National Institute of Mental Health.

Umberson, Debra. 1987. "Family Status and Health Behaviors: Social Control as a Dimension of Social Integration." *Journal of Health and Social Behavior* 28:306–19.

Umberson, Debra and Meichu D. Chen. 1994. "Effects of a Parent's Death on Adult Children: Relationship Salience and Reaction to Loss." *American Sociological Review* 59:152–68.

Umberson, Debra and Walter R. Gove. 1989. "Parenthood and Psychological Well-Being." *Journal of Family Issues* 10:440–62.

Umberson, Debra and Kristi Williams. 1999. "Family Status and Mental Health." Pp. 225–53 in *Handbook of the Sociology of Mental Health*, edited by Carol S. Aneshensel and Jo C. Phelan. New York: Kluwer Academic/Plenum.

Valenstein, Elliot S. 1988. *Blaming the Brain: The Truth About Drugs and Mental Health*. New York: Free Press.

Van Willigen, Marieke. 1996. "Social-Psychological Benefits of Voluntary Work: The Impact of Participation in Political Activism, Community Service Work, and Volunteering on Individual Well-Being." Ph.D. dissertation, Department of Sociology, The Ohio State University.

Van Willigen, Marieke and Patricia Drentea. 2001. "Benefits of Equitable Relationships: The Impact of Sense of Fairness, Household Division of Labor, and Decision Making Power on Perceived Social Support." *Sex Roles* 44:571–97.

Verbrugge, Lois M. 1985. "Gender and Health: An Update on Hypotheses and Evidence." *Journal of Health and Social Behavior* 26:156–82.

Veroff, Joseph, Elizabeth Douvan, and Richard Kulka. 1981. *The Inner American: A Self-Portrait from 1957 to 1976*. New York: Basic.

Vinokur, A. and M. Selzer. 1975. "Desirable versus Undesirable Life Events: Their Relationship to Stress and Mental Distress." *Journal of Personality and Social Psychology* 32:329–37.

Vonnegut, Mark. 1975. *The Eden Express*. New York: Bantam.

Wade, T. J., V. D. Thompson., A. Tashakori, and E. Valente. 1989. "A Longitudinal Analysis of Sex and Race Differences in Predictors of Adolescent Self-Esteem." *Personality and Individual Differences* 10:717–29.

Waite, Linda J. 1976. "Working Wives: 1940–1960." *American Sociological Review* 41:65–80.

Waksberg, Joseph. 1978. "Sampling Methods for Random Digit Dialing." *Journal of the American Statistical Association* 73:40–46.

Waldron, Ingrid. 1983. "Sex Differences in Illness Incidence, Prognosis and Mortality: Issues and Evidence." *Social Science and Medicine* 17:1107–23.

Waldron, Ingrid and Jerry A. Jacobs. 1988. "Effects of Labor Force Participation on Women's Health: New Evidence from a Longitudinal Study." *Journal of Occupational Medicine* 30:977–83.

Walster, Elaine, G. William Walster, and Ellen Berscheid. 1978. *Equity: Theory and Research*. Boston, MA: Allyn and Bacon.

Warheit, George J., Charles Holzer, and John J. Schwab. 1973. "An Analysis of Social Class and Racial Differences in Depressive Symptomatology: A Community Study." *Journal of Health and Social Behavior* 4:291–99.

Webster, P., T. L. Orbuch, and J. S. House. 1995. "Effects of Childhood Family Background on Adult Marital Quality and Perceived Stability." *American Journal of Sociology* 101:404–32.

Weiss, R. S. 1984. "The Impact of Marital Dissolution on Income and Consumption in Single-Parent Households." *Journal of Marriage and the Family* 46:115–27.

Weissman, Myrna M. 1987. "Advances in Psychiatric Epidemiology: Rates and Risks for Major Depression." *American Journal of Public Health* 77:445–51.

Weissman, Myrna M. and Gerald L. Klerman. 1980. "In Reply." *Archives of General Psychiatry* 37:1423–24.

Weissman, Myrna M. and Eugene S. Paykel. 1974. *The Depressed Woman*. Chicago: University of Chicago Press.

Weissman, Myrna M., Diane Scholomskas, Margaret Pottenger, Brigitte A. Prusof, and Ben Z. Locke. 1977."Assessing Depressive Symptoms in Five Psychiatric Populations: A Validation Study." *American Journal of Epidemiology* 106:203–14.

Wethington, Elaine and Ronald C. Kessler. 1986. "Perceived Support, Received Support, and Adjustment to Stressful Life Events." *Journal of Health and Social Behavior* 27:78–89.

Wheaton, Blair. 1978. "The Sociogenesis of Psychological Disorder: Reexamining the Causal Issues with Longitudinal Data." *American Sociological Review* 43:383–403.

Wheaton, Blair. 1980. "The Sociogenesis of Psychological Disorder: An Attributional Theory." *Journal of Health and Social Behavior* 21:100–24.

Wheaton, Blair. 1982. "Uses and Abuses of the Langner Index: A Reexamination of Findings on Psychological and Psychophysiological Distress." Pp. 25–53 in *Psychosocial Epidemiology: Symptoms, Illness Behavior and Help-Seeking*, edited by David Mechanic. New Brunswick, NJ: Rutgers University Press.

Wheaton, Blair. 1983. "Stress, Personal Coping Resources, and Psychiatric Symptoms: An Investigation of Interactive Models." *Journal of Health and Social Behavior* 24:208–29.

Wheaton, Blair. 1985. "Models for the Stress-Buffering Functions of Coping Resources." *Journal of Health and Social Behavior* 26:352–64.

Wheaton, Blair. 1985. "Personal Resources and Mental Health." Pp. 139–84 in *Research in Community and Mental Health*, edited by James R. Greenley. Greenwich, CT: JAI.

Wheaton, Blair. 1990. "Life Transitions, Role Histories, and Mental Health." *American Sociological Review* 55:209–23.

Wheaton, Blair. 1999. "The Nature of Stressors." Pp. 176–97 in *A Handbook for the Study of Mental Health*, edited by Allan V. Horwitz and Teresa L. Scheid. Cambridge and New York: Cambridge University Press.

Williams, Ann W. John E. Ware, and Cathy A. Donald. 1981. "A Model of Mental Health, Life Events, and Social Supports Applicable to General Populations." *Journal of Health and Social Behavior* 22:324–36.

Wilson, William Julius. 1987. *The Truly Disadvantaged: The Inner City, the Underclass and Public Policy*. Chicago: University of Chicago Press.

Wilson, William Julius. 1996. *When Work Disappears. The World of the New Urban Poor*. New York: Alfred A. Knopf.

Wojtkiewicz, R. A. 1993. "Simplicity and Complexity in the Effects of Parental Structure on High School Graduation." *Demography* 30:701–17.

Wolinsky, F. D. and T. E. Stump. 1996. "Age and the Sense of Control among Older Adults." *Journal of Gerontology: Social Sciences* 51B:S217–20.

Woolcock, Michael. 1998. "Social Capital and Economic Development: Toward a Theoretical Synthesis and Policy Framework." *Theory and Society* 27:151–208.

Wright, Eric R., William P. Gronfein, and Timothy J. Owens. 2000. "Deinstitutionalization, Social Rejection, and the Self-Esteem of Former Mental Patients." *Journal of Health and Social Behavior* 41:68–90.

Index